CENSORSHIP OF LITERATURE
IN POST-REVOLUTIONARY IRAN

CENSORSHIP OF LITERATURE IN POST-REVOLUTIONARY IRAN

Politics and Culture since 1979

Alireza Abiz

I.B. TAURIS
LONDON • NEW YORK • OXFORD • NEW DELHI • SYDNEY

I.B. TAURIS
Bloomsbury Publishing Plc
50 Bedford Square, London, WC1B 3DP, UK
1385 Broadway, New York, NY 10018, USA
29 Earlsfort Terrace, Dublin 2, Ireland

BLOOMSBURY, I.B. TAURIS, and the I.B. Tauris logo are trademarks of
Bloomsbury Publishing Plc

First published in Great Britain 2021
This paperback edition published in 2022
Copyright © Alireza Abiz, 2021

Alireza Abiz has asserted his right under the Copyright, Designs and
Patents Act, 1988, to be identified as Author of this work.

For legal purposes, the Acknowledgements on p.vi constitute an
extension of this copyright page.

Series design by Adriana Brioso
Cover image © Kaveh Kazemi/Getty Images

All rights reserved. No part of this publication may be reproduced or
transmitted in any form or by any means, electronic or mechanical, including
photocopying, recording, or any information storage or retrieval system,
without prior permission in writing from the publishers.

Bloomsbury Publishing Plc does not have any control over, or responsibility for, any
third-party websites referred to or in this book. All internet addresses given in
this book were correct at the time of going to press. The author and publisher
regret any inconvenience caused if addresses have changed or sites have
ceased to exist, but can accept no responsibility for any such changes.

A catalogue record for this book is available from the British Library.

A catalog record for this book is available from the Library of Congress.

ISBN:	HB:	978-1-7845-3807-1
	PB:	978-0-7556-3494-1
	ePDF:	978-0-7556-3491-0
	eBook:	978-0-7556-3492-7

Typeset by Integra Software Services Pvt. Ltd.

To find out more about our authors and books visit www.bloomsbury.com
and sign up for our newsletters.

CONTENTS

Acknowledgements	vi
Note on Transliteration and Translation	vii

INTRODUCTION — 1

Chapter 1
A BRIEF HISTORY OF CENSORSHIP IN IRAN FROM THE EARLY
DAYS OF THE PRESS UNTIL THE 1979 REVOLUTION — 17

Chapter 2
LAWS, THEORIES AND POLICIES OF CENSORSHIP IN THE
ISLAMIC REPUBLIC OF IRAN — 27

Chapter 3
THE CENSOR MACHINE: STRUCTURE AND MECHANISM,
OPERATORS, CHANGES AND VARIATIONS — 43

Chapter 4
CENSORS AT WORK — 59

Chapter 5
REWARD AND PUNISHMENT: DIFFERENT TOOLS FOR THE
SAME END — 105

Chapter 6
HOW DO WRITERS AND POETS REACT TO CENSORSHIP? — 123

Chapter 7
HOW IS CENSORSHIP AFFECTING IRANIAN LITERATURE? — 133

Chapter 8
CONCLUSION — 145

Notes	160
Bibliography	186
Index	204

ACKNOWLEDGEMENTS

I am immensely grateful to WN Herbert and Tina Gharavi who played an important role in shaping the study which was later transformed into the present book. Thanks are also due to the following faculty at Newcastle University who read part of my material in different stages: Jackie Kay, Peter Reynolds, Margaret Wilkinson, Laura Fish, Andrew Shail, and Cynthia Fuller. Their feedback was always encouraging and extremely helpful.

I would also like to thank Sean O'Brien and Ahmad Karimi Hakkak for their support and in-depth criticism of the manuscript in its early stage.

It was a pleasure and a privilege working with editors at I. B. Tauris; Sarvat Hasin, Sophie Rudland, and Rory Gormley to whom I would like to extend my heartfelt thanks and gratitude. The three anonymous reviewers offered extremely helpful suggestions. I would like to extend my appreciation for helping me improve the quality of this book.

My lovely wife, Vida, and my children Behafarid, Mehrafarid and Bardia have been a source of extraordinary joy and strength during the years I worked on this project. I know I should have spent much more time with them. They are my guiding light and my endless treasure of happiness and I thank them for their understanding and love.

NOTE ON TRANSLITERATION AND TRANSLATION

I have used the transliteration scheme of the International Society for Iranian Studies as described below:

Consonants

Z	ض	B	ب
T	ط	P	پ
Z	ظ	T	ت
'	ع	S	ث
Gh	غ	J	ج
F	ف	Ch	چ
Q	ق	H	ح
K	ک	Kh	خ
G	گ	D	د
L	ل	Z	ذ
M	م	R	ر
N	ن	Z	ز
H	ه	Zh	ژ
V	و	S	س
Y	ی	Sh	ش
'	ء	S	ص

Vowels

Short	Long	Diphthongs
a (as in *ashk*)	ā or Ā (as in *ensān* or *Āb*)	–
e (as in *fekr*)	i (as in *melli*)	ey (as in *Teymur*)
o (as in *pol*)	u (as in *Tus*)	ow (as in *rowshan*)

Other rules:

- The *ezafeh* is written as *-e* after consonants, e.g. *ketāb-e* and as *-ye* after vowels (and silent final *h*), e.g. *daryā-ye* and *khāneh-ye*
- The silent final *h* is written, e.g. *Dowleh*
- The *tashdid* is represented by a doubling of the letter, e.g. *takhassos*
- The plural *hā* should be added to the singular as in *dast-hā*

Proper names of persons and places have been recorded based on the most common spelling which may or may not comply with the above transliteration scheme.

All translations are mine unless noted otherwise.

INTRODUCTION

Sara and I were the top students in year three in Manuchehri Primary School. We enjoyed constant rivalry and each claimed to be brighter than the other. We had a small library at school – one shelf of children's books – and Sara was in charge of it. I wanted to borrow a book and chose *Babrhā-ye Gharibeh* (The Foreign Tigers). She asked me the name of the book to fill in the borrowing card. I read it wrongly as *Babarhā-ye Gharibeh*, which is a meaningless phrase. She ridiculed me and I was really embarrassed. The following year, I wanted to borrow the same book for my cousin, however, it was no longer available. So I asked my teacher, Mr Afshang, about it. He said: 'We removed that book because it was published by the Farah Foundation and encouraged the spirit of surrender to the strangers. Such books are not good for the Revolution kids'. Revolution was in its stormy days and even our remote village was burning with the fever. Mr Afshang was a lovely man with a beautiful thin moustache and eyeglasses. I admired him and accepted what he had said wholeheartedly. After all, he was a close friend of my brother, too.

I had myself participated in demonstrations against the Shah and considered myself a young revolutionary. A revolutionary kid was expected to read revolutionary literature and that was exactly what I was doing on an unforgettable sunny afternoon in May 1980. At breaktime, children were playing in the yard of Khayyam Junior High School, which had newly changed its name to Vali-ye Asr.[1] A first-grade student, I was reading the last pages of the Persian translation of *Nous Retournerons Cueillir les Jonquilles* (We Will Return to Pick Daffodils) by Jean Laffitte, the French writer. It was a great story about a group of French resistance partisans during the Nazi invasion of France. Mr Nowruzi, the school bookkeeper, came towards me, grabbed the book from my hand and tore it apart in many pieces! I cried and said that I had not finished the book. It was such a lovely story. He smiled – a bitter smile it was – and left, limping away.

This was a very sad experience. The fact that I was unable to finish the story I loved was terrible but what made it worse was the fact that I didn't understand the reason behind this and Mr Nowruzi didn't give any explanation. However, I consoled myself with the fact that there were other books available to read. My brother and his friends had collected their books and opened a library in our village. They named it *Ketābkadeh-ye Shariati* (Shariati Library), after Dr Ali Shariati who they considered the martyred Teacher of the Revolution. The library was a room near the gendarmerie on our way to school. It had a black signboard, metal bookshelves, and two folding metal chairs. Saādat and I were the librarians. We were very enthusiastic about our jobs. We felt incredibly special and important. My brother and his friends used to come to the library every afternoon and talk passionately about revolution. After a short while, whispers of worries and concerns were heard about this library. Some older people warned that the library contained communist books which should not be offered to children. The library was closed down and the books moved to our house. Now I had a large quantity of books from which to choose. That summer was one of the best summers in my life. In autumn of the same year, our neighbour informed us that the books had been reported to the Islamic Revolutionary Committee and that one of these nights they would come and search our house. He suggested that we get rid of the books. Late that night, my brother, my father, and I took the books to the basement. A disused water canal had been flowing under our house and there was a dried well in our basement. My father opened the mouth of this well and the two of them threw sacks of books into it while I was holding the lantern. Balzac, Stendhal, Maxim Gorki, Chekhov, Ahmad Mahmoud, Mahmoud Dowlatabadi – all went into the well. In an atmosphere of fear and frenzy, I only managed to save one book *Mohammad, Prophet to Know Anew* ('La Vie de Mahomet') by Constantin Virgil Gheorghiu. I told my father that this book was about the Prophet. 'It is an Islamic book; let me take this.' My brother also took a very thick book with tiny fonts entitled *Collected Works of Lenin*. He said that it was a particularly important book and that we needed to keep it. So we went to the garden attached to the house, dug a deep hole, wrapped the book in plastic, put it in an old leather bag and buried Lenin in our garden under a sour cherry tree.

The above experiences are not unique. Many people in my generation have had similar experiences being denied free access to books. As I grew up, I discovered that there was a censored part to nearly any debate, be it literature, art, politics, history, religion, philosophy, and so on. There was a part that the state didn't want us to see and there was another part that the state magnified before our eyes. There were books that were removed from school libraries and there were books for which we could win prizes if we read them. In my adult life as a poet and writer, I was reminded every day of the restrictions on free expression in various forms. I was asked not to read some particular poems in university poetry readings on numerous occasions. My first collection of poetry was rejected a publication licence and no one cared to explain why. When I finally managed to publish, I was forced to cut out nearly one fourth of each collection. I learnt to use different pseudonyms and adopt various personas to avoid censorship and its consequences. Gradually, censorship became a major preoccupation. I couldn't help but spend much time thinking about it and I found out I was not alone. In almost every gathering of Iranian poets and writers that I have attended during the past two decades, one major topic of discussion has been censorship. People had different perceptions of censorship and different evaluations of its effects. In some cases, immediate consequences of censorship were relatively easy to observe. When a newspaper was banned, I could see that a group of journalists lost their jobs and I lost one source of my information. But to understand how censoring a novel or a poetry collection affects me or anyone else was not that easy. How will censorship affect the corpus of literature produced in the country? Will this effect be lasting? What are the effects of censorship on my creativity? Would I have written differently if I didn't fear censorship? What is the purpose of censorship? Can the government achieve their goals through censorship? Is there any good coming out of censorship? Who supports censorship and why? There were lots of questions and I didn't have a definitive answer to any of them.

My study always took me back to a seemingly simple question: what is censorship? What definition best describes my experience as a censored reader, writer, and publisher? I found out that the main approaches to censorship debate are in fact centred round this same question: definition.

Although my initial intention in writing this book was not a theoretical debate on the nature of censorship, I discovered that any study of censorship will ultimately face the difficult question of definition. I am aware that there is no theoretical consensus on what amounts to censorship. The traditional definitions have seen it within the binary opposition of repression versus free expression. The historical cases of book burning, torture and murder of authors, and direct acts of governments in preventing free dissemination of art, literature, and information has shaped this general understanding of censorship as institutional acts of prohibition through the use/misuse of power. This definition warrants moral judgement both on the actions of the censor and the reactions of the censored. The state, the church, and other sources of authority have been judged based on their degree of tolerance and poets and writers have been praised or vilified for their perceived resistance or complacency towards censorship. This approach represents the dominant view in contemporary societies. In this view, censorship is 'external, coercive and repressive'.[2] It is external to the text and to the communication process between writer and reader and is imposed by force and aimed at silencing. This approach assumes the existence of 'free' exchange of information which is then interrupted by the external force of censorship. There is a long history of struggle between opponents and proponents of censorship in this sense, that is, between the writers and intellectuals who wished to freely convey their messages and the authorities – state, church, and their supporters – who wanted to silence them. While the first group believed in freedom of speech as a human right, advocates of censorship justified their opposition on the assumption of harm which could result from free speech. And harm was one main reason which divided the opponents of censorship as well. The liberal notion of censorship which has been around since the Enlightenment resisted censorial authority of the church and state but their utilitarian approach allowed some justification for censorship of speech acts that cause undue harm if the supposed 'harm caused by the speech outweighed the harm caused by violating the general proscription against censorship'.[3] The issue of harm which is central to major arguments in defence of censorship caused different practical problems in measuring and calculating harm. Another shortcoming of this notion was its disregard to other sources of authority which didn't fit in the description of 'external, coercive and repressive'. Market or economic relations, for instance, came to be seen as a major force regulating speech and creating the same result as that of state censorship. Therefore, this liberal notion of censorship came under different criticisms. According to Matthew Bunn, Marxism was the first school of thought which made a principal critique of the liberal conception of censorship. It didn't challenge the understanding of censorship as a repressive external action to control thought but questioned the existence of a domain of 'free speech'. In Marxist theory, the function of the state is to secure people's compliance with unequal social arrangements. It is, in fact, a protector of social structures formed by market relations which constitute exploitation disguised as consensual behaviour.[4] It is therefore these social structures which dictate censorship, and the act of coercion by state is just a manifestation of prior social contradictions in the realm of production. Antonio Gramsci developed this notion and introduced new tools for suppression of thought and speech in addition to direct repression by state. The education system, intellectual allies and supportive publications were all seen as forces to exercise a hegemony which would lead to a consensus of thought thus eliminating the need for direct state coercion.[5] He thus sees censorship by the state as one method of controlling speech and not even the most important one.

As governments in liberal democracies become less and less involved in direct acts of censorship, scholars focus on other sources of power/authority which restrict free speech. Althusser sees the ideological production and dissemination as the primary tool for control of society and direct acts of state censorship as secondary and marginal. In his view, a successful censorship regime would make direct coercive control of speech unnecessary. Instead of one repressive state apparatus, there will be a plurality of ideological state apparatuses. This will make dangerous thoughts unthinkable in communicable forms rather than unpublishable.[6] Althusser's view opens new avenues for thought. In his view, the existence of state repression indicates the failure of censorship and the total lack of such external repression shows the absolute victory of censorship. One would therefore conclude that in Western democracies where the state is less involved in direct suppression of speech, censorship has been more efficient than in totalitarian states. Althusser's approach opened the way for a range of new censorship theories focusing on social structures and seemingly consensual forms of speech regulation ignoring the state role as insignificant. These theories which have emerged in recent decades have been variously described by scholars as contemporary, postmodern, or new censorship theories. Matthew Bunn uses the term New Censorship Theory to identify a set of diffused and relatively uncodified arguments and practices 'which stresses the multiplicity of forms of censorship and the generative effects of censorship'.[7] I am inclined to avoid using any specific term and will use new censorship theories – in plural form – to include the commonalities of all theories labelled under New Censorship Theory, postmodern, or contemporary theory. By doing this, I save myself and the reader an endless dispute over naming and ownership of these uncodified arguments which are very often used interchangeably.

Whatever approach we subscribe to, there is no escape from the fact that censorship is defined in its relation to power. A conventional approach sees the power in the form of external authority which tends to restrict the resistant free will of the creative mind. Postmodern thinkers are inclined to alternative definitions of power. Michel Foucault's theory of power/knowledge changes the perception of power in terms of sovereignty and law. He sees power as omnipresent, a phenomenon coming from everywhere and immanent in all types of relations. He thus negates the binary opposition between ruler and ruled thereby changing the perception of power as an instrument of coercion. In his view, power is what makes us what we are.[8] Foucault's notion of power as a circulating entity which only functions in the form of a chain and is exercised through a netlike organization shifts the focus of attention from a singular source of authority, such as the state, to an infinite number of individuals. Individuals who 'are always in the position of simultaneously undergoing and exercising this power. They are not only its inert or consenting target; they are always also the elements of its articulation. In other words, individuals are the vehicles of power, not its points of application.'[9] Foucault calls for a shift of attention from state apparatuses and their accompanying ideologies towards the domination and material operators of power. His analysis of power as an array of techniques and tactics of domination and his discursive approach has been utilized by contemporary scholarship to highlight the complex interrelationship of censor and censored and to get further away from the binary of oppression versus freedom of expression. According to Foucault, individuals are caught within the net of power acting both as victims and agents of suppression. There is therefore no escape from censorship as there is no possibility of free expression.

Sue Curry Jansen asserts that control of knowledge is an inevitable consequence of any social structure and therefore censorship is an ever-present force in any society. Inspired by Foucault's theory of power/knowledge, she argues that there is no knowledge free of power, and censorship is equally visible in liberal market societies as in totalitarian systems.[10]

Taking a cue from Foucault, Michael Holquist notes that censorship may be inescapable and the removal of repressive institutions is no more than a palliative measure. He writes: 'Censorship *is*. One can only discriminate among its more and less repressive effects.'[11] According to him, the conventional approach is actually helping those who want to control culture because it masks the more obscure and subtle forms of censorship.

Other new censorship theorists have challenged the conventional notion of censorship in numerous ways. Richard Burt sees it a monolithic, narrow, abstract, ahistorical, and moralistic approach and calls for a broader definition to consider the varying players including market forces. He suggests that censorship should be considered as a mechanism for legitimating and delegitimating discourse.[12] This mechanism acts in more complex and contradictory ways than is allowed under a conventional definition.

In another line of argument, Nietzsche's recognition of the indirect forces such as market incentives in the production of speech and selective silences[13] is used by numerous scholars to stress the multiplicity of the forms of censorship, as is Pierre Bourdieu's conception of the 'field' of cultural production determined as much by rules and structures as by the actions and intentions of the participants.

Bourdieu regards censorship as an unavoidable structural necessity and speaks of the determining role of structure in the form which, in turn, dictates the content. In his essay *Censorship and the Imposition of Form* he writes: 'The metaphor of censorship should not mislead: it is the structure of the field itself which governs expression by governing both access to expression and the form of expression, and not some legal proceeding which has been specially adapted to designate and repress the transgression of a kind of linguistic code'.[14] These structural forms of censorship can be attributed to market force, literary genres, education system, canonization, and so on. Therefore, censorship is no more viewed as an external repression of free speech but rather as an inevitable part of communication. According to Bourdieu, it is the censorship exercised by the structure of the field that determines the form and necessarily the content.[15] In his view, external state censorship is less significant than the structural forms of censorship which function through a process of selection and exclusion. Judith Butler sees censorship as necessary for the act of communication which, in her view, is possible only through processes that structure people's thought. In *Excitable Speech: A Politics of the Performative*, she argues that the speaker cannot exercise complete control over words because the words are open to interpretation over which the speaker has no control. The words are in fact structured within larger cultural relations. An idea shared by Stanley Fish who suggests that every statement's coherence lies firmly within the 'interpretive community' that receives it.[16]

Butler negates the agency of the speaker/writer and holds the language responsible, writing: 'The one who speaks is not the originator of such speech, for the subject is produced in language through a prior performative exercise of speech: interpellation. Moreover, the language the subject speaks is conventional'.[17]

The dichotomy of censorship versus free speech is irrelevant here because the speech perceived to be free is actually the result of 'prior performative exercise of speech'.

Going back to Foucault, we can see his influence in another set of arguments that portray censorship as a generative, productive force in literature. As we saw earlier, Foucault's theory of power makes any attempt at fighting the censor apparatus look futile as it offers no escape route from the net of power and the censorship it imposes. Yet, Foucault's influence on new censorship theories doesn't end here. In Helen Freshwater's words, 'any recent scholarship which highlights censorship's constructive nature – or draws out the complete interrelationship of censor and censored – owes a considerable debt to his (Foucault's) examinations of wide-ranging networks of disciplinary power and discursive practices'.[18]

In Foucault's view, power is not just a negative or repressive force but can also be productive. 'We must cease once and for all to describe the effects of power in negative terms: it "excludes", it "represses", it "censors", it "abstracts", it "masks", it "conceals". In fact power produces; it produces reality; it produces domains of objects and rituals of truth'.[19] Power, thus becoming such a complex phenomenon, makes the use of power in shaping discourse – i.e. censorship – equally complex and challenges the conventional perception of censorship as regulatory intervention aimed at silencing.

In the *History of Sexuality*, Foucault claims that the Victorian censorship of sexuality encouraged discourse about sex: 'A censorship of sex? There was installed rather an apparatus for producing an ever greater quantity of discourse about sex'.[20] New censorship theories generalized this idea and portrayed other forms of repression as incitements to discourse.

In *Ruled Out*, Judith Butler argues in favour of censorship as a productive form of power: 'It is not merely privative, but formative as well. I want to distinguish this position from the one that would claim that speech is incidental to the aims of censorship. Censorship seeks to produce subjects according to explicit and implicit norms, and this production of the subject has everything to do with the regulation of speech'.[21] Regulation of speech is, in her view, the regulation of the social domain of speakable discourse, that is, the social structures of speech.

The wide application and the expanded meaning of the word 'censorship' has come under criticism by numerous scholars as it seems to have taken away the explanatory force of the concept. More importantly, it ignores the living experience of censored writers in different parts of the world. Helen Freshwater writes:

> Although the inclusive mode of censorship seeks to recognise variety, it does not conflate extreme violations of human rights with the refusal of grant money, or the criticism of a reviewer. Censorious events should be analysed with critical emphasis upon their sociohistorical specificity: Such an approach foregrounds the *differences* between different types of censorship and the decisions taken by numerous censorious agencies, as well as their interaction.[22]

It is this approach that I find useful for the study of a particular censorship regime which is different from all other censorship regimes and it's those *differences* which make all the difference.

Judith Butler also found it useful to 'view censorship as a continuum, upon which it is possible to place the brutal extremes of incarceration or murder at one end, and the shadowy operations of constitutive exclusion at the other. Their connection is thus established, without negating their differences'.[23] The differences alluded to by Butler can be properly understood only if the experiences of those who see themselves censored are considered. The feeling of a writer whose book is denied publication licence by the Iranian Ministry of Culture and Islamic Guidance should not be equated with the one whose book is rejected by a publisher because it is predicted not to sell or the one whose article is rejected by a journal's editor. Although all these cases are common in the fact that they don't get published, there is one major difference. In the first case, the ban is final and the writer can do nothing about it. In the latter case, the writer can try their luck with other publishers or polish their article to meet the journal's editorial requirements. The importance of political and historical context in studying censorial acts has been also emphasized by Beate Müller in *Mapping the Territory* who writes:

> All censorial actions, whether they concentrate on a writer, his or her text, its code, its recipient, or its medium, need to be seen in their political and historical

context because it is this context which structures the way in which censorship can operate, ranging from the legal framework of a given society – especially its constitution, but also its penal code – to the political system.[24]

It is in line with these observations that Helen Freshwater suggests a move towards a redefinition that is based upon a responsiveness to the experience of those who are subject to censorship.[25] Her argument that historians ought to focus upon the subjective experience of feeling censored is helpful in offering productive alterations to both conventional definition and the new, postmodern, contemporary theories. I personally find it truly relevant to the subject at hand. I believe any definition of censorship which ignores the experience of the censored author is a failed attempt which will lead to an endless debate on the binary concepts of repression versus free speech. If we manage to get away from this sort of debate, we will probably end up in a different battleground of ideas which tend to ignore evident and direct use of political power and prefer to see the constitutive or linguistic forces at play; analyses which do not recognize censorship as an act of oppression.

As we can clearly see, there is a wide gap between the ways censorship is defined by scholars and theorists. If we view censorship as a structural imposition of language or the omnipresent unavoidable destiny of text, a large number of lived experiences would have to be ignored. It therefore seems appropriate to consider the element of time and place. While in some parts of the world, external repression might have ceased to exist or might be acting very subtly, there are still parts of the world where extreme forms of outside suppression and silencing are practised alongside subtler forms of censorship. Helen Freshwater makes a useful observation:

> While the term censorship is still used to describe human rights abuses […], it may seem inappropriate to promote a wider application of the term. By interpreting censorship as a constitutive, productive power, there is certainly a danger that we negate any attempt to use the term for political mobilisation. If censorship is everywhere, unavoidable, and ineluctable, then it is hard to believe that it is possible to intervene to counter it.[26]

So, once again I go back to the idea of personal experience. Those on the receiving end of censorship know that it can take diverse shapes. It is as diverse as the experiences of every censored individual. It is therefore these individual experiences which should form the basis of any meaningful study. Ultimately, all censorious acts by the state are aimed at creating that experience and can be understood and expressed in light of that experience of feeling censored.

As this book studies state-imposed censorship, I have adopted the conventional definition of censorship as 'external', 'coercive', and 'repressive'. My choice of this approach should not imply that alternative definitions under new censorship theories are inapplicable. It is just that this definition rightly serves my purpose. In light of the experience of feeling censored, I view censorship as a process; a continuous relationship between censorious agents and the creative force. In literature, censorship may be defined as a set of measures by the sources of authority aimed at influencing representations of literature. Such measures include suppression of undesirable literature and may also include promotion of desirable literature through public sponsorship. In my experience of the contemporary Iranian censorship regime, censorship is not limited to the requirement for prepublication licensing or the act of a *momayyez* (censor) crossing out some lines and suggesting alternative words and phrases. It also includes an enormous set of actions and inactions ranging from economic hardships to prosecution, imprisonment, and murder. Subtler forms of censorship are exercised through cultural institutions, market forces, patronage and sponsorship, boycotting, and disregard.

Censorship in Iran is an extremely sensitive issue and access to official documents on this subject is extremely restricted. It is no wonder that a large portion of the material written on censorship of literature in Iran consists of personal reports and relies on few facts. It was therefore especially important to me to gather as much information as I could and to analyse it objectively in order to offer a clear picture of the censorship of literature in Iran today. I knew that an unbiased scholarly research on such a sensitive subject was unlikely to get published in Iran. If it ever finds a chance of publication in Iran, I will welcome it as a sign that censorship the way I experienced has become history.

This book confines itself to the study of censorship in Iranian literature from 1979 through 2016. It investigates the politics of culture in contemporary Iran to show how cultural policies have influenced the trends in literature and affected the creativity of poets and writers during the said period.

No single study can answer all the questions I raised earlier and any attempt at presenting a comprehensive map of censorship at this stage is a failed attempt for the simple fact that the official documents on censorship are not available and the study of censorship is itself subjected to strict censorship. Nevertheless, the amount of data which is publicly available as well as the information I personally gathered is enough to provide a relatively thorough picture of the interactions between censorship apparatus and authors and the way censorship has influenced and continues to influence contemporary Iranian literature. When we have drawn this picture, we may then be able to enter a different area of debate on how to judge censorship based on the experience of feeling censored. Is censorship good, bad, or insignificant? So, the purpose of this book is to first provide as genuine a picture as possible of the censorship of literature after the 1979 Revolution and then to discuss the effects of this unique censorship regime on the Iranian literature of the time. In doing so, I will discuss the conflicting views of opponents and proponents of censorship as well as the spectrum of ideas within each camp.

Censorship and the debates around censorship go back to ancient times. Every society has social values which some might like to protect and promote. There are social taboos which some might similarly tend to suppress and restrain. Governments, among other institutions, have usually undertaken this role throughout history and have used different techniques and arguments to justify their act of censorship. The development of print and publication made censorship a task of major proportion and many governments created censorship departments to keep publications clean of undesirable material. The centralized censorship in modern Iran coincides with the birth of the press and the technical advancements which made publications accessible to a wider public in the mid-nineteenth century.

Although censorship is vastly different today, both in scope and in effect, some underlying factors remain the same. The first official censorship department established in the mid-nineteenth century laid the foundation for the complex censorship apparatus at work today. There is a similar battle of ideas between advocates of freedom of speech versus the supporters of censorship which can be traced back to the early days of press and publication in Iran more than 150 years ago. Although the main focus of study in this book is the post-Revolutionary censorship, a short history of censorship in Iran will be of immense benefit to the readers and will help them understand the complexity of censorship regime in present day Iran.

Chapter 1 offers a concise history of censorship in Iran from the beginning of the press – mid-nineteenth century – until the 1979 Revolution. As demonstrated in this chapter, during this period, Iran underwent huge social and political changes. The Constitutional Revolution (1905–1911) replaced an ancient idea of absolute rule with a constitutional monarchy and brought along new ideas such as liberty and equality. Censorship was lifted and publications boosted dramatically. When Reza Shah came to power in 1921, he decided that freedom of press had led to anarchy and a little control wouldn't harm. As he progressed on his project of modernization, he gradually became less tolerant of opposition views. Although Reza Shah hugely modernized Iran, freedom of expression suffered under his reign and censorship reached unprecedented levels of harshness. His successor Mohammad Reza Shah, who ruled between the years 1941–1979, took a different approach. He appeared to be committed to parliamentary constitutionalism and respected freedom of expression. Censorship was therefore relaxed and remained so until the 1953 coup and the overthrow of Dr Mosaddeq's government. The success of the coup not only interrupted the democratic functioning of the country but changed the Shah's attitude towards democracy and freedom of expression dramatically. He became suspicious of the intelligentsia and religious forces at the same time and adopted a strict censorship regime. Freedom of expression was seen as a security threat and silencing opposition voices was assigned to the infamous SAVAK – Secret Police – founded in 1957. The Revolution ended the monarchy in 1979 and a short-lived freedom characterized by abundant publication of previously banned books arrived. For around two years, there was rarely any control on the press and publications but as the new rulers seized power and overcame their secular opposition, they re-established a censorship regime to enforce their cultural policies. The first step was to pass laws and regulations to gain control over cultural institutions. The second chapter studies the laws on freedom of expression and how these laws shaped the policies which were then translated into projects and dictated guidelines for cultural authorities. The Constitution of the Islamic Republic of Iran guarantees freedom of expression except where 'it is detrimental to the fundamental principles of Islam or the rights of the public'.[27] It is assigned to ordinary laws to define the boundaries of free expression. The Press Law and the laws passed by the Supreme Council of Cultural Revolution are attempts at disambiguation and clarification. The SCCR – originally named the Cultural Revolution Headquarters – was established shortly after the victory of the Revolution to implement an ambitious plan aimed at transforming the cultural face of the country making it 'Islamic'. A plan so big that it was called the Cultural Revolution. Gradually, this Council was assigned the power of policymaking for all cultural activities including press and publications. In addition to these laws and regulations, anything said by Ayatollah Khomeini and his successor, Ayatollah Khamenei, is to be treated as a permanent guideline which should be obeyed. Views of the leaders have added to the confusion of legislation especially since both expressed contradictory opinions on freedom of expression.

The founder of the Revolution believed in the prevalence of culture over all other aspects of social life. His successor Ayatollah Khamenei also regards culture as the main element in human identity and the backbone of the society. Culture is so important to him that he says he is prepared to die for it. On a trip to the Caspian Sea coast in the summer of 2015, I saw a large billboard on the entrance to the Chamestan Forest. The billboard contained a picture of Ayatollah Khamenei with this sentence: 'Culture is the thing that I am ready to sacrifice my life for'.[28]

Ayatollah Khamenei misses no chance to emphasize the significance of culture and its priority over economics and politics. His understanding of the cultural conditions is summed up in his theory of Cultural Invasion which has been the driving force behind all cultural policymaking in the country. According to this theory, the external world, especially the West, is in a constant cultural war against Islamic Iran and uses every available means to undermine Islamic culture. Literature is thus a weapon and should be carefully guarded. Iranian cultural authorities must do whatever they can to ensure that cultural products are not contaminated by the toxic influences of the enemies and their cultural agents, the so-called intelligentsia.

Ayatollah Khamenei shows a genuine interest in literature, especially in poetry. He is closely associated with some pro-regime poets and spends much time talking about literature. His personal relationship with literature may have also contributed to its perception as a powerful medium of expression which therefore requires strict control. In order to enforce the type of control demanded by the cultural policies, a complex censorship machine has been created. The structure and mechanism of the censorship apparatus including prepublication licensing is discussed in Chapter 3. One major element in the functioning of the censorship machine is the operator, that is, the censor. The identity of censors has always been a matter of interest to the writers and to the public. Every censored writer is curious to know their collaborator who sometimes plays an even more important role in the final shaping of their book. I have tried to shed some light upon the ideas and mentality of censors whose identities are usually kept secret. Censors are important because they are the ones who interpret and enforce the laws based on their understanding.

Although the rules and regulations of censorship haven't changed much during the lifetime of the Islamic Republic, there have been some variations in how these laws are interpreted and applied under different administrations. Variations of censorship under different administrations are also covered in Chapter 3. In the first two years after the Revolution, a relative freedom of publications prevailed. From 1981 towards the end of war in 1988, cultural production suffered due to war conditions. The publishing industry was revived by the end of the war and gradually improved until 1992 when Mohammad Khatami was pressured to resign from his post as the Minister of Culture and Islamic Guidance. From 1992 to the beginning of the reformist government of Khatami, censorship was generally extremely strict with some minor fluctuations between the term of Ali Larijani (1992–1994) and his stricter successor, Mostafa Mirsalim. Khatami was elected president in 1997 and promised to open up the cultural space. His administration worked hard to reform many policies and procedures and achieved change in some practices. Press and publications blossomed and many books previously banned were granted publication licence. The opposition was, however, immense and forced him to gradually retreat from his ambitious plans, especially during his second term in office. As Mahmoud Ahmadinejad took power in 2005, another term of strict censorship began. Many believe that Ahmadinejad's two terms in office (2005–2013) has been one of the darkest periods for culture and literature in contemporary Iran. The election of Rouhani in 2013 was welcomed with some reservations by intellectuals. Many had openly criticized the censorship of the previous administration and hoped that the new government would improve the conditions considerably. Censorship relaxed a little and some procedures improved but the struggle is far from over. Rouhani faces opposition from two opposite sides. The intellectuals complain of censorship and the conservatives criticize him for not censoring enough. Although his re-election in 2017 boosted his popular support, it has also increased the opposition and open hostility of hardline conservatives towards his cultural policies. This is yet another sign of the complex and challenging nature of cultural policymaking in Iran.

Censorship is not acknowledged in the official discourse of the Islamic Republic as such. Instead, the authorities prefer to use euphemisms such as *momayyezi* (auditing/appraisal) or *barrasi* (valuation) which I have also used interchangeably throughout the book. A censor is called either *momayyez* (auditor/appraiser) or *barras* (valuer). Avoiding, if not censoring, the word 'censorship' is a clear indication of the sensitivity of this issue. Documents on censorship are strictly guarded and rarely disclosed. The only book-length study that relies on documents from within the archives of the Book Office – the department in charge of book licensing within the MCIG – is called *Momayyezi-ye Ketāb: Pajuheshi dar 1400 Sanad-e Momayyezi-ye Ketāb dar Sāl-e 1375* (Censorship of Books: Research on 1400 Documents of Book Censorship in Year 1375 by Ahmad Rajabzadeh). This book provides an exceptional insight into the archives of the Book Office and studies the censorship of books received by that source during the Iranian year 1375 (21 March 1996–20 March 1997). Understandably, independent academic research on such sensitive issues is not easy from within Iran. In addition to this book, I researched hundreds of newspaper reports, personal accounts and interviews, and online material written by different writers, poets, translators, journalists, publishers, and government officials in various positions, in order to gather the necessary information for Chapter 4. Chapter 4 categorizes the reasons which might make a work of literature unpublishable or render its licensing conditional. This chapter provides censorship information on hundreds of books of poetry, fiction, drama, and literary criticism both written in Persian or translated from foreign languages. Censorship of children's literature is also discussed and two unabridged sample reports of censors provided.

Censorship – in the conventional sense – is only one tool among many used for the control of culture. The Iranian government promotes the type of literature that can best serve its objectives and uses all available means to suppress alternative literatures. There are numerous cultural institutions funded by the government that sponsor favourable literature. Writers and poets who support the system enjoy many advantages including financial rewards, government positions, fame and recognition, and so on. There is also another set of punitive measures aimed at nonconformist writers and poets. Economic censorship, intimidation, imprisonment, murder, defamation, and vilification have all been parts of this extensive system of punishment. They are all aimed at silencing one group of writers so that another group can be heard louder. Rewards and punishments are studied in detail in Chapter 5.

What do you do if you are a writer under a strict and extensive censorship regime like Iran? How do you react? You may surrender to censorship and try to comply with the rules. You may stop publishing or even writing altogether. You might even leave the country and choose a life in exile. Iranian writers and poets can be found in any of the above categories. A large number, however, have remained in Iran and have tried to fight back. Chapter 6 studies the collective and individual acts of defiance against censorship. It studies different ways of unlicensed publication including publishing overseas, underground, and online. Blogging was a major attempt by Iranian writers a decade ago to set themselves free from the chains of censorship. The phenomenal expansion of Persian Blogistan brought together different generations of Iranian writers and poets both from within the country and the diaspora. In addition to all such attempts, writers have always adopted innovative ways to outwit the censors and get their message across.

One wonders how this cat and mouse game will end. What will be the outcome of this troublesome relationship between writers and the state? How is contemporary Iranian literature affected as a result of such interactions? The effects of this unique type of censorship on the form and content of literary products is covered in Chapter 7. Government patronage has given rise to some literary genres, for example, sacred defence stories or religious–ritualistic poems while undermining others, and state intervention has made it extremely difficult for Iranian contemporary literature to be a true mirror of Iranian contemporary life. Another outcome of this extensive and long-lived censorship regime is the normalization of self-censorship. When self-censorship becomes the norm, censors will have achieved their ultimate objective and can rest.

There is not a single day when there is no report, interview, talk, or story on the topic of censorship. Some attribute their failure to achieve their literary ambitions to censorship, while others claim that this is merely an excuse to hide a lack of talent or the perseverance necessary for a successful literary career. In Chapter 8, I discuss the conflicting views on censorship and analyse these views in relation to post-Revolutionary literature in Iran. As described earlier, I deal with the traditional notion of censorship as perceived in light of its binary opposite, 'freedom of expression'. I will not, therefore, go back to the endless debate on definition. Thus far, I would have hopefully provided a clear picture of the censorship of literature in Iran, enabling me to pave the way to discuss conflicting ideas about the benefits and harms of censorship and to offer my own opinion, which is nonetheless shaped by the experience of feeling censored as previously discussed.

Freedom, including freedom of expression, was one of the main demands in the 1979 Revolution. Freedom of expression is sanctioned as a human right by international conventions.[29] Not everybody, however, recognizes this as such. Since the time of Plato, many thinkers have defended censorship as good and necessary. The ruling clergy in Iran see it as the duty of the state to censor material they deem harmful to society. To them, culture in its widest sense is defined only in its relation to religion – Islam. Anything which they find that doesn't conform to their perception of Islam is therefore bad culture and should be suppressed. There is a second group of thinkers who believe in freedom of expression but they see censorship as being unable to harm literature. Some of them claim that censorship can even help literature flourish because it motivates the writers and makes them feel important in challenging the obstacles put forward by the authorities. Writers may work harder to find new ways of expression to bypass the censors thereby enriching their literary experience. Banned subjects attract a lot of attention which in turn lead to increased production of art and knowledge. A number of new censorship theories support this same idea and stress the productive power of censorship, albeit from a completely different theoretical background. The use of Aesopian language and a wide array of figures of speech aimed at deceiving the censor is to them conducive to a richer literature.

There is also a slightly different view – that a writer writes if they have something to convey no matter how suppressed they might be. Ivan Klima believes that the only duty of writer is to write and writers should not concern themselves with publication.[30] Although this view might appeal to some, I believe it has a lot to do with the type and scope of your censorship experience. The Iranian example of censorship is so confusing that even those who were supposed to shine in the absence of independent literature and who were given all the opportunities and advantages to produce works favoured by the state are seen criticizing censorship. Even authorities in charge of censorship keep complaining about it. I want to uncover how genuine the claims are that censorship is preventing Iranian literature from the growth and recognition it deserves, or the contrary claims that censorship is nothing but an excuse for lack of talent, or the view that there is nothing wrong with censorship and it can even help, as it has arguably helped Iranian cinema gain international recognition.

There is a third opinion to which I subscribe that sees no good in censorship. In my view, censorship is a force that is always destructive and damaging to literature. The worst effect of censorship is the preoccupation of generations of Iranian writers and poets with the idea of censorship; the fact that we spend so much time and energy talking of censorship, thinking about censorship, and finding ways to avoid or adapt to censorship. Writers like to speak about what they do, that is, writing, and censorship is against writing. Borrowing Salman Rushdie's words 'censorship is the thing that stops you doing what you want to do, and what writers want to talk about is what they do, not what stops them doing it'.[31]

Surrendering to censorship can be seen as an immoral act, a hypocritical behaviour in which authors sacrifice the genuineness of their work and the truthfulness of their creativity in exchange for a publication licence. When a censorship regime is so vast and lasts for so long it definitely leaves its mark on the creative minds of authors. To face fewer problems, they are driven increasingly into self-censorship.

Censorship is a kind of reading and is always temporary, but the effect of censorship on the text is permanent. A censored text remains censored forever as does a censored writer or poet. The experience lives on and becomes a constant internal struggle for the censored person. It becomes part of the linguistic experience of the creative mind and does not readily go away even by choosing a life in exile.

Writing this book in English was itself a challenge caused partly by censorship. During the process of writing, there were many instances when I had to overcome my fears and consciously fight self-censorship. The internal struggle to overcome the inclination for self-censorship is important in the process of writing this book. Inability to write this book in Persian originates from my past experiences and the fear that unconsciously, I will have the Persian reader in mind and will censor myself. In the current circumstances, this book has no chance of publication in Iran as writing about censorship is itself subject to strict censorship.

Some of the key terms in this book might need disambiguation. Terms such as independent authors, dissident intellectuals, regime supporters, state poets, and the like are used throughout the book to distinguish between two major groups of literati in Iran based on their proximity to power. These terms are not precise and are generalized notions adopted for the convenience of debate. There is no intention to pass moral judgement on any of these groups or assumed members.

Chapter 1

A Brief History of Censorship in Iran from the Early Days of the Press Until the 1979 Revolution

A historical study of censorship is not the aim of this book, but a brief history of censorship in modern Iran will help understand the present situation better. It will give the reader a background knowledge of the early foundations of the censorship apparatus and its development until today. It will shed some light on the continued battle of ideas and the never-ending war between proponents and opponents of freedom of expression. State-imposed censorship, which is the focus of study in this book, is regulated and implemented by the state and is therefore best studied in line with major political and social changes which shape power relations. Events such as the Constitutional Revolution, the rise of Reza Shah and Mohammad Reza Shah as well as the 1953 *coup d'état* hugely changed censorship practices and consequently affected the literature produced in their respective eras. Although these procedures and practices have considerably changed, fundamental principles of censorship remain the same.

Censorship is not a unique characteristic of modern times. It has been around, in one form or another, throughout history. The widespread, state-governed, centralized censorship of the type that is the subject of this book, however, came with the technical advancements which made publications accessible to the wider public. The first Persian language newspaper printed inside Iran dates back to May 1837. It had no title and was simply called *Kāghaz-e Akhbār* (newspaper). This newspaper was not published regularly and did not last long. Some scholars therefore, consider the publication of the second newspaper, *Ruznāmay-e Vaqāy-e Ettefāqiyeh* – established on 7 February 1851 – as the beginning of press and publication in Iran.[1] Whether we agree or disagree on the birthdate of press and publication, censorship soon became an integral part of life for this newcomer. According to Ahmad Karimi Hakkak, shortly after the publication of the second Persian newspaper, the *Ruznāmay-e Vaqāy-e Ettefāqiyeh*, Nāser al-Din Shah appointed one of his court functionaries, a British subject named Edward Burgess, to oversee the contents of the paper.[2]

Goel Kohan, who has researched the history of the Iranian press, believes that Burgess prepared two different newspapers; one which was openly published and sold to the public and a second confidential paper only for the king and the prime minister. Although no copy of the confidential bulletin has been found, Kohan believes it was intended to inform the king of the news and political reports without any censorship. This, he claims, is the foundation of unofficial censorship as it manifests the will of the state to prevent free publication of news. Therefore, Edward Burgess, whose main job was translating news and features from European newspapers, could be called the first modern censor in Iran.[3]

However, the first official department for censorship was created a decade later in 1863. By then, translation and authorship as well as the publication of books and the press had expanded and the ruling court felt the need to create a system to prevent the use of this developing means of communication by undesirable elements. Nāser al-Din Shah appointed E'temadolsaltaneh as the head of the newly-established Department of Government Press and clearly ordered that 'all printing houses and newspapers in Iran should come under supervision of this department'.[4] Although this department was responsible for monitoring the press and publications, there were no set guidelines for censorship and it was all at the discretion of the head of the department himself; a duty which he willingly embraced. Karimi Hakkak writes that 'On at least one occasion he personally burnt all the copies of a book of poetry which he had not checked himself, although its publication had been sanctioned by his deputy'.[5] As the number of presses and publications increased and political divisions appeared to enter into newspaper columns, the government thought about creating a legal framework to control and censor publications. In 1879, Cont de Monte Ferte, the Chief of Police – who was of Italian citizenship – was assigned the duty of writing a set of rules and regulations which would ensure the successful suppression of free speech. The code that he wrote is known as 'The Penal Code of the Italian Count [The Count Code] and is the first official law for censorship of the press and inspection and censorship of free expression'.[6] This Code criminalized publishing any book against religion, the state, or the nation and stipulated various punishments for any criticism of the king or the monarchy.

The restricted conditions in these years gave rise to a new phenomenon which became instrumental in the history of the Iranian press as well as the political and social changes that ensued. A group of reformists and intellectuals who found it extremely difficult to continue their active involvement in public life left the country and chose a life in exile. Many Persian papers were consequently published outside Iran; in India, Turkey, Egypt, Afghanistan, the Caucasus, Transcaspia, and even in London and Paris. These papers and the books authored by those intellectuals were then sent into Iran and familiarized the educated class with new ideas of modernism and constitutional monarchy.[7] They openly criticized the despotic ruler and different government officials. Although censorship prevented the publication of anything undesirable inside the country, the materials published overseas continued to stir anger and displeasure among the ruling class. A satirical piece targeting the king himself and published in Bombay made the king very angry and he ordered the postal service to inspect the books and newspapers. E'temadolsaltaneh, who was in charge of the government press, took it upon himself to find a solution. He writes:

I told the king that in Europe, the governments have created special inquisition departments called 'censorship' to prevent this problem. As I explained the requirements and the functions, His Majesty favoured it very much and ordered the censorship office to be created in Iran under my supervision and since then, this fault is cured and the line of this business interrupted.[8]

The King thus officially announced the birth of the 'Censorship Department' on Thursday 5 February 1885.

In spite of all the efforts at banning books, newspapers, and periodicals from reaching Iran, the number and variety of such publications increased. They continued to be smuggled into the country and a group of writers from inside Iran cooperated in writing articles and disseminating news. The struggle between censors and advocates of free speech continued until the Constitutional Revolution. In fact, many scholars believe that newspapers such as *Akhtar* (published in Istanbul), *Ershād* (published in Baku), *Qānun* (published in London), *Hekmat* (published in Cairo), and *Habl-al-Matin* (published in Calcutta) as well as books and other publications written by the intellectuals of the time played a significant role in informing the people and encouraging them to demand the rule of law and limit the absolute powers of the monarchy. By the death of Nāser al-Din Shah and the beginning of the reign of Mozaffar al-Din Shah (AD 1896), the press and publications had developed inside Iran and although the censors were at work as before, their success in suppressing the opposition was falling. The victory of the constitutionalists meant the defeat of the censors. The Constitutional Revolution (1905–1911) replaced the absolute monarchy with a constitutional monarchy and led to the establishment of the first parliament in the country. The Constitution of 1906, which was the outcome of the Constitutional Revolution, outlined a democratic path for the country which aimed to transform the centuries' old absolute rule to constitutional monarchy based on secular nationalism while preserving Islamic principles and the religious structure of the society. In Shireen T. Hunter's words, 'the 1906 constitution was based on a political compromise between the two groups that cooperated in Iran's constitutional movement – between the secular-nationalists and the Islamic forces'.[9]

As in other revolutions, the lifting of censorship opened up the floodgates. The Iranian press and publishing industry experienced an unprecedented freedom. The number of newspapers jumped from six at the eve of the revolution to more than ninety at the opening of the Constituent Assembly (October 1906).[10] Abrahamian notes that intellectuals seized the opportunity to debate concepts deemed too dangerous in previous decades:

These concepts, especially liberty, equality, and fraternity, inspired the names of many of the new publications – *Bidāri* (Awakening), *Taraqqi* (Progress), *Tamaddon* (Civilization), *Vatan* (Fatherland), *Ādamiyyat* (Humanity), *Omid* (Hope), *'Asr-e Now* (New Age), *Nedā-ye Vatan* (Voice of the Fatherland), *Esteqlāl* (Independence), *Eslāh* (Reform), *Eqbāl* (Progress), *Hoquq* (Right), *Haqiqat* (Truth), *Adālat* (Justice), *Āzādi* (Liberty), *Mosāvāt* (Equality), and *Okhovvat* (Fraternity).[11]

According to Ahmad Karimi Hakkak, 'The period between the signing of the Constitution (December 1906) and the passage of the first Press Law (March 1908) was marked by the fervent activity of the Persian press. Backed by the newly opened *Majles* (parliament) the press immediately broke free from virtually all forms of prior official control.'[12] The few papers that existed before the Constitution were, in Edward G. Browne's words 'lithographed sheets appearing at irregular intervals, and containing no news or observations of interest, but only panegyrics on various princes and governors, and assurances that everybody was contented and happy'[13] while a short while after the granting of the Constitution, all this changed. A number of daily, weekly, and biweekly papers appeared and soon 'every important town in Persia had its paper or papers'.[14]

The first parliament drafted a supplement to the Constitution within its first year of activity which also included articles about freedom of expression and guaranteed a free press. According to Article 20 of the Supplement to the first Constitution:

> All publications are free except the misleading books and those harmful to the religion [Islam] and censoring them is forbidden, but if they contain anything contrary to the Press Law, the publisher or writer will be punished according to the Press Law. If the writer is known and resident of Persia [Iran] then the publisher and printer and distributer will not be prosecuted.[15]

Article 22 of the same supplement guaranteed freedom of postal correspondence: 'All postal correspondences are protected and immune from inspection and confiscation unless in exceptional cases set by law'.[16]

Although freedom of expression was one of the fundamental demands of the constitutionalists, the conservatives who supported the absolute monarchy were actively opposed to it. They tried to depict freedom of expression as a dangerous weapon which would eventually lead to freedom of religious belief and freedom of alternative ideologies. Their purpose was to invoke religious sentiments against the constitutionalists. When Mozaffar al-Din Shah died in January 1907 – shortly after he had signed the Constitutional Decree – his son Mohammad Ali Shah succeeded to the throne. The new king was no fan of constitutionalism and was adamant in his determination to maintain absolute power. From the very beginning of his reign, he took a strong stand against the nominal adoption and application of a constitution that limited his power.[17] The constitutionalists had the majority in the parliament and enjoyed wide support by the public and actively fought back until the Shah dissolved and bombed the parliament in a coup. Many of the famous constitutionalists fled or were arrested, executed, or jailed. The period from the *coup d'état* of 23 June 1908 until the arrival of the pro-constitutional forces into Tehran and the deposition of Mohammad Ali Shah (16 July 1909) is known as the 'Lesser Despotism'; it was a period of strict censorship and many newspapers and periodicals were closed or went underground. However, Constitutionalism was restored soon after the abdication and escape of the Shah in July 1909 and the press and publications boomed again. Reformist ideas including on the status of women were publicly debated and promoted. Hamid Dabashi notes that 'Tehran and other major cities were the site of an astounding growth of radical and reformist papers, including, an avalanche of periodicals committed to the cause of women's emancipation'.[18]

Persian literature, especially poetry, experienced a revival during and after the Constitutional Revolution. Literature was now perceived to be at the service of the people and consequently required a language simple enough for ordinary people to appreciate. Malekolshoara Bahar, Aref Qazvini, Seyyed Ali Ashraf Gilani (Nasim Shomal), and Jafar Khamenei were some of the poets who 'wrote about the social and political events in the everyday language of people and would sometimes read aloud to uneducated groups'.[19] This was a major shift from previous poetry. This development of writing is exemplified with a social and political orientation. 'Political poetry, satire, and critical journalism constituted a remarkable body of Persian literature in the nineteenth century and the Constitutional period.'[20] Literature of the Constitutional era is one of the most interesting in the literary history of Iran. According to Hassan Javadi, the shift from the previous literature was considerable not only in view of content but also in view of genre, language, and form. It aimed at and attracted a more general public and more varied audience. Generally speaking, it changed the relationship of poet and writer with their readers.[21] The cultural outcome of the Constitutional movement was perhaps its most significant contribution. Writers and poets succeeded to establish themselves as a force of enlightenment and gained a social position enjoyed hitherto only by the clergy. They could now speak to the masses. In Dabashi's words:

> The lasting significance of the Constitutional Revolution was in its unleashing of a cultural effervescence that overcompensated for the absence of economic vigour with an overwhelmingly creative literary imagination. Persian poetry of the Constitutional period... exudes a peculiarly powerful fusion of eroticism and politics, of earthly and material love injecting beauty and passion into the subversive violence at the root of all collective defiance of tyranny.[22]

A similar idea is shared by some other notable scholars. Mangol Bayat believes that the Constitutional Revolution failed politically, but that the secularism which was one of the main tenets of the Revolution triumphed in the social policies of subsequent governments. However, she admits, 'the poet, the man of letters, the new breed of intellectuals, as a result of the vital role played then and the national fame acquired, was able to ensure the triumph of his word over the *mojtahed*'s [the high Islamic cleric], thus displacing the latter in public opinion'.[23]

Although the Constitutional Revolution failed to accomplish the dream of a free democratic Iran, it brought many new ideas into the public debate and was a significant step towards building a new nation based on the ideas of nationalism, patriotism, and Islamism. It could probably be seen as the first step towards the establishment of secular law since it marked a break with the old system whereby law had been religious.[24] This break with the past came at a high price though. It created and surfaced much chasm between groups of influence.

Constitutionalism succeeded in overthrowing the old order and establishing some democratic institutions, but power struggles came to the surface after a while and administrative deficiencies showed up. Unrest and rebellions, especially among nomads and in the provinces, increased. The outbreak of the First World War and the subsequent war conditions contributed to more confusion and somehow led to chaos in the political scene. Homa Katouzian writes:

> Even some leading intellectuals of the Constitutional Revolution confused liberty with licence, and thought that law meant complete freedom from the state. The legislature was claiming all power to rule, reducing the executive to the status of a docile civil service. The press behaved as if there was no bound to the freedom of expression, not only in their lack of display of social responsibility, but in their liberal recourse sometimes to the vilest language against anyone, including ministers, Majlis [Parliament] deputies, even the Shah himself.[25]

Perhaps Iranians were not accustomed to free speech. Maybe they didn't acknowledge the responsibility which comes with freedom. Whatever the reason, in the absence of a powerful government and strong civil institutions, this newly-gained freedom was under permanent threat from the absolutists as well as foreign powers. People wanted order and security and wished for a strong man to end the chaos. Reza Khan was exactly that man; a strong autocratic leader whose rise to power was itself indicative of the prevailing anarchy.

The state of chaos played a major role in the success of the *coup d'état* of 1921 which brought Reza Khan to power, first as the Minister of War and later as prime minister. Reza Khan succeeded in ending the chaos and re-established order and stability, mainly by way of military power. In 1926, and in the absence of Ahmad Shah of Qajar who was undergoing a lengthy treatment in Europe, the Iranian parliament elected Reza Khan as the Shah of Iran, thus ending the Qajar dynasty which had ruled Iran since 1794 and creating the rule of the Pahlavi dynasty. As a king, Reza Shah led the country towards modernization. Modern public and higher education flourished and the literary and cultural progress that had started before the Constitutional Revolution continued and was further stimulated by the stability and optimism of the mid-1920s, although censorship gradually began to tighten as the Shah demanded more absolute power. The Shah's growing grip on power disillusioned many intellectuals even some of his former supporters such as Bahar, Taqizadeh, Eshqi, and Farrokhi Yazdi. The pressures on poets and writers increased and many intellectuals were detained, including the group known as fifty-three prisoners who were arrested on charges of membership in a Marxist organization.[26] Mirzadeh Eshqi, a leading poet and much admired journalist who had turned from a supporter of Reza Khan to a harsh critic of his autocratic policies, was assassinated and some placed the blame on Reza Khan and his supporters.[27] Mohammad Taghi Bahar, renowned classical poet of the twentieth century was imprisoned repeatedly and forced to compose poems in praise of the Shah and his rule.[28] Farrokhi Yazdi, constitutionalist poet and journalist endured police harassment or imprisonment on numerous occasions and eventually died in prison in October 1939. Those who survived the repression either succumbed to poverty and desolation – such as Abolghasem Aref (d.1933) – or had to show their allegiance to the Shah and his system as did Bahar.[29] Other literary figures such as Jamalzadeh – the founder of modern Persian fiction – and Nima Yushij – nicknamed the Father of Modern Poetry – ceased to publish.[30] The most famous Iranian work of modern fiction to date – *The Blind Owl* – was published in Bombay and carried the notice 'The publication and sale of this book in Iran is forbidden', so that if a copy somehow fell into the hands of the censors, the author would have an excuse to avoid prosecution.[31]

Censorship during Reza Shah's reign reached unprecedented levels, sometimes to the brink of absurdity. Abdulrahim Zakir Hussain writes that even before publication the press were controlled in two or three different departments, however, the pressure of police and censorship was so strong that the press were ordered to only publish poetry which reflected the public's happiness and satisfaction with their new ruler and the new conditions.[32]

The reign of Reza Shah hugely transformed Iran. His government focused on 'modernization, centralization, and nationalism'[33] and he pursued these three objectives with the determination of a military commander. He hoped that nationalism could replace Islam as the principle of social cohesion.[34] His policies brought about economic development, secularization of the state, improved public education, better living conditions, and legal rights for women, but many believe that literature and creativity suffered. In Mehrzad Boroujerdi's words, 'The lack of intellectual vitality is generally attributed to such factors as the state's monological discourse, its use of censorship and repression against critics, its reliance on propaganda, and its ability to co-opt a great number of the literati.'[35] Boroujerdi provides a list of intellectuals and writers who accepted offers of various positions in government and spread the ideas of constitutionalism, nationalism, and secularism and holds that the picture was not as bleak as it might seem. However, he admits that, due to the censorship, 'many intellectuals decided to devote themselves fully to historical, literary and folkloric research';[36] in other words to areas which carried less risk of censorship or prosecution. Mohammadreza Shafiei Kadkani confirms the growth and development of literary research during the time of Reza Shah. He names the government's idea of nationalism as one factor and the fact that this was a hazardless pastime for men of letters at the time as the second reason. He writes: 'You can find criticism in the literary works during Reza Shah's rule but this criticism is mainly directed toward superficial things. There is no criticism targeting the fundamental issues. The regime does not allow anybody to write about the fundamental problems. Political literature can be found only in underground publications.'[37]

Reza Shah's rule ended in 1941 when he was forced to abdicate in favour of his son, Mohammad Reza. Although Reza Shah had hugely modernized Iran, this modernization was of a centralized dictatorial nature. Freedom of expression suffered under his reign and censorship was strict and harsh.

The new Shah was young and naïve and even the British who had deposed his father and brought him to power treated him – in the words of Edward

Posnett – 'like a recalcitrant schoolboy'.[38] In contrast with Reza Shah, Mohammad Reza Shah followed a more liberal political attitude. Many political prisoners were released and oppositional organizations, trade unions, and protests began to emerge. The atmosphere of a relatively free press led to a rapid increase in the number of newspapers which in turn promoted political and social debates.[39] One major change was the rejuvenation of the press. More than 150 newspapers appeared in Tehran almost overnight.[40]

In his first speech after taking the oath of office in parliament on 17 September 1941, the new king promised to respect the Constitution and to abide by constitutional law.[41] Immediately after the abdication of Reza Shah, the press started publishing critical articles against him and against dictatorship.

Once the sixteen years of autocratic rule of Reza Shah had ended, the intellectuals found a renewed opportunity for social, political, and literary experiences similar to that of the Constitutional era. A free press allowed an increase in the number of translations from European languages which, in turn, contributed to the overall broadening of the intellectual vision.[42] Literary activities of all types increased considerably. European-style cafes became gathering points for intellectuals where new ideas were debated and literary groups were formed. The two most well-known of such cafes were *Café Naderi* and *Café Firouz*. Although pioneers in modern literary styles had begun their work during the Reza Shah's time, it was during the 1940s that modern literature began to assume its present form.[43]

The relaxed censorship continued until the 1953 coup which saw the popular Dr Mosaddeq's government overthrown. The period 1941–53 can be called a period of free expression and parliamentary constitutionalism, a period on which, even today, 'many intellectuals look back with deep nostalgia'.[44] Political parties were actively at work both in Tehran and in provincial centres. Between 1941 and 1946, there were twenty-two major political parties and many more associate parties and student branches active in Iran. They catered for all types of political and social appetites from radical left to centre to right, from religious to secular. Every political group had at least one newspaper. When Dr Mosaddeq became prime minister in 1951, there were around 700 papers in print in Tehran alone.[45] As Fakhreddin Azimi states, 'In this period the hampered spirit of constitutionalism preserved in defiance of all obstacles, and the political culture of the country showed signs of enrichment[…] freedom of expression, including criticisms and challenges directed against the ruling elite, encountered no systematic curtailment.'[46]

The Iranian Constitutional Revolution of 1906 had come a long way by then. In spite of all obstacles, including the various conflicting ideologies at work in the political scene, the country experienced a secular constitutional monarchy where the religious forces were unable to threaten the secular nature of the political institutions. Especially during the premiership of Dr Mosaddeq (1951–1953), parliamentary government and the spirit of constitutionalism ruled at its best. Mosaddeq 'reduced [the] Shah to a position of near redundancy, contained the royal family and its clientele, and deprived the Court of its pivotal position in the Iranian body politic'.[47] The freedom was short-lived though and soon came under threat with the fall of Mosaddeq. The success of the coup was a severe blow, not only to the political administration but also to the intelligentsia. Intellectuals were extremely disappointed at what was perceived to be the defeat of secular democracy and intellectual freedom. This trauma had an enormous effect on Persian literature sending waves of despair and hopelessness to the ranks of the literati. Peter Avery writes:

> After 1954, it was no longer possible for writers and artists to meet in cafes opening off one of Tehran's most thronged streets, as throughout the War and for nearly a decade after it they had been in the habit of doing. Until 1951 Sadiq Hedayat had been of their number and was generally to be seen, at about six o'clock in the evening, chatting with friends in a teashop or one of the bars in the centre of the city[…] Hedayat decided to leave the country; […]saying that the 'vileness' and political 'obscenity' of Tehran had become intolerable. There was, he said, no hope any longer that political freedom or decency might prevail, and he was leaving never to return. In fact some months later news of his suicide in Paris was heard.[48]

For a few years following the coup, the Court concentrated its efforts on consolidating its rule. Part of these efforts included strict censorship of the press and a crackdown on political parties and intellectual activities. Yervand Abrahamian writes:

> Although the Shah helped modernize the socioeconomic structure, he did little to develop the political system – to permit the formation of pressure groups, open the political arena for various social forces, forge links between the regime and the new classes, preserve the existing links between the regime and the old classes, and broaden the social base of the monarchy that, after all, had survived mainly because of the 1953 military *coup d'état*.[49]

The SAVAK – the Shah's secret police – was founded in 1957 and, among other security tasks, took over the duty of silencing critics. Freedom of expression was to be viewed as a security threat. Compared with the direct straightforward censorship of the Reza Shah period, the new system adopted a subtler censorship regime which, in many cases, led to self-censorship on the part of the poets and writers.

It took Iranian literature a few years to recover from the shock of *coup d'état*. When grief and despair were finally overcome, it found itself in completely different settings. Open political and social debates were driven underground as the crackdown on political parties and their affiliated press began. Literature was again in a position to assume the responsibility of carrying political and social messages. Writers saw it as their duty to observe and record the problems of society such as social inequality and political repression in their work and to encourage the reader to engage in activities for future change.[50] As a result of the new socio-political conditions, a large part of the literature written in this period was politically and socially committed. Once again, Iranian society saw their writers and poets as prophets and as torchbearers of social progression, and even leaders of social change. As M. R. Ghanoonparvar indicates, 'Social commitment in literature and other extraliterary concerns became major factors in the evaluation of literary works and particularly the popularity of the literary artist.'[51]

In spite of all pressures and efforts of the censor machine, resistance continued. The Iranian Writers Association (*Kānun*) was established in April 1968 as an independent forum for writers and since the very beginning defined its duty to combat censorship and to fight for freedom of expression. Their efforts sharpened criticism against the government but the censorship machine was by now very well organized, structured, and efficient. Literature was viewed as a security threat partly because of the fact that many writers and poets were – or had been at some point in their lives – active members of oppositional political parties and advocated a socially committed type of literature. Authors had no means to publish unless figurative language was used to get their message across. In the 1960s and 1970s, the amount of symbolism, allegory, metaphor, and allusions used to avoid the institution of censorship is striking.[52]

Freedom of the press was also being limited in a persistent manner and the number of papers fell considerably, as is shown in an article by Hossein Shahidi:

> The 1978–1979 Revolution found the Iranian press in a state of deep hibernation, with about 100 newspapers, twenty-three of them dailies, compared to around 300, including twenty-five dailies, in 1952, a year before Mohammad Mosaddeq's government was overthrown in the coup organized by the United States and Britain. The fall in the number of newspapers was all the more remarkable since over the same period Iran's population had doubled to 35 million – 50 per cent of them living in cities, a rise of around 70 per cent – and the literacy rate had risen by five times, to just over 50 per cent.[53]

The Pahlavi regime came to an end by a popular revolution in 1979 which brought about another short-lived wave of freedom in the absence of any controlling power. The government had actually lost its grip earlier and censorship had been relaxed since 1977.

Chapter 2

LAWS, THEORIES AND POLICIES OF CENSORSHIP IN THE ISLAMIC REPUBLIC OF IRAN

The Constitution of the Islamic Republic of Iran defines its goal as the creation of a perfect Islamic state where mankind can be modelled 'according to the Divine morality'.[1] Consequently, all types of publications and mass media are seen as a means to achieve this goal. Radio and TV are exclusively state-owned, and the Guardian Council, which has the authority to interpret the Constitution, has ruled on numerous occasions that they should remain under direct supervision of the Supreme Leader. Hence, no private radio or TV broadcasting is allowed although one religious channel affiliated to one of the influential clerics has recently obtained a licence and there is some speculation that others might follow. The mass communication media are expected to serve the diffusion of Islamic culture and, to this end, the media should be used 'as a forum for healthy encounter of different ideas, but they must strictly refrain from diffusion and propagation of destructive and anti-Islamic practices'.[2] Article 24 of the Constitution defines the boundaries of freedom of expression as follows: 'Publications and the press have freedom of expression except when it is detrimental to the fundamental principles of Islam or the rights of the public'.[3] The Constitution, however, fails to define the kinds of material which may disturb the fundamentals of Islam or the rights of the public. It leaves this to ordinary laws and regulations to decide.

The legislative arm, the Islamic Consultative Assembly (ICA) (parliament) is the main source of legislation. Laws passed by this assembly are then required to obtain the seal of approval of the Guardian Council, an assembly of high-ranking jurisprudents and lawyers. The most relevant law to the subject in hand passed by the ICA is the Press Law. The Press Law was first ratified on 19 March 1986 and later modified on 18 April 2000. It defines the main objectives of the press to include 'fighting against the manifestation of colonial culture – profligacy, love of luxury, rejection of religiosity, immorality and debauchery – and propagating and promoting genuine Islamic culture and sound ethical and moral principles'.[4] Article 4 of this law forbids all official and unofficial authorities from exerting any pressure on the press regarding the publication of any material or article or from attempting to censor or control the press.[5] However, article 6 criminalizes publishing any material which might create division among the different strata of society or 'may harm the basis of the Islamic Republic'.[6] While supporting freedom of the press except in cases where the publication is deemed to be harmful to the principles of Islam or to the public interest, the law does not give clear guidance on what material might be seen as harmful to either or both considerations.

Although the ICA is the principal lawmaker, it is the highest cultural authority in the country, the Supreme Council of Cultural Revolution (SCCR), which is the main source of legislation when it concerns culture. The SCCR passes the relevant laws and defines the legal boundaries of free expression. Approvals of the SCCR do not go through ordinary legislative channels. They are instead submitted directly to the Supreme Leader for approval. So, one can say that the SCCR is actually the legislative arm of the Supreme Leader in cultural affairs. The history of SCCR goes back to the early days after the Revolution. Soon after the victory of the Revolution in February 1979, the new rulers felt the need for a second revolution, a cultural revolution. In his New Year's message on 21 March 1980, Ayatollah Khomeini called for 'revolutionizing all universities, firing professors linked to the East or West, and changing the universities into a proper environment for authoring and teaching Islamic sciences'.[7] Subsequent to the official closure of universities following a period of political unrest, Ayatollah Khomeini ordered the establishment of the Cultural Revolution Headquarters in June 1980 and assigned a number of professors at theological schools and universities to lay the foundations of a council to make cultural policies according to Islamic values. Reopening the universities and development of higher education centres required a more permanent body with enhanced powers and capabilities. Therefore, in November 1984, Ayatollah Khomeini promoted this organization by appointing new high-ranking members to whom he assigned the duty of spreading cultural revolution in every field and area throughout the country and fighting what he called 'the deeply-rooted influence of the West'.[8] The SCCR gained more influence during the leadership of Ayatollah Khamenei and became the major policymaker not only for universities and academic centres but also for art, literature, public space, science, and culture. Khamenei changed SCCR to the main body 'at the centre of the national campaign to fight illiteracy, scientific backwardness, and cultural imitation'.[9] He demanded the 'compilation of [a] scientific map of the nation, cultural engineering and renovation of the educational system' in an attempt to prepare the ground for 'emergence of a society enriched with the Divine blessings'.[10]

A document entitled 'Objectives, Policies, Rules and Regulations for Publishing Books' ratified by SCCR in 1988 acknowledges that books can be a manifestation of social and human freedoms but warns that they may also act as a 'vehicle for encouraging intellectual insouciance and disturbing the rights of the public'.[11] This document requires government officials, including the Ministry of Culture and Islamic Guidance (MCIG), to 'enforce the legal regulations on publishing books and protect the healthy and constructive atmosphere for publications'.[12] The law further lists the contents which make a book 'unworthy of publication':

A. Publicizing and promoting blasphemy and denial of religious fundamentals
B. Promoting prostitution and moral corruption

C. Instigating an uprising against the Islamic Republic of Iran and enmity towards it
D. Publicizing and promoting illegal and hostile groups, followers of deviant religious sects, also supporting monarchical and tyrannical systems of ruling
E. Provoking sedition and ethnic or religious conflicts or to bring about discord in social solidarity and territorial integrity
F. Ridiculing national pride and patriotic spirit, encouraging submission to Western or Eastern cultures and civilizations or colonial systems of government
G. Promoting dependency on one of the superpowers in the world, animosity towards strategies aimed at safeguarding independence[13]

Such wide-ranging regulations provide a framework whereby every book needs to be submitted to the MCIG if it wishes to obtain a publication licence. The mechanism for achieving this is a department within this Ministry (the Book Office) which is responsible for approving or disapproving the publication of books. Once a book is approved, a licence is issued and the publisher is authorized to print the work. A second permit is needed for distribution of the published book which is issued by the Book Office after ensuring that the printed book is an identical reproduction of the approved copy.

In addition to statutory laws, the acts and words of Ayatollah Khomeini, founder of the Islamic Republic, are considered permanent guidelines. Freedom, including that of thought and expression, was one of the fundamental slogans during the Revolution in which Khomeini presented himself as a strong advocate of freedom of thought and expression. He regularly criticized the Shah for a 'lack of freedom' and promised that, under a new system, freedom of expression would be protected. In a speech delivered on 15 April 1964, he condemned censorship and urged the Shah to respect freedoms as envisaged in the Constitution: 'We say you should act according to the Constitution; the press should be free; the pen should be free; let them write'.[14] In response to the Shah's accusations of the clergy being a regressive force, he emphasized the independence of the pen, asking rhetorically: 'We say the press should be free; are we regressive'?[15] A few months before the victory of the Revolution, a reporter from *Die Welt* newspaper asked Khomeini, still in exile in France, about proposed freedoms: 'How about the rights of the religious, ethnic, and political minorities? Will the Communist parties be free'?[16] In response, Khomeini asserted that Islam gives more freedom to religious minorities than any other school of thought and that, in the Islamic Republic, communists would be free to express their views.[17]

Contrary to what had been promised, freedom of the press after the Revolution didn't last long. With conflicts between political factions widening, the regime felt threatened by a free press and tried to ban newspapers which expressed views less favoured by the clerics, most notably by Khomeini himself. On 8 August 1979, *Āyandegān*, a major newspaper, was closed down by the order of the Islamic Revolution Prosecutor General. A short while before this event, Khomeini had expressed dissatisfaction with *Āyandegān* by saying that he no longer read it. In addition to this casualty, more than fifty other periodicals were closed down.[18] Soon after this, in September 1979, in an interview with Italian journalist Oriana Fallaci, Khomeini said that in Iran there was freedom of thought, freedom of pen, freedom of expression but no freedom to commit conspiracy or corruption.[19] Fallaci mentioned the tens of thousands of people who were killed during the Revolution, shouting slogans for freedom, and asked if they had died for freedom or for Islam. Khomeini answered: 'For Islam. The people fought for Islam. And Islam means everything, including those things that, in your world, are called freedom and democracy'.[20]

As time passed, Khomeini became less tolerant of nonconformist opinions. The political rivalries and militant journalism of the time might have contributed to his more restrictive approach but the war conditions gave him the best excuse to crack down on free expression. Iraqi forces invaded parts of Iran on 22 September 1980 and started a war which lasted for eight years. During, and even after the war, the Iranian authorities frequently emphasized the sensitive and critical nature of time to justify shortcomings and silence opposition. Pointing to the critical condition in the country in an address to government officials on 30 August 1986, Khomeini warned those whose writings might weaken the Republic. He recommended that they should always be careful of the harm their writing might bring to the country. The Islamic Republic was the focal point, he opined, with everyone, including writers, having the duty to protect it.[21]

One could conclude that Khomeini's opinions merely added to the confusion. He expressed contradictory opinions about freedom of expression, at times praising free speech while at other times threatening to break the satanic pens. His notorious fatwa against Salman Rushdie,[22] author of *The Satanic Verses*, however, is a clear indication of his true stance, namely, that freedom is good but only for those who confine their expression within the boundaries prescribed by Khomeini's own religious views.

In general, there appears to be no shortage of laws on the limits of free speech – but what these laws are short of is clear, unambiguous language which can show what is legally permissible and what is not. The vague terminology and different sources of legislation make it exceedingly difficult for an author or a publisher to predict what will be censored and what will pass the censor's pen. This jumble of legislation has so far served the purpose of opponents of free speech since they can justify their acts of censorship by arbitrary interpretation of the laws and pseudolaw.

More important than the legislation is how the legislation is construed and acted upon. In an assessment of the actual influence that laws and regulations bring to bear on censorship, the way they are translated into policies and projects is much more important than how they read. The prevalence of culture over economics and politics is rooted in the ideas of the founder of the Islamic Revolution. Ayatollah Khomeini believed that culture is the most significant element in any society and the principal factor in forming its identity; it can lead human societies to happiness or doom.[23] Hence, shortly after the victory of the Revolution, the authorities sought to transform the cultural face of the nation through a project so extensive that it was called the Cultural Revolution. Khomeini believed that the

Revolution would not be complete until the social and cultural foundations were also revolutionized. A change in the ruling system seemed unimaginable without a change in the ruling culture. Similarly, Ayatollah Khamenei, who succeeded Khomeini as the leader in 1989, regards culture as the backbone of society and the main element in human identity. One of the most recurring topics in his speeches and statements is the importance of culture and its priority over economics and politics. On 18 May 2004, after visiting the Islamic Republic of Iran Broadcasting (IRIB), Khamenei addressed the significance of culture, terming it the 'spinal column of nations and the identity of nations'.[24] In another speech, he used the analogy of culture as the air we breathe – whether we want to or not.[25]

The new Islamic rulers soon succeeded in defeating the secular opposition. As soon as Khomeini had established his rule, he gradually obliterated the diverse political groups that brought down the Shah in favour of clerical rule and Islamic governance.[26] The clerics recognized that in order to stabilize their rule they needed to reinforce their ideology and used all means at their disposal to do so. Ali Mirsepassi remarks:

> After the Revolution of 1979, the new ideological regime and its intellectual ideologues found an unprecedented opportunity not only to formulate but also to try and enforce their notion of a pure and just religious community of believers based on the Platonic idea of a republic of virtue. They attempted to 'Islamicize' all aspects of culture, education, media, and even economy.[27]

The new leaders launched the Cultural Revolution to establish their cultural and ideological hegemony. They closed all the universities in order to purge faculties and student bodies. They rewrote the textbooks and tried to create anew an entire educational system based on Islamic visions and virtues.[28] The universities remained closed for a full four years. The clerics also established different organizations such as the *Sāzemān-e Tabliqat-e Eslāmi* (Islamic Propagation Organization) and its art subsidiary, *Hoze Honari* (The Art Council) and took over existing cultural institutions such as National Radio and Television and the Children and Young Adults Intellectual Development Organization. The aim of all these carefully planned interventions was to promote the cultural values of the Islamic Republic, to control the cultural space, and to censor cultural products.

Cultural Invasion

Another very important issue in understanding these cultural policies is the theory of cultural invasion, which is also called cultural aggression, cultural attack, cultural offensive, cultural destruction, cultural infiltration, cultural annihilation, cultural looting, cultural massacre, cultural genocide, cultural imperialism, cultural NATO, soft war, and many other names. According to this theory, the external world, especially the West, is attacking the cultural foundations of Islamic Iran and the Iranian cultural authorities must do whatever is necessary to fight back.

The idea that the West and East have been trying to influence Iran is not a novel idea and goes back to pre-Revolution times. The Shah accused his leftist opposition of undermining the independence of the country and trying to turn Iran into a Soviet puppet state. A negative approach towards Western influence was also common and was partly rooted in the anti-imperialistic stance of the leftist movements. Jalal Al-e Ahmad, the renowned secular intellectual, popularized the term *gharbzadegi* (Westoxification) to describe the fascination with the West and what he perceived to be Western values to the detriment of traditional, historical, and cultural ties with Islam and the Islamic world.[29] Ali Shariati, one of the main ideologues of the Revolution, borrowed this term from the secular and leftist discourse and incorporated it into his circle of Islamic revolutionaries. Shariati attacked the Shah's modernization programme as a vehicle of cultural influence of the West which had brought all the evils of capitalism including cultural imperialism and political domination.

Ayatollah Khomeini summed up the identity of the newborn ruling system of Iran in his famous phrase as 'Neither the East, Nor the West / Islamic Republic'. Communist groups were very soon suppressed and the Eastern threat thus weakened. The fall of the Soviet Union in 1991 was welcomed by the Iranian authorities as it also meant the demise of communism in Iran. However, the end of the war and the reconstruction and development programmes that ensued brought fear and paranoia back to the political scene of Iran. Any idea slightly different from the mainstream ideology favoured by the religious leaders could be judged Westernized and the result of Western cultural influence.

Ayatollah Khamenei, the Supreme Leader, is the main architect of the theory of cultural invasion. Since the early days of his leadership, he has warned of the dangers of Western cultural influence and the threat posed by what one might call Westernized intellectuals. Ata'ollah Mohajerani, a former Minister of Culture and Islamic Guidance, believes that Khamenei has a military–security attitude towards culture and politics, and uses military terminology in reference to culture. For instance, he likes to refer to university students as officers in a soft war.[30]

Speeches by the leader have a snowball effect and are broadcast and discussed in the media by different groups. The same ideas are amplified by hundreds of Friday prayer Imams all over the country. The legislative, judicial, and executive forces then translate these sayings into regulations, bylaws, guidelines, policies, and protocols. For the purpose of brevity, a few examples of the leader's statements are cited to show how focal the issue of cultural invasion is in the cultural politics of Islamic Iran. Talking to the students in Qom Seminary on 28 November 1989, Khamenei compared cultural aggression to a chemical attack: 'It acts like a silent, unfelt chemical bomb. Imagine a chemical bomb falling somewhere silently, so that no one can feel a bomb has fallen, but after 7–8 hours they see all faces and hands are burnt'.[31] In a meeting with students at Shahid Beheshti University on 12 May 2003, Khamenei asserted that cultural aggression is more dangerous than military aggression: 'In military aggression, you know your enemy, you see your enemy; but in intellectual aggression, cultural aggression, soft aggression, you don't see your enemy before your eyes'.[32]

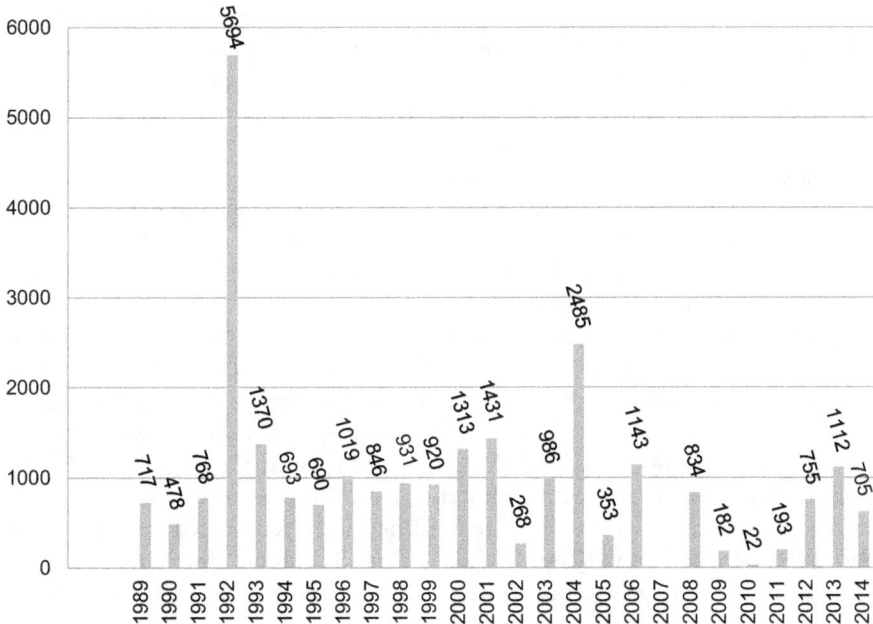

Figure 1 Frequency of use per year of keyword 'cultural invasion' by Ayatollah Khamenei

Khamenei's official website has published ninety-seven public speeches, Friday prayer sermons, and messages on the subject of cultural invasion delivered between 1987 and 2014.[33]

It also provides statistical analysis of the use of the expression 'cultural invasion' by Khamenei during the years he has served as leader (see Figure 1).

According to Figure 1, Khamenei has devoted a considerable part of his public utterances to the issue of cultural invasion. In 1992, he used this term on no fewer than 5,694 occasions, that is, an average of almost sixteen times a day! In second place is the year 2004 (2,485 times).[34] This graph shows how focal the issue of cultural invasion is in the theoretical frameworks of the Islamic Republic.

Ayatollah Khamenei sees cultural invasion as a historical phenomenon going back for more than 200 years. His website has published an infograph based on the views and ideas of the Supreme Leader which chronicles the history of cultural aggression. It divides the modern history of Iran into different periods under the following titles: 'beginning of colonization', 'cultural humiliation', 'cultural imposition', 'cultural propaganda', and 'reinforced cultural propaganda' to describe the 121 years of Qajar rule and the Constitutionalism era. The fifty-eight years of Pahlavi rule (1921–1979) is divided under 'intensified cultural imitation', 'countering Islam', 'contempt for culture and belief system of Iranian people', 'undermining religion and secluding clerics', and 'promotion of corruption'. According to this infograph, the cultural invasion was interrupted in 1979 and re-emerged in 1983 during the Iran–Iraq war. In 1983, wrong ideas started to get published. In 1988 as the war ended, a new cultural front was created and progressed to a cultural looting and massacre in 1999 when foreign satellite media increased their cultural bombardments in a campaign similar to that which ended the Soviet Union. Year 2000 marks the looting of theoretical and spiritual resources and 2009 saw the creation of a cultural NATO and unified media attack on Iran in an attempt to create a velvet revolution. Year 2016 is the time of intellectual and cultural influence when the enemy attempted to shatter the foundations of the belief system of Iranian people. This latest phase of cultural infiltration is accompanied by a picture of Coca-Cola, McDonald's fries, cheeseburger, and double burger in the infogram.[35]

In a speech delivered to the cultural authorities on 12 August 1992, he delivered a short history of cultural invasion in Iran and blamed it on the genealogy of intellectual movements in the country: 'Iranian intelligentsia was unfortunately born dependent and in malady. There were a few elements who were healthy and uncorrupted but they were lost. The rest were dependent, some on Russia and some on Europe and the West'.[36] In his view, the cultural invasion was interrupted by the Islamic Revolution; but as the West became disappointed at its failure to defeat the Islamic Republic on the military and economic fronts, it decided to wage a cultural war against Iran. This war also targeted Islamic art and literature:

> One of their projects was to humiliate and seclude the revolutionary art and culture in Iran [...]. One important work accomplished by the Revolution is that it has trained a group of writers and artists who have cultural authority and – thanks God – are not few in number. Many poets, many story writers emerged who wrote good Persian [...]. One of the works of the enemy is to seclude these loyal groups. The so-called artistic and literary journals show no interest in their work [...]. Another method is that global organizations award prizes to anti-Islamic and anti-revolutionary works. Why is it that among all these works which have received international prizes, there is no revolutionary work? Don't we have revolutionary films? Don't we have revolutionary poetry? Don't we have revolutionary plays? Of all these revolutionary products that our youth have produced, do none have any artistic value? I think that if they could, they would even be ready to award a Nobel Prize to one of these anti-Islamic and anti-revolutionary elements – to make them famous around the world, to seclude the revolutionary figures! Isn't this cultural aggression?[37]

The open enmity towards one group of Iranian artists and writers whose works are not favoured by the Supreme Leader sends out an important message with massive repercussions. On the other hand, Khamenei's unreserved support of those whose art and literature are deemed to be at the service of the Islamic Republic acts as the guiding principle for cultural policymaking in the country.

Some might argue that Khamenei is using the theory of cultural invasion to suppress domestic opposition and promote his idea of cultural identity. They might say that he needs external justification to sell his cultural policy of homogenization to the public and to his potential critics. He regularly points the finger at intellectuals as agents of the enemy thus increasing the risk of any opposition. His supporters treat his concerns as genuine. They say that he genuinely and truthfully worries about culture. He is quoted as saying: 'I sincerely and truly worry about culture. It is that sort of concern that wakes you up in the middle of the night and makes you pray to God for help. My concern for culture is of this type'.[38] Shahab Esfandiyari, a researcher at Art University in Tehran rejects the claim that Khamenei's cultural policy is aimed at homogenization of culture. He describes Khamenei as an exceptional political and religious leader who is also well-versed in arts and literature. A man who has a deep knowledge of classical and modern literature of Iran and the world; someone who indiscriminately reads works by Tolstoy, Sholokhov, Hugo, Stendhal, Bulgakov, and Umberto Eco, and even pursues the works of Iranian *degarandish* (secular) writers and intellectuals, cannot be so narrow-minded. On the contrary, he argues, his special position as the highest political and religious authority has provided an exceptional historical opportunity for cultural growth and development. Moreover, as secular artists and writers are still more powerful and continue to dominate in spite of all the support for Islamic art and literature, it is fair and just to continue to support the Islamic discourse. It is in such an unequal historical and social background that the authorities in the Islamic Republic support 'the minority', that is, those loyal to the Islamic Republic.[39] So, according to him, although the Islamic Republic is in power, the cultural and artistic sphere represents different power relations.

In spite of all warnings and advice by the Supreme Leader, it seems that the Islamic Republic has not been very efficient or successful in its mission. That is the reason why Khamenei keeps criticizing not only the West and secular intellectuals but the authorities in government and especially in the cultural institutions. He has been championing the fight against cultural invasion for nearly three decades, yet he is not happy with the outcome at all. In fact, he has repeatedly complained of negligence and recklessness of cultural authorities.[40]

Khamenei and his supporters believe that 'cultural engineering' is the solution to the cultural problems of Iran. They see culture as an amorphous entity which is unpredictable and therefore dangerous. Cultural engineering will shape this entity making it predictable and safe.

In 2013, The Cultural Engineering Map was approved and published in 120 pages. Ayatollah Khamenei had assigned this task to the SCCR that he called the Cultural Command Centre. More than 300 researchers were employed full-time at the project and 2,000 other experts collaborated partially.[41]

Theory of cultural invasion has been the driving force for cultural policymaking since the early 1990s. All types of cultural and artistic activities have been affected including literature. Literature was perceived by the authorities – and especially by the main architect of this theory, that is, the Supreme Leader – as a fertile ground for cultural infiltration of the enemy which required careful scrutiny and surveillance. The written word received undue attention and control – compared with other forms of cultural or artistic expression – and I believe the peculiar relationship of the Supreme Leader with literature and the literati have contributed to this image. I therefore find it necessary to shed some light on this relationship.

Ayatollah Khamenei: The Poet and the Critic

Khamenei shows a particular interest in literature in general and poetry in particular. The founder of the Islamic Revolution, Khomeini, also wrote poetry and a collection of his Sufi-style poems was published posthumously. Khamenei, signing his poetry as 'Amin', has also published poems in the classical style of ghazal.[42] He has a handful of friends among poets. Annual poetry readings are organized in his presence where he acts both as an appreciative listener and an occasional critic. The annual meetings with poets are one of the most significant single literary events in the official discourse of the Iranian regime. The way these meetings are conducted and broadcast crystallize the leader's expectations of his favoured poets and writers. The timing is always Ramadhan to emphasize the religious and moral aspects of literature. The participants include a distinct group of supporters of the regime who regularly attend. Every year a large group of young and emerging poets from different parts of the country and other Persian-speaking communities are invited. Ayatollah Khamenei clearly enjoys these readings. He pays careful attention and offers feedback. He sometimes enters into a dialogue with some, asking personal questions about their life, their family, or their poetry. In these readings, people see a less formal, more ordinary face of the leader. Poets give him signed copies of their books and he indulges in friendly conversations. In the meantime, he uses every opportunity to draw a line between the type of literature that he approves of and the type of literature that he believes is harmful and non-Islamic. Every year, some major decisions are announced informally which are then acted upon by the cultural institutions.

In the words of Reza Esmaili, a poet who regularly attends these meetings, they are aimed at 'strengthening the discourse of the Islamic Revolution in the literary community. They are also a networking opportunity and a place to discover new talents who require help to gain fame and recognition'.[43] The meetings get wide coverage including on radio and TV and full reports are published in print and online media.[44]

Both in these and other meetings with cultural authorities, Khamenei announces the expectations he has for poets and elaborates on the type of literature he hopes to see. In one such meeting on 15 September 2008, he recommended the need for ethical poetry, adding that 'Religious poetry which you call ritualistic poetry is good'.[45] As seen in 2009, he frequently advises poets to put their art to the service of the Revolution, also recommending that sentiment is not overindulged and romantic feelings are dealt with discreetly: 'Of course, I never recommend any poet not to write love poetry[...] but I can recommend to be careful not to exaggerate in this area'.[46] In a message to the ceremony commemorating Moshfeq Kashani, a well-known pro-regime poet, Khamenei praised his poetry and wrote: 'One good characteristic of Moshfeq's poetry is that it is at the service of objectives, serving religious and revolutionary objectives'.[47] The outcomes of these annual meetings are translated into guidelines for cultural institutions and the approved poets of the Islamic Revolution.

While Khamenei admires revolutionary poets for their loyalty to Islamic and revolutionary values and for the literary merit of their works, he expressly condemns secular poets and loathes the most renowned Iranian poets. In a meeting with producers on Iranian state radio in 1991, Khamenei praised young poets and recommended the authorities use their poetry more frequently on radio at the expense of others: 'Now our revolutionary young poets write poems which are much better than the poems of former secular poets who are unfortunately more famous'.[48] He has shown his contempt for and dislike of secular poets on other occasions, too. Yet Khamenei is known to have been associated with secular poets as a youth in Mashhad, Khorasan Province, where he was a regular visitor to different poetry circles. He once said that Mehdi Akhavan Saleth had been a friend of his when they were young and that he admired poets like Amiri Firoozkoohi, Rahi Moayyeri, Shahriar, and Malekolshoara Bahar – classical poets – as well as modernist poets such as Nima Yushij, Mehdi Akhavan Saleth, and two others whom he preferred not to name.[49] The fact that he avoids naming two of his past favourite poets shows that he has become more judgemental over time and less tolerant of nonconformist literature.

Khamenei seems to take much pride in his association with poets in Khorasan, especially his friendship with Akhavan Saleth. His official website has published pages of his notebook containing a poem, along with a short commentary, written and autographed by Akhavan Saleth in 1962.[50] This old friendship did not, however, stop him from harshly criticizing Akhavan Saleth. In a meeting with artists and cultural authorities on 19 October 1994, Khamenei complained that no famous author or journalist – not even one – had been attracted to the Islamic Republic regime. He accused the Iranian intelligentsia of opposition to Islamic values and recounted a story about an old poet friend. Khamenei had telephoned and asked the friend to join the new Islamic system and use his pen in the service of the Revolution and Islam.

> I called that famous friend and said: 'How are you; do you know that the Shah is gone and that everything has changed?' [...] He answered in a very grave tone and said: 'We are always against dominance, not for dominance' [...] I said: 'That is a very bad approach! [...] If the dominance is good dominance, you should serve such a dominance and be "for dominance".'[51]

Even though Khamenei does not name the poet, he seems to be referring to Akhavan Saleth. Commenting on this, Faraj Sarkoohi writes: 'Mr Khamenei leaves the rest of the story untold, but Akhavan told me and another friend that a few days after he rejected Khamenei's offer, a group of men attacked him in the street and severely beat him up. Soon after, his retirement pension was terminated'.[52]

Sarkoohi believes that the frequent poetry readings attended by Khamenei is a reflection of his inferiority complex and his inclination towards censorship and Islamizing culture, as well as a strong delusion about his own ability as a poet and his love of being recognized as a 'book-loving, literary scholar [and a] cultivated poet'.[53] This idea is supported by the propaganda that Khamenei is an avid reader of poetry and fiction and has been praised by many important poets in the past. Hojjatoleslam Ali Shirazi, a representative of the Supreme Leader, writes that when Khamenei was a young man in Mashhad, Amiri Firoozkoohi, the well-known poet, had frequently praised his poetic knowledge, telling Gholamreza Ghodsi, another renowned poet, that Khamenei was Iran's greatest connoisseur of poetry.[54]

Many leading poets and writers have been the target of Khamenei's anger. In an annual meeting with that profession, he said that the poetry of Forough Farrokhzad was not acceptable to society and that even intellectuals of the time had not approved of it because it was outrageously licentious. However, he said some other female poets were even worse than Forough: 'I'm not naming some other female poets. I've mentioned Forough because, firstly, Forough is dead and, secondly, I believe that she achieved redemption toward the end of her life. But some others did not achieve and will never achieve redemption.'[55] Again, he refuses to name because he thinks even naming those poets give them some official recognition. Of course anyone who follows the poetry scene in Iran knows that he is referring to Simin Behbahani, a major voice for social change and a passionate advocate of women rights. On 12 September 2014, after undergoing a surgical operation, Khamenei was visited in hospital by a group of Iranian filmmakers. He read a poem by Parvin E'tesami, an early twentieth-century female poet, and used the opportunity to attack Forough Farrokhzad again, observing that some people undermine E'tesami with the intention of exalting Farrokhzad.[56] The truth is that he and his cultural machine have actually been trying to fabricate such a dichotomy. E'tesami and Farrokhzad belong to two different schools of thought and poetry and lived half a century apart. In a failed attempt to undermine the fame and influence of Forough Farrokhzad, who represents an emancipated woman and a rebellious modern female poet, they tried to portray Parvin E'tesami as a homely modest poetess advocating moral and ethical poetry. In such an attempt they ignored the fact that E'tesami was also a progressive poet of her time in a more conservative and traditional society. She frequently wrote about the importance of education, social justice, and gender inequality and although she is mainly silent about major social and political events of her time, she exceptionally 'wrote about the unveiling of women in 1953, which she commemorates approvingly'.[57]

On another occasion, he criticized the efforts of independent literary circles to commemorate literary figures of the past. Using what amounts to abusive language, he said:

> They bring forward a miserable fossilized name and try to discuss his poetry and his name and his so and so [...]. This poor man is a fossil now and even when he was young, he did not follow a good path! Now, should we commemorate such people? What service did they do to this country? What good story – good novel – good essay and good poem did they write on behalf of this nation? Other than attracting people towards moral corruption with their poetry, did they do any positive work? So why should we commemorate this gentleman or that lady?[58]

The above examples show how personally involved Khamenei is with literature. He is an originator and promoter of the concept of *khodi* (insider) and *gheir-e khodi* (outsider). He frequently recommends all cultural institutions to rely on those who are faithful to the Islamic regime and are, therefore, *khodi*. '*Khodi* elements can resist aggression. Esteem the *khodi* elements wherever they are. This is my word. I tell all the cultural authorities in the country, from the Ministry of Education to the Ministry of Islamic Guidance, the Islamic Propagation Organization, other cultural institutions, and foundations: rely on *khodi* elements'.[59]

A direct outcome of this divisive policy is that independent authors lose any chance of government patronage and sponsorship. Employment in cultural organizations is offered only to *khodi* elements. Anyone who wants to benefit from cultural sponsorship needs to prove that he belongs. Such policies institutionalize discrimination and stigmatize those who think differently, namely '*degarandish*' writers. *Degarandish* literally means someone who thinks otherwise. This type of naming assumes the existence of a mainstream way of thought to be the ideology of the Islamic Republic and brands those who do not conform to this mainstream ideology as '*degarandish*'. This brand also helps cultural organizations to ignore and refuse to support independent literature. The discrimination has become the norm so that even *degarandish* authors themselves see it as normal and natural. They try to avoid any association with state patronage. These conditions have created another stigmatization from the opposite side. Poets and writers who benefit from public patronage or who are associated with public cultural organizations are branded as *dowlati* (state) poets and writers. Independence or dependence – actual or assumed – from/on the state has become a major criterion in evaluating authors and state sponsorship has become a highly conflicted and divisive territory.

Khamenei has literature under his radar and sometimes interferes in the smallest matters related to literature. He recommends books and those books suddenly become bestsellers. During the presidency of Khatami, the MCIG initiated a procedure to reconcile independent writers with the system. The Minister of Culture and Islamic Guidance, Ata'ollah Mohajerani, himself a writer, was keen to open up the cultural scene and show a more positive approach to writers and poets who had been disillusioned and isolated for so long. Although many of the independent writers were suspicious of his intentions, some met with him and agreed to cooperate towards a more diverse and inclusive literary patronage. One major initiative was the 'Festival of 20 Years of Iranian Fiction' in 1997. For this festival, some renowned independent authors attended a government-sponsored event for the first time after the Revolution and stood side by side with cultural authorities and regime supporters. The atmosphere was one of hope and the MCIG led by Ata'ollah Mohajerani was the flagbearer of this hope. Mohajerani later left Iran in 2004 and has since been living in exile in London. In 2010 he wrote an open letter to the Supreme Leader and reminded him of his lengthy discussions about that festival.

> You ordered the festival to be cancelled. I talked to you about the writers at length. We discussed every single writer and their works. We specifically talked

about Mahmoud Dowlatabadi and his novel *Kelidar*, about which you are so sensitive and once referred to as a lie during a Friday prayer sermon in Tehran. I talked in detail about Simin Daneshvar and Moniroo Ravanipour and others. Fortunately, you accepted that we award prizes to nineteen people but you didn't concede in the case of *Madār-e Sefr Darajeh* (Zero Degree Orbit) by Ahmad Mahmoud which had, perchance, been selected as the Selected Novel of the past twenty years and I will never forget the astonished and sad face of Ahmad Mahmoud as long as I live.[60]

Mohajerani remarks that Khamenei considered that novel an 'anti-war' novel and therefore didn't approve of it.

Khamenei is a man who clearly appreciates poetry. He sees himself as an insider in literature and, consciously or unconsciously, in competition with others in the circle. Although he has huge power and popularity, he clearly values the admiration of the intelligentsia, of the type of people he associated with as a youth. He believes in the power of the word and is aware of the special position of good wordcraft. Great poets such as Ferdowsi, Hafiz, Sa'di, and Rumi are revered fanatically in Iran. There is a volume of *The Divan of Hafiz* next to the Koran in nearly every Iranian home.[61] Hundreds of visitors every day visit the graves of Hafiz, Ferdowsi, Sa'di, Khayyam, Attar, Rumi, and others. Tens of thousands of the Divans of these poets are sold every year. I witnessed the funerals of major contemporary poets such as Ahmad Shamlou, Manouchehr Atashi, and Simin Behbahani blocking the traffic. As the main medium of culture for centuries, poetry remains the most popular form of cultural expression today. Poetry is present everywhere: at religious ceremonies, funerals, and political rallies, on gravestones, and on the back of lorries and buses. Iranian culture has strong ties with poetry and readers are aware of its aesthetics. Edward G. Browne spoke of the Iranian nation's love of poetry more than a century ago:

> I doubt if there be any people in the world to whom poetry comes so natural as to the Persians, or whether any poets so truly live in the hearts of their people as Persian poets. Even the humble and often illiterate muleteer will often beguile the tedium of the road by singing or reciting not merely popular rhymes and ballads but the classical poetry of Hafiz and other great poets of the past.[62]

In a book on Iranian contemporary cinema, Khatereh Sheibani attributes the success of post-Revolutionary Iranian cinema and the works of renowned filmmakers such as Kiarostami and Beyzayi to inspiration they gained from classical and contemporary Persian poetry.[63]

In recent history, poetry has been used to promote political ideologies and mobilize the masses. The poetry nights of *Dah-Shab* (Ten Nights) in the Goethe Institute of Tehran (autumn 1977) were attended by tens of thousands and some scholars claim they contributed significantly to the Revolution.[64] In a matter of ten nights of public readings, sixty-one poets and writers read poetry and delivered talks. Many of those poems were perceived to be critical of the system and highly provocative.

Edward G. Browne states that poetry to the Persian people 'is a real incentive to action or endurance'.⁶⁵ He counts numerous examples of Iranians, especially religious and political dissidents, who recited lyrical and mystical poems at the moment of their execution and thereby endured torture and 'confronted death with verses on their tongue'.⁶⁶

Prisoners write poetry on their cell walls, as Mehdi Aslani, a former political prisoner, notes:

> The prisoner records their being with the help of poetry and shares their being with others by writing poetry on the walls [...]. Considering the fact that no pen or pencil is available to prisoners during interrogations, it was extraordinary to see so many lines on the walls of the cell. Poetry was pouring from the door and walls of the cell.⁶⁷

I was twenty-two years old and an undergraduate student when I was first interrogated by the Intelligence Department in Mashhad. After lengthy interrogations by the Disciplinary Committee of my university over several months, I was ordered to introduce myself to the Intelligence Department on a certain day. When I arrived at the building, knocked on the aluminium window and was let in, I was taken into a room, sat on a chair facing the wall, and told not to look back. Those first minutes were full of fear and anxiety. My mouth was dry and I was trembling. Suddenly, I saw a small piece of writing in blue on the wall. I leaned forward and read part of a line of a poem by Fakhreddin Araghi, a fourteenth-century Persian poet: *'in niz begzarad'* (this too shall pass). It gave me huge comfort. It reminded me that other people have been in my position before. They had sat on this very chair facing this very wall. The power of those words united me with all those people who had undergone interrogations in that room and I suddenly felt strong and was able to overcome my anxiety.

Iranian authorities are aware of this significance and as we saw earlier, both leaders of the Islamic Republic, Khomeini, and Khamenei, have shown a personal interest in literature in general and poetry in particular. This personal relationship – especially Khamenei's – with poetry could also have contributed to its perception as a powerful medium of expression. If Khamenei was not so personally involved, Iranian contemporary literature might have experienced less scrutiny by the state.

Chapter 3

THE CENSOR MACHINE: STRUCTURE AND MECHANISM, OPERATORS, CHANGES AND VARIATIONS

Structure and Mechanism

The Ministry of Culture and Islamic Guidance (MCIG) is the principal authority responsible for censorship. The Cultural Affairs Division within this Ministry has the duty of 'policymaking, planning, standardizing and engineering of cultural affairs in compliance with the objectives of Islam and the Islamic Revolution'.[1] Part of this duty involves control of the entire process of publication including issuing and revoking business licences for publishers, issuing pre- and post-publication licences, setting the standards of licensing, selection, and purchase of books for public libraries, and other relevant activities. A subsidiary department within this division, the Department General of Book and Reading – unofficially called the Book Office – carries out the censorship of books including literature. Under the relevant laws and regulations, printing houses are not permitted to publish any book or similar item which has not been issued a valid publication licence. In order to obtain a licence, a final copy of the book (print + CD) is submitted alongside an assessment form which contains the specifications of the book – title, author/translator/editor, publisher, circulation, edition, number of pages, size, ISBN, DDC, printer, binder, and a short description of the book. At the end of the form, the author signs a statement undertaking not to make any changes in the text or cover of the book – if passed – and to ensure that the printed version will be identical to the copy submitted for licensing. A current version of the form (2016) includes the following text:

I, … … author/translator of … … …, being fully aware of the Law on Objectives, Policies and Standards of Book Publications as amended by the Supreme Council of Cultural Revolution in their meeting number 660 dated 13 April 2010 hereby undertake to avoid making any change or alteration/correction in the text or the cover of the book after obtaining the publication licence and to fully abide by the said regulations and the contents of this form.[2]

The above form also includes the address and contact details of the author and should be signed and dated. Publishers use a similar form.

The book is then passed by the Book Office to a *momayyez*. *Momayyez* literally means auditor and is the same word used in economic literature. In the same way as a tax auditor, a *momayyez* is expected to examine the texts, identify the defects, and approve or disapprove. They may also offer corrections or amendments. The process is called *momayyezi* (auditing) which is presented by its supporters as a necessary measure to protect the public against harmful literature. The euphemism was intended to conceal the derogatory implications associated with the word censorship and make it more palatable both to those who take the job and to the public. Nevertheless, as with any other euphemism, it gradually revealed its true nature and needed to be replaced with a new euphemism. *Barras* and *barrasi* (valuer and valuation) are more recent terms preferred by the officials in charge although *momayyez/momayyezi* and even censor- censorship are frequently used both by proponents and opponents of censorship.

Censors assess the book and enter their comments in an assessment form. The assessment form includes entries such as a brief summary of the book, the censor's critical view, facts to be considered for final decision- making, overall assessment of the censor, negative and positive aspects of the book, corrections needed – if any – final assessment, and final comment. The last two items are filled by a senior censor (team leader). The views are summarized in a table which describes the book as either 'authorized', 'conditional', or 'unpublishable'. The director then looks at these views and acts accordingly.

Due to the sensitive nature of censorship, there has been little access to the archives of the Book Office, and thus far no official document has been released. The censorship criteria are not fully clear and the identity of censors is kept a secret. However, one scholar was able to obtain exceptional access to the censorship documents for Iranian Year 1375 – March 1996 to March 1997. Ahmad Rajabzadeh and his colleagues studied 1,400 different documents on censorship of a wide range of books in fiction, poetry, drama, literary criticism, history, religion, and so on. They included books written in Persian and those translated from foreign languages. Although Rajabzadeh does not provide any information on how he accessed these documents, there are some indications that this was made possible under the progressive policies of the reformist President Mohammad Khatami. Khatami came to power in 1997 and during his time, the MCIG became one of the strongholds of reformists. The publisher, Mohammad Javad Mozaffar (Kavir Publishers) was close to the reformists as were the authorities of the Book Office at the time.

He studied the censorship documents of 499 'unpublishable' and 1,289 'conditional' titles. Some of the conditional books were later reviewed in light of corrections made by the authors or agreements with the censors. The final number of books which failed to obtain a publication licence were 1,373 titles. These titles made up for around 10 per cent of the entire titles published that year. It should be noted that a large number of books which passed censorship were scientific or religious books such as the *Qur'an* which are normally immune from censorship. As one may expect, the majority of censored books were in the category of literature. With a total of 1,528 titles, literature counted for 10.6 per cent of the total books published that year. In the same year, 705 books in literature were branded 'unpublishable' or 'conditional' which accounts for 51.3 per cent of the entire books censored (1,373 titles).

From the total of 1,528 titles in literature, 73.9 per cent (1,129 titles) was Iranian literature, 10.3 per cent (157 titles) was made up of English and American literature, 4.7 per cent European literature, 5.4 per cent literature from other parts of the world, and 5.8 per cent (eighty-eight titles) were general topics related to literature. Two hundred and thirty-four titles in foreign fiction – mainly English and American – were assessed unpublishable which exceeds the number that passed censorship. Non-fiction international books in the fields of literary criticism, literary history, and poetry were not spared.

Persian fiction was one of the heavily censored areas. The total number of books in this category which were granted publication licence was 129 titles while the number of unpublishable titles was nearly double that figure (257 titles).

Persian poetry endured substantial censorship too. Around 71 per cent of books published in the category of literature were classified as Persian poetry (802 titles). Four hundred and twenty-eight of these were the divans of classical poets – poetry written before the 1940s – many of which were reprints. Three hundred and thirty-one books belonged to post-1940s poets. Approximately 21 per cent of these books (seventy titles) were elegiac or panegyric poems for the Shi'a saints, which are not usually categorized as poetry in the conventional sense since they are only verses read in religious rituals. Around 100 of the books belonged to those who are known as poets of the Islamic Revolution – including Khomeini, Gheisar Aminpoor, Shafaq, Joolideh Neishabouri, and Moosavi Garmaroodi. These poets are known to be staunch supporters of the regime. Only around 160 collections were the works of independent contemporary poets. According to Rajabzadeh, 105 collections of poetry were assessed by the censors as either unauthorized (23 per cent) or conditional (77 per cent). Seventy-one per cent of the censored poetry books belonged to post-1940s non-panegyric poets, mainly the works of less famous figures. Famous poets – contemporary or classic – were also censored. The *Divan* of Mohammad Taghi Bahar, the renowned poet of the Constitutional era, as well as a collection of lyric poetry by Fereidoun Moshiri and a collection of poems by Abolghasem Lahouti were labelled as unauthorized. The list of conditional books included a variety of classical poets, those of the Constitutional era and the most famous poets of the Iranian modernist movement.[3]

The statistics indicate that 46 per cent of all literary books submitted to the MCIG that year were deemed unauthorized or conditional. The ratio of works that were either banned or sent back for revision to those approved was as follows: literary criticism, 2.43 to 1; Persian fiction, 1.99 to 1; foreign fiction, 1.17 to 1; Persian folk or local poetry, 1.21 to 1; satire, 1.43 to 1; and 1 to 1 for anthologies. In the same year, 107 poetry collections, mainly modern contemporary poetry, were refused a licence, some 13 per cent of the total of 802 books published. We should also bear in mind that many of the books published were multiple prints of classical works such as the *Divan* of Hafiz (eighty prints), the *Shāhnāmeh* (seventeen prints), Baba Tahir poetry (seventeen prints), and Rumi (forty-four prints). Moreover, many other books classified as poetry were versified sermons or religious hymns. If we deduct these books, we will see that the actual percentage of censored contemporary poetry was much higher.[4]

As shown in the next chapter (Chapter 4), the censors appear to enjoy abundant freedom in censoring anything they assess problematic. The problem arises from the fact that the guidelines are vague and lack specificity. The main guideline on censorship – 'Objectives, Policies, Rules and Regulations for Publishing Books' – offers seven conditions which can render a book unpublishable.[5] These conditions range from promotion of blasphemy and moral corruption to encouraging dependence on superpowers. No further specification or exemplification is given. How are these criteria going to be understood? How does one define moral corruption? What type of writing encourages dependence on superpowers? This especially important duty is vested on censors to decide. Censors have their own understanding of the law. Their subjective taste and their ideological and political affiliations influence their judgement. Blake Atwood describes censorship in Iran as,

> an act of interpretation that occurs on two levels. First, the resolution itself must be interpreted. What, for example, might contribute to the corruption of morals? Then, the books undergoing inspection must also be interpreted. Ultimately, the process of censorship boils down to the interpretive skills of a single individual, who determines which books receive permits. The interpretive aspects of the process mean that censorship in Iran is a truly subjective procedure, and the system as a whole is highly susceptible to current waves in the political ocean.[6]

The censors' views and remarks and their demand for corrections are so wide and varied that little is left untouched. They censor books for political, ideological, religious reasons, and the like. Moreover, they also censor books if they feel some historical facts are not right or the rhyme and rhythm in a poem is poor. Sometimes they tend to adopt the role of an editor and comment on the literary merit of the work. Reasons for censorship are so varied and vast that no comprehensive listing is possible. In some cases, censors are not inclined to provide reasons and guessing their thought is not always easy. They have a say on nearly everything and therefore an accurate classification of all the items which might be censored is practically impossible. In the area of politics, for example, any critical view on the Constitution, the leaders – past and present – the clergy and religious figures, people of high office in the government, judiciary, or elsewhere may get censored. Criticism of the Iraq–Iran war and its consequences; social, political, or economic conditions in the country; contempt or insult of different social and ethnic groups, foreign nations, Islamic and liberation movements; or insulting the major press and media or public institutions is not permissible. Promoting liberal and secular views or socialist and communist ideologies, liberalism and technocracy, radical nationalism, and racism are all censored, as is any praise for intellectuals – even Islamic intellectuals such as Shariati and Sorush. Any support of the monarchy, Israel, or America can face censorship.

With regard to religion, the confusion is also immense. A large number of views or topics may get censored. Any material deemed to promote religions other than Islam or glorify non-religious or anti-religious movements, promote mysticism or

Sufism, support Judaism or Zionism, or deemed to invoke sectarianism is censored. Casting doubt on the divine origin of Islam, Christianity, or Judaism; assuming divine origin for non-Abrahamic religions such as Buddhism; insulting religious principles or rituals; or promoting Baha'i, Babi or Ismaili faiths are censored, as is any doubt cast on the existence of soul or the idea of a saviour (*Imam Mahdi*). Insulting the Sunni Imams is not permitted while promoting Sunnism or praising Sunni Imams is also frowned upon. Although promoting Sufism is not permissible, insulting or ridiculing Sufis is not authorized.

Abusive language, indecent diction, any mention of alcohol or alcohol-related activities or jargons is usually censored. Any literature which can be viewed as promoting smoking or narcotics is banned and pictures of pipes or cigars and cigarettes may get censored. Cultural references to narcotics and smoking – even in a critical context – is sometimes censored.

Music has been a contested area in the Islamic Republic of Iran since the very beginning. In the early years after the Revolution, except for revolutionary songs, music was banned. Even now, many types of music in Iran is underground and official concerts are regularly cancelled under threat from the hardliners. Female solo singing is still officially forbidden and Iranian national television avoids showing musical instruments even when broadcasting a music concert. In literature, promoting music, names of instruments, descriptions of Western music styles – pop, jazz, etc. – names and pictures of some musicians – for example, pre-Revolutionary pop singers – have been subject to censorship.

Sex and sexuality are probably the widest area of censorship in contemporary literature in Iran. Depending on the censor, sometimes a simple reference to love is even considered sexual and is censored. In general though, sex is a large forbidden ground. Incest, homosexuality, rape, sodomy, paedophilia, masturbation, and unconventional sex are not to be named or described. Weakening conservative ideas on marriage gets censored as does the promotion of open sexual relationships or promiscuity. Abortion, sex education, sexually transmitted diseases and social interactions of men and women – parties, social gatherings, sport events – are areas best to be avoided. Generally speaking, anything of a sexual nature carries the risk of censorship. It should be noted that censors' views on sexuality are not always identical so while one censor might reject a book for its sexual content, another censor might assess it as non-sexual. Romance and platonic love is sometimes treated as erotic and may be censored.

Historical novels or any book with historical references can be subject to censorship if they contradict the official narratives of the Islamic Republic. The Islamic Republic is not particularly fond of the pre-Islamic history of Iran. In a reaction to the Shah's glorification of pre-Islamic Iran, the Islamic Republic is more in favour of the Islamic civilization and the role of Iranians in the wider Islamic history. Criticizing the Islamic Arab invasion of Iran, insulting Arab invaders or history of Islam, insulting historical Islamic figures, or praising Iranian Anti-Islamic resistance movements is censored. Marxist or non-religious approaches to modern history are not favoured and any indication of historical injustice towards religious or ethnic minorities might get censored.

Social interactions and lifestyle, including interactions of opposite sexes which might be viewed as Westernized or capitalistic, for example, words like girlfriend-boyfriend; names of items of clothing which are deemed to be Western such as tie or bowtie; references to female underwear or immodest apparel; pets – dogs or cats; reference to pigs or ham; dancing – ballet, tango, disco, club, etc.; references to gambling and betting; violence and violent behaviour; promotion of suicide; description or promotion of violence; and terror or praise of criminals are usually censored.

The Islamic Republic has a contradictory approach to women. On the one hand, it portrays women as a very noble and highly esteemed group in society, while on the other, it limits their social functioning and social freedoms. It expects a similar approach from Iranian writers and poets. Therefore, any negative description of women as cheating or deceitful and any insult to girls and women even in the form of proverbs may get censored. Insult to traditional images of women or hijab, negative views on the man–woman relationship in Islam or Iran, description of relationships between Muslim women and non-Muslim men, writing about prostitution, or indicating women's lack of freedom in Iran and Eastern countries may also be subject to censorship.

As we can see, there is nearly no area of human culture which is untouched in one way or another. Censors approach the books looking for the above examples. Regardless of the type of book, they may censor it if they find anything objectionable. They may censor a poem because they found the word 'wine' in it. They may censor a novel because one of the characters is a gambler or a drunkard and it doesn't matter if this character is the protagonist or the antagonist.

Operators of the Censor Machine

This broad and rather incoherent application of censorship regime is particularly important in view of the experience of feeling censored. While trying to categorize the wide variety of instances of censorship, I discovered that it is practically impossible to provide an exhaustive list. It is consequently impossible for an Iranian contemporary writer to predict what will or will not be censored. Such a writer will pause on any scene and any line and even choice of word during the writing process. The significant role that censors play in shaping contemporary literature in Iran cannot be stressed enough. They are very often the first and, in some cases, the only readers of books. It comes as no surprise, therefore, that writers are curious to know them and to discover their disposition. Their identity is, however, strictly protected. Iranian authors have no idea who reads their manuscripts and who collaborates towards the final shape of their creative productions. Many Iranian writers and poets have expressed their interest to meet with the censors. They hope that a face-to-face dialogue might help save some of the books from censorship. They hope too that censors might help them to understand the censorship rules and standards. However, there is no mechanism in place to meet censors. If you object to the censor's decision, you can submit a written letter to the Book Office. Your book might then be reviewed again or assigned to a new censor, but the identity of the censor will not normally be revealed to you.

This lack of transparency has led to different speculations. Some believe that censors are among the writers themselves. Some say they are members of intelligence forces and some suggest that the censor department is actually based in Qom and run by the clergy. Some consider censors to be well-versed in literature while others believe that many of them are not qualified for the job and that they sometimes rely on computer programs to detect problematic words and phrases, and that, for that reason, the outcome of their censorship looks mechanical. Some writers prefer learned censors who will not reject their harmless books for imaginary dangers while some others are worried that clever and cultivated censors will discover their tricks more easily and will reveal the hidden content of their books. Both groups are equally curious about the identity of the censors. Ali Shojaei Saein, a former director of the Book Office, describes censors as highly educated experts who work extremely hard to detect threats and protect the cultural integrity of the country. He told news agencies that university professors, PhD holders, and PhD candidates work as censors. In the area of literature, he said: 'Our team comprises university professors in literature and writers and poets'.[7]

In view of some critics, hiding the identity of censors reveals a major paradox: If censorship is a good thing – as is claimed by the Islamic Republic authorities – and censors are serving the people, why should their identity be kept secret? Mohammad Hossein Papoli Yazdi, a geography professor whose edition of an eighteenth-century geography book had been refused a publication licence, wrote an open letter to the Minister of Culture and Islamic Guidance and questioned the Islamic foundations of censorship. He pointed to the views of some clerics who claim that censorship is an act of *Amr-e bel Ma'ruf* (Enjoining Good) and *Nahy-e anil Monkar* (Forbidding Evil) and therefore a religious duty and argued that if it is so, why should the censors remain unknown? Why should a writer accept advice from somebody who he can't see? He adds: 'The fact that they hide their identity shows that they are ashamed of what they are doing'.[8] Some suggest that they are kept unknown for security reasons. The fact that they have antagonized a lot of people by their actions contributes to this assumption. Whether ashamed or scared, withholding the identity of censors has raised questions and speculations to which an unidentified chief censor, who was interviewed by *E'temad* in 2016, tried to provide an answer. He said:

> I don't think writers see us as their enemy anymore. We are now interacting with writers. The Head of the Book Office is meeting authors every Tuesday. If a writer or publisher objects to a censor's decision, the Head calls us into the meeting to speak with the author. By God, we are not monsters. We even sometimes forge close friendships with authors.[9]

One journalist asked the Head of the Book Office in 2014 about this same issue. Elaheh Khosravi Yeganeh told Ali Shojaei Saein:

There has always been a question in my mind and I have heard it from many authors and publishers as well. Why are the *momayyezes* (censors) never introduced? Why is everything so confidential? Why do the lists of corrections given to publishers have no letterhead/ reference number or signature? If *momayyezi* (censorship) is good, why should it not be open? Why are these people always in hiding?[10]

To which Shojaei Saein answered:

What you say is not exactly true. They are here and sometimes they even talk to publishers. But this issue has two different aspects. One is their personal choice. The second is the view of the Book Office. We don't want these people to be known. Because our society is a special society. We don't want these people to be approached through unofficial channels[…]. Don't see this as a security issue.[11]

He is hinting at the likelihood of authors and publishers trying to befriend or bribe censors to have their books approved.

The unidentified chief censor interviewed by E'temad didn't like to be called *momayyez* (censor) and asked to be called *barras* (valuer). Although *momayyez* itself is a euphemism it seems that the overuse of this word has now eliminated the euphemistic features and it is perceived by many to be identical with censor. He therefore wants to introduce a new euphemism. In this interview he states that none of the censors are in regular employment of the Book Office. They are generally professionals such as university lecturers or instructors in religious seminaries, or cultural experts in other organizations. Some of them are even writers or publishers. According to him, *momayyezi* is not a fulltime job and some don't even receive payment for it because they believe they are contributing to the promotion of culture and gain personal gratification from their service. Although censors undergo no training, he believes they learn the trade from their co-workers and more experienced colleagues. Chief censors are nominated by the Book Office and introduced to the Book Supervisory Board whose members are appointed by the Supreme Council of Cultural Revolution. The Book Supervisory Board finalizes the appointments. Chief censors are then free to form their team of censors. He strongly rejects the accusations that censors are uneducated and do not appreciate good literature.[12]

A former official in the Book Office confirmed this claim. Mahmoud Motahharinia worked as the Scientific Secretary in the Book Office and is a strong supporter of censorship. He was interviewed in October 2013 by Mashregh News after he had left office and said: 'During the past 6 or 7 years, we tried to employ specialists with a minimum master's degree and higher. Most of our colleagues are faculty members in universities who devoted their free time to us. They sometimes stay in office until 10 p.m. and work.'[13] He tries to portray censors as highly educated self-sacrificing people who believe in the important and valuable job they do and are even ready to work late into the night. They don't get paid sufficiently and censorship is underfunded. He attributes the failures in censorship to lack of proper funding.

According to him the wages are ridiculous. A censor receives IRR 50,000 for reading and assessing a 500 page book – this is equivalent to just over a pound based on the exchange rate at the time of the interview. 'They are actually doing jihad. More importantly, the authorities fail to pay even these meagre wages' he said.[14]

The unnamed chief censor who was interviewed by *E'temad* expressed the same view. He claims that no one earns a living by this job. Each censor reads four or five books a month and they are paid between IRR 2,000 to IRR 4,000 per page – equivalent to 4–8 pence. Although this is significantly higher than the amount claimed by Dr Motahharinia, it is still not a very attractive income.

The overall understanding based on what few censors have so far revealed is that censorship is not a financially rewarding job. If we accept their claims, we have to agree that censors do not do this job for money and believe they are actually contributing to a sacred cause by promoting Islamic culture and combating cultural invasion. It is, however, clear that censors are not trained for the job and, in the early years after the Revolution, they may not have been highly educated. It is also clear that the outcome of censorship can be vastly different depending on who reads and assesses your book. Although there are rules to be followed, they are too loose and open to subjective interpretation. External pressures on censors are also evident as some authorities within the system might believe in stricter censorship while some others might advocate more lenient or no censorship at all. The censors work in specialized teams each headed by a chief censor and assigned to assess one special category, be it religion, fiction, poetry, art, and so on.

Rajabzadeh, who had full access to censorship documents in Iranian Year 1375 provides a slightly different image. He says that each censor is designated a unique code and based on these codes he concludes that all the books in the study year had been assessed by 188 censors. Some censors had assessed only one and some up to ninety-three different titles. The average number was seven. Only twenty-eight censors had surpassed the average number and some of these were team leaders who had also commented on assessments made by other censors. On average, each had read thirty-five books, with some only nine and others as many as ninety-three titles. From the entire number of 1,276 books whose censors he was able to identify – by code number – 304 titles (22 per cent) had been assessed by 160 censors, and 972 titles (71 per cent) had been assessed by the remaining twenty-eight censors. Five of these twenty-eight censors were team leaders who had the final say in regard to disputed books. So, if a book did not pass the censorship standards in the initial assessments, the decision would fall on these team leaders. If we generalize this finding to the books which passed censorship, we may conclude that more than 70 per cent of all books submitted to the Book Office in that year (14,000 titles) were actually assessed by only twenty-eight censors, thus these censors were responsible for 70 per cent of the entire book industry throughout the country. Rajabzadeh also questions the specialized nature of censorship showing that the twenty-eight principal censors had decided on books in nearly every category. One censor, for example, decided the destiny of eight titles on philosophy, three on religion, two on social sciences, eight on languages, three on applied sciences, twenty-two on literature, and two titles on history.[15]

If censors were really highly educated and cultivated people who work for such meagre incomes, censorship would be a very unpleasant profession unless done for reasons beyond money. In John Milton's words: 'There cannot be a more tedious and unpleasing journey-work[...] than to be made the perpetual reader[s] of unchosen books'.[16]

Censors vary on the type of judgements they pass as well as the ratio of books they pass/reject and the type and frequency of corrections they demand. Rajabzadeh found out that a specific number of censors were extremely harsh and tended to refuse most of the books while some others were less decisive and demanded corrections rather than totally rejecting the books. Some censors try to provide evidence and base their decisions on some sort of reasoning. Others, especially chief censors, pass general statements and make no effort to justify their decisions or provide any evidence for their findings.

He also studied the style of writing of the censors and their occasional mistakes in understanding the texts. His main conclusion is that censors are neither highly qualified nor expert readers. Their style of writing is commonplace and there is little indication that they appreciate literature at a deep level. He therefore concludes that they are probably young and novices in the field of literature.[17] Of course we should bear in mind that his study is limited to only one year (1996–1997) and things might have changed drastically since then.

Changes and Variations

Earlier I said how important the role of an operator can be within the Iranian censor apparatus. It is largely the way censorship laws are interpreted and implemented that affects the severity or ease of censorship experience. Although the rules and regulations on censorship have generally remained the same throughout the lifetime of the Islamic Republic, changes of government have usually brought about some variation in censorship policies. The main policymaking body in culture, that is, the Supreme Council of Cultural Revolution reports to the Supreme Leader and although it is headed by the president, its policies do not necessarily reflect the incumbent president's policies. In addition to the president and a select number of cabinet ministers, SCCR's membership includes the parliament speaker and head of judiciary as well as cultural dignitaries directly appointed by the Supreme Leader. Nevertheless, any change of administration or even change of officials within the same administration has changed the outcome of the censor regime. This changing atmosphere is indicative of the fluid nature of cultural policymaking and the various, somewhat conflicting views on culture among the cultural authorities and influential circles in Iran. In view of the subjective experience of feeling censored, these shifts in policy reveal another dimension of the Iranian censorship experience: uncertainty and unpredictability. Earlier I discussed the depth and breadth of censorship experience and now in this part I would like to focus on the temporary and provisional aspects of censorship experience.

As far as the publication of literature is concerned, the authority in charge, that is, MCIG, acts differently under different ministers. A detailed study requires access to full information including internal directives and procedures within the Book Office and the wider cultural establishment – which could itself be the subject of an independent book. For ease of reference I have contented myself with a demarcation of major shifts in the direction of policies and scope of censorship. The aim is to see how these shifts respond to the experiences of those who were subjected to unstable censorship practices. These shifts have usually occurred simultaneously with major changes in executive power, namely the election of a new president, but even a change of the minister or a senior executive could have major implications. To the censored subject, this is a window for hope. A hope which can end in despair or disillusionment. The factional differences between powerful groups within the system provides a small opportunity when some rules are bent and some books get licensed. Although the cultural agenda of the regime pursues authentication of the Iranian-Islamic culture, there is no consensus as to what constitutes an authentic culture.[18] This lack of consensus usually creates a battleground of ideas and opens opportunities for those on whose territory these factions are fighting. Depending on which faction gains the upper hand, this window might slightly open or close. If the more culturally tolerant faction triumphs, censorship may be relaxed to a certain degree.

The 1979 Revolution ended censorship and led to an unprecedented freedom of the press and publications. Although the crackdown on newspapers resumed a few months after the victory of the Revolution, there was no state-imposed censorship on books during the early years of the Revolution (1979–1981). Governments were short-lived and the regime had more pressing priorities. Pressure groups were openly active but they mainly targeted newspapers and thus literature was not in the forefront. According to a report by Farrokh Amirfaryar, the highest growth rate in book publication – an average of 52 per cent – was seen immediately after the Revolution. He attributes this growth to social changes in addition to the lack of a controlling authority.[19] The outbreak of war and the dominance of war conditions reduced publications and helped the government silence potential critics. Some of the pre-Revolutionary writers and poets had left the country in fear of prosecution while others were uncertain of the conditions and unable to publish much during the war. At the same time, a new generation of writers emerged who defined their mission as spreading the message of Islam and supporting the war effort. It seemed like a good opportunity for those who supported the system to shine under government patronage. Fatemeh Shams who has researched the state sponsorship in post-Revolutionary Iranian literature holds that the regime reached out to a new generation of religious literati as part of its Islamization strategy (1980–1983), 'hoping to train an alternative group of poets and writers who had spurned the secular mindset of the pre-Revolutionary intelligentsia.'[20] The cultural organizations came under government control and new cultural enterprises were created to train and promote the poets and writers of the Islamic Revolution.

Amirfaryar believes that, as with any other commodity, the production of books suffered during the war with Iraq (1981–1988) but recovered after the war: 'By the end of the war, book publication increased about 90 per cent in a matter of one year and reached 7,848 titles in 1988'.[21] In addition to logistical issues, Amirfaryar credits changes in the cultural and social environment for the growth. Mohammad Khatami had been serving as the Minister of Culture and Islamic Guidance since 1982. During his tenure (1982–1992), the MCIG showed a great degree of tolerance although his actions were limited by the more conservative forces. By the end of the war (1988), the MCIG had changed its policies gradually and welcomed a more open cultural atmosphere. New journals obtained a licence and books by well-known writers and intellectuals who had been secluded for years were published. A combination of new policies and the end of the eight-year war with Iraq 'led to a cultural vitality and the more nuanced relations between the state and the intellectual community developed'.[22] These policies, however, were harshly criticized by different sources of power within the system. Mohammad Khatami came under pressure for his relatively liberal approach to culture. According to Amirfaryar, 'Poems and stories published were scrutinized; words and phrases extracted and used in order to attack the MCIG. The sensitivity was mainly directed towards the older generation of Iranian poets and writers'.[23]

The pressures forced Khatami to resign on 22 August 1992 after around ten years in the post. In his autobiography, he attributes his resignation to disputes with the competing and higher authorities and writes: 'Due to difference in opinion and methods between myself and some of the relevant authorities, I resigned in 1992 in favour of freedom of expression, democracy and the rule of law which I deeply believed in'.[24]

Although the resignation of Khatami and appointment of Ali Larijani to the post reduced the pressure considerably, some policies were still being criticized. On 14 February 1994, Mostafa Mirsalim replaced Ali Larijani and held the post for four years. During that time, censorship became extensive and publishing exceedingly difficult. All books were required to obtain a new licence for each print run, even if their previous licence had been obtained only a few months prior. Amirfaryar writes: 'The lengthy process of issuing licences, assessing all books – even books in pure science disciplines – and banning advertisement of books prior to their publication were among the policies adopted during this period'.[25]

Banning advertisements for future publications had financial implications both for publishers and for independent journals who depended on cultural advertising. Mirsalim's approach was extremely conservative and precautionary. Both his predecessors, even the conservative Larijani, had been criticized by some influential clerics for their assumed leniency towards culture. During his term, the Book Office was closed to publishers and authors. If a book was refused publication, the office would issue a short notice on plain paper – no letterhead, reference, date, stamp, or signature. A sample notice, which I personally saw, was as follows:

Mr Ali Abdollahi,
Your book *Bar Pāgard-e Yādhā* (On the Stairwell of Memories) is assessed as unauthorized based on the rules and standards of book publication.[26]

Amirfaryar confirms that during Mirsalim's time, publication of literature decreased considerably.[27] Pressure groups were actively involved in acts of protests, which were not always peaceful, against cultural products such as movies or novels.

The election of Khatami to the presidency in 1997 brought about major hopes for social and political change. Under his rule, newspapers flourished and the publishing industry developed considerably. In 1999, according to Christopher de Bellaigue, the combined circulation of Iranian newspapers and magazines doubled to around 2,750,000 compared with a couple of years previously.[28] Likewise, the publication of poetry and fiction increased. In 1998, 220 new poetry titles were published, most of them belonging to emerging poets.[29] In a study on the publication of books during the first two decades after the Revolution, Alireza Mahdiani and Seyed Hassan Mortezavi wrote: '[...] 1997 through 2002 [the year of publication of their study] saw the highest number of literary books published. The average annual growth of literature publication during this period was about 10 per cent. However, literature is the only category of books that has always had a negative growth rate after the Revolution, in view of the ratio to the total publications'.[30]

Many writers who were unable to publish anything, were now able to publish their books. Although the laws had not changed, the way those laws were enforced changed drastically. In his election manifesto, Khatami emphasized clarity and well-defined regulations for the publishing industry and the protection of the rights and security of authors and publishers.[31] So, while he accepted the necessity of pre-publication supervision, he wanted it to be impartial and fully regulated. One of the main criticisms against censorship was the wide disparity between different censors and the confusion among publishers who were unable to predict if a given book would be licensed or not. The new administration clearly took a different approach. They opened the doors of the Book Office to publishers and authors and one was able to visit the directors and enter into negotiations about their book. My first book which had been rejected before faced many corrections. I managed to reduce those corrections to less than half after a short meeting with the Head of the Book Office who appeared knowledgeable and well-behaved. Amir Hassan Cheheltan, a novelist, believes that censorship was harsh in all periods except for a short while during the Khatami presidency and the first two years after the Revolution when the MCIG was not yet well established. He claims that it was only during Khatami's time that he could negotiate with the censors.[32] Other measures by the MCIG were also very influential. They made book licences permanent so that if a book was licensed once, it didn't need to undergo the licensing process for subsequent reruns. They also relaxed the requirements for obtaining a business licence as a publisher and hence the number of publishers increased considerably to near 8,000.[33] Books purchased for public libraries were now chosen from a more diverse group of authors and publishers. They even had a plan to abolish pre-publication licensing and make publishers responsible for observing the criteria.

At the first stage, a number of 100 more experienced publishers were chosen to take part in this plan.[34] This proposal was rejected by the publishers who feared they would have to face judicial and security authorities if they accepted such a responsibility that would practically turn them into censors. The proposal didn't go ahead and even the minister who was championing these changes, Ata'ollah Mohajerani, was forced to resign under pressure from the conservatives. His successor, Ahmad Masjedjamei, pursued similar policies more cautiously to avoid provoking the hardliners and was content to protect what had already been gained. Independent literary awards such as the Golshiri Award, Mehregan Award, and the Journalists' Award for Poetry came to being and *Kānun-e Nevisandegān-e Iran* (Iranian Writers Association) managed – for the first and last time during the lifetime of the Islamic Republic – to openly hold their annual general meeting. The government's tolerant policies, however, were harshly criticized by the hardliners and conservative factions. Their actions, which included judicial prosecution of a number of writers and even executives in the MCIG, brought back a strict censorship regime during the last two years of Khatami's presidency.[35] The window of hope that had opened by Khatami's election gradually ended in disillusionment and despair because of the upper hand of the conservatives in judiciary and security departments.

The reformist government came to an end in 2005 and Mahmoud Ahmadinejad was elected president. The crackdown on the press entered a new phase and censorship became much stricter. Ahmadinejad's Minister of Culture and Islamic Guidance, Saffar Harandi, a member of the Islamic Revolutionary Guard Corps, undertook to introduce new cultural policies and to put an end to the more relaxed regime of the previous government. According to Payam Yazdanjoo, the result of this new approach was 'unprecedented severity in issuing a publication licence for books of "problematic content", that is, contrary to the Sharia, the Islamic ethics, or the prestige of Islam or the Islamic Republic, as well as obliging publishers to obtain a new licence for reprinting previously published books'.[36] Consequently, many books which would have successfully passed censorship under the former administration were rejected and some titles that had been repeatedly published before were now banned. The new censors also encouraged self-censorship. Harandi openly recommended authors and publishers to delete what he called problematic content from their books before submitting them to the censor. Yazdanjoo writes: 'Submitting any book that would fail to pass the censorship due to problematic content would bring about a negative point for the publisher and frequent negative points would put an end to the activity of the publisher and would eventually nullify the publisher's business licence.'[37] This type of punishment was a permanent threat which endangered the economic sustainability of publishers. As a result, many became extra cautious and avoided the risk of accepting books which might be rejected by the censors. The new administration did not even honour licences it had granted itself. Ramezani Forati, director of the Book Office, observed that a book might obtain a licence and be published but that its distribution might be prevented at any time if it was understood that the Office had made a mistake.[38]

To help the censors search for undesirable material, publishers were also ordered to deliver a CD of every book, in addition to the printed copy. This led to speculation that the censors might be using software to identify problematic words and that many works might be rejected simply because no one even cared to read them.[39] During the presidential debates in 2009, the reformist candidate, Mir Hossein Mousavi, described some of the problems of the Ahmadinejad government in the area of culture: 'Somebody's book has been published fifteen times. The book has obtained a licence from this same government. It is banned in its sixteenth reprint [...]. Every government should honour its signature and stand by what it promises.'[40] Ahmadinejad agreed with his opponent and stated that he had written and spoken to the minister.[41]

Policies did not change during Ahmadinejad's second term. Mohammad Hosseini, his next Minister of Culture and Islamic Guidance, was also a member of Islamic Revolutionary Guard Corps. The BBC Persian has published a list of books which had been licensed and published during Khatami's presidency but were denied a reprint licence by Ahmadinejad's administration. This list, which is incomplete and has been compiled with the help of authors who provided the information, includes the titles and bibliographical information of 103 books written in Persian and forty-two books translated from foreign languages.[42]

Censorship during Ahmadinejad's term was so vast and comprehensive that even supporters of the Islamic Republic, including those known as Islamic revolutionary poets, for instance Mostafa Rahmandoost, Abduljabbar Kakayi, Afshin Alae and Soheil Mahmoudi, criticized it openly. Rahmandoost, a former high-ranking official in the MCIG, considered the period of Ahmadinejad administration a bleak time for culture, saying: 'During the past dark years, a catastrophe struck culture and art which cannot be remedied easily.'[43] Seyed Mehdi Shojaei, a novelist who had previously published a novel in praise of the 1979 Revolution, was censored and the authorities prevented distribution of one of his novels. He then wrote a story castigating the cultural policies of Ahmadinejad and the structure of the Islamic Republic.[44]

Hassan Rouhani was elected president in 2013. He appointed Ali Jannati as the Minister of Culture and Islamic Guidance. Jannati expressed discontent with the censorship system and, in one of his first interviews, revealed his plan to abolish pre-publication censorship and entrust the publishers with *momayyezi*.[45] He expressly criticized the arbitrary censorship of the previous administration and complained that the security and secret services were dictating policy to cultural directors and treating culture as a security concern. He acknowledged that directors in cultural organizations had a security attitude towards culture or were directed by security authorities. He claimed to have a list of fifty publishers who were not permitted to take part in international book fairs – based on instructions from security organizations.[46] He added: 'There were about 400 books which were either refused publication or left undecided just because they had once been published by the publishers who were now on the blacklist.'[47] Although the new administration sparked many hopes, it did not deliver much. Censorship of literature relaxed a little and some books previously categorized as unpublishable found their way to market. Still, there are many books that undergo censorship and a large number remain unpublishable.

President Rouhani has frequently criticized the state of censorship and has asked authors and publishers to teach the authorities how to supervise book publication. He defends censorship but wants it more regulated. In the thirty-second Book of the Year Award Ceremony in February 2015, Rouhani said: 'I don't say whether to have *momayyezi* or not, I am saying that we cannot have a hundred principles for *momayyezi*. *Momayyezi* is necessary but it should be limited to moral standards, sacred principles, and national security issues'.[48] His initiative to assign censorship to authors and publishers has been criticized both by hardliners and authors. The hardliners believe that this would relax censorship while the authors and publishers fear it would add to more self-censorship and compromise their security, because they would be held more accountable than they currently are.[49] The *Kānun-e Nevisandegān-e Iran* (Iranian Writers' Association) acknowledged that some unpublished titles had been published and that censorship had been relaxed, but said it would be too optimistic to congratulate ourselves: 'Let's assume that the books delayed in the MCIG obtained a publication licence and that the licensing is now quicker and censorship less strict. Now, what have we achieved except a more relaxed and speedier censorship'?[50]

In general, we can assert that except for the first two years after the Revolution, literature has been censored during the lifetime of the Islamic Republic. The degree of censorship has varied depending on the political atmosphere and the government in charge. The revolutionary regime had more pressing priorities in the first couple of years and therefore a relative freedom of publications prevailed until 1981, but from 1982 to 1988, cultural production suffered because of the war conditions. The period from 1988 to 1992 saw a revival of the publishing industry which ended with the resignation of Mohammad Khatami as the Minister of Culture and Islamic Guidance under oppositional pressures, while 1992 to 1997 was a period of strict censorship. During the reformist Khatami government (1997–2005), censorship was relaxed to some degree. Ahmadinejad's two terms in office (2005–2013) was one of the darkest periods for culture and Iranian literature experienced an extreme censorship climate. Since Rouhani's election in 2013, censorship is less strict and some procedures have improved but the struggle is far from over. Rouhani's policies on culture are being criticized by two opposing fronts: The conservatives who favour stricter censorship regime and the intellectuals who demand an end to censorship.

Chapter 4

CENSORS AT WORK

In light of what was previously said about the censors, it would be interesting to watch them at work and to see how they implement the policies and carry out their duties. As told earlier, any book which is submitted for assessment is passed to a specialized team based on the category to which the book belongs. A censor will then read the book and offer their general feedback in the form of 'authorized', 'conditional', or 'unauthorized (unpublishable)'. In the case of authorized or unauthorized books, their remarks are mainly descriptive. They will write a summary of the book and cite some examples to justify their decision. In the case of books which the censors assess 'conditional', they usually make a list of corrections and demand those corrections to be made in order for the book to become publishable. The list of corrections can be extensive and may include major changes. They might demand a change of title, or of words and expressions, the deletion of parts in chapters, or the addition of explanatory footnotes or a preface. In some cases, books of undesirable content have been published with an introduction by the editor/translator or publisher condemning the content of the book they have themselves edited, translated, or published.

Literature in all subgroups is censored heavily. Fiction, drama, poetry, children's literature, and even literary criticism are subject to similar criteria. However, due to the different nature of these works, the censorship has some variations in practice.

Fiction is truly problematic. Novelists and storytellers write about ideas, politics, and human interactions. They describe feelings, desires, and sentiments. All these areas can raise the alarm and censors themselves are aware of the problematic nature of fiction. The unidentified chief censor who was interviewed by *E'temad* said:

> Fiction is an area open to interpretation. We tell a writer that what you have written here will spread corruption. They say that they are simply discussing a social problem. Even *barrase*s (censors) have different views with regard to fiction. Allegory, metaphor, symbol, metonymy, and figurative language make our job difficult in assessing fiction. Other areas are not as difficult and don't require as much effort![1]

Motahharinia, a former high-ranking authority in the Book Office, confirmed that fiction is a highly sensitive area. A decision on a novel usually takes much longer than other genres. Many writers complain that their novel has been with the Book Office for years without any decision being made. One reason, Motahharinia says, is the fact that not everyone has the patience to read a novel to the end and therefore fewer censors are willing to accept the job. The second reason, he says, is that it is usually a contested subject where different censors might have opposing views and a work is thus often referred to chief censors to make a final decision.[2]

Plays are censored for exactly the same reasons as fiction as well as the description of the clothing of female characters which may also render a play unpublishable. Books on the history of literature, anthologies, criticism, or commentary on literature are also censored for similar reasons. According to Rajabzadeh's research, there were only fourteen books on literary history and literary criticism published in 1375 [Iranian year] (1996–1997), while in the same year, thirty-four books in this category were rejected. This represents the highest ratio of unsuccessful to successful submissions (2.4:1) among all book categories. The highest ratio is partly due to the fact that an anthology or history of literature is censored even if only one of the authors named/quoted does not pass the censorship criteria.

The nature of poetic language might lead one to expect poetry to undergo less censorship, as poetry usually avoids direct statements and description of any nature is concise and contained. In spite of this, poetry is censored for similar reasons to fiction, with one major difference of which we need to be reminded. Due to the lower translatability – compared with fiction – the majority of censored poetry is Persian poetry.

As we can clearly see, factors which may render a work of literature unpublishable or conditional are extensive and varied. A book might be censored for virtually every reason or none at all. That's what makes the Iranian censor machine uniquely unpredictable. It is in view of this unpredictability as a main characteristic of the experience of censorship that I try to provide a taxonomy of reasons for the censorship of literature. I could have refered to the rules and regulations in a more 'predictable' censorship regime where the censors followed 'objective' procedures and passed 'measurable' decisions. However, my approach to censorship as a sociopolitical phenomoenon which is responsive to the experience of those subject to censorship can only be descriptive. I have therefore looked at the actual examples of censorship rather than the rules or procedures and have tried to categorize them in order to show what can render a book unpublishable and how the censor–author interaction shapes Iranian literature. My taxonomy doesn't follow any specific logic except the frequency and cannot be exahustive as my information is partial. Another researcher with a larger or different pool of examples may get a different picture and offer a different taxonomy. Based on the information available to me, I suggest the following broad categories in order of prevalence: 1. Sex and Eroticism, 2. Politics, 3. Religion. 4. Culture and Society, 5. Technical and Literary Issues, 6. Unspecified, and 7. Extratextual Reasons.

Each of these categories can be divided into subcategories. For example, I have included lyric poetry under sex and eroticism because the censors treat it as such. Cultural and social issues include lifestyle and cultural traits as well as social problems such as addiction, alcohol, gambling, divorce, offensive and abusive language, crime and violence, and so on. Technical and literary issues mainly concern editorial reasons such as the quality of the prose, accuracy of rhyme and rhythm, and historical accuracy which one would expect to be the job of an editor rather than a censor. Unspecified cases include cases of censorship when no reason is given by the censor or the reasons cited are ambiguous and unclear. And finally, by extratextual I mean reasons which may impose censorship on books without any direct link to the content such as when the author or publisher is blacklisted.

I have provided numerous examples in each category to show the process and outcome of censors' work and the way they treat the texts submitted to them for licensing. These examples are selected to show the seemingly indefinite layers of censorship, each representing a new subcategory. Each subcategory then branches into smaller subcategories and this goes on ad infinitum. A majority of these examples have been taken from Rajabzadeh's book as it is the only valid source which relies on documents produced by the censors themselves. The aim of this chapter is to offer an unretouched image of the scope and extent of censorship as far as possible. Censorship is a human experience and, as we can see in this chapter, each experience is unique. It therefore helps me argue my case for a redefinition of censorship based on the experience of feeling censored. I have kept my comments to a minimum so that readers get an uninterrupted picture of censors at work.[3]

Reasons for Censorship: A Taxonomy

Sexual and erotic implications count for the largest number of censorship cases in literature. The censors tend to see sex even in the most unexpected places. In their broad definition of sex, even a simple embrace of people of opposite genders or an exchange of affectionate words is deemed improper and should be deleted. In fiction, this single category is responsible for the censorship of most titles.

The description of relationships between man and woman is severely censored. Any word or phrase which directly or indirectly alludes to sexual or romantic relationships usually gets censored. The censors have a word for such works; *mobtazal*. This is a difficult term to define. In common usage, it means banal, commonplace, tasteless, degenerate, cheap, or clichéd. However, in the official language of the Islamic system, it normally refers to anything of a sexual or erotic nature perceived by the authorities to be degrading, demeaning, or shameful. Hence, we may say that *mobtazal* is a dysphemism aimed at associating any sexual reference with low, vulgar, and commonplace conduct. This dysphemism helps easily reject a large volume of art and literature and leaves the creators of such art or literature defenceless, since few people would want to defend clichéd, stereotype, and commonplace literature. Ida Meftahi traces back the use of the word '*mobtazal*' to pre-Revolution times. Based on her research, *mobtazal* was used by the leftist groups in Iran to 'devalue and dismiss a range of arts, most of which belong to the realm of popular culture'.[4] Considering the historical and wider connotations of this branding, *mobtazal* goes a long way. It not only brands the work but also stigmatizes the author and confuses the readers. Independent authors use the same word to describe works of mediocre taste. The term was adopted by the Islamic Republic and used in a broader context to include any work of art or literature – even of high literary value – with any allusion to eroticism or even lyricism.

All types of fiction, whether Iranian or translated, undergo heavy censorship and Persian classical literature is no exception. Persian classical literature is a universally recognized treasure of stories and anecdotes which have survived centuries of political and ideological turmoil, yet censors in the Islamic Republic have decided that some of these texts cannot be published.

Dāstānhāy-e Delangiz az Adabiyyāt-e Fārsi (Beautiful Stories from Persian Literature), a collection of stories selected from classical literature by a renowned academic, Zahra Khanlari, was rejected for the following reason: 'Collecting such stories cannot have any benefit for the society except stimulating romantic faculties of the youth. It is harmful and the images of the book are mostly *mobtazal*. The book is unpublishable'. The same happened to *Chand Dāstān-e Bargozideh az Shāhnāmeh* (Selected Stories from Shāhnāmeh). This selection of *Shāhnāmeh*, the national epic of Greater Iran written more than a thousand years ago, was assessed 'conditional'. The censor demanded the removal of phrases that indicated 'joy', 'dance', 'wine', and 'woman'. For example, the censor ordered the deletion of phrases such as '... and they all played music and were merry, ate and danced' and 'He asked Rustam to sit with him and drink a glass of wine'. *Hekāyāt-e Mathnavi be Zabān-e Sādeh* (*Mathnavi* Anecdotes in Simple Language) was categorized 'conditional' due to 'sexual content'. According to many scholars of Persian literature, *Mathnavi* is a mirror to the Qur'an and is hugely inspired by the Qur'an and Islamic teachings. But it would appear that even the name of Rumi and the significance of *Mathnavi* does not suffice to persuade the censor to allow an uncensored edition.

Riāzolhekāyāt (The Garden of Anecdotes) is a collection of anecdotes and stories from various classical texts collected by Mullah Habibullah Sharif Kashani, a high-ranking cleric from the nineteenth century. Some of the stories in this collection were branded as '*mobtazal*, sexual, repulsive, shallow'. Again, it is interesting to note that something which was acceptable to a Shi'a clergyman in a much more conservative nineteenth-century Iran is not acceptable to the cultural authorities today.

Some of these classical books are published uncensored in their original unabridged form but their abridged or simplified versions or selections are censored. We may therefore conclude that although the censorship authorities do not approve of such books they see them as harmless as long as they are confined to a limited elite readership.

Contemporary Persian novels as well as foreign fiction translated into Persian are hugely censored for similar reasons. Novels by renowned writers such as Houshang Golshiri, Nader Ebrahimi, Esmail Fasih, Ghazaleh Alizadeh, Javad Mojabi, Jafar Modarres Sadeghi, Rasoul Parvizi, Shahriar Mandanipour, Goli Taraghi, Amir Hassan Cheheltan, Fereshteh Sari, Zoya Pirzad, and Mahmoud Dowlatabadi have been either completely rejected or had numerous corrections demanded, as have many novels by bestseller writers like Nasrin Sameni, Amir Ashiri, Ahmad Ahrar, Manouchehr Moti'e, and a large number of young and emerging writers. Irrespective of the difference in style and readership, many of these works are branded *mobtazal* and immoral.

Based on the type of books that have been rejected under this category, we can assume that any relationship between a couple where love – legitimate or illegitimate, sexual or platonic – is expressed through words or actions is considered *mobtazal* regardless of the overall direction of the story and the author's objectives.

The censors demanded 378 corrections in *Amir Arsalān-e Nāmdār*, a nineteenth-century popular romance demanding that all mentions of wine, dance, and love be deleted.

A sentence like 'Soon the lust emerged, lust caused envy and envy led to cruelty' or 'kiss Lizanka' – in *The Dream of a Ridiculous Man* by Fyodor Dostoevsky – was viewed by the censor as 'arousing'.

'His heart started to beat like a trapped bird and his face turned as red as wine' – *The Dream of a Ridiculous Man* by Fyodor Dostoevsky – was assessed by the censor to be an 'expression of strong sexual desire'.

Kissing is many times viewed as 'immoral and contrary to cultural traditions, against the prestige of Islamic society, against public decency and an expression of worldly desires' by the censors. A translation of *Romeo and Juliet* by William Shakespeare received eighteen corrections, eleven of which were phrases containing the word 'kiss'.

'I kissed him' – in *The Feather* by Charlotte Mary Matheson – was viewed to be 'against morality and culture'.

'She fell in her husband's arms and kissed the man, a long cinematic kiss' and 'The girl rose coquettishly and brought forward her budded lips' – from *Fakhr-zamān* by Eshrat Rahmanpour – are two examples of problems that made this book unpublishable.

Even kissing a picture is branded as 'immoral'. 'The woman kissed the man's picture on the lips and giggled to find a trace of her lipstick on his lips' – from *Begu be Māh Biāyad* (Tell the Moon to Come) by Mostafa Zamaninia – was demanded to be removed. In another novel, *Āstāra* (The Star), the censor demanded a sentence which he found ambiguous to be deleted, writing: 'This is ambiguous, the author means kiss'.

Any indirect reference to kissing or hugging even in figurative language does not escape the censor's eye. In *Firestarter* by Stephen King, the censor viewed 'Apple pie without a piece of cheese is like a smooch without a squeeze' as 'An indecent and improper example'.

'It's just like the kiss. Girls fear it until they experience it' – *A Man is in our House* by Ehsas Abdul Quddus. This sentence was assessed as '*Mobtazal* and shameless example'.

Breast is another problematic word, as are some other parts of the female body. Even hair, arms, tummy, or face may be censored. 'The wavy hair', 'two marble arms', 'Banoo's tummy', 'hair flying in the air', and 'the good-looking well-shaped girl' are some of the phrases the censors asked to be deleted.

Sensitivity to breasts is high to the point of paranoia. The breast is always viewed as a sexual organ. The phrase 'Busty women are more attractive to men' – in *Désirée* by Annemarie Selink – was marked as 'against public decency and social prestige'. But it doesn't end here. In *Siāsanbu*, a collection of short stories by Mohammadreza Safdari, the following sentences were demanded to be deleted: 'The mother was breastfeeding his little sister. Her empty and wrinkled breast was left in the baby's mouth'. In another example, the censor demands deletion of a line describing an old woman suffering from breast cancer. 'The cancer spread to her breasts and then to her entire body … the nurse told me that the old mastectomized woman stared at the ceiling in her last moments.'

Sineh and *Pestān* are Persian words for breast. The former also means chest and bosom. The latter is used in medical terminology too and both are also used in non-sexual idioms and expressions. Very often these words are censored in contexts which have nothing to do with an actual breast. *Pestān be tanur chasbāndan* is an expression meaning 'exaggerated pity'. It literally translates as 'sticking breast to tandoor' but as in all idioms, the overall meaning of the phrase has nothing to do with the individual word of breast. When reading an idiom most people rarely pay attention to the individual ingredients. The censor, however, asked this phrase to be deleted because he spotted the word 'breast' in it. Lili Golestan, a translator, told ISNA (Iranian Students' News Agency) how she was asked to replace the word '*Sineh*' in the phrase '*Dast-e rad bar Sineh-ash zad*' in one of her translations.[5] This idiom means 'rejected' and has no sexual connotation whatsoever. In a collection of satire, the phrase 'a cotton breast' was censored – *Lotfan Labkhand Bezanid* (Please Smile) by Morteza Farajian.

In addition to parts of the body like breast, thigh, arms, and hair, items of clothing such as shorts, skirts, and bra, and makeup such as lipstick and so on are also censored.

'The new lipstick that I bought yesterday is red', 'What does the old woman have to do with my lipstick?' 'Ladies in Lālehzār are applying lipstick on their lips' are three of the sentences ordered to be deleted from a story called '*Mātik* (The Lipstick) in a collection of short stories entitled '*Enjemād*' (Freezing) by Karimpour. The censor assessed these sentences 'immoral'. Even items of furniture such as bed, sofa bed, bedsheet, and quilt have sometimes been censored due to their association with lovemaking. A mention of shower, changing clothes, or a description of a private moment of a female character which might stimulate the imagination is susceptible to censorship. The following passage was censored from Zoya Pirzad's novel *Mesl-e Hameh-ye Asrhā* (Like All Afternoons):

The cloth diapers were hanging from a rope between two cherry trees. The woman started to spread them. It was cold and her hands were getting numb. She thought of ironing […]. The bare and thin branch of the tree kept going into her eye. She now hated the smell of her body. She said, 'I need to heat some water before the baby wakes up. I need to wash my head and body and change my clothes.'

The censors are extremely paranoiac about sex and they sometimes treat a simple handshake between people of two sexes or a kiss on the cheeks as sexual.

'Monro fainted and fell in her husband's arms', 'He put his hand round his wife and walked away', and 'Threw herself into his arms' were demanded to be deleted from the Persian translation of *Steam House* by Jules Verne.

Even scenes of rape or sexual violence are censored on the assumption that they are sexually charged. Books by Milan Kundera, Jean-Paul Sartre, and Mahmoud Dowlatabadi were censored for such scenes.

'He has certainly entered my room to shamelessly assault my honour' is seen by the censor as 'an ugly and outrageous sentence'. 'She lifted the girl's dress. She had no underwear and the red lines on her body shows that they had undressed her by force and raped her' is viewed as 'sexual deviation' and is ordered to be deleted. Here, the censors seem to ignore the context and the writer's attitude toward these scenes. They don't care if the writer is actually criticizing such behaviour. A mere description or mention of any sexual act is enough to alarm the censors.

Pregnancy is not spared, nor circumcision. In the translation of a book by Danielle Steel, the following phrase is marked 'immoral' by the censor: 'All her thoughts were whether she was pregnant or not'. In a translation of *Claudius the God*, a historical novel by Robert Graves, the censor demanded changes to sentences which alluded to circumcision. In the same novel, the following sentence was deleted because it contained the word 'incest' while there was no description of any scene or any sexual allusion whatsoever: 'Herodias had not only committed incest by marrying an uncle but had divorced him in order to marry her richer and more powerful uncle Antipas'.

Flirting is not approved of – even flirting with books. The following sentence was ordered to be removed from *Shirin Hamcho Zendagi* (Sweet as Life) by Mehdi Izadi: 'He saw the girl as one of the few women who read and enjoy literature and who flirt with the works of great writers such as Dostoevsky, Proust and others'.

A description of beauty, praise for physical characteristics of a woman, or any expression of love and affection might get censored. The following are examples of sentences deemed unpublishable by the censors:

'Comb your hair so that I can watch your hair and thank God for the beauty of my wife' – *Hokumat-e Jahāni-ye Mohabbat* (Universal Rule of Love) by Mostafa Javidan.

'Parvin was getting ready for her beloved husband and set the table' – *Asir-e Sarnevesht* (Prisoner of Fate) by Masoumeh Saberpour.

'I recently saw a picture of Elizabeth Taylor in this newspaper. She is really stunning.' *The Way of the Toltecs* by Graciela Corvalan.

'The golden hair and the warm skin of [the] enchanting women of Venice' and 'Her bare shoulders' (*Seven Days*).[6]

'[…]is very beautiful [….] And so are English girls', 'What hair […] the real gold' and 'My friend of whom I spoke was a young man, a man who thought all women good, and most of them beautiful' – *The Murder of Roger Ackroyd* by Agatha Christie.

'She is a beautiful being, really beautiful', 'My dear' – in four cases – and 'My letters were not love letters' – *Crooked House* by Agatha Christie.

'She's beautiful', 'Beautiful face, well-shaped figure', 'You are beautiful', 'Beautiful and attractive', 'Women, however charming, have this disadvantage, they distract the mind from food' – *Death on the Nile* by Agatha Christie.

'Greedy sailors who haven't seen women for long' – *The Silence of the Lambs* by Thomas Harris.

'To me, she specially looked an innocent lady', 'The attractive young woman with that heavenly voice' – *A Love Crime* by Paul Bourget.

'Fredrick greeted her in a loving manner and said: My beautiful lady! I have travelled a long distance. I have heard of your beauty and have fallen in love with you and I want to reveal my love to you.' – *Seven Brides for Seven Brothers* by Gholamreza Alvandpour.

'My clever husband', 'My soul and my heart', 'My beloved', 'My darlings' – *The Mysterious Box*[7] – were noted as 'love and lovemaking' by the censor and demanded to be deleted. The censor who assessed *Bāda-ye Kohan* (The Old Wine), a novel by Iranian novelist, Esmail Fasih, demanded deletion of a section because of 'outrageous words such as smile and olive eyes'.

The censors have ordered deletion of some sentences and phrases where the word 'woman' is mentioned and one cannot establish if it was out of respect for women or if they saw it sexually arousing. For example, the following sentences were ordered to be deleted:

'[…] one of my friends hates women' – *Marcel Proust* by Claude Mauriac.

'I have always believed that full obedience of a woman to her husband makes the woman dull and foolish and diminishes her power' – *N or M?* by Agatha Christie.

In spite of extreme censorship of any material of the weakest sexual indication, there are exceptional cases where books of relatively high sexual content are approved for publishing. One such example is a memoir by Parvin Ghaffari, a former mistress of the late Mohammad Reza Shah. *Tā Siyāhi … Dar Dām-e Shāh* (Into Darkness … Trapped by the Shah) gives a detailed account of the alleged three-year affair of a teenage girl with the Shah and some of his courtiers. The publication of this book broke all censorship rules. Historical books about kings of centuries ago have been censored for mild allusion to sex even in figurative language, but in this book Ghaffari describes in graphic detail how she lost her virginity in the Shah's bed. This example leads us to believe that moral and ethical perfection is not the main reason behind censorship of erotic content, otherwise those values would not have been sacrificed in favour of political gain.

In spite of the fact that Persian classical poetry is brimming with lyricism and, for many poets, lyricism is the core of their creativity, the Islamic Republic has not been kind to lyric poetry. Masoud Ahmadi, a poet and scholar, believes that the censors are against any form of beauty. He told me in an interview:

> Nowadays censorship involves all areas of your thinking. It is not only politics. Your aesthetics, your private ideas such as love, everything is under their radar. They don't approve of lyricism; they don't like it. Although some censors are not

as strict, generally speaking, they have [a] problem with beauty. Therefore, they will not approve any high quality lyric poetry. If someone were to write such poetry, their book will not be published.[8]

Many collections have been censored for what is viewed as sexual implicity. Such books are usually labelled as *mobtazal*.

Dar Āvār-e Daryā (Under the Rubble of the Sea) by Manouchehr Cohen faced seventeen corrections; ten of which were marked *mobtazal* and idolizing love. Examples include: 'Naked water | nude rocks | hurrying wave | endless love' and 'The fire of love | and the peace of your arms | the tumult of whirlwind | and the silence of mountain | the river inevitably | flows into the sea'.

Dar Sarābi Digar (In Another Mirage) by Ziaoddin Torabi required six corrections. The censor marked these lines as follows:

- The woman became naked | between two dreams ('*mobtazal* line and sexually stimulating').
- Berry of pleasure | under the tooth of coitus ('stimulant metaphor, *mobtazal*').

Paranda-ye Bibāl (Wingless Bird) by Mohsen Souri faced four corrections, such as:

- I slept with myself in sleep and while awake ('meaningless and *mobtazal* sentence').
- They tell me you embrace the body of the daughter of fire | the fire poem is a bastard | the fruit of your sin ('*mobtazal* sentences and swear words').

There are many instances where there is no sexual reference. However, it seems that censors treat sex very broadly. Any talk of friendship between the sexes or any reference to love, even platonic, might be censored. Examples include poems by Manouchehr Cohen from *Barā-ye ke Besorāyam?* (For Whom Should I Write?):

- A glance | a desire | a memory | an evening.

In *Che Kasi Bud ke Goft?* (Who Was it That said?) by Hida Eskandari, sixteen pages were ordered to be deleted. According to Rajabzadeh, the content of those pages concerned the unity of lover and beloved and their mutual expectations expressed in a manner which is very common in classical Persian poetry.

Politics is another minefield for contemporary writers in Iran. Few works of fiction with a political plot have been published since the Revolution unless representing the official narrative of the regime. Scholarly works on contemporary history and politics undergo heavy censorship but fiction is subject to even stronger censorship because of its wider audience. The case of *The Colonel* is a clear example of the crippling role of censorship when a writer wants to reflect on a contemporary theme in their fiction.

Mahmoud Dowlatabadi, the renowned Iranian novelist, has repeatedly called upon the authorities to allow publication of his novel, *Zavāl-e Colonel* (The Colonel). German, English, Hebrew, French, and Italian translations of *The Colonel* have been published. This novel was also a candidate for the Man Asian Literary Prize in 2011[9] and won the Jan Michalski Prize in Switzerland in 2013,[10] but the original Persian version has not yet been permitted. Dowlatabadi wrote *The Colonel* in 1983–1984 and waited for twenty-four years before his publisher applied for a publication licence. The Ministry of Culture and Islamic Guidance has so far returned the manuscript to the writer several times and demanded corrections. According to Dowlatabadi, he has agreed to apply changes at least four times, in the hope of publishing his novel in Iran, but to no avail. The minister who had spoken favourably about issuing a publication licence for this book was threatened with impeachment by parliament.[11] According to the BBC, the authorities who had spoken favourably about this novel retracted their statements and Hamidreza Moghaddamfar, a senior Revolutionary Guard figure, warned against publication of *The Colonel*, calling it the 'most anti-revolutionary' novel after the 1979 Revolution and describing any idea of publishing it as a 'major deviation'.[12]

Throughout history, writers have used fiction to communicate their social and political messages. Iranian fiction is no exception. In fact, a large portion of pre-Revolutionary fiction in Iran contained sociopolitical ideas and faced considerable censorship due to this. The type of fiction which was aimed at enlightening the masses and served a mainly leftist ideology, lost its appeal after the Revolution for different reasons. The government's appropriation of 'committed literature' which was perceived to be the property of intellectuals before the Revolution might have contributed to the reduced popularity of political fiction. Kamran Talattof shows how the Revolution led to the emergence of a new type of literature which used the committed literature forms and was based on the same concept of commitment, except this time to revolutionary ideas and Islamic values. While the pre-Revolutionary committed writers were advocating socialist ideas in defiance of the state and suffered for their commitment, the new committed writers promoted the state ideology and were, as expected, state-sponsored.[13]

The censors though, see things differently. A writer may submit a text believed to be totally non-political but the censor might find some undesirable political content. Criticizing government or any government organization, a negative view of the country or community, and criticism of Iraq-Iran war may lead to censorship but it is of course a much broader topic as we will see hereunder.

In *Begu be Māh Biāyad* (Tell the Moon to Come) by Mostafa Zamaninia, the censor demanded the following sentences to be deleted. He found the first sentence 'an insult to people' and the second sentence 'an insult to the country':

'I want to run away from these damned people and this cursed land', and
'I don't want to waste one more day of my life in this miserable, lawless place where the only language understood is force'.
'Cats are like revolutions. Revolutions devour and destroy their dearest, purest and noblest children very early on'.

Although this is a general statement and a widely-held belief, the censor is not happy because it may be viewed by some readers as a description of the Islamic Revolution.

The translation of *L'Engrenage* (In the Mesh) by Jean-Paul Sartre was assessed unpublishable because the censor believed that 'It shows people's revolutions as a futile effort. The political theme of the book encourages readers to look for similarities'. The censor fears that readers might find the Revolution and revolutionary leaders described in Sartre's book too familiar and thus rejects the book as 'unpublishable'.

In *Asir-e Zamān* (Prisoner of Time) by Esmail Fasih, the following sentences were censored:

'We are living in uncertain times. You cannot count on anything especially here in Iran and in the third world countries that do not have stable systems and rule of law.'

Another example is 'In our country, books for children and young adults are not sufficiently supported', *Gorba Siyāh va Dāstānha-ye Digar* (The Black Cat and Other Stories). Author not named in the documents.

Not only are you not allowed to criticize the times and the country, you may be censored if you criticize a city:

'The city is the city of the dead, its nights are dark and its days are burning hot' – *Dāstanhā-ye Panjshanbeh*' (Thursday Stories) by a group of young writers. The censor commented: 'bad description of the city'.
'He bid farewell to the city which could give him many things such as happiness and security' *Gozar az Tanhāyi* (Passage through Loneliness) by Zamanian.

If a text is perceived to be insulting an official in government, it might be censored. The censor found the following sentence in *Moallem-e Madreseh* (The School Teacher) by Jamal Sadeghi 'an insult to the Head of Education Department':

'He didn't bother at all. There were a number of ass-kissers turning round him like flies calling him Haji Āghā, Haji Āghā'.
'My other job is to find one truthful official in this city' – *Āsheq-e Qesti va Ma'shuq* (The Part-time Lover and the Beloved) by Arash Azad – was deleted as well as the following sentences from the same book: 'Fortunately, the conditions of the society have taught us all types of tricks' and 'Our officials pay no attention to these things'.

Hālā Hekāyat-e Māst (Now, it is Our Tale), a collection of satire by Emran Salahi was refused a publication licence for a number of reasons, including insult to the print and publication authorities in the MCIG. Two of the sentences which were considered offensive to the censors are as follows:

'To be able to publish a book, you need to obtain a qualifying card. We should be grateful they don't demand a qualifying card for writing a book.'
'In order for his poem not to get into trouble with the moral police, he should print it like this: I wanted to grab his moustache, I couldn't find a ladder, instead of the original: I wanted to kiss her lips, I couldn't find a ladder' [indicating that the beloved is tall].

The censors seem to have been offended by an indication of what they do and their being compared to the moral police.

The words *Haji* and *Āghā* – a respectable way of addressing men, also used to address fathers among some communities – are sensitive in some contexts. *Haji* refers to a Muslim who has been to Mecca on a *Hajj* pilgrimage. Although *Āghā* is an ordinary word and has no major significance, some censors associate it with the clergy. Ayatollah Khamenei, the Supreme Leader, is called *Āghā* by some of his young supporters. In *Hekāyat-e Ruzegār* (The Tale of Time) by Farideh Golboo, the censor requested that the word 'Āghā', the novel's antagonist, be changed to 'Khan'. The censor demands that the name Haji be replaced with another name throughout the novel *Arz-e Hāl* (Complaint) by Jafar Modarres Sadeghi. These examples show the extended arm of censorship which may ban the use of ordinary words because of a feared connotation or possible allusion to sources of authority. *Khan* is associated with pre-Revolution rural landowners or nomadic chiefs who were perceived to be supporters of the previous regime. It is therefore a preferred title for a villain.

War is another sensitive issue. Different organizations are involved in creating a literature to portray the Iraq-Iran war as the system prefers: a sacred defence. Many stories have been written about war but few offer an alternative perspective. The official narrative refers to the Iraq-Iran war as the Imposed War and the role of Iran as the Sacred Defence. Any view which differs from the official narrative might get censored.

'The sound of music and celebrations undermined the problem of war for a while' in *Gozar az Tanhāyi* (Passage through Loneliness) by Zamanian, was demanded to be deleted.

'We don't know which way the wind is blowing but the turmoil of palm trees warns of the anxiety of an incident approaching' in *Sangrizeh* (Gravel) by Ali Hosseini was also deleted. The censor viewed this sentence as a negative description of war and marked: 'Such writings induce a negative outlook about the victory of the Revolution, the Imposed War and the years of the Sacred Defence'. The following sentences from the same book were also seen as 'negative views on the battlefront' and demanded to be deleted:

'Don't you have a life and a home? Don't you have a wife? Why did you leave her and go to the battlefront? What is [the] battlefront? We didn't have such a thing before'.

While writers should be careful not to insult anything or anybody who might be associated with the Islamic Republic in one way or another, they should also avoid any positive remarks about things or people who are no longer favoured by the system.

Asir-e Zamān (The Prisoner of Time) by Esmail Fasih mentions Hassan Nazih as a patriotic moderate technocrat. It also names Bazargan and Shariati in a positive manner. Bazargan was the first prime minister after the Revolution and Nazih was the first post-Revolutionary CEO of the National Iranian Oil Company. Shariati, nicknamed the Teacher of the Revolution, was an Islamic intellectual perceived to have been influential in the Revolution. When the censors objected to these statements in 1996, all of these former revolutionaries had lost their appeal to the regime.

The same was true of Mohammad Mosaddeq, the popular prime minister (1951–1953). Mosaddeq symbolized a secular nationalism, an alternative not favoured by the Islamic Republic. In *Arz-e Hāl* (Complaint) by Jafar Modarres Sadeghi, the censor asked for the deletion of the following paragraph:

> 'Once Rustam dared himself and asked Mr Nobakht: "Is Mosaddeq dead or alive?" Mr Nobakht turned red and said: "Where did you hear this name?" [...] "It was written on the wall." Mr Nobakht said: "Never utter this name again. Do you want to put us all in trouble?"'

Not only the name of political figures might get censored, even the names of places, books, and movies may be frowned upon.

Gomshodeh va Howz-e Morvārid (The Lost One and the Pearl Pond) by Davoud Ghandchi Tehrani has been assessed unpublishable. In part of the story, the character who has newly arrived from the United States to revolutionary Iran describes a visit to bookshops and names some of the titles of the books he sees. He is enthusiastic about the victory of the Revolution and the fact that many books banned during the Shah's regime are now available. Books such as *18th Brumaire of Louis Bonaparte* (Karl Marx), *The Gadfly* (Ethel Voynich), and many other forbidden titles were freely sold everywhere. 'I thought to myself: *What more does one want from a revolution?* [...] I wanted to write to all my friends in America who are unhappy with the Revolution and let them know what has actually happened.'

The censor notes that 'The books he names belong to the leftists. This book cannot be trusted'. The final assessment of the censor is 'The soul of this novel is based on an insulting and ridiculing approach to the Islamic Revolution and this soul cannot change by any number of corrections and this book is therefore unpublishable'.

Another sensitive political topic appears to be ethnic and minority issues. *Nasim-e- Kārun* (The Breeze of Kārun) by Yousof Azizi Banitorof, an Iranian Arab writer, was assessed 'unpublishable'. The book is a collection of essays, poems and notes on folk culture of Iranian Arabs. The censor has observed:

> As the local problems are being magnified throughout the book and a nationalistic spirit is being propagated, and the author even spreads lies to mobilize the nationalist sentiments of the people, I concluded that it is not expedient to allow publication of this book in the current situation because it will provoke nationalistic [ethnic] sentiments. Such problems exist in all minorities and among all ethnicities, and they have not been created by the regime; and publicizing such problems merely benefits the enemies of Islam and Iran.

A large number of poetry collections have been censored for their political implications. Due to the nature of poetic language, direct political content is rare in poetry. However, censors have found various faults with some poems and have indicated these faults by remarks ranging from direct statements like 'communist content' to ambiguous phrases such as 'argumentative and toxic, dangerous meaning, containing a type of political thought', or simply 'poetry with political meaning' as is shown in the examples below.

Inja Setāreh-hā ham Misuzand (Here the Stars Burn Too) by contemporary poet, Hossein Saffaridoust, was rejected for seven reasons, mostly political, including: 'ambiguous and harsh tone of the poem; political and revolutionary dimension and soft text;[14] political dimension; creating suspicious analogies'.

Sokhan-e Del (Word of Heart) by Khaled Bayazidi faced five corrections, all political. In the line, 'My words are raising the dove of peace and reconciliation in prison. Each word of mine will change into a bullet in a freedom fighter's gun', the censor remarks: 'alluding to prison and freedom fighting'. At 'They closed my eyes, silenced my voice, created fear, hanged me on the rope of ignorance and superstitions', the censor has written: 'poems with dangerous meaning'. As for 'Saturday, execution of one … Thursday, all ropes hanging … Friday, all puppies on the gallows' the censor noted: 'Toxic and provocative poem'.

Khāneh (Home) by Mehdi Akhavan Langroodi faced seven cases of censorship and was denied a publication licence. The censor wrote: 'As the majority of poems are about homesickness and in memory of homeland, these poems contain negative political charge and should be deleted'. Samples of lines to be deleted are as follows:

- Home! | I want to weave a violet dress | for you | from waters
- The sky over my home | is bright | in the commute of those | who have been carrying | their homeland on their shoulders | for years
- These are the flames of your love | burning me | this is me | calling you | fire does not burn my voice.

As the above examples show, even a nostalgic piece by an expat poet admiring his homeland is considered politically undesirable and, therefore, censored.

A collection by Seyed Ali Salehi called *Neshānihā* (The Addresses) is also considered to contain some poems 'full of political allusions'. One example is: 'The prayers of you and that restless bird | both fluttered and flew away | they sat on the arch of a broken tile | I had cried the sorrow of freedom | for a thousand lost birds | and you knew not'.

The way censors treat poetry indicates a presumption on their part that poets are using allegory and symbolism to attack the Islamic Republic because of a perceived lack of freedom of speech and that, therefore, they have the duty to 'discover' and 'neutralize' such attacks. This is, in fact, an admission of censorship by the censors, who offer extreme interpretations of texts which are not necessarily political and would not be perceived as such by the ordinary reader. In the example of *Khāneh* by Langroodi, an ordinary reader would view those poems as evidence that someone is missing their homeland. However, the censor who deeply, though unconsciously, acknowledges the lack of freedom of speech in the country, reads them as political statements.

Religion is and always has been a major battleground of ideas and interpretations. It is a remarkably interesting subject for literature and there are great works on and around religion. However, there is an inherent risk in bringing religion into literature. Iranian contemporary writers are aware of the sensitivity around the topic of religion and usually avoid religious discussions in their work. Nevertheless, the censors read way beyond the ideas expressed in the books. They do not tolerate any phrase, dialogue, or depiction of a scene which might, in one way or another, associate any negative qualities to religion, especially to Islam. If a character is portrayed as a religious man, then he is expected to be virtuous, otherwise it will be censored. Anything which is somehow associated with Islam or religious people is sensitive. Islamic names, Islamic dressing (hijab and chador), turban and so on, and Islamic symbols such as prayer beads and even beards should be respected.

'*Sāl-e Dohezār be kojā Miravad*' (Which Direction Does the Year Two Thousand Go?) was unpublishable because 'The writer has portrayed Haj Hassan who is a religious man as a negative character'.

'*Sāli ke Tufān Shokufeh Dād*' (The Year the Storm Blossomed) by Ne'mat Saremi Rad was regarded unpublishable because '1. The revolutionary characters have mainly non-Islamic names such as Sohrab, 2. Thieves and drug dealers have religious names such as Zabih, Hamid and Hossein, 3. [A] Muslim woman is ridiculed for being a housewife'.

As we can see here, a novelist should even choose the names of his characters with caution. A negative character cannot be given an Islamic name. Sohrab is a popular Persian name deeply rooted in Persian culture. Sohrab is actually a major character in *Shāhnameh*, the national epic of Iranian people.

Erāda va Sarnevesht (Will and Destiny) by Nasser Mirdamad was assessed unpublishable with sixty-six problems including the following:

- 'You can choose the path of Hossein or Kaveh, the blacksmith'. The censor objected to this sentence as he deemed it improper to see Kaveh in the same position as Imam Hossein. Kaveh, the blacksmith, is a mythical figure who led a popular uprising against a foreign tyrant and re-established the rule of Iranians. He is the symbol of resistance against oppression. Imam Hossein is the third Shi'a Imam who is similarly a symbol of resistance and struggle for justice. Here again, we can see the conflict between Iranian identity and the Shi'a Islamic identity. The censors take side with the latter.
- 'Haji was obsessed with sexual thoughts'.
- 'They admitted the *Ākhund* in their gang'.

The above two sentences were regarded to be offensive. *Ākhund* is a title for Islamic clerics which is common in its original honorific sense in Afghanistan and parts of Iran but has gradually become derogatory in most parts of Iran. A similar title such as Mullah is also treated as offensive even in an historical context when it was an honourable title for learned men and women.

The following dialogue in *Eshq va Zendagi* (Love and Life) by Gholamhossein Akhavan is regarded as 'ridiculing religious people and religiosity, ridiculing and belittling the word Ayatollah':

- 'Since when did you become religious? Religion was the last thing in your mind. Do you remember how often we fled from school and watched porn movies? What happened that you are now talking of religion and enjoy religious talks? Ha Masoud? Sorry, Ayatollah Masoud Khan!'
- No Saeed, I am not an Ayatollah, but to a wise man, all creatures are Ayatollah (sign of God).'

In *Tondbād-e Sarnevesht* (The Storm of Fate), the following sentences were demanded to be deleted:

'This was God's will and may be to the benefit of us all'
'His words made no sense. Baseless and empty words that he himself didn't believe'
'God wanted me alive to punish me with the torture of conscience'
'I have been ungrateful to God; you shouldn't complain'

Insulting the clergy, ridiculing Islamic rituals, and falsifying the truth of religion are among the reasons that censors refused to allow publication of *Diyār-e Man Hamisheh Khazān Ast* (It is Always Autumn in my Home) by Mohammadreza Zaker. Some of the problematic phrases are as follows:

'Dark clothes, dark night, dark heart, God help us out of all this darkness' (The censor saw this as ridiculing Islamic rituals of mourning)
'Mullah Taghi is worse than Ibn Ziyad'

Ibn Ziyad is hated by the Shi'a muslims as the leader of the army who killed Imam Hossein and his family in Karbala. So the censors treated this as an insult to the clergy. They also found the word 'Mullah' offensive.

'Like an obsessive mullah' – *Passenger to Tehran* by Vita Sackville-West – was viewed 'offensive' by the censor and ordered to be deleted. 'A crimson velvet robe, and a shawl turban' from *Jane Eyre* (Charlotte Brontë) was deemed offensive and demanded to be deleted. The censor seemed to take no interest in the fact that the 'turban' in this English novel is not the same turban the Shi'a clerics wear.

In '*Neveshtahāy-e Farāmushshoda-ye Hedayat*' (The Forgotten Writings of Hedayat) by Maryam Danayi Borumand, the censor demanded the following:

- Delete the word '*Ākhond*'
- Add 'PBUH' (peace be upon her) after the name of Fatemeh Zahra
- Add 'PBUH' (peace be upon him) after the name of Muhammad
- Delete 'In the name of *Yazdan*' which is undoubtedly an insult
- Change the word '*Ākhond*' to 'priest'. It is 'priest' in the original text

It is worth noting that the word *Yazdan* is today used interchangeably with *God* but has its cultural roots in pre-Islamic religions. The censor seems to be wary of the cultural connotations and associations of this word.

In another book, *Bād-e Musā* (The Wind of Musā) by Shirin Farahi, the censor demanded the change of a character's name because 'The servant is called Fatima. Her name should be changed'. Fatima (Fatemeh) is the name of the Prophet's daughter. The censor seems to be ignoring the fact that Fatima is a popular Islamic name and in real life, many women in various jobs, including servants, are called Fatima.

In *The Journey to the East* by Hermann Hesse, the protagonist is in love with a girl called 'Princess Fatima'. The censor demanded that the name Fatima be changed because it is a sacred name.

One reason for refusing the publication licence of *Not-e Zendagi* (The Life's Note) is that 'In spite of the fact that the girl character is portrayed as an observant Muslim, she keeps contact with people of opposite sex'.

The opposite is also true. If you have a character who is not a perfectly pious person, then they are not allowed to speak favourably of religion. In *Sāyahāy-e Mohabbat* (The Shadows of Love), a girl says: 'We are followers of Fatima [...]. Followers of Ali should resist oppression and it's the duty of us, followers of Fatima, to support them to our last breath'. The censor demanded this sentence be deleted noting that 'Talking of Ali and Fatima – The first Shi'a Imam and the Prophet's daughter – is not acceptable from a morally loose girl.'

Gozari Tā Maslakh (A Passage to the Slaughterhouse) by Tabrizian was rejected because the censor believes: 'The main characters are the parents who are both teachers. The mother is a practising Muslim who says her prayers but the father does not say his prayers. This plot sends the wrong message and causes ethical and religious deviance among the readers and the youth'.

Censors are sensitive to any mention of Islamic hijab, Islamic rituals – prayers, fasting, preaching, pilgrimage – and even facial hair.

'Buy a prayer book from me' is seen as an insult to praying and was demanded to be deleted from *Lotfan Labkhand Bezanid* (Please Smile) by Morteza Farajian.

'Why are you wearing a black headdress girl? It is a bad omen!' – *Enjemād* (Freezing) by Karimpour. Here the censor is acting against the popular belief of many Iranians who perceive wearing black as a sign of mourning and are not generally in favour of black colour garments.

'She dried her tears with the edge of her chador and emptied her nose with a fartlike loud noise.' – *Fakhrzaman* by Eshrat Rahmanpour. The censor might have seen it unfit for a woman clad in chador to blow her nose loudly or he might have censored this sentence because of the word 'fartlike', especially when attributed to a woman.

Any reference to the historical roots of hijab which might challenge the official discourse on hijab is also censored.

The censors demanded the following sentences to be removed from a collection of essays '*Jadāl-e Naqsh bā Naqqāsh* (The Struggle of Painting with the Painter) by Houshang Golshiri:

'Chador – the veil – and niqab in the manner that had been common in Iran has nothing to do with Islam', 'Justice and security should prevail and a re-establishment of order will not lead to acceptance of Hijab. On the other hand, removing [the] veil does not mean lack of chastity and nobility of women', 'No form of radicalism is good. It is surprising to wrap yourself in a black or white sack. Similarly, it is astonishing to walk among men, half-naked, mirror in hand, applying makeup'.

The following two sentences were censored from the Persian translation of *Passenger to Tehran* by Vita Sackville-West:

'Little girls wearing chador were imitating grown up girls' – censor's remarks: 'insulting little girls clad in chador'.
'Because Iranian women are very bold under their chadors and always talk to each other like this' – censor's remarks: 'insulting Iranian women and women wearing chador'.

In the same book, the censor demanded deletion of two other sentences with the word 'beard' in them: 'Aren't you ashamed of yourself! You are a big man with a beard and moustache!' The translator has used an idiom here which actually means: 'You are not a child anymore; you are a grown up man'. The second example is also an idiom which means 'He is laughing at me, stupid me!' The Persian phrase used by the translator is *'be rish-e man-e hālu mashang mikhandeh'* which can literally be translated as 'He is laughing at my beard, stupid me'. This phrase has nothing to do with beard. It's a well-known expression.

'You fast one full year and at the end you have to break your fast with dog poo' – *Asir-e Zamān* (Prisoner of Time) by Esmail Fasih. The censor regarded this as 'an insult to fasting'. It is interesting to know that this is a popular proverb and has nothing to do with fasting. The proverb is used in conditions when someone destroys their hard-earned achievements with one single foolish or morally unacceptable act. Again, it seems that the censor either didn't know the proverb or didn't want to take the risk.

General utterances of anger or frustration or complaints addressed to God are sometimes perceived as blasphemy and are censored.

'Bibi Gul raised her hands to the sky and cried: What God? What world? Why? What wrong had I done? Why did you take away my young son? Why? – *Sangrizeh* (Gravel) by Ali Hosseini. The censor found this utterance blasphemous.

'She was telling herself: Great God! Why did you create woman if you wanted her to be so hopeless and suppressed? Of course I am not talking about all women, I am talking about myself, Setareh. Wouldn't it be better if you created us men as well?' – *Āstāra* by Mostafa Mohammadi. The censor assessed this sentence as 'blasphemy and anti-religious'.

'Because she was a woman and weak' in the same book was deleted. The censor wrote, 'Wrong view of women'.

'The cruel God of death' and 'the Son of God in the arms of Virgin Mary' – both phrases from *Begu be Māh Biāyad* (Tell the Moon to Come) by Mostafa

Zamaninia – are described by the censor as 'blasphemous'. In both cases, the censor seems to have no regard to the context and is just looking at the word. In the first example, the writer has a mythological god in mind. The God of Death is not the same God or Allah in the censor's understanding of the word. In the second sentence also, the censor is inattentive to the fact that the Son of God is a common reference to Jesus Christ in Christian literature.

In *Safar be Kora-ye Merrikh* (A Trip to Mars) by Kazem Khalkhali, the censor found the two following sentences 'blasphemous and ideologically wrong':

'Sinners may appeal to God on the day of resurrection. His Divine grace may find them innocent in a retrial', 'The Qur'an says we ornamented the sky with stars and made it so as to be protected from any rebellious Satan'.

'Whoever God wanted to destroy, will first make them insane' – *Moallem-e Madresa* (The School Teacher) by Jamal Sadeghi. The censor viewed this sentence as 'Blasphemy and an insult to the Almighty'.

Any allusion to the futility of life or complaining of fate may be described as nihilistic and is censored: 'nothing is divided justly in life, not even its pains and sufferings' – *Khāneh-ye Dardhā* (The House of Pains) by Farideh Rahnama. The censor marked: 'Emphasizing futility of life' and demanded that it be deleted.

'Be patient, it will be OK. Bad times have made everyone fight someone' and 'The time does not adapt to your needs, you adapt to the time' – *Dāstanhā-ye Panjshanbeh'* (Thursday Stories) by a group of young writers – and 'Tired of the cruelty of time, he arrived at the bus terminal' – *Qessa-ye Zendagi* (The Tale of Life) by Parvaneh Mohtasham – were regarded as 'complaining of times, negative description of times' and were demanded to be removed.

Sometimes the censors are uncertain of their understanding. However, they don't take risks and demand censorship even when in doubt. 'We could hear the voice of Allah-u Akbar from one of the classrooms, loud and harmonious' – *Gāvkhuni* by Jafar Modarres Sadeghi. The censor remarks: 'It is irrelevant and there is a possibility that the writer is ridiculing Allah-u Akbar. It should therefore be deleted.'

A sentence like 'Machin has nothing to do with beliefs' – *Machin-e Ajib* (The Strange Machine) by Amirkhani – is assessed as problematic and the censor demands that it is amended.

Expression of an idea which might seem to contradict some Islamic principles is another reason to censor a book. In *Ātash-e bedun-e Dud* (Fire without Smoke) by Nader Ebrahimi, the censor asks the following dialogue to be deleted:

'In March 1946, a renowned historian who was famous for his enmity with Islam was killed in the Palace of Justice.'

'In my view, killing men of knowledge is not right, even if a nonbeliever.'

The censor marked this as 'supporting Ahmad Kasravi'[15] and demanded for it to be deleted.

Religious ideas that differ from the censor's understanding of 'true Islam' are challenged by the censors. In some texts, there is nothing contrary or offensive to Islam. Just having a different approach or phrasing might put the text in danger. Some of these samples seem to have been difficult for the censors to comprehend. In such instances, they appear to be taking the words at surface value and do not appreciate the literary diction or figurative language when used in discussions on religion.

The censors asked for the following parts from *Jane Eyre* (Charlotte Brontë) to be deleted:

'I am sure there is a future state; I believe God is good; I can resign my immortal part to Him without any misgiving. God is my father; God is my friend: I love Him; I believe He loves me.' 'Now, he continued, again addressing me, 'I have received the pilgrim – a disguised deity, as I verify believe!'

'Truly I envy the eternal God' – *Dustān-e Hemāsa* (Friends of Courage) by Hossein Salehi – was marked as 'improper' and ordered to be deleted.

'I now know how it feels to be like God' – *Cinamā-ye Dāyereh* (Circle Cinema) by Nasser Jadalzadeh – was assessed 'improper' as was the following sentence from *Tālārhā* (Halls) by Ghazaleh Alizadeh: '[...] I have abandoned the world; I look at mortal poor mankind through the eyes of God'.

In the translation of foreign novels, the censors very often tend to correct topics in Christianity or other religions based on their Islamic approach. In *Of Love and Other Demons* by Gabriel Garcia Márquez, the censor demanded the following sentence to be deleted: 'We are the sons of Joseph the Carpenter'. The dominant Islamic view is that Mary remained a virgin throughout her life and was never married to anyone. It is possible that the censor saw this phrase as either historically incorrect or offensive to Mary.

Mysticism – be it Islamic or non-Islamic – is not usually favoured by the censors. Hermann Hesse's books are heavily censored for their unorthodox ideas on religion. The following sentences were deleted from *Demian*:

'Every religion is beautiful; religion is soul, no matter whether you take part in Christian communion or make a pilgrimage to Mecca.'

'Drink wine from a chalice.'

'That some people considered Cain a better person than Abel.'

'Do you know that there must be a god who is both god and devil at one and the same time?'

'On occasion they would say it was ridiculous, unworthy of a person to believe in God, that stories like the Trinity and Virgin Birth were absurd, shameful.'

'But that we ought to be able to worship the whole world; this meant that we would either have to have a god who was also a devil or institute a cult of the devil alongside the cult of god.'

'And he is God and Satan'.

These sentences seem to be contradicting the censor's understanding of Christianity and other Abrahamic religions. They assessed part of this text as an insult to Christianity and Islam.

In *Narcissus and Goldmund* by Hermann Hesse, the censor marked some parts as 'blasphemous'. Among them are the following:

'But I'm really curious about it. Not of the beyond, Narcissus. I think about that very little, and if I may say so openly, I no longer believe in it. There is no beyond. The dried-up tree is dead forever; the frozen bird does not come back to life, nor does a man after he has died.'

'Do you mean peace with God? No, that peace I have not found. I don't want any peace with Him. He has made the world badly; we don't need to praise it, and He'll care little whether I praise Him or not. He has made the world badly.'

The same happens to books by Carlos Castaneda and novels by Paulo Coelho. The following sentences were cut from *By the River Pedra I Sat Down and Wept* by Paulo Coelho:

'So he began to tell me about the visions of the Virgin Mary at Fátima. I don't know why he came up with that...'

'All of the great religions – including Judaism, Catholicism, and Islam – are masculine. Men are in charge of the dogmas, men make the laws, and usually all the priests are men ... I believe in the feminine side of God.'

Although these are phrases from dialogues and are not necessarily the author's view, the censor demanded them to be removed.

The following sentence from *The Fire from Within* by Carlos Castaneda was censored because it was perceived as an approval of reincarnation which Islam rejects:

'He then guided my assemblage point until I could isolate the crows' band of emanations, which resulted in my changing into a crow.'

Sufism is an integral part of Persian classical literature. In spite of this, some Sufi writings have been a victim of censorship in a manner which reflects the overall opposition of the Islamic Republic to Sufism and dervish sects. *Az Nim Negāhi Digar* (Through Another Glance) by Pourkashani was assessed 'unpublishable' for the following reason: 'The book follows the idea that Khanqah, mosque and dervish are all vehicles of spirituality. The hero finds truth by visiting Khanqah. As the book is short and can be read by a large public, it is unpublishable.' This example shows an opposition to Sufis and dervishes. The censor has found no fault with the book except the fact that the seeker of truth finds it in Khanqah, a gathering place for Sufis. In another example, *'Shāhed-e khiyāl'* (The Witness of Dream) by Fatemeh Khoshro, the censor disapproves of the use of an honorific title for Shah Nematollah Vali, the renowned Sufi poet of the fourteenth and fifteenth centuries. He remarks: 'Mentioning Shah Nematollah Vali and using [the] title of *Hadhrat* and discussing Sufi ideas' as reasons for rendering this book 'unpublishable'.

In *Tārikh-e Tahlili-ye She'r-e Now* (The Analytical History of Modern Poetry) by Shams Langroodi, the censor demanded seven instances of corrections for matters related to religious rituals. They included the deletion of 'Reza Shah's using a prayer bead', which the censor described as 'an insult to sacred things and Islamic rituals'; apparently because Reza Shah – the First Pahlavi King – is not supposed to be depicted as somebody who is interested in religion. Another example from the same book is, 'I have been captive in this black cloth for more than a thousand years', concerning which the censor marked: 'About the restrictions on women'.

In *Seiri dar Divān-e Shams* (A Survey through the Divān-e Shams) by Ali Dashti, the censor required the word *mullah* to be replaced, since he found it an insult to the clergy. The line reads: 'At that time, the mullahs were very influential and were against the Sufis'. The censor also wanted the following sentence corrected: 'Due to his perfectionist nature, he could not remain content within the narrow frame of religious systems.'

The above examples show that censors have little respect for, or knowledge of, historical facts. As the Islamic Republic intended to portray the Pahlavi dynasty as a corrupt system, anything that might allude to a religious interest in the Pahlavi kings is censored, even the simple act of holding a prayer bead – which is not necessarily a religious act, for many people in Iran keep one and turn the beads as a habit or for pastime. Critical views on the clergy, especially if perceived to be of an offensive nature, are not allowed publication. The word *mullah* is today considered derogatory by some but this was not so in the past. In fact, it means 'knowledgeable' and was considered a very respectful title for learned people. However, the censor seems to pay no regard to the historical period that is the subject of the book in question.

In *She'r-e Now* (Modern Poetry) by Mohammad Hoquqi, the censor adds the comment 'untrue and improper analogy' to a line which reads: 'The Davidian voice of Abdul Basit flew side by side with the song of Parisa'. Abdul Basit is a well-known Egyptian Qur'an reciter and Parisa is a female Iranian classical singer. The censor, it appears, dislikes the idea of comparing reciting the holy book to singing, even though Parisa's lyrics are usually spiritual and the mystical poetry of classical poets.

The Islamic Republic has tried hard to promote an Islamic culture and lifestyle and spends vast sums of money to fight elements perceived to be of Western origin within both Iranian public and private life. The system accuses intellectuals of being instruments of cultural infiltration of the West and does not approve of their lifestyle. With regard to literature, there are many cultural elements which are treated as non-Islamic and Westernized that are demanded to be deleted or changed. These include intellectual ideas such as humanism, feminism, and nihilism to more practical things like keeping pets, eating ham, or socializing. Drinking, dancing, and gambling are censored not just because they are sins and should be avoided but also because they allegedly represent a Western lifestyle which needs to be kept out of reach. Deleting these scenes from fiction, especially foreign fiction, renders an unnatural image of the communities about which these books are written. In many cases where the plot contains a problematic theme, the censors reject a publication licence altogether. In other cases, they demand too many corrections leaving the translator/publisher no choice but to withdraw the book and forget about its publication.

Culture, lifestyle, and social issues are therefore subject to heavy scrutiny and censorship. *My Life in Pictures* by Charles Chaplin translated by Jamshid Navaei, faced forty-eight cases of correction all related to Charlie's personal life, his loves, and his relationships with women. If the translator had accepted these corrections, Charlie Chaplin would be a quite different character in the Persian copy of his autobiography.

Wings, Crossings, Impossible, and *Safe Harbour* by Danielle Steel were all refused licence. In addition to corrections demanded in each case, the censor also made the following judgements:

'The overall texture and atmosphere of Danielle Steel's stories is immoral.' 'She shows illicit relationships of a woman with multiple men as something natural and ordinary. These books spread and promote the Western licentious culture, are contradictory to the moral principles and communal values, they promote lack of restraint, promiscuity, corruption and debauchery.' 'Not only is there no necessity to publish such books, but the private life of Westerners and their lifestyle can not be a model for anybody.' 'This book has a feminist theme, that is, it allows women to do anything to succeed. It describes the marital and non-marital relationships of a woman with five men or husbands. It frequently describes hugging and flirting and lovemaking.'

Not only is wine and drinking alcohol censored but also any item related to the wine culture such as 'glass' and 'bar' may also be censored. Compound words or figurative use even in the absence of any link to alcohol is censored. For example, the word '*Sarmast*' – meaning happy and joyful – is censored because it contains the word *mast* (intoxicated). The word *Araq* – an alcoholic drink – is also used for other types of extracts including medicinal herb extracts which are extremely popular and widely consumed in Iran. Sometimes the censors have deleted *Araq* used in this second meaning which adds to the suspicion that they might have used a computer program and searched the text for specific words. The following examples show the wide range of situations that the censors found problematic:

'Once a beautiful girl went blind in my home because of the consumption of smuggled alcohol' – *I Was a Male War Bride* by Howard Hawks.

'Neither is new wine put into old wineskins. If it is, the skins burst and the wine is spilled and the skins are destroyed. But new wine is put into fresh wineskins, and so both are preserved' (Matthew, 9.17). The censor remarks: 'Instructions for winemaking from the Bible!'

'He passed in front of the bar', 'Beer, drinks, casino, cards, gambling, abortion …' – *Theodore Boone: The Fugitive* by John Grisham.

'The door opens and Joe throws out a man who seems to be drunk', 'You shouldn't come here and drink beer' – *East of Eden* by John Steinbeck.

'Her wine-colored eyes' – *The Silence of the Lambs* by Thomas Harris.

The words 'dog' and 'pig/ham' have been deleted even when used idiomatically or in combination with other words.

'Peter said: We don't need salted ham' – *The Mysterious Box*.[16] The censor marked: 'Eating *harām* (forbidden) meat'.

'You were snoring like a pig; may be you were having a nightmare' – *The Mysterious Box*.[17] The censor marked: 'Immoral'.

'Starling was trembling like a dog' – *The Silence of the Lambs* by Thomas Harris.

'I was sweating like a beaver' – *The Art of Dreaming* by Carlos Castaneda – was viewed 'Immoral' by the censor. Beaver in Persian is '*Sag-e Ābi*' which is a word combined of *Sag* (dog) and *Ābi* (water). This is another example of mechanical censorship when the censors appear to have no regard for the context.

In *The Land I Lost: Adventures of a Boy in Vietnam* by Quang Nhuong Huynh, the censor demanded the following text to be written on top of the first page in a large font:

'Attention: In some countries – including in Vietnam – people eat some animals which are not allowed to be eaten in Islam and our people do not approve of eating them. Some of the animals indicated in this book belong to this group.'

In spite of this instruction, the censor did not tolerate the word 'pig' and demanded it to be replaced by 'cow' throughout the book.

Some censors expect fiction to show a society with no social problems. Although sociological studies have indicated that problems like addiction, prostitution, divorce, suicide, gambling, and crime are not rare in Iran, censors do not like to see such issues reflected in literature.

In *Ākharin Negāh* (The Last Look) by Fatemeh Salamat, the censor requested that the following two sentences be deleted:

'He had nearly become isolated and started smoking opium.'

'Eskandar Khan was smoking opium.'

Nāmahā-ye Āsheqāna-ye Mādaram (My Mother's Love Letters) by Manouchehr Haghgou was censored because of sentences such as: 'I took the urine sample to the laboratory. They found out that he is an addict. I asked: "Addict to what?" She said: "Heroin."'

'Classic furniture, opium pipes, gilded burner' was ordered to be deleted from *Sho'la va Shab* (Flame and Night) by Razieh Tojjar.

Not only items related to narcotics get censored, but tobacco, cigar, cigarette, lighter, and other words related to smoking may also be censored. In *Tālārhā* (Halls) by Ghazaleh Alizadeh, a character is writing a letter to her friend and reminds her of some of their common memories from their university days:

'Qadami took Gitanes cigarettes out of his pocket', 'He lit the cigarette with a lighter'. These sentences were removed by the censor.

Gambling and playing cards are other causes for censorship. Cards are censored even if used on occasions other than gambling. Examples include: 'Do magic card tricks on Christmas days', 'Never surrender to the temptation to play cards with strangers in trains or onboard ships or in any other place', 'He drew three cards' – *The Mysterious Box*.[18]

'I even know what types of gambling you are into. One type you do with cards is called Poker and another type is Rummy and another is Blackjack' – *Ātash-e bedun-e Dud* (Fire without Smoke, Vol. 4) by Nader Ebrahimi. The censor marked: 'Teaching gambling'. The censor also asked for the following sentence to be deleted from *Bokhāra-ye Man, Eel-e Man* (My Bukhara, My Tribe) by Mohammad Bahman Beigi remarking that it 'Explains the ace cards': 'There are four other cards: The black card is called Ace, the green card is called King, the white is called Queen, and the yellow one is called Jack'.

Suicide is another sensitive subject. Some censors reject books on the claim that a description of suicide in a story might encourage readers to attempt suicide. *Jazira-ye Tanhāyi* (The Island of Loneliness)[19] was banned from publication because, according to the censor, 'The conclusion of the story is undesirable and leads to suicide of the protagonist. It induces disappointment and hopelessness and cannot be published'. An example of problematic parts in this book is, 'Once I wanted to commit suicide. I went near Jajrood river. But I changed my mind when I saw a rabble of beautiful butterflies dancing'.

Dāstān-e Javān (The Story of the Young) by Mehdi Taj Langroodi raised the question in the censor's mind 'Does the narrator approve of suicide?' The problematic sentence was: 'He cannot afford to buy heroin anymore. Therefore, he has no way to save himself except suicide.'

'I attempted suicide many times because I couldn't live anymore, useless to others and very dangerous to myself' – *Shāhed-e khiyāl* (The Witness of Dream) by Fatemeh Khoshro. The censor marked 'Suicide because of disappointment in love' and refused to issue the publication licence for this book.

The Picture of Dorian Gray by Oscar Wilde was assessed unpublishable because the censor believed 'Instead of patience and perseverance, this book encourages suicide when faced with difficulties in life'.

Writing of divorce can also be problematic especially in children's and young adults' literature. *Strider* by Beverly Cleary is a novel for young adults which was assessed unpublishable by the censor because of 'the promotion of dog-keeping culture, too many references to the parents' disputes and their divorce, and the promotion of a Western lifestyle'. As in the case of many other sensitive issues, sometimes the censors have no regard for the context and meaning of the words and tend to censor the text as soon as they see an undesirable word. In *Hokumat-e Jahāni-ye Mohabbat* (Universal Rule of Love) by Mostafa Javidan, the following sentence was one of the reasons which made the book unpublishable: 'I have divorced the world unconditionally'.

Abusive or indecent language and slang may sometimes get censored. As different people have different views of what is rude or indecent and what is not, this is another vehemently contested area of censorship. Some censors see words such as idiot, shit, and burp as rude and demand that they be deleted. Examples include:

'He kicked the bucket' and 'Such a twit!' *Fakhrzamān* by Eshrat Rahmanpour.

'He was coming back to the shop, burping all the way' – *Nāmahā-ye Āsheqāna-ye Mādaram* (My Mother's Love Letters) by Manouchehr Haghgou.

'Don't lie, stupid girl!', 'You are lying like a rug' – the Persian idiom has dog instead of rug. 'Wake up big bear and say your prayers' – *Gozari Tā Maslakh* (A Passage to the Slaughterhouse) by Tabrizian.

'They have shitted on Godot' – *Tālārhā* (Halls) by Ghazaleh Alizadeh.

'Charlatans' – *Safar be Kora-ye Merrikh* (A Trip to Mars) by Kazem Khalkhali.

'Get lost', 'Son of a bitch', 'Goddamn it', 'Shut up', 'Hey loser!' were some other examples of words and phrases marked by censors as reasons to reject a publication licence for *Dāstān-e Jāvid* (The Story of Javid) by Esmail Fasih.

Crime novels have also been censored. *Sābeqeh-dār* (Professional Criminal) by Hamidreza Goodarzi was refused a publication licence because the censor concluded that it 'justifies and normalizes crime' and 'promotes corruption'. *Kosuf dar Zendān* (Eclipse in Prison) by Reza Seyedmohammadi was assessed unpublishable because 'It portrays prisoners as noble and innocent people who have been forced to a life of crime because of their social conditions. It sees society as the only culprit'. Nevertheless, description of crime and violence in itself does not account for much censorship when compared with issues such as sex or religion. In view of the extensive and strict censorship regime in place, censorship of crime is less than expected.

A similar attitude to cultural norms and lifestyle is seen in censoring poetry. In *Kolliyāt-e Mirzadeh Eshghi* (Collected Works of Mirzadeh Eshghi), the censor demanded the picture of Adib Boroumand to be deleted as he was wearing a tie.

Four poems from the *Zemestān* (Winter) collection by Mehdi Akhavan Saleth were ordered to be deleted. One of the poems included the following line 'Toward Venus, this thoughtless bad whore wolf widow'. The censor observed: 'ugly and improper words'. The Persian word for Venus is Nahid which is also a name for women. It may well be that the censor didn't recognize Nahid as the name of a planet or, if he did, he was against abusive language even when addressed to planets. A poem by Mehdi Soheili from his collection '*Ganjvāra-ye Soheili*' (Soheili's Treasure) was demanded to be deleted on the grounds that it was an insult to the poet's father and was therefore unethical.

In *Chehel Sāl Shāeri* (Forty Years of Poetry Writing) by Fereidoun Moshiri, the censor demanded that the author add diacritical marks to a line of poem by Hafiz for disambiguation. The word in question was *Kown* and the censor appeared to be worried that someone might wrongfully read it as *Kun* –both words are spelled identically in Persian. While the correct form (*Kown*) means universe, the incorrect form (*Kun*) means ass or anus.

Hajv (invective or lampoon) is a major tradition in Persian classical poetry. It is a harsh satirical piece aiming at ridicule and has little reservation when it comes to diction. It normally uses strong language and taboo words. Major classical poets have written *hajv* some of which have shown their best art in *hajv*. All these works get heavily censored and in the rare cases that they get published, they are full of blank spaces or dots as substitutes for the taboo words.

Piāno-ye Sukhteh (The Burnt Piano), a collection of poetry by Amin Kashani, received a lengthy list of corrections which included deletion of the following phrases: 'you are dancing', 'dance didn't allow me to', 'this cigarette was', 'cigarette tasted', 'I am smoking', 'where in the cigar', 'I sell them my cigarette', 'you come and you go and I am smoking', 'I didn't smoke to bother you', 'with a cigarette between lips', and 'the bastard was a prostitute'. Most of the lines that made this book unpublishable had to do with smoking.

One of the interesting functions of censors is the role of editor, copyeditor, and even literary critic they sometimes assume. Occasionally, they deny publication licence to books on purely technical or literary grounds. It is not a rare practice for censors to base their judgements on the strength or weakness of prose, the quality of rhyme and rhythm, and the literary value of the books or even historical accuracy in fiction.

Technical and literary issues may thus endanger the publishability of a book. Historical novels are very often among the bestselling works of fiction. They are fiction in a bed of historical events and some censors expect historical accuracy in this genre. They also expect to see a historical narrative which conforms to the ideas and goals of the Islamic Republic. As the numerous examples show, the Iranian censorship regime is not much in favour of pre-Islamic history of Iran. *Eshq va Saltanat* (Love and Monarchy) by Mousa Nasri Hamedani was rejected because the censor judged that: 'The book is not a documented work of history' and 'It is a myth about the life of Cyrus'. Another historical novel about Yaqub Layth Saffār, the founder of the Saffarid dynasty in the ninth century AD titled '*Farzandān-e Layth Saffār*' (Children of Layth Saffār) by Asadollah Soleimani was denied publication licence. The censor marked: 'The author is either ignorant of historical events or pays no attention to them. The book is written as desired by the writer and is therefore not real. It is full of nationalistic sentiments of Yaqub Layth.' Here once again we see the dualism of Iran versus Islam. These two examples show that the censors are not happy with materials which they perceive nationalistic while they might also be seen as patriotic. Nevertheless, historical fiction is first and foremost fiction and no one expects it to be 100 per cent true. Historical novels may also be censored for the same reasons as other forms of fiction. *'Princess: A True Story of Life Behind the Veil in Saudi Arabia'* by Jean Sasson was diagnosed with ninety-six scenes perceived to be 'immoral' by the censor. Hamza Sardadvar is a bestselling author of historical novels in Iran. In 1997, six of his novels were censored each with an average of 290 corrections. Most of these corrections involved scenes of lovemaking, dancing, drinking, or other vices of the historical rulers.

Muyeh-ye Shabāneh (The Nightly Cry) by Arezoo Rahimi was rejected because the censor deemed, 'It is very weak and has no literary value'. *Khāmushān* (The Silent Ones) by Gharib was described as *'Mobtazal* plot, disjointed and feeble poems, amateurish, unclear and weak'. 'A distorted and uneasy prose, feminist approach, and questioning beliefs' are the reasons for rejecting *Sefidbakhtān* (The Happily-Married) by Shakoori. Ameneh Ghazanfari's novel, *Hāla-ye Porrang-e Gham* (The Bold Aura of Sorrow) was described as 'Extremely *mobtazal*, degrading public culture, superficial, and baseless school child composition'. *Faryād* (Call) by Taher Talebi was rejected because of its 'Inability to provide information and a shallow tackling of the subject matter'. *Tanhā yek Mo'jezeh* (Just a Miracle) by Hamideh Sedaqat, *Tajviz-e Eshq* (Prescription of Love) by Masoud Shahrokhian, *Ta'qib* (Stalking) by Ahmad Mottaghi, *Bā Cheshmān-e Geryān* (With Tearful Eyes) by Roqieh Firoozi, *Morvārid Khātun* (Morvārid Khātun) by Fereshteh Sari, *Asir-e Eshq* (Prisoner of Love) by Mohammad Latifi, *Gomshodeh dar Ālam-e Khiyāl* (Lost in the World of Dreams),[20] *Not-e Zendagi* (The Note of Life) by Maryam Asadi, *Shāhed-e Khiyāl* (The Witness of Dream) by Fatemeh Khoshro, and *Shabhā-ye Khākestari* (The Gray Nights) by Nasrin Sameni were all rejected for reasons such as 'Lack of any literary value, illogical sequence of events, repetition of useless events, lack of a proper theme, report-like nature of the story, poor writing, weak link between different parts of the story, meaningless sentences' and so on.

Chekād-e Dayti (Dayti Peak) by Bahram Tavakoli was assessed unpublishable because of what the censor described as 'Ambiguity, bewilderment, incoherence, incomprehensibility, depiction of imaginary settings'.

Ebrat (To Set an Example) by Aziz Tavili was rejected because of 'The shallow and *mobtazal* texture of the story' and 'Unjustified preference of government employee over business owner'. The censor was rejecting a publication licence because the writer had preferred one of his characters over another and had not been able to persuade the censor to agree with his decision. In the case of another novel, *Ākharin Gol* (The Last Flower) by Houshang Ashtarani, the censor interferes in the structure of the novel and recommends the following:

'The description of Nargina government in this novel is paradoxical. Once it is introduced as a totalitarian government, another time as a nationalist and in yet another part it is described as a patriotic state. How can one government have so many different faces?'

'It will be better to delete the quotation on page 15 because it damages the coherence of the story which is fictional.'

'It will be better to change the names of places like Paris and River Seine to imaginary names. The same is true of names of characters.'

Using real names in *Man az Jāpon Miāyam* (I Come from Japan) by Hamid Mobini was also criticized by the censor. The censor recommended that the writer change the name of the horse character in *Bād-e Musā* (The Wind of Musā) by Shirin Farahi because 'it is not acceptable to call horses by names which represent calmness'. *Tandis-e Zendagi* (The Statue of Life) by Eniseh Tajik was rejected because the censor claimed, 'it contains reasoning which is not rationally acceptable', 'the subject matter is old and repetitious', and 'it introduces money as the solution to all problems'. One of the reasons for censoring *Āref va Favvāreh va Chand Dāstān-e Kutāh* (The Mystic and the Fountain and A Number of Short Stories) by Banafsheh Hejazi was that the censor believed 'The theme is not interesting'.

As is clear from the above examples, censors sometimes forget their role and interfere with things which should not be their business. They act as editors and comment on the literary value of the works. They might be right to say that some of these works are of little or no literary value or that the prose is not good and so on but they seem to ignore the fact that they have not been appointed by writers or publishers to judge the quality of their books. They are not literary critics and even if they were, no literary critic is in the position to ban publication of a book just because he finds it to be of poor taste.

A large number of poetry books are rejected a publication licence because the censors believed them to be of poor quality. The victims are mainly works by young and aspiring poets. Rajabzadeh lists numerous poetry collections in this category in 1996–1997. The list is summarized in the following table. The feedback left by the censors is very interesting and shows the amount of freedom they had at their job. They could reject a book without bothering to justify their decision or referencing any legal regulation. Some of the comments are offensive and many of them are vague.

The censors' reaction in some cases shows anger or frustration with a work they clearly don't like or to which they are unable to relate.

Sometimes the censors give no reason for their decisions or issue general statements which make it difficult for the author to understand what was actually wrong with their book. *Farzand- khāndeh* (Adopted Child) by Ahangarian was rejected as the censor believed '80 per cent of the content contradicts publishing rules'. Another novel, *Mitra* by Fereshteh Sari, was rejected with the censor's feedback as 'It is a tacit and creeping cultural aggression against the current policies of the country'.

Table 1 Poetry collections refused a publication licence in 1996–1997 for technical reasons

Title of Poetry Collection	Name of Poet	Comments by Censor
Ārezu (Wish)	Gholamreza Yamani	Lack of basic principles of poetry
Fardā Parandeh-yi be Harf Miāyad (Tomorrow a Bird Will Start to Talk)	Unknown	Lack of a notable poetic essence
Golbāng-e Shādi (The Call of Happiness)	Narguess Mousavi	Inability of the poet in composing poetry and satire, ignorance of the quality of satire and inability to distinguish feeble and weak poetry from satiric verse
Rāyeha-ye Reyhāneh (The Fragrance of Reyhaneh)	Behzad Kashani	Cheap and commonplace in view of content, defective rhyme and rhythm
Divān-e Ghazaliyāt-e Ghasemi (Divan of Ghazals of Ghasemi)	Haj Sheikh Mohammad Ghasempour	Weak rhyming, coarse verses, lack of attention to meaning of words in the verse
Divān-e Eshq (Divan of Love)	Aziz Fattahi Poldashti	Many problems in respect of composition
Tefl-e Khāki va Mām-e Aflāki (The Terrestrial Child and the Celestial Mother)	Delneshin Shali	Weak language, lack of any clear message, poet is a beginner
Divān-e Eshq (Divan of Love)	Ali Rangamiz	Poor content
Az Kelid tā Ākhar (From Key to the End)	Abbas Habibi Badrabadi	Lack of meaning
Qadah-e Zarrin (The Golden Cup)	Sona Allahyarzadeh	Too many technical defects
Entezār (Waiting)	Aminolsharia Najafi	Defective rhyme and rhythm
Zemzemahāyi dar Esārat-e Ghorbat-e Zamin (Whispers in the Nostalgia of Earth)	Javad Abolfazli	1. Absurd poems; 2. Void thought; 3. Defective and mixed-up forms; 4. Dispersed verses lacking proper rhythm. This book resembles the first writings of schoolchildren and has no artistic and literary value
Sokhan-e Āmuzandeh (Didactic Words)	Karamali Khosroshahi	1. Weak writing; 2. Uncanny defence of the values in parts of the collection, which seems as if the publisher himself has intended to write poetry. Except for a handful of poems, the rest is very weak and suffers from various problems in form and content.
Feqdān (Loss)	Lorestani	This is not She'r (poetry), it is Me'r (bullshit)!
Montakhabol Ashär (Selected Poems)	Forghanparast	The book is a mixture of different types of poetry and prose, from satire and lampoon to the praise of Imam Ali. The author has not followed any specific purpose. It is, therefore, unpublishable

At other times, the censors give contradictory accounts of the books they reject. *Kolihā va Afsāneh-hāyeshān* (Gypsies and their Myths) was rejected for the following reasons:

1. 'The book targets young adult readers and as the text is full of demons, sorcerers, ghouls, and so on, it has undesirable effects on the souls and minds of young adults.
2. It helps superstitions to take root among the younger generation.
3. It is highly exaggerated and has assumed extraordinary powers for humans and considers beauty as the only objective in life.'

The censor rejected the book because it is scary and might disturb young readers while at the same time criticizes its emphasis on beauty.

There are some poetry collections that have undergone censorship without the censors indicating any reason. In some cases, censors have written 'ambiguous or twofold meaning', as in a poem by Hafez Mousavi in *Satrhā-ye Penhāni* (The Hidden Lines) or considered the text to induce 'absurdity and nihilism' as in *Sayyāreh-ye Bitaskin* (Restless Planet) by Mehdi Ghahhari. However, many poems are refused a licence without any reason being cited and there is little to suggest why these poems were considered undesirable.[21]

There are also numerous instances of censorship which do not fall within any of the categories previously discussed. They are one-off examples which indicate the broad scope of censorship and demonstrate the wild imagination of the censors.

In *Kashkul-e Attār* (The Attār's Sack) by Mohammadtaghi Attarnejad, the censor assessed the following text as an 'insult to names' and ordered it to be deleted:

'A man called Bāqer was friends with a man called Tāher. Tāher asked Bāqer about the origin of his name. Bāqer said it is derived from the name of an animal whose excrement is Tāher. Bāqer is derived from *baqar* meaning "cow" and because cow's meat is halal, its excrement is clean (meaning Tāher).'

In *Gozida-ye Asār-e Mohammad Ali Jamalzadeh* (Selected Works by Mohammad Ali Jamalzadeh), the censor asked for the word '*Mashhadi*' to be deleted. *Mashhadi* means someone who comes from the city of Mashhad or who has visited the holy shrine in Mashhad on a pilgrimage. The following sentence from *Kenār-e Takhtekhāb* (Beside the Bed) by Cyrus Ganjavi was assessed as 'somehow insulting the creation':

'First edition error: They say woman was created after the man and that's why she is more beautiful, more accomplished and better because all first edition errors were rectified.' In the same book, the censor demanded that the picture of a goat merged with that of a bearded man be deleted.

A translation of *Gulistān* of Sa'adi into Pure Persian was assessed unpublishable. *Gulistān* is itself a Persian text but includes many Arabic words and phrases. The censor marked: 'Since this book is the outcome of double ignorance and persistent insanity of the author [translator] and will smear the sacred reputation of Persian science and literature, its publication is a waste of money and is therefore unauthorized.' The censor's anger is evident by this decision as is his assumed authority. I believe a political stance is also evident behind this decision. It is again the dichotomy of Islam versus Iran which is translated into Arabic versus Persian language. A group of Iranian intellectuals discourage the use of words of Arabic origin in favour of words of Persian origin. Many officials including the clergy who revere Arabic as the language of the Qur'an and whose world view of Islamic Umma does not favour nationalism see such efforts as enmity with Islam and the Islamic Republic rather than linguistic preferences.

In a collection of Russian folktales *The Adventures of Strong Vanya*, by Otfried Preussler, the following sentence was perceived as 'publicity for Russia' and its deletion demanded:

'Once upon a time, a peasant lived in the sacred land of Russia.'

In the same book, the following sentence was assessed as 'publicity for Turks': 'Military instruments of Turks were playing and making sounds like bells.'

In *The Dream of a Ridiculous Man* by Fyodor Dostoevsky, the following sentence was described as 'catcalling a lady': 'You and your cup are only good for the Devil'. Another sentence in the same book was perceived as 'an insult to the barracks': 'The uncle who had been silent for a while told an indecent joke which smelled of the barracks and the Father didn't like this joke'.

'There are no good films in the cinemas except a number of films by Kiarostami, Hatami kia, Makhmalbaf, Hatami and others. The rest are just ugly, nauseating imitations of foreign films or the product of poor, sick, and deviant minds.' The above text from *Yek Āsheqāna-ye Ārām* (A Gentle Love Story) by Nader Ebrahimi was demanded to be deleted because the censor saw it as 'an insult to all filmmakers'.

Censorship of Children's Literature

Censorship in children's literature is a divisive issue throughout the world. Since the early days of print and publication, there has been a conflict of ideas between the more conservative and the more liberal approaches to childhood and what children can read. Every society places much emphasis on protecting children as they are considered vulnerable. Parents control their children's exposure to certain texts and ideas to protect their innocence and contemporary Iran is no exception. The regulations (MCIG bylaws) recognize the sensitive nature of books for children and young adults and require the setup of a specialist committee called 'Children and Young Adults Books Supervisory Board' to undertake censorship of children's literature. Although many Iranian writers of children's literature agree that a degree of control is needed, they believe that the writers themselves are the best judge of what is and what is not good for children. They agree that childhood is a sensitive age and authors need to be cautious when writing for children. Mehdi Rajabi, a writer of children's and young adult literature states:

> Writers are aware that children are undergoing character development but there is a huge gap between the writers' understanding of the needs of young readers and the authorities' perception. For example, emotions such as love are

subject to dispute. As writers, we believe that love is one of the most important sentiments that a young adult experiences. If we cannot write about love in our novels, young adults will read adult books on the subject which may harm their character development.[22]

Writers of children's literature complain that they are limited by the subjects they can write about. Adaptations of classic works for children and young adults are extensively censored.

If a children's story indicates the presence of a dog as a pet in a house, it will be censored. The word 'pig' must be deleted as should any indication of card games or dancing. Farid Moradi – senior editor at Negah Publishers – believes that the censors are illogically sensitive to any word with a sexual connotation in children's literature even if it is a mother breastfeeding her baby. He also recounts the story of an illustrated book for children which was kept in the Book Office for years. They finally discovered that the problem was the illustration of a pine tree. 'The censors said that the tree was the problem. We didn't understand and asked for more explanation. They said: "Why did you use a pine tree? You should have used another tree. Pine trees promote Christianity".'[23] The censor was probably alluding to the fact that pine trees are also used as Christmas trees.

As children's books are usually illustrated and thus expensive to produce, publishers need to be extra cautious not to put their investment at risk. Extreme censorship therefore has led to self-censorship on the part of both writers and publishers.

The policies toward children's literature has been described by some writers as cruel and inhumane. Mehdi Rajabi believes that the cultural authorities constantly promote religious messages through all channels of communication; in schools, in the media and through literature. What is lacking is literature that tackles the social problems faced by children and young adults; problems which are intentionally ignored by the system. He says:

> The age of drug abuse is very young. You can see drug addiction in junior high schools. We should be able to write stories about this issue so that children and young adults are informed of the depth of the catastrophe. We need to write fiction to raise awareness. The cultural authorities should be smarter and allow free discussion of social issues such as addiction, poverty, divorce of parents, and so on. 'Dog' is not the concern of our authors. Our main concern is the emotional upbringing of children and the destruction of family structure.[24]

The censorship policy has led to an increase in the number of books on safe subjects such as science or education. Books with a religious, scientific, or educational theme are easily licensed and supported. They are published in high circulations and make huge profits. But if a book indicates a social problem, it may undergo censorship. Farid Moradi says: 'Most of the books for children are scientific or educational books. Authored or even translated books are fully neutralized or pasteurized and this adversely affects children's literature.'[25] Children's books are expected to be didactic and to promote the official ideology of the state offering little space for creative freedom.

Extratextual Censorship – Censoring Authors rather than the Work

There have been speculations that some writers have been blacklisted for long periods and their books rejected publication licence regardless of the content. Writers whose books were kept too long in the Book Office for a decision have sometimes blamed this on such lists. It was usually denied by the authorities until Ali Jannati, Minister of Culture and Islamic Guidance under President Rouhani (August 2013–October 2016) acknowledged for the first time that there existed a long blacklist of writers whose works were banned, regardless of what they wrote. He said: 'It was enough for a book to have a name from this list on its cover to be banned from publication'.[26] Some writers and poets welcomed this as a confession and claimed that they belong on that list.[27] Authorities during the previous administration, however, strongly rejected this, calling it a propaganda tactic to win the favour of the intellectuals. Mohammad Hosseini, Jannati's predecessor who had served under President Ahmadinejad rejected the existence of a list while defending censorship. He said that such accusations were unfair and provide fodder for antagonistic foreign media and so-called human rights organizations.[28] Other previous authorities, including a former vice minister and a head of the Book Office, have rejected or denied any knowledge of a blacklist. Consequently, Jannati's deputy said that there was no official written blacklist but blacklisting of writers – and less frequently of publishers – had actually happened based on oral and unofficial instructions. He told the *Iran* newspaper that: 'During the past few years, there were books which had been previously published and there was no problem with their content. Yet, they were not allowed publication. There existed no directive or written instruction. It was oral and unofficial. Both in the case of blacklisted writers and suspended publishers, the banning was enforced with no written or formal document'.[29]

Although the existence of any blacklist cannot be verified and may be reasonably contested as publicity of a new incoming administration against their predecessors, there is other evidence that supports that censorship is not merely a process of examining the book in isolation. Censors definitely have an image of the writers in mind as does the entire cultural establishment. They also categorize authors based on their overall perception of their relationship with the Islamic Republic. The unnamed chief censor who was interviewed by *E'temad* admitted that the names of authors were a major factor when deciding the destiny of a book. Asked if the name of the author had any effect on the outcome of their assessment, he said: 'The name of the author definitely affects the view of the *momayyez*. It is actually one of the elements of quality evaluation. There might come a day when the texts are delivered to the *momayyez*i without the name of the author, but for the time being, *momayyezes* have their subjective view of a writer'.[30]

One of the reasons given by the censor in refusing to offer publication licence for *Six Characters in Search of an Author* by Luigi Pirandello was that 'the author is laic'. *Memoirs* by Pablo Neruda was rejected and the censor marked: 'The author is a Chilean Communist Poet'. The *Captain's Daughter* by Alexander Pushkin had frequently been published before but was considered unauthorized in 1996 because its translator was 'Parviz Natel Khanlari', an academic who had served in some high positions during the Shah's regime. We do not know if his alleged affiliation with the Shah's regime was the reason the censor rejected Pushkin's work or any other reason associated with his name, but in doing so, the censor was ignoring the fact that other translations of the same book were being regularly reprinted. Khanlari's translation was later published and has run numerous reprints since.

There are numerous instances where books were censored because of the past records of the writer regardless of the content of the book at hand. Books by Gholamhossein Saedi – aka Gohar Morad – and Houshang Golshiri were once refused publication because the authors were perceived to be anti-Revolutionary. The censor rejected one book by Golshiri 'Due to the content of most of his stories and due to Golshiri's stance against the Revolution and the regime'. A play by Gholamhossein Saedi was rejected because, according to the censor, 'The author is an anti-cultural and anti-Revolutionary element who has fled the country'. A bestseller novel by Nasrin Sameni called *Shiftagān-e Mohabbat* (Enchanted by Love) was rejected and the censor marked: 'To prevent easy read books which are also *mobtazal*, republication of the book – for a fifteenth reprint – is not allowed'. *Gozargāh-e Turak* (Turak Passageway) by Amir Ashiri, another bestselling author, was rejected because, according to the censor, 'Publishing works by Amir Ashiri is destructive, his works bring down the cultural level and general information of the readers'.

There have been instances where a political act by an author has led to a ban on their books even on those previously licensed under the same administration. After the Khomeini's fatwa against Salman Rushdie, some Iranian diaspora writers who didn't fear prosecution openly criticized the fatwa. Consequently, all books by such writers including Shojaoddin Shafa and Fereidoun Tonekaboni were banned because they had 'supported Salman Rushdie'. The name of Bijan Asadipour, one of the editors of *Tanzavaran-e Iran-e Emrooz* (The Contemporary Satirists of Iran) was deleted in the fifth edition of the book because 'he was one of the fifty exiled intellectuals who signed a letter condemning the death sentence against Salman Rushdie.'[31]

Arash Hejazi, a translator and publisher, had his publishing company closed and his licence revoked after he appeared on international news outlets testifying about the murder of Neda Āghā Sultan in the post-election protests in 2009. Hejazi, who is also a medical doctor, was recorded on camera trying to resuscitate Neda after she was shot. Consequently, all books that he had translated, including many bestselling titles by Paulo Coelho, were removed from bookstores.[32] In this case, the ban had nothing to do with the content of the books. A similar example is the request of a censor to delete names of authors or translators who are considered politically undesirable. Adel Biabangard Javan, a poet and translator, told me that the authorities had asked that the name of Kian Tajbakhsh, a political prisoner, be deleted from the Persian translation of Rudyard Kipling's *Epitaphs of the War*, which he co-translated with Adel in order to allow the publication to see the light of day. The translators refused the request, so the book was never published.[33] Another book, a Persian translation of *The Dance of Genghis Cohn* by Gary Romain was republished in 2015 three decades after its first publication. The book had two translators but carries only one name as the translator in the second print; one of the translators, Nasser Zera'ati, was omitted. Zera'ati stated in an interview that when the publisher called him to inform that the MCIG authorities would issue republication licence only on condition that his name be deleted, he insisted that the publisher shouldn't waste his time bargaining with the censors and should accept the condition as he preferred the book to be published, with or without his name: 'I told Mr Karimi (Niloofar Publications) that for me the book is important not my name. You have spent money on the book's preparation and moreover, the readers will notice this and it will reveal yet another ugly face of censorship'.[34]

The censors demanded that the names and poems of Nader Naderpour and Esmail Khoi should be deleted from an anthology called *Az Panjerahā-ye Zendagāni* (Through the Windows of Life) edited by Mohammad Azimi. They also sought the omission of the poetry and name of Simin Behbahani from another anthology *Golchin-e She'r-e Farsi* (Selections of Persian Poetry) edited by Abbas Sahabinia. A collection and critique of the poetry of Abolghasem Lahouti edited by Mohammad Ali Sepanlou was refused a licence and the censor wrote: 'This book is unauthorized for publication because it glorifies the poetry of a communist poet of the Constitutional era. Bringing up his name as a freedom-seeking poet by Sepanlou is worthy of attention'. There is a tacit threat in this remark addressed to Sepanlou for editing this collection. The censor is questioning the motives behind this scholarly work and is taking on the role of the inquisitor rather than a censor.

In *Bāzandishi-ye Zabān-e Farsi* (Rethinking Persian Language) by Daryoush Ashouri, the censor demanded the removal of the names of Ahmad Shamlou and Mehdi Akhavan Saleth from the phrase: 'In the poetry of major poets of this time, Shamlou and Akhavan'. *Talā dar Mes* (Gold in Copper), a collection of essays on Persian contemporary literature by Reza Baraheni, was assessed as unauthorized for the following reason: 'The author has frequently commended anti-regime thinkers such as Faraj Sarkoohi, Gholamhossein Saedi, Mirza Agha Asgari, Eslam Kazemieh, Khosro Golsorkhi, and Nader Naderpour'.

Āshenāyi bā Adabiyyāt-e Moāser (An Introduction to Contemporary Literature) by Hormoz Rahimian was unauthorized on account of:

> Praising Talebov, Akhondzadeh, Malkam Khan, Bozorg Alavi, Mohammad Ali Foroughi the freemason, and Sadegh Hedayat. […]; whitewashing the corrupt faces of literary figures such as Reza Baraheni, Simin Daneshvar, Gholamhossein Saedi, Samad Behrangi […] and Bahram Beyzayi; distorting the history of contemporary literature through magnifying the influence of anti-Islamic writers, and ignoring the healthy literary figures.

This comment reveals a way of thinking which goes much beyond the censorship of literature. The censor claims that a scholarly book distorts the history of contemporary literature because it discusses works by authors who do not favour and are not favoured by the Islamic regime. But the second claim, 'ignoring the healthy literary figures', is even more important, in other words 'the supporters of the Islamic Regime'. As we will see in other parts of this book, the Islamic regime goes to extreme lengths to promote its brand of literature and to deny non-conformist literature as valueless and insignificant. In fact, one of the reasons frequently given in support of censorship is to promote wholesome literature which is being ignored and discriminated against by the dominant voices of the dissident intelligentsia. Similar views frequently expressed by cultural authorities and the camp of regime supporters have significant influence on the experience of those who feel censored. Independent writers watch as the supporters of the regime receive generous patronage and yet complain about lack of support. The anger and frustration evident in the act of this censor is indicative of one of the major paradoxes of Iranian cultural policies: the more they sponsor their brand of literature, the less they succeed and then they blame their lack of success on the victims of these policies, that is, independent writers.

Gohar Morād va Marg-e Khodkhāsteh (Gohar Morād and Self-Inflicted Death) by Esmail Jamshidi, an account of the life and works of Gholamhossein Saedi (Gohar Morād), was assessed unpublishable. One of the reasons cited for rejecting this book was 'introducing the members of the Iranian Writers Association and people who have escaped the country such as Simin Daneshvar, Homa Nategh, Houshang Golshiri, Gholamhossein Saedi, Siavosh Kasrayi, Bagher Parham, and Javad Mojabi and reflecting their views'. This book was about the life and works of Gholamhossein Saedi yet the censor complained that the name of Saedi is mentioned.

The censor demanded that two of the sources referencing works by Ehsan Yarshater be deleted from *Kherad-e Eshq dar Tārikh-e Iran* (The Wisdom of Love in the History of Iran) by Mohammadhassan Shahkouyi. Two other sentences containing the names of Sadegh Hedayat and Ehsan Yarshater were also demanded to be deleted from the same book.

Az Saba tā Shahriar (From Saba to Shahriar) by Sheibani is a handbook of twentieth-century Persian literature. The censors asked the writer to delete the entries on a large number of influential writers and poets from the twentieth century and demanded that the author 'correct' their biographies. The censors, however, did not offer any guidelines on how to correct someone's past life. They also demanded that the author delete any praise or admiration towards some other writers.

The biographies of Tahira Qurrat al-Ayn and Ghamar Beigom Sheida were deleted from *Azerbaijan Āshiq va Shāer Khānimlar* (Female Musicians and Poets of Azerbaijan) by Aziz Jafarzadeh; the former because of 'her support of Bābism' and the latter because of 'her involvement in communist activities and her call for abandoning Hijab'.

In *Seiri dar Tārikh-e Zabān va Lahjahā-ye Turki* (A Survey through the History of Turkish Language and Dialects), the censor demanded that the title of Ustād (Professor) be deleted from the names of Zabihollah Safa and Reza Baraheni.

In *Forough Farrokhzad* by Jalali, the censor demanded the following:

- Name of Nader Naderpour to be deleted and his status clarified[35]
- The essay by Mahmoud Tayyari to be deleted because he is anti-revolutionary
- The essay by Ahmad Shamlou to be deleted because he describes Forough as a worldly poet who does not see spirituality as important
- The essay by Fereidoun Tonekaboni to be deleted because he has supported Salman Rushdie
- The essay by Shojaoddin Shafa to be deleted because he has supported Salman Rushdie
- The rumour that Nader Naderpour married Forough Farrokhzad must be deleted.

The enmity of censors towards some names is to the level that they demand that reference to the late Ahmad Kasravi be changed to Ahmad Kasravi in *Nuh-e Hezār Tufān* (The Noah of a Thousand Storms) by Bastani Parizi.

Although the censors in the above cases disallowed the naming or commendation of a large number of influential writers and poets, this should not be seen as an indication of the existence of a sweeping ban on these names or their works, many of which have been granted publication licence at different points in time after the Revolution.

APPENDIX: TWO CASE STORIES OF CENSORED BOOKS

The best way to obtain a clear picture of how censorship works in practice is to look at some real examples of censorship reports. I have personally received four such reports for my collections of poetry published in Iran so far. I applied for a publication licence for my first collection of poetry in 1996 and received no reply. Emboldened by the victory of reformist President Khatami, I resubmitted my book in 1997 and received a long list of corrections. I visited the MCIG and was able to negotiate with the Head of the Book Office. Finally, I had to remove eighteen pages from the book and accept some minor changes to the remaining poems. In 2004 my second book had a similar experience and I was forced to remove around twenty pages and make changes to some other pages. The report from the Book Office on my third collection is discussed below. Once again, I had to delete some of the problematic poems and make changes to others. The revised version was eventually published in 2014. Although there is a large time gap between the three books, they all faced similar problems for similar reasons. In 2017 my publisher requested a publication licence for *The Pomegranate of Bajestan* comprising two long poems. The book came back with four corrections. The publisher recommended that I write a letter and ask for a review of the censor's decision. This time, the book came back with a demand for twelve corrections. I visited the Book Office with my publisher and asked to see the Chief Censor for Poetry, a gentelman called Dr Ismail Amini. After a few months, we managed to meet him in his office. Himself a poet and satirist,

Dr Amini said he didn't believe in censoring poetry because nothing is more harmless than poetry. However, he said that sometimes they had to censor books so as not to provoke the powerful clerics. Anyway, I read the whole book with him and he suggested some changes to make the book publishable. I accepted his suggestions to save the book and he promised that the book would receive a publication licence. To my dismay, a few days later, the publisher received a new and even longer list of corrections which would be impossible for me to accept. In the same year, I submitted another book *Black Line, London Underground* which was issued a licence with no corrections. But of course my publisher and I had already handpicked poems which were expected to pass censorship and left the rest to be published overseas.

The censor's report on one of my books is presented here as a sample:

In the name of God
Conditional Items Notified to the Publisher

Date: March 26, 2013
Print Run: First
License Application Ref.: 1197898
Respected Manager of Negah Publishers

With due respect and gratitude for the valuable cultural activities of that respectable publisher, please be informed that some of the material in the book '*I hear a tree from my desk*' does not conform to the rules and regulations of publishing. You are therefore requested to revise and rectify the following cases in the said book and resubmit the CD along with a print out of the corrected pages.

[A] list of the conditional cases are as follow:

Page	Line	Description
20	last two lines	delete
54	last two lines	delete
56 and 57	full pages	delete
64	last four lines	delete
72	lines 2 and 3	delete
75	full page	delete
81	line 2	delete
84	full page	delete
86	from line 4 to the end	delete

Please present this list when submitting the corrected copy. Please also deliver a PDF file of the complete book in CD format.

The letter was not signed nor stamped.
A printout of the concerned pages was attached to the above letter which read as follows:

Page 20:
Plain of Paradise
I've been invited to a wedding party in Dasht-e-Behesht
Does this mean anything to you?
I've been invited to a wedding party in Hotel Evin
Does this mean anything to you?
When the waiters in frock coats and white gloves
Place large dishes of lamb and paulo on the table
When the battle of forks and plates breaks out
On the long table as the guests move round
What is happening next door?
On the other side of this wall? Under these watch towers?

Note: The censor demanded the last two lines to be deleted. Deleting these lines would render the whole poem pointless, so I decided to remove the whole poem instead. This poem alludes to notorious Evin Prison which is home to the largest population of political prisoners in Iran. *Dasht-e-Behesht* (Plain of Paradise) is the name of a set of banqueting halls adjacent to Evin Prison. Hotel Evin is a 5-star hotel across from Evin Prison.

Page 54:
I have many things

Glass	teapot	sugar bowl
Table	chair	central heating
Gas oven	dishwasher	fridge-freezer
Socket	napkin	ashtray
Dining room	sitting room	kitchen
Staircase	bathroom	bedroom
Sheet	pillow case	blanket
Toaster	coffee maker	ironing board

I don't have human rights
Freedom, a happy heart

Note: The censor demanded the last two lines to be deleted. I removed the whole poem instead.

Pages 56 and 57:
Behboudi Street
It is a time of mourning
The young are in jail
And the mills are turning with blood
The wine press is empty of red grapes

It is a time of mourning
The young are on the gallows

And the mills are turning with blood
The wine press is empty of white grapes

I crossed over the Kāshmar plain
Heads were scattered in every direction
I passed through the Balkh meadows
Bodies were heaped in Hāmoon Lake
I gave vent to a bitter song
The mills were turning with blood

I crossed the river, crossed the desert
I crossed the burnt mountain
I crossed the bolting plain
On the horizon, the sky is blue

In my sleep I saw a bloodied axe
In my sleep I saw a white rope
In my sleep I saw a clean garment
I rolled from one dream into another
Sleep stole my dreams

In my sleep I saw a slaughtered camel
In my sleep I saw a beheaded sheep
A white swan flew from my chest

The night reached its midst and the time for sleep arrived
I tore my clothes
Dishevelled my hair
Took up residence in the alley

From nightfall till the morning, weeping was heard from my desk

Note: This poem is about the 2009 post-election uprising. Behboudi Street is a street off Azadi Avenue in Tehran which was the scene of much violence on the part of police and pro-government militia. The censor demanded that the whole poem be removed.

Page 64:
The Old Warrior
I was the gardener here for forty years, Crow

Remember that
Tell them to plant a tree in my memory at this corner
And a red rosebush
In the shade of the tree, a wooden bench
And on the bench, a plaque in my name:
"No one may sit on this bench except for lovers
And nothing may be drunk here except red wine"

Thus said Alireza Abiz
That old warrior

Note: The censor demanded the last four lines to be deleted. I decided to remove the whole poem instead.

Page 72:
In the Botanic Gardens
On the notice-board, there is a photo of a poet
Who died when he was fifty
And beside it, the poster for 'The 400 Blows'
Which I saw at the cinema last Thursday
To the right of this poster,
An invitation to a poetry reading in the botanic gardens
Beneath it, the instructions for operating the Venetian blinds
And beside those, the recycling schedule
In the centre, is my daily schedule
According to this, I am now asleep
At 11:00 hours, I have breakfast
At 13:00 hours, I translate
At 15:00 hours, I am in the library
At 19:00 hours, I do whatever pleases me

For a few years now, I have resided at 19:00 hours.

Note: The censor demanded lines 3 and 4 to be deleted. This is a good example to see how far the censor's imagination might go. In this poem, I am alluding to the film *The 400 Blows* by French filmmaker François Truffaut. I never thought this would be problematic. But the censor clearly thought differently. He either didn't know of the existence of such a film or he knew. Nevertheless, he overinterpreted this poem and read something which was not my intention. Public flogging for various offences, mainly alcohol drinking or so-called illegitimate relationships, was very common in the early years after the Revolution. The censor probably thought that I am alluding to this form of Islamic punishment. I agreed to remove these two lines because I didn't see them vital to the understanding of the poem but I certainly regretted having to compromise the integrity of my poetry.

Page 75:
Qezelhesar
Years ago, they took your brother to Siberia
Your sister to Qezelhesar

Note: The censor demanded this short poem to be deleted. Qezelhesar is a prison in Karaj, Iran.

Page 81:
The Legends
I am sitting in Legends
In a dark corner of the bar
Nursing a glass of beer
And thinking
In a hundred years – just one hundred years –
None of these people will be alive

Not that one up there on the little stage
Playing a new track every few minutes
Nor those young boys and girls skilfully filling glasses
And taking money
Nor this crowd moving their bodies un-rhythmically

And not me
– The melancholic scribbler of these lines –
And the almighty god of these words
Not one of us will continue to be
We'll all be lost in Legends

From the window of my basement room
Only the topmost wintry boughs are visible
I hear the crying of the crows
A cold morning envelops me
In the mirror another man looks at me
With puffy eyes and white hairs in his temples
A two-day beard
He says: Look at the world with fresh eyes
Tomorrow night there's a seminar "Rejuvenate with Love" in the Methodist church
"People of all faiths and no faith welcome"
The man in the mirror asks me in English:
"What is your faith?"
I reply: Speak in your mother tongue
With the words that you carry in your mind from the distant past
Speak with the words of your ancestors
Did my grandfather suffer any doubt in his faith?
Does my father ever think about this?

The world is too brief an opportunity for thought

Note: The censor demaned the third line to be deleted because of the word beer in it. The original Persian word is '*Zahr-e Mār*' (snake venom) which is slang for alcoholic drink. The Persian equivalent that I used for 'bar' in the first line is *Nushgāh*, a lesser known word mainly common among the literati. The censor didn't find it problematic which might imply that he didn't know the meaning. This is one sample of the use of Aesopian language which has been a common practice of writers under censorship.

Page 84:
The Soul of my Souls
The soul of my souls, my bright world!
You move before my eyes like a crystal wine jar
A happy dream grows in me
To take you to my bed.

Note: This poem was demanded to be deleted in full.

Page 86:
College Girls
There were many loves in me
The kettle was boiling
I drank tea after tea and was in love

Where did those ravishing girls go
The college girls on the bus
In poetry nights
On benches in the parks?

I would find happiness in them
They would find happiness in me
We would press each other's hands stealthily in the streets
We would steal kisses in the shelter of doors and wall corners
I would go to my room in rented homes, intoxicated and dancing
I would sit between my books and my spread prayer mat
And would repent every single night

Note: The censor demanded that this part be deleted from a longer poem. I decided to remove the entire poem.

The 'Plain of Paradise', 'I have Many Things', 'Behboudi Street', 'The Old Warrior', 'In the Botanic Gardens', and 'The Legends' are translated by the author and W. N. Herbert.

Translation also undergoes similar censorship. My second example is the story of a Persian translation of Vladimir Holan's poetry. The book was published in 2015 by Cheshmeh Publishers and is titled *Budan Āsān Nist* (To Be is not Easy). It is a complete translation of 'Selected Poems' by Vladimir Holan from the English translation published in the Penguin Modern European Poets series. The translator, Alireza Hassani, told me that he did not delete/add anything from/to the book. He translated the poems without any thought of censorship. The editor, Ahmad Pouri, or the publisher, didn't censor anything before submission to the MCIG. However, the Book Office returned the manuscript and demanded revisions. The translator was forced to revise some parts two or three times. He wrote to me: 'I made some changes which would harm the poems less but the Book Office didn't accept them. So I had to make more drastic changes to see the book published.'[36] He then suggested to the publisher that he visit the Book Office and negotiate with them but the publisher warned that this was not possible as only they were permitted to communicate directly with the Book Office. He therefore didn't insist on seeing the authorities. He later prepared a PDF file of the uncensored translation of affected pages apologizing for the changes which, in his own words 'have rendered some of Holan's poems ambiguous or meaningless' and asked the readers to amend their copies accordingly. He used social media to inform readers of what had happened and to mitigate the damage. The parts demanded to be deleted are given below. The note under each part reflects on the final shape in which it appeared in the published copy of the Persian translation. Page numbers are based on the English copy of Selected Poems:[37]

Page 20: No, Don't Go Yet
I too will hold back
words that rush like the serpent's sperm
to the woman in Eden.

Note: The revised text reads like this: I too will hold back/ words that rush like the serpent/ to the woman in Eden.

Page 45: Night After Night
Only a virgin can enter by a closed door
her own bedroom
in which everything that is called assurance
has long smelt of masturbation's sheets,
of violence, of spittle in a well or wreath of resin
flung voluntarily on the tower of man.
If he is a poet, all will be ruined,
if a murderer, then nakedness will reign here
and there will be an applauder, an applauder
hired from the marble quarries of Aeschylus

Note: This poem does not appear in the published copy

Page 54: To the Enemy
It's evening, you would say: sexually ripe,
and the lady has such firm breasts
you could easily break
a pair of brandy glasses on them, but that's another
story.

Note: The revised text reads like this: It's evening, you would say: maturity/ and a perfect woman/ you could easily break a pair of wine glasses on that side, but that's another story.

Page 55: To the Enemy
To be is not easy…. Shitting is easy…

Note: The revised text reads like this: To be is not easy…

Page 63: A Night with Hamlet
On the way from nature to being
walls are not really kind,
walls soaked with the urine of talents, walls running with the spittle
of eunuchs in revolt against the spirit, walls no smaller
for not yet being born

Note: The translator was forced to remove two lines, which he substituted with two lines of dots. This is a familiar technique frequently used by Iranian authors to indicate that something is missing and that some lines have been censored. The revised text reads like this: On the way from nature to being/ walls are not really kind, …/…/ walls no smaller for not yet being born.

Page 64: A Night with Hamlet
as through a blind man's sex nipped by music
Nature merged our contempt for the town
with the rock urine of mosses uprooted

Note: The revised text reads like this: as through a blind man's sleep, nipped by music/ Nature merged our contempt for the town/ with the homeless parasites

Page 66: A Night with Hamlet
He was face to face with the holy spirit of music
and had to live for the takings of a whore
or the price of a dog

Note: The revised text reads like this: He was face to face with the holy spirit of music/ and [had to] live with an impure income

Page 68: A Night with Hamlet
A man cannot bear to look at cotton wool.
And woman? No sooner born in the dry season,
she is already flattering the rains

Note: The censor demanded the words 'cotton wool' be deleted. The translator replaced this with 'women problems' and changed the verb 'look at' to 'think of' in order to make some sense. So the Persian reads something like this: A man cannot bear to think of women problems/ And woman? No sooner born in the dry season/ She is already flattering the rains

Page 68: A Night with Hamlet
But I have known convicts.
For some of them it's enough to imagine
huge backsides

Note: The revised text reads like this: But I have known convicts. For some of them it's enough to imagine/ huge bodies

Page 68: A Night with Hamlet
you, I mean, who like a ship
leave in you under you a continuous line

Note: The revised text reads like this: you, I mean, who like a ship/ leave a continuous line

Page 68: A Night with Hamlet
Yes…. Whereas virgins, yes,
they know when a tree is unwell…. And the cloth
of their innocence
always covers the male graftings,
even if their stockings are made from the hair of whores…
Freedom, you know, is always kin
to voluntary poverty…

Note: The revised text reads like this: Yes…whereas virgins, yes,/ they know when a tree is unwell…. And the cloth/of their innocence / always covers the male's abuse/ Freedom, you know, is always kin/ to voluntary poverty…

Page 107: The Virgin
The party is over at which there were so many lights
the dark was perfect.
And he was there. She didn't mind
If his feelings were wine and his thoughts
grapes.
Towards morning he left her. She sat gazing
through the small hole in her dress
at Monday's naked nail.

Note: This poem does not appear in the published copy.

Chapter 5

REWARD AND PUNISHMENT: DIFFERENT TOOLS FOR THE SAME END

The Ministry of Culture and Islamic Guidance (MCIG) is the official body responsible for culture, but it would be wrong to assume that it has everything under its control. As a matter of fact, there are many other institutions active in the cultural scene which operate independently of this ministry and do not necessarily share the same approach to art and literature. Some such organizations, for example, the Islamic Republic of Iran Broadcasting (IRIB) have a larger budget than the MCIG. Based on some reports, the MCIG's share is less than one-seventh of the annual budget on culture while more than six-sevenths of the budget is given to organizations which do not directly report to the government.[1] Some of these organizations are affiliated to religious leaders while others are responsible only to the Supreme Leader. Therefore, MCIG's influence has always been limited. Even when governments tried to open up the cultural space, these rival cultural institutions pressed for more control. It needs to be noted that many of these organizations have other sources of income as well as the annual government budget. A report in *Shargh* lists eighty-seven different organizations which are officially financed by the state, and their activities include a wide range of cultural, religious, recreational, and research initiatives.[2]

Although varied in size and scope of activities, all these cultural organizations have one common goal: the promotion of Islam and Islamic culture as understood by the ruling clergy. They make movies, publish books and magazines, run schools and summer schools, organize festivals, conferences, and cultural contests, and carry out a wide range of other activities. Their prime purpose in all these activities is to control the cultural space. Control of culture is the focal point and a key objective in the strategic plans of the Islamic Republic. This is an aim shared by the entire system and in order to enforce this control, all elements of the state including judiciary and security forces cooperate. Ahmad Karimi Hakkak describes the Islamic Republic's censorship regime as 'one of the most comprehensive, most aggressive, and harshest systems of censorship that that country has experienced'.[3] State policies in regard to control of culture are not limited to censorship of books, movies, and audio recordings. There are a large number of other policies and measures in place. The state attempts to 'cover all public spaces – city walls, the human body, the printed page – with messages propagating its ideology, so much so that little visible territory is left to oppositional expression'.[4] State policies for control of culture can be broadly divided into two main categories: rewarding policies – tokenism – and punitive policies – intimidation. Both of these sets of policies influence the experience of feeling censored in unique ways. Although different in approach, both pursue the same objective: control. Earlier I discussed the significance of censorship experience in censorship debates and argued in favour of an inclusive approach to respond to all forms of the censorship experience. However, I narrowed down my definition of censorship to include only the censorious acts which are 'external', 'coercive', and 'suppressive' and excluded other structural or constructive forms of censorship such as market forces. I also argued that state-imposed censorship in Iran includes a large array of rewarding policies which are used extensively to control culture through selective patronage. Some forms of tokenism target independent writers and poets in an attempt to bribe them into conformity or silence. The system puts intellectuals and independent authors under enormous economic and social pressures for years and when they become weak and old and vulnerable, they are offered small rewards to either attract them to the regime supporters' camp or force them into silence. For some, this is the last nail in the coffin because it takes away their self-esteem and antagonizes their friends and fans. So, in my view, intimidation and tokenism are two sides of the same coin, as are punishment and reward, and both should be treated as censorship.

Part of what is discussed in this chapter falls within the subjective experiences of feeling censored. Official data on cases of torture, imprisonment, murder, and other major breaches of freedom of expression is not openly accessible. In such instances, I have relied on published information as well as the narratives of the victims or witnesses.

Acts of punishment include closing down newspapers and literary periodicals, revoking business licences of publishers, financial hardships and economic censorship, violation of privacy, interrogations, imprisonment, vilification and defamation, murder, preventing memorial services, and interfering in funerals and burials. There are numerous organizations and forces involved in these acts. On the other hand, the system rewards its favoured poets and writers with financial incentives, positions in cultural institutions, political establishments, and academia, through fame and recognition, literary awards, foreign trips, official memorial services, and by commemorating them permanently through the posthumous naming of public places.

Reward has been recognized by some censorship scholars to produce the same effects as repressive censorship. Matthew Bunn argues that 'positive' press politics can be used

> to induce the same kinds of behavior as repressive prohibitions. Whereas censorship represents 'negative' press policy, the repression of undesirable speech, 'positive' press policy refers to the methods by which the state seeks to advance ideological and political goals through collaboration, manipulation, and co-operation of the press. Such practices include manipulation of stories through selective leaks, cultivating friendly relations with 'loyal' journalists, and financially subsidizing press organs.[5]

These 'positive' policies include a large set of incentives which I call 'reward' to indicate their discriminatory nature. They are rewards and need to be earned through loyalty to the system. Their aim is to achieve the same objective as the repressive policies: control of speech.

The state has many tools at its disposal to effectively reward and punish whoever it desires. Financial and economic tools are used extensively. Independent press and publishers have to struggle for survival while those who openly support the regime have access to vast public funds. Dissident writers and poets are regularly dismissed from their positions and are left with minimal employment opportunities. At the same time, there are lucrative job opportunities in state and public sector cultural organizations for any writer or poet who agrees to comply with the state policies. Reward and punishment policies are studied in more detail in this chapter. Rewards include financial incentives, fame and recognition, employment opportunities, tours and travels, honorary titles, and so on. Literary awards, state publicity and broadcasting agencies, cultural institutions, and public and governmental organizations are the means by which the Iranian regime awards its supporters. As many of the awards come as a package, it is not easy to categorize them. For example, fame and recognition is the outcome of state-sponsored publicity and at the same time leads to financial gain. I therefore discuss rewards under two subheadings of 'literary awards' and 'other forms of patronage'.

Literary Awards

Literary awards play a significant role in promoting literature and are usually seen as a major source of recognition for writers throughout the world. They are equally attractive to those in power who want to utilize them for their benefit. In his essay, 'When they Beat Us, We Suffer', Dario Fo writes: 'There exists another kind of censorship, to do with prizes, grants, opportunities to tour [...]. It is a kind of blackmail which governs the selection of texts'.[6]

During the early years after the Revolution, there was rarely any literary award. After the election of Khatami and as a result of a more open political environment, Iranian writers and poets established a few independent literary awards. The Mehregan-e Adab Award was founded in 1999 and was sponsored by a cooperative of private publishers (PEKA Co.) until this cooperative was closed down in 2006 and sponsorship was limited to a couple of interested individuals. Haft Eqlim is another privately-sponsored award scheme for novels and short stories. Yalda was sponsored by Karevan Publishers and since 2002 awarded novels and short stories; however, the publisher was closed down in 2009 after its owner, Arash Hejazi, was forced into exile. The Sadegh Hedayat Foundation established the Sadegh Hedayat Award in fiction. This is a private foundation run by the family of the late Sadegh Hedayat. The Golshiri Award was established by the Golshiri Foundation, which was founded after the death of novelist Houshang Golshiri in June 2000, and stopped its activity in 2014.

Independent literary awards in Iran receive no government support and rely on private sponsorship. They mainly serve as a source of recognition and have very little or no financial value. For example, even the prestigious Golshiri Award is insignificant moneywise. The Best Novel and the Best Short Story Collection each receive only IRR 10,000,000 which is roughly equal to £220[7] based on the average exchange rate in 2016 – the last year covered by this study. Iranian Poetry Today (also known as the 'Karnameh Award') was an award enterprise of Karnameh magazine established in 1999. When this magazine was closed down by the government in 2005, the Karnameh Award was also interrupted. The Nima Poetry, Khorshid Poetry, and Journalists' Poetry Award are three other independent poetry awards with small financial reward. In 2013, the latter's awarding committee announced that it could not afford any financial payment and might consider giving some 'pistachio nuts' to its award winners.[8] Facing such obstacles, the Golshiri Award halted its activities in 2014.[9] Numerous other initiatives to establish literary awards by independent writers have also failed during the past years either as a result of financial problems or due to state intervention.

The government, on the other hand, grants lucrative awards. Jalāl-e Āl-e Ahmad, established in 2008, rewards authors in categories such as novel, short story, literary criticism, history, and life writing, with each winner receiving 110 gold coins. The market value of each coin in 2016 was around IRR 10,000,000, which means each winner received an amount equal to IRR 1,100,000,000 (roughly equal to £24,000).[10] This is over 100 times higher than the financial value of the Golshiri Award.

The Jalāl-e Āl-e Ahmad Literary Award defines its aim as the promotion of language and national-religious literature through acknowledging the creators of new works that are distinguished and progressive.[11] Parvin is another award scheme managed by the MCIG. This prize is aimed at 'paving the way for the growth and development of women'[12] and is awarded biannually to female authors and translators. *Gām-e- Avval* (The First Step), the *Ketāb-e Fasl* (Book of the Season), and the *Ketāb-e Sāl* (Book of the Year) Awards are other awards granted by that ministry, which also organizes an annual literary criticism festival. The Fajr International Poetry Festival is another major cultural event which has been running annually since 2006 and awards winners in the three categories of 'Poetry', 'Children's and Young Adult Poetry', and 'About Poetry'. The financial value of this award is thirty gold coins. This festival commemorates the victory anniversary of the Islamic Revolution.[13]

Hoze Honari (The Art Council) is in charge of thirteen annual festivals and awards including the *She'r-e Enqelāb* (Revolution's Poetry) and *Dāstān-e Enqelāb* (Revolution's Story) international festivals. The competition for these awards is subject-based and every year the topics are advertised on the award's website. The 2016 poetry festival (Sixth International Festival) considers poetry on the subjects of 'justice and humanity, unity of Islamic *umma* and national elevation, ethics and religious knowledge, Islamic Revolution and Islamic awakening discourse' and issues thirty different awards to national and international contestants. Winners in each category receive IRR 70,000,000 in cash. Three winners in the international section – single poem contest –receive US$ 1,500 each.[14] The Fiction Festival in 2016 – Revolution's Story Festival – issues the Amir Hossein Fardi Award which is named after a writer of religious and war stories who passed away in 2013. In 2016, this award will consider novels and short stories in different categories which are written on events preceding the Revolution to the events today including the war with Iraq, the Kurdistan conflicts, acts of terror and sedition, national identity, the influence of the Islamic Revolution in the region and the Islamic awakening – Iran's name for the Arab uprisings, otherwise called the Arab Spring – as well as opportunities facing the Islamic Revolution in social, political, economic, and cultural areas, the role of the leadership of the Islamic Revolution in national unity and cohesion, and the anti-imperialist movements among Muslims of the world. Awards include a cash prize of up to IRR 140,000,000.[15] There are numerous other topic-based awards, such as the Sacred Defence (war) Literature Award, and various religious and ritualistic poetry awards supported by governmental or semi-governmental organizations all spending considerable amounts of cash and gold on literature.

During Ahmadinejad's two terms as president – from August 2005 to August 2013 – nearly 18,000 gold coins were awarded in literary festivals.[16] Based on an average value of IRR 10,000,000 for each coin, the amount paid out is around IRR 180 billion – roughly equal to £4.2 million in the 2016 average exchange rate.

In spite of the financial value of state-sponsored awards, they are not popular with the literati. Mohammad Javad Jazini, a novelist and researcher and himself a judge in a number of state-sponsored awards, told the Iranian Book News Agency that while the state literary awards were worth a lot of money, what they lacked was prestige because they follow the official policy of the state which might not be popular with the people.[17] Sarkoohi believes that literary awards are a tool in the hands of the government to continue its suppression of independent writers. He accuses the judges in such awards of sponsoring censorship and believes that even if a relatively independent poet or writer wins an award, it is actually the result of a trade-off, with the state bestowing the distinction buying the reputation of the recipient in exchange for the money that accompanies the prize.[18] Sarkoohi is not alone in his dislike of state-sponsored awards. When my name came out as the winner of the Book of the Season Award for the Best Translation in Visual Arts in 2006, I didn't feel very happy although the category of winning was merely technical and only recognized my translation skills. I even considered rejecting the award but I was afraid it might put me in trouble. At last, I attended the award ceremony and received my award but it was not the most pleasant experience.

Literary awards are part of the state's policy of tokenism and are sometimes aimed at attracting vulnerable authors into the camp of the regime supporters or neutralizing their influence as independent voices in literature. Good or bad, association with any cultural project sponsored by government undermines the integrity of independent writers and damages their social influence among some groups, especially young idealist readers. The government knows this and tries to use it to their advantage. Masoud Ahmadi told me that he had been approached a few times to appear on literary programmes on TV or judge government-sponsored awards. He said: 'I asked them: Am I allowed to talk – in your program – about the reasons my book was rejected a publication licence? They said: This is out of our control. Then I said: In that case, goodbye! and I hung up'.[19] Doing this, the independent authors lose money but protect not only their dignity but their social position as independent intellectuals.

Other Forms of Patronage

In addition to literary awards, the government has many other ways to reward writers and poets who support the system. Many young and aspiring authors enjoy easy fame through public broadcasters. The fame gained through appearing on TV or frequent interviews on radio helps build up a career for some whose only advantage over those who are deprived of this opportunity is their different stance toward power. With this fame comes money and financial success elsewhere. While pro-regime poets and writers enjoy prime-time TV shows and extensive radio interviews, independent authors are rarely invited to appear on TV or to talk on radio. On the rare occasions that they are invited, this may lead to criticism. One example is the appearance of Ali Dehbashi, editor of *Bukhara*, a literary journal, on TV. Tasnim News Agency reported criticism of national TV's Channel 4 for inviting him:

> Questions arise about the logic behind the appearance on Islamic Republic TV of those who do not believe in the fundamentals of the Islamic Revolution [...]. Last night the presence of Ali Dehbashi, editor of *Bukhara*, which is a main tribune for the intellectual movement in Iran, on a TV programme called *Be Vaqt-e Mahtāb*, sent waves of objections toward the station.[20]

Independent authors have no share of the arts and culture budget nor do they get the chance of any official recognition. Based on an unwritten law, a number of publishers have not been allowed to publish pictures of living poets and writers on their book covers. This is a shared experience of some publishers and although I haven't encountered any written regulation on this, it has been the norm throughout much of the history of the Islamic Republic. Pictures of deceased or foreign writers sometimes appear on their book covers.[21]

In order for the Islamic Republic to promote its cultural goals, it has established or taken control of many cultural institutions. The most important of all is National Radio and Television, which was later renamed the Islamic Republic of Iran Broadcasting (IRIB). The president of this organization, which controls all internal and external television and radio broadcasts, is appointed by the leader.[22] In addition to TV and radio, this massive organization owns a major film production company and a university, and publishes a variety of books and journals.

According to the Constitution, radio and TV are exclusively state-owned and state-run, and must serve for the 'diffusion of Islamic culture in pursuit of the progressive path of the Islamic Revolution. To this end, they should draw upon a healthy debate of different ideas, and strictly refrain from diffusing and propagating destructive and anti-Islamic traits'.[23]

In addition to IRIB, there are many other institutions advocating the type of literature favoured by the regime and consequently undermining independent literature. Such institutions have abundant financial resources and are highly subsidized by the state and promoted by the official media. *Hoze Honari* (The Art Council) is an institution affiliated to the Islamic Propagation Organization. It has offices in all provinces and undertakes various literary projects through its Centre for Literary Creativities.[24] In the annual budget table of 2015–2016, *Hoze Honari* was granted IRR 55 billion to spend on its artistic and literary programmes.[25] It defines its function as one of the major authorities in art and culture to work in extensive and varied fields including publications, training, conferences, and other activities to maintain and promote the ideals of the Islamic Revolution and the Islamic government.[26] It has numerous departments including the Centre for Literary Creativities, the Centre for Research and Study of Resistance Culture and Literature, and the Islamic Revolution Literature Centre, the Islamic Culture and Art Research Centre, the Ashura Art and Literature Centre, and the Satire Centre. A look at their website shows that many of the directors of these centres are poets and writers who are well known for their support of the regime and its policies, although not so much for their literary achievements. The current head of the *Hoze Honari* (2016) is Mohsen Momeni Sharif, a story writer. Vice-president for Art and Director General of the Music Centre is Fazel Nazari, a best-selling poet whose collections of classical style *ghazals* run above forty reprints each, selling a combined total of more than 100,000 copies. Born in 1979, he has held numerous cultural positions and been involved in various festivals.[27] Alireza Qazveh, the head of the Centre for Literary Creativities is a hardcore supporter of the Supreme Leader and is believed by many to be the closest poet to the leader. The remaining directors are writers, poets, or satirists who have one thing in common: they don't criticize the regime openly and are regarded as loyal to the system. These poets and writers are everywhere. They are on TV, in literary festivals, in international congresses, and in poetry readings with the Supreme Leader. Their books are purchased in large numbers by public libraries, cultural centres, schools, and universities. It is therefore not surprising to see a collection of poems by an emerging poet like Fazel Nazari reprinted forty times while many established poets cannot sell even the first print of their books. *Hoze* organizes thirteen different festivals including the Young Poetry and Fiction, Revolution's Poetry, Revolution's Story, and Sura Satire festivals, the Shafaq Ritualistic Poetry Congress, and so on.

The Children and Young Adults Intellectual Development Centre, the cultural departments of the Islamic Revolutionary Guards and the Baseej Organization, the Supreme Leader's Representative Office in universities, and Islamic societies in universities and mosques are all fully or partially funded by the state. They organize numerous festivals and events, and publish many journals and books.[28] Independent poets and authors have very little or no share in these activities.

The Tehran Municipality Cultural – Art Organization owns thirty-four cultural centres (*Farhangsarā*) in Tehran.[29] An examination of its website shows that there is at least one programme on poetry or fiction in one of its cultural centres every day. Municipalities in other major cities have similar facilities and offer comparable activities. In Tabriz, it organizes the Annual Book Festival and manages the Tabriz Literary Award.[30] These organizations provide employment opportunities for poets and authors who are not openly critical of the system and they are required to follow the standards of desirable literature prescribed by the system in their public duties.

There are more than 19,000 cultural-art centres in mosques throughout the country. Only in 2014, the MCIG spent IRR 140 billion equipping the libraries in mosques. It also supported 9,000 cultural centres in rural mosques and created 149 centres in campus mosques.[31]

In addition to the above institutions, there are many smaller organizations working more specifically on poetry and fiction.

Anjoman-e Qalam-e Iran (Iran Pen Association) is one such organization. The founding members include political figures such as Ali Akbar Velayati (adviser to the Supreme Leader), Ali Larijani (Parliament Speaker), and Mohsen Parviz (former Deputy Minister of Culture and Islamic Guidance). Some of its activities include nominating a day as the Universal Day of the Pen in the Islamic World; granting academic equivalent degrees to poets, writers, and literary critics; recommending the publication of a hundred books authored by emerging poets and writers, and 40,000 pages of poetry and fiction by established poets and writers. It has also established the literary award of *Qalam-e Zarrin* (The Golden Pen); granted numerous interest-free loans to members; organized the literary festival of 'Salam Nasrullah'; published *Ashāb-e- Qalam* (Friends of the Pen) quarterly; created an initiative to establish an 'Islamic World Writers Union', and organized meetings with international writers' clubs, including the Arab Writers Union.[32]

The above list of activities shows the full range of facilities at the disposal of this body and the immense financial benefits of joining it. Many writers believe that this association was established to undermine the activities of *Kānun-e Nevisandegān-e Iran* (Iranian Writers Association) which is the only independent association of authors in Iran and to create a direct confrontation with PEN International. When the latter criticized the use of its registered name, the Iran Pen Association reacted fiercely. It asserted that God had sworn on a 'Pen' in the Qur'an, and that PEN International and other PEN organizations should be questioned for the unauthorized use of this word which was undoubtedly under the absolute ownership of Muslim nations, including Iran.[33]

Khāneh-ye Shāerān-e Iran (Iranian Poets Society) is another organization devoted to the promotion of poetry. Established in 1999, its range of activities include poetry readings, poetry courses, and the publication and translation of poetry. Its charter defines its role as supporting poets whose work evinces the values of Islamic culture.[34] A subsidiary organization, *Daftar-e She'r-e Javān* (Young Poetry Office), recruits young poets (15–25 years of age) from all over the country[35] and offers them training, support, and publication, thus investing in the future generation of poets.

Kānun-e Adabiyyāt-e Iran (Iran Literary Centre) was established in 2002. So far it has organized more than 600 different workshops, thirty international gatherings, three major international congresses each with more than fifty foreign guests, and the first international congress on Latin American literature, attended by thirty Latin American poets and writers.[36]

Another such organization is *Bonyād-e She'r va Adabiyyāt-e Dāstāni-ye Irāniān* (Iranian Foundation for Poetry and Fiction) which acts as the literary arm of the

Cultural Deputy in MCIG. This foundation organizes the Fajr Poetry Festival and administers the Jalāl-e Āl-e Ahmad Literary and Parvin Literary Awards. Other activities of this foundation include:

- Theory construction in the area of poetry and fiction based on indigenous and religious patterns
- Expert study of different literary trends, overseeing, and analyzing the status of poetry and fiction throughout the country
- Training elite poets and fiction writers
- Introducing the literature of Islamic Iran to the global publishing markets
- Translating Persian literature
- Liaising with writers and literary foundations around the world
- Discovery, coaching, and support of young talents[37]

Although all of the above institutions are supported by the system, they do not have an identical approach to independent literature. In fact, some of them are rivals and do not get along very well. For example, Iran's Pen Association is a very conservative organization supporting the hardline approach to independent writers and poets while the Iranian Poets Society is a pro-reformist organization and has a more liberal approach to literature. The leading figures in this society supported the opposition leader, Mir Hossein Mousavi, during the 2009 post-election uprising. Nevertheless, they act within the boundaries of the official discourse and their publications never reflect the nonconformist views of a large number of independent authors.

Punishment

The second and more extensive sets of policies in control of culture are punitive measures which are 'external', 'coercive', and 'repressive' and are aimed at silencing and punishing dissident and/or independent voices in literature. Punishment includes a wide range of financial pressures that I call economic censorship and more repressive forms of persecution including human rights violations, arrest, interrogations, surveillance abuse, imprisonment, torture, murder, and defamation. I will discuss these non-economic punitive acts under the subheading of acts of repression. The variety and scope of this set of harsh treatments has forced a large number of Iranian intelligentsia out of the country and has led to a community of exiled authors adding to the complexity of censorship experience.

Economic Censorship

Economic censorship is a very efficient tool and one that the Iranian government has utilized extensively. In spite of some efforts at privatization during recent years, the government is still the leading player in the Iranian economy. According to some studies, public sector economy counts for more than 80 per cent of the Iranian economy.³⁸ The government has exclusive control over the paper market and the paper ration acts as a controlling apparatus. While pro-regime press and publications have generous access to subsidized paper, independent publications have often had to struggle to purchase paper from the free market. Mehrangiz Kar, a lawyer, writes:

> Since 1981 paper was provided to the publishers at two different rates. The cheap subsidized rate was accessible only to publishers who published books conforming to official policies and the political taste of the MCIG. The free market rate was so expensive that publishers who did not receive subsidized paper were unable to buy and they, therefore, decided to stop publishing books. Consequently, economic censorship was imposed on books.³⁹

In addition to paper, the government discriminates in cash subsidies paid to the press. The amount of direct government aid is enormous and its distribution kept secret, yet unconfirmed reports indicate unequal treatment of the press. Another financial tool at the disposal of the government is the distribution of official advertisements, which are a main source of income for newspapers and magazines. Saeed Leylaz, an economist, writes: 'Exclusive rights […] in ordering advertisements is not to be ignored when government companies are practically banned from offering advertisement to reformist newspapers such as *Shargh* or *E'temād*; […] and even the directors of such companies are prosecuted if they place advertisements with these newspapers'.⁴⁰

Buying books for public libraries is another massive financial tool in the hands of the government. Public libraries are controlled by a body called the Public Libraries Institution. Based on their portal, this institution is the biggest buyer of books in the country. On average, they spend IRR 200 billion a year on the purchase of books, the majority from governmental or semi-governmental publishers.⁴¹ According to their mission statement, they purchase the type of books 'containing material which strengthens the fundamentals of Islam, the Islamic Revolution, the *Velayat-e Faqih* and the components of Iranian national identity, and those which promote family values, obedience to God, spirituality and the unity of God'.⁴²

The Tehran International Book Fair attracts more than five million visitors and is an especially important opportunity for publishers to sell their books and gain much-needed cash for their struggling businesses.⁴³ There are hundreds of similar book fairs in provincial capitals and other cities around the country every year. The governmental publishers and publishers of religious books are normally given the best and largest stands, while undesirable publishers are regularly banned from attending the book fairs to sell their books.⁴⁴

The above measures have a significant impact on the publishing industry in Iran. With the exception of a few governmental publishers or those affiliated to semi-governmental organizations, publishers in Iran are generally small or medium-sized enterprises. They cannot financially compete with government or with publishing arms of major religious organizations. When faced with such discrimination and restrictions, they either have to abandon publishing or change their policies for publishing independent literature. Those who remain committed to independent literature have no way but to struggle for survival.

Acts of Repression

As we saw above, the government uses its powers to put independent press and publications under unbearable financial pressure. When financial pressures fail, the government resorts to its licensing power. Hundreds of newspapers and magazines including many leading literary journals have been closed down by the government or by the judiciary. *Gardun, Takāpu, Ādineh, Donyā-ye Sokhan*, and *Kārnāmeh* are some of the literary journals in this category. *Takāpu* was closed because it published an open letter against censorship, which became known as the 'Letter of 134 Writers' (1994).[45] Mansour Kooshan, editor of *Takāpu*, observes: 'The MCIG did not sell *Takāpu* subsidized paper. They knew I had to sustain at least IRR 5 million loss for each issue, as I had to buy paper from the free market, and they knew the economic hardships we were facing. They, therefore, expected *Takāpu* to be closed for economic problems'.[46] When this did not happen, the authorities put the magazine under pressure by giving regular notices. Finally, they revoked its licence after fourteen issues.

Ādineh was taken to court and tried for a number of pieces published in different issues, including a poem by Nima Yushij which, the complainant claimed, 'showed all modes of woman'.[47] The court fined the licence holder and permanently annulled the magazine's licence, for 'publishing materials which compromised public decency'.[48] *Gardun* was closed down for its cover design, which was perceived by some to be insulting to Hijab. In court, *Gardun* was accused of enmity toward the Islamic Republic, spreading rumours, and insulting the authorities, the clergy, the Sacred Defence [Iraq–Iran war] and the Hezbollah,[49] as well as promoting royalist ideas.[50] In addition to *Gardun*, at least five other newspapers and magazines (*Shargh, Phārād, Hayāt-e No, Āzād*, and *Zan*) have been closed down for publishing controversial cartoons.[51]

Kārnāmeh was shut down after forty-nine issues. Saeed Taghipour, Director General of Press in the Ministry, confirmed that *Kārnāmeh* was closed because it published some poems and other texts which were found by the Supervisory Board to be incompatible with public decency.[52]

Books have been perceived to be dangerous by numerous political systems throughout history. Rebecca Knuth, who has researched cultural destruction, writes:

> As regimes consolidate control, often becoming totalitarian, they tend to cast libraries and books in a suspicious light, as either inherently seditious or the tool of the enemy or a scapegoat for a nation, an ethnic group or class of people that thwarts their policies. Looting, co-option, censorship, neglect, and violent destruction of books and libraries are therefore sanctioned practices.[53]

Although there is no record of destruction of library or libricide by the Islamic Republic, there are countless examples of library cleansing. During the early years of the Revolution, many people destroyed their books for fear of prosecution. My elder brother threw more than 500 books into a dried-up water well running under our house. This was a common story in many families. Nasser Zera'ati, Iranian writer and filmmaker, has made a documentary called *Khāneh-ye Pedari* (Ancestral Home) about the books he buried in his family home's basement during the 1980s, which he hoped to return to soon and recover. He was able to visit that house twenty years later by which time most of the books had rotted.[54]

In 1990, the publisher *Noqreh* was set on fire after publishing *Zanān bedun-e Mardān* (Women without Men) and the writer, Shahrnoush Parsipour, was imprisoned and all her books – even those published during the Shah regime – were banned.[55] In September 1995, *Morgh-e Āmin* Bookstore was set on fire after publishing *Va Khodāyān Doshanbeh-hā Mikhandand* (And Gods Laugh on Mondays) by Reza Khoshbin Khoshnazar. Although the culprits were never identified, the fact that in both cases the books in question were banned might indicate a sort of coordination between the government and its zealot supporters. Masoud Noghrehkar, a researcher, believes that both acts were organized libricide decided upon by security officials and carried out by Hezbollahi thugs.[56]

Pressures from different hardline groups for more strict censorship have also been enormous. There has even been speculation that major censorship policies are adopted outside the official organization responsible for censorship, that is, the Ministry of Culture and Islamic Guidance. Ali Asghar Ramezanpour, a former Vice-Minister of Culture and Islamic Guidance, revealed that all types of censorship are supervised by institutions that prioritize censorship based on their assessment of social, political, and cultural conditions: 'Institutions affiliated to the leader, the part of clergy which is supported by the regime and the commanders of the Islamic Revolutionary Guards Corps are on top of this "Supreme Supervisory System".'[57] The security forces and the judiciary are also very active in suppressing independent writers and poets. Faraj Sarkoohi, editor of *Ādineh* and a victim of torture and imprisonment, recorded that the censorship authorities and staff cooperate openly with the security services.[58] In 1998, *Salām* revealed that the press law which was being debated in the parliament had been actually drawn up by the intelligence forces. It published a top-secret letter by Saeed Emami, Vice-Minister of Intelligence, which proposed further legal restrictions on the press to enable the judiciary and security forces to prosecute not only the directors and licence holders in the media but anyone involved in content production.[59]

When the censorship failed to bring about the desired outcome, the authorities decided to physically remove the undesirable elements from the cultural scene, as Sarkoohi notes:

> The tools of physical removal included murder, imprisonment, torture and crushing your personality. The goal was to seclude and neutralize active writers and poets. The methods used included: spreading rumours; magnifying real or fictional weaknesses of individuals; creating internal disputes and rivalries

between intellectuals; discrediting; false accusations; forced televised interviews; censorship and imposing self-censorship; promoting false critics who would appear to be advocating the same messages as the independent intellectuals but who were, in fact, related to security forces or various factions within the system; fabricating secretly dependent institutions to monopolize independent activities or institutions which allow limited activity to others but keep the key areas exclusively to the state; neutralizing the influence of independent writers and poets by luring them into programmes and projects affiliated to the government in one way or another [...]. The theory of cultural invasion was the guiding light of religious despotism in Iran for two decades and had all capabilities of the country at its service.[60]

Sarkoohi claims that he suffered flogging, hanging, handcuffing, sleep deprivation, and psychological tortures in prison: 'The same tortures of the Shah regime were common during the Islamic Republic, but some new tortures such as Chicken Kebab[61] had been added. Psychological torture had aggravated and had become quite common. I myself underwent three mock executions'.[62]

Seyed Ali Salehi claims that, in 1984, his publisher was threatened for publishing his rendering of parts of *Avestā*. Salehi himself was allegedly attacked with the book – a thick and heavy volume: 'They hit me on the neck with the book so forcibly that I lost my balance. One of them said to me: "Are you Zoroastrian? You are a Seyed [believed to be descendants of Prophet Mohammad] and now you follow Zoroaster?"'[63] One very influential form of torture is overt stalking. The security forces stalk writers and poets in a manner certain to be noticed by the victims, who will ask themselves why they are being followed and what wrong they have committed? This leads to further self-censorship. It is also a common pre-arrest practice to frighten the victim and make them ready to sign a confession. In Sarkoohi's words, 'As a result, the victim becomes his own interrogator. He tortures himself and is torn from within. Then he gets arrested.'[64]

The events of autumn 1998, which became known as 'chain murders', revealed an extensive programme of extrajudicial killings and the disappearances of political and religious dissidents, including a number of well-known intellectuals, writers, poets, and translators. The number of extrajudicial killings is subject to speculation. Akbar Ganji, who researched the killings and was imprisoned for six years for the publication of his findings, believes that the murders were part of an ongoing government project decided on at the highest level and ordered directly by the Supreme Leader. He claims that when summoned to the Ministry of Intelligence, they informed him that they were aware of over 300 assassinations but were unable to investigate them.[65] Saeed Emami, who was named as the man behind these murders, is quoted as saying: 'Fighting cultural invasion is a jihad against the enemies. In war, any tactic is allowed. We don't like homicide, but we cannot allow the Revolution and the country to be played with by a bunch of corrupt liberal intellectuals'.[66]

Amir Fasrhad Ebrahimi, a defector from *Ansār-e Hezbollah* – a hardline pro-regime cell – has described how the intelligence forces tortured Ali Akbar

Saeedi Sirjani, a writer, essayist, and poet, forcing him into self-loathing televised interviews and then killing him by injecting air into him.[67] Moreover, Akbar Ganji believes that the security forces intended to eliminate all major intellectuals in a public gathering, such as a funeral. He holds that the system saw intellectuals as security threat: 'Based on the theory of cultural invasion, intellectuals are the main agents of the cultural aggression of the West. They act as catalysts for change through cultural activities and turn loyalists into revisionists and make people indifferent toward the sacred fundamentals of Islam'.[68]

Although these murders apparently stopped in 1999 when President Khatami ordered an investigation and the Ministry of Intelligence admitted the wrongdoings of a number of its agents, the true scope of the plot was never revealed. Emami, the highest-ranking suspect, allegedly committed suicide in prison. Some experts believe that he was murdered to block the investigations and to save people at the top; Akbar Ganji commenting that they 'closed the dossier midway' by killing Emami.[69] However, Emami's arrest and subsequent events prompted some writers to disclose horrific events which nobody had dared to talk about before. One was the story of the trip to Armenia, after the Armenian Writers Union had invited Iranian writers to a gathering in that country. The Iranians decided to hire a bus for the journey. According to Sarkoohi, at first thirty-five people decided to go. Some then cancelled their trip for different reasons. Seventeen or twenty-one – according to Sarkoohi and Kooshan, respectively – got on the bus. Sarkoohi alleges that the Iranian intelligence forces took control of the trip either from the very beginning or sometime in the middle of the planning.[70] The bus driver – Khosro Barati, who was later named as one of the killers in the chain murders – tried to throw the bus down the valley twice in the middle of the night when most of the passengers were asleep.[71]

In April 2004, a letter faxed to *Kārnāmeh* office threatened to 'wash the territory of the Islamic Iran with the blood of the corrupters on Earth [who use their] dark pens to annihilate Islamic culture'. The letter contained a list of sixty-one names – my name included – whom the writers promised to kill, pursuant to their 'revolutionary executions' of 1998.[72]

In order for the killers' message to work particularly well, they added humiliation and defamation to murder. When Saeedi Sirjani was arrested in March 1990, the newspaper *Keyhān* reported the cause of his arrest as addiction and drug dealing, and later added the crimes of sodomy and espionage. He was later killed in one of the safe homes of the Ministry of Intelligence.[73]

Ahmad Miralayi, a literary translator, was found dead with two bottles of home-made vodka by his side.[74] When the intelligence forces raided a party at the home of the German cultural attaché, they arrested six poets and writers, filmed the dinner table, searched the guests and, after planting something in the pocket of a novelist, found it and declared it to be opium.[75] Dissidents who were of religious backgrounds, even clerics, were usually accused of sodomy, addiction, and espionage, and those who had no religious background were accused of illegitimate relationships, promiscuity, addiction, and espionage.[76]

Ever since the early years of the Revolution, some pro-government newspapers, especially *Keyhān*, have published defamatory material about writers, poets, and intellectuals. *Keyhān* used to run a series of articles called *Nima-ye Penhān* (The Hidden Half), in which they tried to portray intellectuals as agents of the West and spies of Israel, people who indulged in promiscuity, and who lacked any moral standards. These articles were later made into books and distributed in large circulations with lurid subtitles.[77]

On occasions, Iranian national TV has broadcast self-loathing confessions recorded during detention. *Cherāgh* (Light) and *Hoviyat* (Identity) are two examples of TV series that targeted intellectuals. *Hoviyat* was broadcast in 1995. Ahmad Pournejati, Vice-President of IRIB at the time, later wrote:

> Ali Larijani, President of IRIB, contacted me and told me that a programme had been made about the conduct of some of the anti-revolutionary and problematic cultural elements and that it's good to be broadcast on Channel One [the most watched Iranian TV channel]. From the taste and colour of the programme, I knew in what kitchen it had been cooked! I told Larijani that this work was more a dark, one-sided piece of propaganda by the intelligence forces rather than a work of the media.[78]

In recent years and as a result of the spread of the Internet, hundreds of websites and weblogs carry out the same role. They publish derogatory articles about writers, poets, translators, and cultural figures with details of their private lives – fact and fiction mixed – portraying them as immoral, promiscuous, non-Muslim, agents of the West, spies, and so on.

Faraj Sarkoohi claims that his interrogators played an audio file secretly recorded in his bedroom and that he was forced to listen repeatedly to his orgasmic sounds during interrogations.[79] He considers that one of the most effective psychological tortures is the use of the victim's personal information, whereby the tortured, flogged, and sleepless victim is hauled into the interrogation room and put under psychological pressure by disclosing details of his private life.[80]

Personal writings such as letters, diaries, sketches, and unpublished material have been used against their writers and others. If, by any chance, you get into trouble with the state, the content of your diaries or your personal notes can further aggravate your situation or be used as evidence against others. I was an undergraduate student when my room was raided and my diary seized. I was interrogated about the contents of my diary for days. As a student of English Literature, I had written some parts of my diary in English to practise English writing. The intelligence forces had these parts translated and questioned me about them as well.

In writing about the Soviet Union under Stalin, Irena Maryniak quotes Vitaly Shentalinsky, who believed that there were many informers amongst his fellow writers and that even the Writers' Union had been created by Stalin and used to spy on its own members.[81] In the interrogations of the suspects of the 1998 chain murders, one of the security agents disclosed the name of one of their informers, called – or nicknamed – Dariush, who is claimed to have belonged to the small circle called the Advisory Group that was managing the Iranian Writers' Association (*Kānun*) in the absence of an elected committee. In a chilling narrative, Mehrdad Aalikhani, Director General of the Ministry of Intelligence during the chain murders, retells how he and his colleagues killed Mohammad Jafar Pouyandeh, the celebrated translator. As he told his interrogators: 'While en route, the source (Dariush) called me on my mobile and informed me of his friends' analysis. He said that the Advisory Group are of the analysis that this type of action contains a message by the killers. The message is that we want to kill and we want to kill openly. It's serious. They have panicked'.[82]

Memorial services for dissident poets and writers are sometimes disturbed by the security forces and pro-regime pressure groups. Security forces attend these ceremonies and openly film the participants. In 1995, I attended the memorial service for Siavosh Kasrayi, an exiled poet who had died in Austria. The security forces filmed everyone, then raided the mosque and beat the participants while the *Ansār-e Hezbollah* group were marching on the pavement shouting slogans through their loudspeakers. My friends and I were sworn at and asked to leave the venue by young members of *Ansār-e Hezbollah*. I tried to chat with them and entered into a row with two of them when a tall man in his forties approached me. He had dark sunglasses and a black beard. He approached me and in a very authoritative voice told me: 'This is the third time I am seeing you. If I ever see you again, I will send you to a place of no return!' I opened my mouth to answer him but my friend, Mehrdad Fallah, pulled my sleeve and said: 'Alireza, let's just leave!' Years later, I saw the picture of that man in the newspapers. He was the infamous Saeed Emami, the Vice-Minister of Intelligence in Domestic Security and the mastermind of the chain murders. Mahmoud Dowlatabadi recalls that *Kānun* had intended to hold a memorial service for Ahmad Shamlou, the most celebrated Iranian poet of our time, but that this had not been allowed and that the deceased's family had been also forbidden to hold a memorial service.[83]

Funerals and burials of poets and writers in recent decades have not been without problem. Two of the victims of the chain murders – Pouyandeh and Mokhtari – were buried in Imamzadeh Taher Cemetery in Karaj, near Tehran. Consequently, that cemetery gained a symbolic significance and some other independent poets and writers expressed their wish to be buried there. Houshang Golshiri and Ahmad Shamlou died in June and July 2000, respectively, and were both buried in this cemetery. The government felt threatened by the popularity of this cemetery and tried to prevent it becoming a gathering place for dissident intellectuals. They therefore decided to forbid further burials of writers there.

The funeral of Manouchehr Atashi (November 2005) turned into a confrontation between mourners and the security forces. According to a report by Alireza Jabbari, Atashi had repeatedly requested to be buried near his dead friends in Imamzadeh Taher Cemetery. On the day of the funeral, the authorities ordered the body to be transported to the southern city of Bushehr – Atashi's birthplace – a decision that caused huge dissatisfaction and stirred protests among the participants.[84] M. Azad, a poet, died in January 2006 and his family decided to bury him in Imamzadeh Taher Cemetery. They obtained the necessary permit but the security forces would not allow the burial. Simin Behbahani remembers how the body was stranded for hours while his friends and family were negotiating with different authorities. At last, Behbahani herself urged the participants to put the body into the grave and not to wait for permission: 'Should we put the body of a poet on the mountain to be eaten by vultures? Azad was born without permission and we will now bury him without permission'.[85] Simin Behbahani's death in 2014 led to confusion and controversy. An advocate of freedom of expression and a major force in women's rights movement, Behbahani was openly disliked by the Supreme Leader. However, the MCIG under President Rouhani wanted to give her a state funeral. Her body was buried in Behesht Zahra against her express will and in spite of the fact that she had previously bought a grave for herself in Imamzadeh Taher Cemetery, beside her husband's and grandchild's graves. As a result, some members of *Kānun* decided to boycott the funeral of this leading member in order to show their objection to the government's interference.[86]

The disrespect to the dead bodies and the graves goes against all cultural norms of Iranian society. Iranians revere their dead and it therefore requires much hatred to disrespect the dead and destroy gravestones. Nevertheless, some gravestones have been frequently destroyed by anonymous people and vandalizers have never been caught. The gravestone of Ahmad Shamlou has been broken a number of times.[87] The gravestone of Iraj Afshar, the renowned bibliographer and Iranologist was stolen from Behesht Zahra Cemetery. The grave of Mohammad Ali Sepanlou, a poet who died in 2015 and was buried in Behesht Zahra against his will – he also wanted to be buried in Imamzadeh Taher – was completely covered in concrete so that no sign of his grave was visible. The authorities of the cemetery didn't react to the news at the time.[88] Sepanlou's niece, described her numerous efforts to talk to the authorities in the cemetery – which is governed by Tehran's municipality – and they told her that such things do happen and they can't be held responsible even if 'the gravestone had been made of Indian ruby'. Shabnam Sepanlou ordered a new gravestone with an ordinary design so that it might not provoke those who vandalized the first gravestone which was an artwork inspired by Sepanlou's poetry. The Cultural and Social Deputy of the Cemetery then took a selfie with this new stone and published it in the media claiming that there had never been any vandalism.[89]

Although there is no hard evidence to prove the regime's involvement in such acts of vandalism, these acts are congruent with other forms of disrespect to the dead such as interference in their burial or memorial services. For the past sixteen years, the security forces have prevented a gathering at the grave of Shamlou on his death anniversary. In 2016, I was present when they severely beat up and arrested three members of the Iranian Writers Association and forced the participants to leave before they could enter the cemetery.

Chapter 6

HOW DO WRITERS AND POETS REACT TO CENSORSHIP?

Independent writers and poets in Iran have reacted differently to censorship. Some left the country and started a life in exile. Others preferred to stay but were driven into a self-imposed seclusion. They stopped publishing or even writing. Some others decided to resist censorship and find ways to fight back. Those who stayed and continued writing adopted two distinct policies. On the one hand, they criticized censorship and did whatever they could to show their dissatisfaction publicly. They wrote open letters, signed statements and petitions and tried to organize collective acts of protest. On the other hand, they tried to use every means to publish their work and circumvent censorship. Both of these measures are described in more detail below.

Open Protest

The idea of writing to the authorities and demanding the rights of free speech dates back to pre-Revolution time. The most recent example before the Revolution is probably the letter sent by a group of writers to Premier Abbas Hoveida in June 1977, eighteen months before the victory of the Revolution. Ervand Abrahamian, a historian, writes: 'The letter denounced the regime for violating the constitution, demanded an end to censorship, protested that SAVAK [the Shah's secret police] stifled all cultural, intellectual, and artistic activity, and argued that many citizens were in prison for the "crime" of reading books disapproved of by the police'.[1]

After the Revolution, some writers published open letters demanding civil and democratic rights, and objected to policies such as censorship. One such writer was Ali Akbar Saeedi Sirjani, who published letters addressed to the leader and paid the price with his life. The most important public declaration protesting censorship after the Revolution was that known as the 'Letter of 134 Writers' of 1994, initiated by Kānun-e Nevisandegān-e Iran and signed by that number of writers and poets, which became a landmark for the struggle against censorship in Iran. Some of the signatories took back their signature under pressure from the security forces; nevertheless, it remained a document of defiance and resistance. In part of the letter, we read:

We are writers. By this, we mean that we write our feelings, imagination, thoughts, and scholarship in various forms and publish them. It is our natural, social, and civil right to see that our writing – be it poetry or fiction, drama or film script, research or criticism, or the translation of works written by other writers of the world – reach the public in a free and unhampered manner. It is not within the capacity of any person or organization to create obstacles for the publication of these works, under whatever pretext these may be.[2]

Ali Ashraf Darvishian, a novelist, believes that the huge success of the letter was due to the fact that it came out during a period of absolute silence, a time that no one dared to oppose censorship openly. It was broadcast through satellite television and radio stations overseas, and was hugely copied and distributed inside the country. In an interview with M. Ravanshid, Darvishian says: 'Some friends were arrested and some withdrew their signatures under duress. But others resisted. Regressive newspapers which were influenced by hardliners started to build up cases against the members of Kānun and wrote many articles against them [...]. They wrote more than 1,000 pages against Kānun and the signatories to the Letter of 134 Writers'.[3]

The Letter of 134 Writers was a very brave act and the fierce reaction of the regime showed how vulnerable are the theoretical foundations of censorship. In spite of the problems that it brought for signatories, it continued to inspire many others to stand up to censorship and to write about it. On numerous occasions, Iranian poets and writers criticized the arrest or prosecution of authors, expressed their views on social issues such as women's and children's rights and expressly emphasized their right of free expression. On 16 October 2012, a letter entitled 'Annul the Book Publication Licence' was signed by more than 170 authors and widely published online. This letter called on the government to annul not just the pre-publication licensing but all relevant laws and regulations.[4] In addition to such letters, individual poets and writers have written letters to stress their independence from the system. When a novel by Amir Hassan Cheheltan was nominated for Book of the Year Award, he wrote an open letter and asked his book to be withdrawn. He considered it immoral to accept a governmental award for literature as long as even a single book remains unpublished because of censorship.[5]

Although the Letter of 134 Writers caused many problems for the signatories, it brought Kānun back to the forefront of struggle against censorship. Since its foundation in 1968, Kānun has continued to stand by the principle of free expression with no exclusion or exception. Kānun has never been recognized by the government and has always been viewed as an illegal institution. Except for a short while during President Khatami's government, Kānun has been unable to form an open assembly and has been confined to the homes of its members. Even these private meetings have been raided on numerous occasions and members arrested and jailed. Nevertheless, Kānun didn't compromise on its ideals and has survived all these obstacles. It has published different issues of its bulletin *Andisheh-ye Āzād* (The Free Thought) and has defiantly resisted any attempt to keep silent. Kānun regularly publishes its statements in reaction to different cultural and social issues, and strongly rejects any censorship. Although any gathering of independent writers could not escape the watchful eyes of the security forces, they tried to organize public readings and talks where censored materials were read and discussed.

In November 2008, Kānun declared 4 December – the anniversary of the murder of Mohammad Mokhtari – as the Day to Combat Censorship and independent Iranian authors have commemorated this day ever since.[6] Furthermore, the Iranian diaspora has created Iranian Pen in Exile[7] and The House of Free Speech,[8] among other initiatives, with the aim of promoting free expression and fighting censorship.

Laughing at censorship might not look like a genuine protest, but satire is one of the ways in which Iranian authors have reacted to it. There is a huge potential for comedy around the topic of censorship; something that Iranian writers and poets have seized on to expose it. Emran Salahi, the celebrated satirist, frequently targeted censorship in his writings, while many others have written satiric pieces addressing the absurdity of censorship rules. One example is a piece in Qanun newsapaper titled 'I censor, therefore I am' – reminiscent of Descartes's phrase 'I think, therefore I am'.[9] Another satirist mocked the ban on the use of 'wine' in literature by changing this word in the famous poems of Persian classical poets to other words such as 'water, cucumber, pomegranate, chewing gum, Vitamin C, Hype and RANI [brands of juice], Delster [a non-alcoholic beer brand], sour cherry juice, shampoo, fake Chanel perfume', and so on resulting in funny but absurd verses.[10] In the following poem, the poet mocks the use of ellipsis (three dots) as a sign of words omitted and uses the 'beep' sound as a sign of alarm when describing different parts of his beloved's body:

> Oh my beloved, your stature three dots!
> Your face in all modes, three dots!
> Your lips beep, your mouth beep, your head and body beep!
> What more can I say, your entire being beep![11]

Circumventing Censorship

Iranian poets and writers use different tactics to publish their work in spite of censorship. These tactics can be categorized into two groups: getting round censorship and outwitting the censors. They have ignored censorship by making their work accessible to readers through unofficial channels. They have also employed different innovative techniques to present their work in a manner to pass censorship or undergo as little change as possible.

Underground publication has been a common practice of writers under totalitarian regimes. Samizdat played a key role in preserving and publishing dissident literature during communist rule, especially in eastern Europe. Throughout the history of modern Iran, many books have been published away from the eyes of the state. Underground publication of political material was common during the Shah's rule, and even many works of literature were published in unmarked printing houses and distributed secretly. During and immediately after the Revolution of 1979, many white-cover books appeared on the market. They became popular because of the fear of persecution. According to Abdolhossein Azarang, many books were published uncensored and without being registered anywhere during 1977 and 1978. A few months before the victory of the Revolution, underground publication turned into open publication. Books with circulations of hundreds of thousands and even above a million were published. A new generation of readers appeared who, Azarang notes, would devour any book or journal previously forbidden.[12]

As the new regime established its control and censorship intensified, some publications went underground again. However, it should be noted that the majority of pre-Revolutionary underground publications were carried out by political parties and were distributed through their extended networks of supporters and sympathizers throughout the country. As the Islamic Republic heavily suppressed opposition political parties and destroyed their networks, underground publication of political pamphlets and books diminished and became a solitary act by a few brave souls. One such person was Pirooz Davani, a writer and translator who printed his highly provocative anti-regime material and distributed them personally sometimes using the state-owned postal service. He paid a high price for his activities and has been missing since 28 August 1998. Although the Iranian government has not officially admitted any role in his disappearance, there are numerous indications from defectors of the regime that he probably died under torture or was killed by a religious decree and buried by the Intelligence forces.[13]

Some banned books are also published illegally and sold by street venders or second-hand book sellers. These are the books of high demand which have not been officially published for years and are illegally offset and sold. Although many of these books have been around for decades, some well-known works of literature by contemporary poets and writers also find their way into this black market. Authors of such books earn no income from the sale of their books, however many have no objection because, in most cases, it is the only way they can reach the reader. In reacting to the news of the illegal sale of his collection of poetry, *Madāyeh-e Biseleh* (Reward-less Panegyrics) on street corners, Ahmad Shamlou said: 'Do you expect me to complain against these poor booksellers? And to whom should I complain? To the censors? [...]. These brilliant people have broken the barrier of censorship with their work over the years. They have kept many valuable books circulating'.[14]

Some writers and poets have themselves chosen to publish underground. They either do it out of disappointment at never getting a licence or because they do not want to go through the hassle of getting one. Seyed Ali Salehi submitted his collection of poetry *Yek Nafar Injā Dustat Dārad* (Someone Loves You Here) to the Book Office in 2009. In June 2013 he was informed that his work has been rejected and he, therefore, decided to publish it underground.[15] Some others knew in advance that their books would never get a licence because of the content. Reza

Khandan Mahabadi published *Enferādiyeh-hā* (Memos of Solitary Confinement) underground, as did Rouhollah Mehdipour Omran who wrote the novel *Ān ke Nevesht* (The One Who Wrote) about student uprisings. Hassan Asghari and Farkhondeh Hajizadeh illegally published a novel and a collection of short stories, respectively. Baktash Abtin published an audio CD of his poems called *Muriāna-yi ba Dandānhā-ye Shiri* (A Moth with Baby Teeth). Most of the poems reflected a critical view of the Iran-Iraq war which challenged the official narrative of the state.[16]

Alishah Mowlavi published his collection of poems, *Kāmelan Khosusi barā-ye Ettela'e Omum* (Totally Private for Public Information) in defiance of the licencing procedures. He used every opportunity to express his refusal of censorship and promised that he would never publish a book if it meant he had to submit to the will of censors. His resistance acted as a political and intellectual statement and inspired some of the new generation writers and poets to follow suit. These authors didn't fear to publish their books under their own name. Some of their books might have even passed censorship without any problem. They, however, didn't recognize the institution of censorship and opposed the Iranian publication industry and its submission to the will of the state. Although the extent of this practice is not known, it should have been big enough an issue to have forced authorities to react. The MCIG announced on numerous occasions that they would fight against unauthorized publication of books and in 2015, the speaker of the ministry told the press about the creation of a special taskforce to monitor the illegal printing and distribution of books.[17] On other occasions they collected such books from bookshops and book fairs.[18]

Some books are published in neighbouring countries and smuggled into Iran. The publication of *'Man-e In Nasl'* (Me, from this Generation) by Mohammadreza Asadzadeh in the Republic of Azerbaijan and its distribution in Iran caused major debates as to the degree of control the MCIG exerts over the book market. Asadzadeh was the editor-in-chief of IBNA (Iranian Book News Agency) which is the official news agency of the MCIG. He had published the book in Baku in 2012 but the book entered the Iranian book market in 2015 and was harshly criticized by the conservative media as an 'anti-revolutionary work' which makes nasty sarcastic remarks about 'different institutions of the Islamic system'. The conservatives were outraged that the writer of such a book should be in a culturally important government position.[19] As the publishing industry in neigbouring Afghanistan is reviving, some Iranian writers have opted to publish their books in Afghanistan where no pre-publication censorship is exercised. An uncensored translation of *Lolita* by Vladimir Nabokov was one of the first books by an Iranian translator published in Afghanistan. The distribution of this book in Iran stirred anger among some of the hardline conservatives which perceived the book to be sexually explicit. One news agency, Student News Network, called for stronger control in the bookstores calling *Lolita* a 'monster which showed up in Tehran bookshop windows'.[20]

Banning a book attracts attention and acts as good publicity. When Judge Mortezavi summoned Dr Cyrus Shamisa to court and ordered him to collect all distributed copies of his scholarly book *Shāhedbāzi dar Adab-e Farsi* (Male Homosexual Love in Persian Literature), or face prosecution, the book became an instant sensation on the black market. As reported by Sayer Mohammadi, the news spread and led to a cheap print of large numbers of the book. The following day, all booksellers near Tehran University were making a fortune from sales of it.[21]

As a result of the Revolution and the subsequent events, many writers and intellectuals left the country and started a life in exile. Some of them set up small publishing houses and published Persian literature. Publishers like Arash, Baran, Ketab-e-Arzan, and Bokarthus in Sweden; Asr-e-Jadid, Forugh, Gardun, and Sujet in Germany; Khavaran in France, and Dena in the Netherlands, as well as those in North America, such as Ketab Corp and Ibex, publish Persian books in many different areas.[22] During recent years, publishing outside Iran has become more popular. As more poets and writers become frustrated with censorship, they choose to publish their works overseas. Increasing popularity of electronic publication has greatly contributed to this trend. Nogaam, a company in London, mainly publishes books previously censored or forbidden in Iran. The company was established in December 2013 and, up to October 2016, had published thirty-six titles, all of which are downloadable for free.[23] H&S Media, an on-demand publisher based in London, has published 661 books by 414 authors since its inception in May 2011.[24] Naakojaa has been publishing traditional and electronic books since February 2012 in Paris. This is a rising trend and every now and then new publishers emerge. These publishers are now one major platform for uncensored publication. Since many of them offer electronic versions, their books can be easily accessed by readers from inside Iran.

Anonymity is one way to stay safe and publish potentially dangerous materials. By publishing anonymously, the writer loses their right to be recognized officially as the creator; however, this can sometimes be a life-saving tactic. Although many authors adopt pen names which are different from their birth names for reasons of choice, some do this to create a separate identity and protect their private lives from the risks and undue attention of their literary career. There are writers who are well-known by their adopted names, but they keep this fame away from their neighbours or their co-workers. There are samples of extremely popular books whose writers have never been ascertained, such as '*Shāh-e Siāhpushān*' – attributed to Houshang Golshiri – and *Kahrobā* – published under Joseph Babazadeh's name and believed to have been written by Mohammad Ali Sepanlou. The Internet has made anonymity easy. Many online writers are only known by their chosen alias.

Iran accessed the Internet in 1990s but it was in the early 2000s that it gained cultural and political significance due to the popularity of blogging. In 2001, Hossein Derakhshan, a young journalist published a blogging guide in Persian in his weblog. Soon after, the number of Persian blogs increased considerably and blogging gained enormous popularity. This new phenomenon and the community formed around it was called Weblogistan/Blogistan. Iran's highly educated population and the free software made it easy for writers to blog but the number one reason for the rapid growth of blogging was the strict censorship in traditional media. In such circumstances, the Internet was the only safe space which provided a free platform for expressing critical views on social and political issues and to publish material which could not be published elsewhere. Blogging was viewed not only as a new and exciting method of communication, but also as a tool for the promotion of democracy and freedom of expression. Although the exact size of Blogistan could not be measured, numerous studies and reports astonished the world by the assumed size of blogging some reporting Persian to be the third most popular language on the Internet.[25] A 2013 report by the Iran Media Center summarizes former reports on the size of Persian Blogistan in the previous decade which range from 13,000 blogs – in a report dated 2003 – to 700,000 blogs – in another report dated 2007. Other reports indicate a number between these two.[26] The number of active blogs written by Iranians and regularly updated was estimated at around 70,000 in 2009.[27] In other years the estimate varies from 52,000 to 100,000 active blogs.[28] Regardless of the different estimates, it is clear that blogging had become very popular and was perceived as a huge potential. Blogs were seen as platforms for dialogue between different ideas; a space to practise tolerance and read alternative views. In a closed society such as Iran where public interactions, especially between the sexes, were limited, the Internet provided a space where dialogues could form beyond gender and class barriers. Censorship of traditional media boosted blogging as a way to circumvent censorship. It was difficult for the state to control the Internet. It also gave extra security than traditional media because you could hide behind an alias and write whatever you wanted without the need to disclose your identity.

Ordinary people who had never written before found a platform to get their voices heard. Many writers and poets took to blogging both to present their work and to be in direct contact with their readers. Literary blogs and websites also created a bridge between Iranians inside and outside the country. A large number of Iranian diaspora writers used weblogs to reach out to readers inside Iran. Likewise, the Internet enabled the Iranian diaspora to read the literature being produced by the younger generation inside the country. Diaspora writers published works from within the country on their websites which were out of the Iranian censor machine's reach. This was a very important benefit because it connected different generations of writers who lived physically far apart. Literary contests were held in Blogistan and even a café was opened in Tehran called Café Blog which acted as a community centre for the bloggers. There is no way to understand what portion of Iranian Blogistan was devoted to literature, but numerous studies indicate the large clusters of blogs around cultural topics, notably Persian poetry and literature.[29]

The blogging spring didn't last long though. A phenomenon which was first seen as a vehicle for practising tolerance and a medium for freedom of expression, was soon perceived by the government as a new threat. The government imposed a complicated censorship regime on the Internet. Strict laws for ISPs and coffee nets, filtering or blocking unfavoured websites and blogs, cyberattacks, negative publicity, and vilification of the Internet, keeping the Internet speed low, and intimidating its users were some of the tactics the government used to control cyberspace. The crackdown on the Internet and blogging intensified, especially after the 2009 elections and the post-election protests. In addition to punitive measures, the government also trained a large group of bloggers and sponsored pro-regime online activism. As a result of the government measures, the face of Persian Blogistan changed considerably. The writers of the Iran Media Program Report remark:

The changes have resulted mainly from the efforts of the regime and its allies to influence online communications in their own favor, by suppressing dissenting voices and promoting friendly ones. The suppression has taken the form of blocking and forced removal of blogs, as well as intimidation of critical voices. The second approach has included efforts to flood the network with Basijis and other pro-regime bloggers.[30]

Once again we witness the same pattern of censorship; a mixture of punitive and rewarding policies. The efforts of the government, the emergence of newer social media such as Facebook and Twitter, combined with some other social and cultural factors, brought Persian Blogistan into decline. Although there are still some literary weblogs which are updated from time to time, many former bloggers use their blogs as a form of storage for their writings. Mehdi Jami, a journalist and himself a well-known blogger told in 2015: 'Blogistan is a dead city. It is a living document of the life of people who were seeking a way to express their untold stories. It is now a museum of memories for all of us. We made our voices heard louder and sharper. We recorded our diaries in hundreds of thousands of pages, publicly and openly.'[31]

Although blogging lost its unique position in Persian language and literature, Iranian writers found new ways to utilize the Internet to their ends. In addition to the use of social media such as Facebook to publish their short works and share links to longer works, they are increasingly using messaging and file sharing platforms to promote literature. One platform is particularly popular in Iran for its capability of sharing large files and working with limited Internet speed; Telegram. Telegram today hosts hundreds of literary channels, groups, and supergroups where writers and poets discuss various subjects and share all types of files. There are numerous literary magazines which are regularly produced – some weekly – and then uploaded onto Telegram and other messaging systems for free. Furthermore, there are many online journals and websites dedicated to publishing Persian literature which are based overseas and are therefore safe from censorship. Although some get regularly filtered, readers know how to circumvent the filtering. Book sharing clubs offer free downloads of banned books and are a great help for the readership inside Iran to access censored materials.[32] Iran is not a member of universal copyright and copying foreign products will not be considered a breach of intellectual property. Nonetheless, Iranian copyleft is also on the rise where some groups actively distribute Iranian literature and art as a way to challenge the establishment and make books accessible to financially disadvantaged readers.

Outwitting Censors

The above examples show that many Iranian authors are constantly seeking new ways to circumvent a censorhip regime of which they don't approve and publish their works intact. Nevertheless, none of these measures, even online publication, has been able to substitute the need for official presence on bookshelves in Iranian bookshops and libraries. Many writers still prefer to have their books published officially to be able to benefit from their creative products, financially and otherwise. That's why they continue to submit their books to the censor authorities and apply for pre-publication licences. This is where the second group of tactics come into play. How to outwit the censor and pass your book with no or minimum censorship?

A familiar way is to employ Aesopian language. Aesopian language aims at circumventing the censor, putting him in the dark while communicating with the reader. It is 'a special literary system, one whose structure allows interaction between author and reader at the same time that it conceals inadmissible content from the censor'.[33] It functions like a code system based on a common knowledge between a writer and fairly learned readers. Writers use different tools such as allegory, parody, periphrasis, euphemism, ellipsis, quotation, shifts, or writing in genres other than what they are known for, for example, authors who have established themselves as writers of children literature writing adult themes.[34] Aesopian language techniques were overly used by Iranian writers and poets before the Revolution. Metaphors were used to describe the social and political conditions of their time. Some ordinary words and phrases found highly symbolic connotations as a result of the works of those authors. 'Dark night' meant repression, 'rose' was the martyr, and 'wall' indicated prison. The secret for Aesopian language to work is in repetition. At first the authors use an allegory which is communicable to a selected group of well-read readers. Through repetition in other works, it gradually becomes accessible to the public. As these metaphors become known to the censors, the authors have to coin new ones. Samad Behrangi is a very good example of a writer of children's literature who used the genre to convey adult themes of political significance.[35] Censors would read such books as children literature ignoring the serious nature of the material.

Some scholars claim that censorship encourages metaphorical language and therefore can – paradoxically – be useful to literature. In an interview about censorship in Soviet Russia, Joseph Brodsky says: 'If there is censorship [...], then one must avoid it; that is, censorship is unwittingly an impetus to metaphorical language. A person who might under normal conditions speak normal Aesopian language is speaking Aesopian language at a third remove. This is remarkable, and the thanks for it must go to the censorship'.[36] Whether we decide to thank censorship in agreement with Brodsky or reject the literary value of such language – as some of Brodsky's critics have done – it is undeniable that writers have employed figurative language as a tool to overcome censorship. Frequent use of Aesopian language can, however, alarm the censor. The censors learn to decipher the elements of this language and gradually begin to 'read into' innocent works a hidden meaning. The suspicion of Aesopian language could lead to the entire repertoire coming under suspicion. Lev Lifshitz-Losev argues that the same practice by Soviet writers, for example, alarmed the censors who then banned studios from accepting scripts with historical or fantastic plots without special permission, as the ideologues had been wary of allusions and parallels.[37] As some of the examples of censorship presented in Chapter 4 show, Iranian censors have very often treated perfectly innocent texts with suspicion.

After the Iranian Revolution, the focus of censorship shifted from word to the entire text. The post-Revolutionary censors were not as naïve as their pre-Revolutionary counterparts and could not be deceived by solitary metaphors and illusions. Authors therefore had to find more elaborate and comprehensive ways of employing figurative language. Some writers shifted the setting of their stories to historical periods. For example, the majority of Reza Jolayi's stories take place in recent or old history.[38] He has exiled his characters to history in order to be able to write more freely. Aboutorab Khosravi, another novelist, writes fiction with contemporary themes in unspecified times and locations.[39] Many writers use a distinctly complex prose and densely figurative diction to pass censorship. Some poets also employ different techniques to make their poetry less accessible to the censors which, in turn, makes it less accessible to the general public. Although some do this for aesthetic reasons, there are some who see it as a way to outwit the censors.

Another technique is to use words or phrases which are not easily comprehended, are obsolete, or only found in books. By experience, Iranian writers know that words related to alcohol or sexual organs/acts would normally get censored. They, therefore, use less known or outdated equivalents. In my latest collection, the word *Nushgāh* is used instead of the more ordinary equivalents of *bār* (bar) or *Meykhāneh* (tavern) and it seems the censor has not worked out the meaning. The novelist Mohammadreza Pourjafari showed me a glossary he had compiled which provided less known equivalents for a list of forbidden words and phrases.[40] He had made copies and distributed them to his writer friends.

In addition, many poets and writers make use of ellipsis in their books to denote that something has been censored. In many cases, the reader is able to guess what the missing word or phrase might be. I used this tactic in one of my collections, *Spāgeti bā Sos-e Mekziki* (Spaghetti with Mexican sauce), where I was forced to delete some words considered taboo. Some other writers use ellipses to indicate to the reader that something has been censored even when the missing text cannot be guessed from context. Mohammad Ali Sepanlou told *Mardomsālāri* newspaper that when he was asked to delete the word 'bare' from a line of his poem 'I rolled down the bare woman of the tree', he decided to use [...] in place of the deleted word. He wrote: 'I rolled down ... woman of the tree' in order to attract the reader's attention to the fact that censorship is still happening.[41]

Some books were able to obtain a publication licence by the author after changing the title and sending it to a different censorship department in the provinces. Jalil Shahcheshmeh's collection of poetry *Saqanqur* (Sandfish) was rejected at first. He then changed the name to *Rigmāhi* – which is another name for the same animal – and obtained a publication licence from the representative branch of the Book Office in Mashhad. Sometimes, publishers find a censor in a provincial city who is more sympathetic and send rejected books there for a decision. There have also been some rumours – unverified – of favouritism and bribery in obtaining publication licences for problematic books.

Chapter 7

HOW IS CENSORSHIP AFFECTING IRANIAN LITERATURE?

In previous chapters, the structure and performance of the censorship machine were investigated and the reactions of Iranian writers and poets delineated. This section will analyse the outcome of this interaction, in order to see how censorship has affected Iranian contemporary literature.

It is probably too early to be able to provide a definitive answer to the title question. The Iranian censorship machine is still working at full speed and creates new experiences of censorship among authors. In the same way as other ongoing situations, consequences only appear later. We will need much more information than what is currently available to pass final judgements. Along with other social phenomena of such proportions, there are conflicting views on how censorship can affect literature in any given language. But as I discussed in the introduction, my approach is to avoid theories that universalize experience and instead, focus on specific characteristics of the censorship regime in question. The experience of feeling censored is the key here because it is the only way we can study the effects of censorship on creative minds and consequently on their literary output. Censorship of texts cannot and should not be studied in isolation. Both historical and sociopolitical circumstances need to be fully investigated and the complexity of censorship experience properly acknowledged. We therefore need to consider the special characteristics of censorship in Iran and bear in mind the differences between this unique type of censorship and what has been experienced elsewhere.

In previous chapters, I tried to portray a realistic picture of the specific characteristics of the Islamic Republic's censorship regime. I showed how widespread, arbitrary, and strict it is. It is both prescriptive and proscriptive; punishes and rewards, suppresses and promotes. Any of these functions leave their mark on the corpus of literature of the time.

The Islamic Republic has tried very hard to advocate some forms of literature perceived to suit their cultural objectives. In doing so, some forms and styles are promoted to the detriment of other types. Schoolchildren are exposed to only a fraction of contemporary literature. Poems and stories in textbooks are selected to promote the values of the state. Public libraries, especially libraries in Children and Young Adults Intellectual Development centres, youth festivals, and thousands of cultural centres throughout the country are controlled by the government or semi-governmental organizations. Not only the content, but even the forms and genres fall within the contentious field of cultural policymaking. Promotion of religious songs, ritualistic poetry, war (Sacred Defence) poetry and fiction, didactic literature, and biographies of religious figures and war veterans are only partially reflective of the effects of selective sponsorship policies by the state.

In poetry, for example, many organizations advocate classical style poetry. This is partly rooted in the way poetry has been perceived by the state. The state sees poetry and, in a wider sense, literature as a tool for promoting its social values. With this outlook the social status of the poet and its associated responsibility is constantly emphasized. The poet is seen as responsible to the nation and to history. The cultural policy of the Islamic Republic encourages committed literature and to them, a committed literature is a literature which advocates values of the Islamic Revolution and the Islamic regime. Literature becomes a tool to convey messages to the masses of people. Therefore, the form and language become significant. Poetry should be in a form and language that relates to the masses and can be easily appreciated by them. Classical poetry can easily be turned into songs and set to music to feed the state-owned radio and television outlets. Consequently, classical forms get exceptional sponsorship through festivals, poetry contests, and poetry awards. Fatemeh Shams argues that the importance of rhetorical and verbal skills for clerics as well as Ayatollah Khomeini's personal inclination toward mystical poetry contributed to the expansion of classical forms of poetry after the Revolution.[1] As we saw in Chapter 2, personal interest of both leaders of the Islamic Revolution in poetry has considerably affected cultural policies and influenced the way poetry has been perceived. It can be safely argued that their personal interest in classical forms of poetry made those forms more popular among supporters of the regime. It could also be seen as an attempt at appropriation of the rich corpus of Persian classical poetry which is open to conflicting interpretations in favour of religious reading. Ahmad Karimi Hakkak views the posthumous publication of Ayatollah Khomeini's ghazals 'as an attempt to force a determinate religious reading on the entire tradition of lyrical poetry in the Persian language'.[2] Khomeini's divan was published a few days after his death and attracted enormous attention. Other classical forms such as *qasida*, *masnawi*, and the quatrain became predominant forms, especially during the Iran-Iraq war.[3] These forms employed simple diction and could best appeal to emotions in that turbulent time and entice people to volunteer for the war effort. The rhyme and rhythm were pleasing to the ear of a nation brought up on classical Persian poetry.

Ayatollah Khamenei's famous poetry gatherings are also another official occasion which reveals the Supreme Leader's preference for classical forms of poetry. Fatemeh Shams writes:

> Examination of a large corpus of poems that have been presented in front of the leader between 2003 and 2013 shows that in terms of form *qasidas*, *masnawis*, ghazals, and quatrains enjoy a marked preponderance compared to modern poems. In this set of one hundred poems, only two poems were written in the modern style and two others in a folk style. Such an apparent imbalance of forms is rooted in the leader's personal interest in classical forms, specially the ghazal.[4]

Even critical content is more tolerated if written in classical forms. Every year, a couple of satirists take part in Ayatollah Khamenei's poetry readings and read satirical pieces often critical of the system or the government. One reason could be the fact that classical poetry is so concerned with rhyme and rhythm and is so overwhelmingly present everywhere that it has somewhat lost its expressive power and communicative force. Readers are more fascinated by the craft rather than the content.

It would be a mistake, however, to think that anybody who writes classical poetry is a supporter of the regime or his poetry is favoured by the regime. Actually, neoclassical, progressive, and post-modern ghazals are three alternative styles of modified classic forms which challenge this notion in novel ways, both in form and in content. Poets in these schools employ everyday language to write about taboo subjects such as religion, politics, drugs, and sex. Their poetry is extremely notorious in view of its sexual content. Some of these poets were imprisoned or forced into exile because of their work.[5] Nevertheless, this revival of classical poetry can be partially attributed to the efforts of the government.

It would be equally wrong to assume that classical poetry has managed to marginalize other styles. In spite of all the patronage it receives, it is still the free verse which dominates the mainstream and attracts much of the theoretical debate in poetry.

Earlier I discussed the Aesopian language as a characteristic of literature produced under censorship. I argued that while it sometimes helps avoid censorship and creates elaborate metaphorical texts, it can also alarm the censor and then new, more complex set of metaphors will be needed to deceive censorship. In response to severe censorship, some Iranian poets adopted extremely complicated figurative language. Some have written poetry with either a very obscure meaning or none at all. Although many consider this an aesthetic choice, some believe it to be a reaction to the censorship. Houshyar Ansarifar, a poet, told the BBC's Tamasha programme that one of the reasons why a number of young Iranian poets were attracted to a radical version of language poetry and wrote poetry that nobody could understand was the fact that:

> After the Revolution, poets were faced with powerful commands such as to write poetry which should be at the service of the Revolution or the Sacred Defence. When you are not given a choice of how to express any given subject other than that prescribed, one solution is to challenge the expression itself, that is, to challenge the idea that poetry should carry any meaning. The natural solution would be to avoid expressing anything.[6]

Ansarifar's position is congruous with some other scholars on Aesopian language. Lev Loseff's study on Aesopian language in modern Russian literature points out that Aesopian language doesn't convey any specific information. It tells attentive readers what they already know from other sources. Its function is therefore not in the expression but in its opposition to expression. As one reviewer of Loseff's book puts it 'It [Aesopian language] stands in opposition to the ritual celebration of the power of the state embodied in propaganda and censorship. It is the celebration of anti-censorship, the intellectual's catharsis'.[7]

Censorship has forced many writers into silence. Discussing the will of censorship regimes to conceal their acts of censorship so that no one could even notice its existence, Karimi Hakkak claims that:

> something close to this did happen a few years after the Revolution. Having violently quashed the intellectual resistance to its rule, the Islamic Republic of Iran saw itself confronted with the near total silence of the poets and writers whose presence on the scene was associated in the mind of a significant portion of the reading public with the climate of relative freedoms which prevailed in the years immediate preceding and following the events of 1979.[8]

The large number of writers and poets who left the country indicates the severity of the conditions. Many of them couldn't publish inside Iran and it was only during the last decade or so that some were able to reconnect with their readers through online publishing or other digital forms of communication.

The acts of censorship are not only addressed at texts but, as we have seen in the Iranian experience, at creators of the texts, that is, authors. While disrupting the relationship between the author and the reader of the censored text, censorship also threatens other texts by sending indirect messages to other writers. The aim is to scare others and force them into self-censorship. Beate Müller writers:

> If censorial measures are directed against the sender of a message, they can be regarded as strategies ad personam. As far as censorship of literature is concerned, all actions taken to threaten, influence, or punish an author come under this heading, whether they be ideologically motivated negotiations with an author about a text, the exertion of psychological pressure, the levying of fines, or the imprisonment, exiling, or even assassination of an unruly author. Obviously, many such measures are intended to deter other authors from overstepping their limits, which means that the censoring of one writer can, at least indirectly, affect other writers too.[9]

Iranian security authorities make no secret of their intention to 'make it a lesson' for others when they deliberately leave coded messages of their acts of punishment or broadcast self-loathing forced interviews on national television.[10]

Tiring the authors to the point of exhaustion is another tactic used frequently by the censorship authorities. Sometimes a book is kept undecided for years until the writer loses their interest in following up and forgets about publication for good. Fanoos Bahadorvand has explained how a translation of Federico Garcia Lorca's poetry was submitted for a publication licence in 2004 and how she struggled until 2011 to obtain a response to her application, finally giving up in 2011 after much correspondence, changing publishers, visiting the Book Office, and numerous censorship interventions.[11] Moreover, many authors claim that they would have written much more if it were not for their frustration with censorship.

Reza Jolayi, a novelist, said in an interview that the conditions didn't allow him to write more. 'I could have written better but losing hope in the audience, in the critics, in myself and the censorship – add the fear of tomorrow to this list – did not let me write better'.[12]

Censorship makes publishing a book a joyless experience for many. When a poet or writer submits a manuscript and waits for years for publication, only to find out that one-third or a quarter of their book is deleted, little room remains for happiness. Describing his meeting with an Iranian novelist and journalist Mehdi Yazdani Khorram, who had just received a licence for release of his novel, de Bellaigue wrote: 'Even now, permit in hand, his satisfaction was mitigated. One regret was that the book would appear with some two hundred changes'.[13]

The writers repeatedly ask themselves why they should continue to write? What hope remains for spending years on a book without knowing if it will ever see the light of the day? Mansour Khalaj, a playwright and researcher on theatre, describes how the censors asked his publisher to delete pictures and entries on some of the most celebrated Iranian playwrights in the first volume of his book '*Namāyeshnāmeh Nevisān-e Iran (Az Akhondzadeh tā Beyzayi)* (Iranian Playwrights – from Akhondzadeh to Beyzayi). He told *Namāyeshnāmeh* (quarterly journal of Iranian Playwrights Association):

> These people are playwrights in different historical periods and are historically important. Now that they do this to the first volume, what will they do to the second volume which covers more contemporary playwrights? When they delete the biography of playwrights of the past, what will they do with the rest? What hope do I have to work? What will be the outcome of all my toils and suffering?[14]

Such disappointments force some writers to stop writing thus bringing early death to their literary careers.

The economic pressures caused by censorship have affected the creation and publication of literature significantly. Mahmoud Dowlatabadi complained about the economic hardship he had suffered and how it had affected his creativity: 'Imagine that my books have been banned for four years. I have not been allowed to publish them. During these four years, I have had no income. This has, in fact, changed the fate of my economic life; and when I object to this, they treat my objection as a crime'. Asked whether the economic problems directly influenced his creativity, Dowlatabadi answered 'Yes, definitely'; he had been writing for forty years but still needed to borrow money to make ends meet. That hindered his work. Furthermore, he felt that part of the purpose of censorship is to force writers to admit defeat.[15]

Economic hardship is an immensely powerful tool, one the Iranian government uses very effectively. Unable to pay for their basic needs, some writers feel extreme pain and humiliation. A page out of Ahmad Mahmoud's diary shows how one of the greatest contemporary writers felt crushed under financial pressures. On November 23 1985, he writes:

Once again I felt the strong hand of poverty today. I felt this monster growing again. My wife informed me that we need to pay the water bill. I asked how much time we had. She said: Four days. I said we've still got time. My wife felt I did not have the 348 Tumans (IRR 3,480) to pay for the bill. I didn't want her to worry thinking that I have no money. I gave her 1,000 Tumans. She said: I thought you didn't have any. Well, in fact, I didn't have any money. I had only put aside a few thousand Tumans so that if one of us falls ill, we might not die in front of the hospital. If you don't pay, you are not admitted into hospital and many people have died because of this. I don't know when my books will be allowed to be published. We have to be patient and fortunately we are all content people'.[16]

A majority of independent poets and writers have no regular job. Based on my personal knowledge, many live on a meagre income earned by occasional teaching in private institutions, proofreading jobs, or completely irrelevant professions such as driving a taxi or working as shop assistant. Many of them prefer to live in poverty rather than compromise on their principles. Masoud Ahmadi told me that he was offered to judge a poetry contest in a cultural centre belonging to Tehran Municipality for a decent amount of money. Masoud declined to accept this job in spite of financial hardship and told them, 'I cannot accept any money for literature- related activity from any government organization in a country which does not allow my books to be published'.[17]

On 30 April 2013, Philip Roth received the Literary Service Award at the PEN Gala in New York. In his speech, he told of his memories of travels to Czechoslovakia and described how writers and thinkers had been deprived of proper jobs:

Some whom I met and spoke with were selling cigarettes at a street-corner kiosk, others were wielding a wrench at the public waterworks, others spent their days on bicycles delivering buns to bakeries, still others were washing windows or pushing brooms as a janitor's assistant at some out-of-the-way Prague museum. These people, as I've indicated, were the cream of the nation's intelligentsia.[18]

Roth ended his talk by describing Ivan Klima being interrogated about the reason for Roth's annual trips to Czechoslovakia. Klima had answered: 'He comes for the girls.' This saved him and ended the interrogation. However, if Klima had been interrogated in Iran, this answer could have put him, Philip Roth – and even those girls, if any – into still further trouble. This is yet another example of the importance of socio-historical specificity in censorship experience.

Notwithstanding these conditions of extreme poverty for Iranian intelligentsia when the most celebrated novelists are struggling to make ends meet, governmental organizations pay hefty sums for commissioned books. According to unconfirmed reports, *Bonyād-e Adabiyyāt-e Dāstāni* (Fiction Foundation) paid IRR 550,000,000 to Ali Moazzeni to write a novel about the life of the twelfth Imam of Shi'a (The Absent Imam). This is more than twenty times the amount an ordinary Iranian novelist might receive for one book of a similar size (c. 300 pages). The novel sparked much controversy over the writer's handling of the subject and its literary quality, and in the end the government decided to collect all copies from the bookstores.[19]

The Epic of Imam Ali is another such project sponsored and managed by the Islamic Propagation Organization. Hojjatoleslam Mohammad Baghizadeh, the project manager, called it the second *Shāhnāmeh*. 'The poet received the material and historical information from us and converted them into poetry. He then brought the poetry to the Islamic Propagation Organization where an expert team inspected the content. The research on this project lasted six to seven years. At the end, the poet spent one more year editing the book.'[20]

Mohammad Hassani, CEO of Fiction Foundation, told of fifty contracts for commissioned novels and defended offering high remuneration to writers by saying that they received insignificant amounts compared to professional footballers.[21]

Distorting Mirror, Distorted Image

Iran has undergone major social and political changes during the past forty years but these changes have scarcely been reflected in Iranian literature. Revolution, war, political struggles, and class conflicts which have been an integral part of the Iranian life are mainly absent from the pages of books. The intellectual life of Iranians has been full of hot debates on religion, identity, sex, drugs, ethnicity, and many other topics but these debates have rarely found their way into literature in the same manner in which they are discussed in private circles of writers and poets. Many writers painstakingly depict images of the society in a manner to be true to their instinct or artistic perception. When an outsider interferes in this process, the image cannot be trusted.

Censorship thus distorts the image of the society. Literature cannot function as a true mirror anymore. When the censorship lasts for a long period, many writers choose to avoid problematic themes and write harmless stories instead. That's probably one of the reasons that gave rise to a genre of 'apartment' fiction around themes of domestic relations. Fiction which leaves public life out of the picture. They rarely discuss major social and political issues and the outdoor landscape is usually absent. Kaveh Mirabbasi, novelist and translator, says: 'Most of these novels reflect the routine life of the urban middle class with limited dramatic interactions.'[22]

Iran was involved in an eight-year war with Iraq. A war which claimed hundreds of thousands of lives and brought destruction to many infrastructures. Many Iranian writers who write today have first-hand experience of war, whether as soldiers on battlefronts or as children affected by war at home. The government massively sponsors war literature provided that it shows the war as the regime wants it portrayed; a sacred defence, a holy war between good and evil, between Islam and *Kufr*. Any alternative narrative is frowned upon. Ahmad Mahmoud's novels *'Zamin-e Sukhteh'* (Scorched Earth) and *Madār-e Sefr Darajeh* (Zero Degree Orbit) were both harshly criticized by the conservative media as anti-war novels. Ayatollah Khamenei personally prevented an award for *Madār-e Sefr Darajeh* because he considered it to be an anti-war novel.[23] *Rozay-e Nuh* (Noah's Sermon), a novel by Hassan Mahmoudi, is a story of a young boy who scores the first top place in nation-wide university entrance exams but his place is withdrawn for ideological reasons. He then goes to the battlefront. This is one of the few novels by the younger generation of writers which provides an alternative view of the Iraq-Iran war. Many parts in the story are left ambiguous. The writer explained that this book is actually the middle volume of a trilogy. Books One and Three have not been granted publication licence. He further said that he left part of the story untold and ambiguous because he felt the book would not pass censorship if he had written more clearly.[24]

At the same time, Sacred Defence literature is sponsored disproportionately. *Dā* (Mother) is an example of a book on war which won the favour of the Supreme Leader. This book is a memoir of an Iranian young woman during the first weeks of the war in Khorramshahr, a city under the Iraqi siege. Ayatollah Khamenei praised the writer and said: '*Dā* is truly and justly a very good book and is suitable to be presented in a global level'.[25] This book was published in 2009 and was reprinted eighty times in its first year of publication. In May 2010, the publisher announced that the book was going for its 110th reprint.[26] The book won numerous awards including the *Shahid Habib Ghanipour*, the *Jalāl-e Āl-e Ahmad*, and the Book of the Year Awards. The publisher's website shows that in June 2014, the 153rd reprint was released.[27] It was made available on all electronic platforms. It was made into a 120-part animation narrated by more than forty of the most famous female actors and celebrities and broadcast on national TV Channel One. A thirty-part radio adaptation was broadcast on Radio Iran. *Dā* was translated into English (titled *One Woman's War*[28]), Arabic, Spanish, Turkish, Urdu, and into Tajiki Cyrillic script. All these translations were made possible by government sponsorship through Iranian cultural centres and consular missions. Hundreds of meetings were organized in public libraries, mosques, and cultural centres throughout the country to read and discuss this book. This extensive campaign to make this book a universal success is deeply rooted in the fact that the Islamic Republic is desperately looking for literature to show a picture of war as they desire. Ayatollah Khamenei's seal of approval mobilized the entire cultural establishment behind this book which was written by an amateur writer recording the memories of a seventeen-year old girl twenty years after the actual events. It is not a novel and even the supporters of the book believe its value lies in its realistic portrayal of the events of the early days of war which can be utilized by other writers as raw material.[29] Some other books have also benefited from this exceptional favour in different scales.

The efforts to portray Iranian society, lifestyle, and values in a manner approved by the state, prompted Amir Hassan Cheheltan to say in June 2016:

> They want us to write novels which portray a distorted image of Iranian life [...] We as writers need to be ourselves and write of our own experiences. I cannot imagine literature outside the realm of our experiences as human beings. Literature speaks of everything which relates to human being. It is like a house which has a bedroom and a bathroom as well. If we limit a house to the kitchen and dining room, it cannot be called a house anymore. No one can live in such a house.[30]

He said that he had not been able to publish in Iran since 2005. During this period, he has published numerous novels in German while none of those have had any chance of uncensored publication in the language in which they were written in, that is, Persian. One of his novels, *Tehran, Shahr-e Ākharolzamāni* (Tehran, the Apocalyptic City) waited for three years to get a licence and the censors demanded so many changes that would destroy the novel altogether. One of the corrections demanded was to delete one full chapter from a book with only six chapters. Another novel, *Tehran, Shahr-e Bi-Āsemān* (Tehran, the Skyless City) was published in 120 pages while the German translation is 200 pages. The writer had to cut around eighty pages of his novel to publish in Iran. Cheheltan believes that the government doesn't trust the intellectuals and it sees literature as a means for intellectuals to strengthen their position amongst the public. The state doesn't want this and that's why they censor literature which, in turn, leads to people losing trust in the books that get past censorship.[31]

Lack of trust especially comes up in regard to translations. How can one know if a translation is genuine when every book has to pass censorship? Faraj Sarkoohi wrote about three different translations of a single book, *Notebook*, by José Saramago, the Portuguese writer. One of the translators, Ali Ghaderi, compared his translation with the other two and found that most of the parts censored in his translation were published uncensored in one of the other two works. He told ISNA News that the Book Department had treated each differently and that this proved the arbitrary nature of censorship.[32] That's why very often you see different translations of the same book with variations in content as they may have been approved by different censors.

In another example, Mohammad Hashem Akbariani wrote about a dialogue with a book-loving relative. He wrote in *E'temād* newspaper that one of his relatives was angry with censorship and was swearing at the translator of the book he had just read. He was complaining about the fact that the translator had compromised the quality of the book in order to obtain a publication licence, noting that the 'omissions and alterations were so annoying and insulting to the reader's intelligence that it would be wise to crush the translator under my feet'. He threw the book into the rubbish bin so that the smell wouldn't stink out the whole house. Akbariani believes that censorship causes the reader to lose trust in the genuineness of a work and thus lose interest in reading. He concluded that reading would not be as pleasant an experience if you feel that what you are reading is not 'genuine'.[33]

When a large portion of literature is ignored by the officials in power and never finds its way into schools or university textbooks and is absent from the mass media, ordinary people suffer. They are deprived from the diversity and variety of styles and it may even adversely affect the language. In his interview with *Tajrobeh* magazine, Cheheltan accused the national broadcaster of bringing harm to the Persian language by its censorship of independent writers: 'Radio and TV should not omit the juice of the Iranian contemporary literature from their programmes. Somebody who lives in a remote city has no other means to know independent authors'.[34] He argued that 90 per cent of people nowadays watch TV or listen to the radio and that the state-run media use a neutral, formal Persian in which good literary works are not represented: 'Literature that carries the manoeuvrings of the Persian language creates a very thin margin and this is one of the catastrophic results of censorship'.[35] Therefore, the Persian language suffers. Whether censorship can actually harm language in the long term is a matter of much speculation. It is true that official media in Iran advocate a special type of language usage. TV talk show hosts employ a type of flowery language not very common in everyday Persian. The public speakers and religious figures use too many Arabic words in their speeches and a large portion of language usage is kept in the dark. Masoud Ahmadi believes that official language has failed to suppress the dynamic and lively language of the people in the past and it will fail this time as well. He believes that as soon as this system is gone and the official language advocates are replaced, this type of language usage will also die out because it doesn't belong to the people.[36]

On the other hand, censorship and persecution act as a kind of publicity for some poets and writers. When Alireza Roshan, an emerging poet, was arrested and put into prison, sales of his book soared. In a short period, his book reached eight runs and was the second bestselling book of his publisher for the entire year.[37] The same thing has happened to other authors whose arrest or wide publicity surrounding censorship of their work has attracted attention to their books. Mehdi Moosavi and Fatemeh Ekhtesari are two other examples. After their arrest and confinement, public interest in their poetry increased considerably.[38] The policies of cultural control in Iran made the work of these poets much admired, a popularity that cannot be attributed to their literary merit alone. Another side effect of such conditions prevailing is the turning of poets and writers into heroes. Without asking, poets and writers become heroes in society, which then expects them to represent social and political issues of popular interest through their art. Wole Soyinka, the Nigerian poet and writer, has described how Salman Rushdie, by then a novelist, suddenly became a hero in the forefront of 'Jihad for freedom', in the aftermath of Khomeini's fatwa.[39]

As a result of a globalized world, news of persecution spreads very quickly and brings instant fame and recognition. It is not unlikely in such conditions that some writers might exaggerate their personal conditions to seek attention. The highly politicized and polarized status of literature fuels such misrepresentations and can even show a distorted image of Persian literature to the outside world, an image made more by politics rather than literature.

Self-Censorship, the Absolute Victory of Censor

According to many scholars of censorship, the most effective and lasting type of censorship is self-censorship. A successful imposition of self-censorship is the ultimate goal of censor systems. Breyten Breytenbach, himself a victim of censorship in South Africa, believes that it is fatal for a writer to consent to censorship because 'It takes root inside you as a kind of interiorized paternalism [...]. You become your own castrator'.[40] In a different passage, he observes that once someone yields to the restrictions imposed by those who seek to manage one's thoughts, the game is lost.[41] If censorship succeeds in establishing itself as a regime of writing and reading, then the writers have only two options – either obey or disobey. Effim Etkind, who has studied Soviet writers, describes the first option as a form of 'self-regulation via what Isaac Babel called "the genre of silence" or "via writing for the desk drawer"'.[42]

The Iranian censorship machine lacks clear guidelines and indirectly places responsibility onto the writer and publisher. Consequently, writers tend to apply self-censorship to avoid getting into trouble. The harsh treatment of independent writers and the government's decision to ban most of the independent journals in the early years after the Revolution scared large groups of writers so that 'when the regime finally agreed to allow publication of a few independent journals […] the intellectual community had sobered up to the reality of the violence of which a revolutionary Islamic state was capable. The resultant prudence was what officials would count on in allowing the voice of the opposition to be heard.'[43]

It is a belief shared by a number of Iranian poets and writers, including some of those interviewed for this study, that long-term, state-imposed censorship encourages self-censorship. Nasser Taghvayi, a prominent Iranian writer and filmmaker, said in an interview:

> Censorship has continued for so long and has been so overwhelming that it has infected everybody's mind. In the process of writing, you are always thinking about censorship and who will be offended and who won't […], to Hell! You should be able to write and just let it go, but all the time you are worrying about what disaster will befall your work. You think more about censorship than what you are actually writing […]. You work hard day and night to publish a good work and then somebody crosses it out! As simple as that! Therefore, I decided that whenever I face censorship, I either find a solution for it or don't do the job at all.[44]

Mohammad Hashem Akbariani criticizes the arbitrary nature of censorship and holds it responsible for self-censorship:

> You hold the pen and set your imagination free to wander and do its job, but in each paragraph and on each page you are confronted with fear about whether this sentence, or this description, or this scene will be approved for publication? And you keep deleting and changing sentences and scenes and descriptions. At the end, you see yourself turned into a censor who is sometimes stricter than the official censor.[45]

Some writers hold a different opinion on self-censorship. Abdoljabbar Kakayi, a poet, believes that every knowledgeable creative person deletes part of the text based on their own perceptions which is rooted in their understanding of the social ethics and their personal characteristics. He says:

> This goes back to moral, familial and social upbringing as well as the religious beliefs and even rational thinking of writers. A writer deletes whatever he/she

feels might limit the freedom of others. Therefore, it is natural to me because otherwise we will encourage anarchy in writing which might hurt others. I call this 'self-control' rather than 'self-censorship'[….] and I personally follow it as a moral principle.[46]

However, in the same interview, he confesses to self-censorship in fear of radical and fanatic groups who 'react to our literature selectively and create problems'.[47] Although he says he doesn't support state-imposed censorship, he doesn't approve of the sudden removal of censorship and he blames society for his idea. 'With our current cultural upbringing which doesn't make clear distinction between social and individual freedoms, it can have dangerous psychological damage – the same as removing hijab. But if it is done gradually so that censorship changes from a state-imposed apparatus to an ethical and moral contract between the author and the reader, it is acceptable to me.'[48]

His approach is not unique. A large number of supporters of the Islamic Republic who do not wish to openly oppose freedom of expression but want to draw a line between their political and ideological stance and that of the more conservative elements, adopt the same approach. They claim that they are in favour of freedom of expression but the society is not ready for it. Kakayi believes that the Iranian society cannot be compared with the developed world. We are not living in ideal conditions. If Iranian society had higher ethical standards and people were more knowledgeable, censorship would look really bad. But for the time being, it seems that the benefits of censorship outweigh its harms. He compares censorship to hijab and says that we need to adopt a gradual approach and purge both in a well-planned slow process because a sudden removal of either could have catastrophic consequences. Abdoljabbar Kakayi considers himself a poet of the Revolution and admits that he and people like him are viewed by independent literati as state writers but he says he is a realist and supports the reformists.[49]

Whatever your view on self-censorship, it is evident that a long-lasting and all-inclusive censorship regime, such as that of Iran, can lead to self-censorship. If any censorship regime succeeds at self-censorship, then there will be no need for 'external', 'coercive', and 'suppressive' censorship. In Bourdieu's words, 'the more effective the process of regulation and repression is, the less apparent it becomes, as it begins to appear as the natural "way of the world". The need for explicit prohibitions, imposed and sanctioned by an institutionalised authority, diminishes as the mechanisms of internalisation take hold.'[50] Self-censorship is one of the major mechanisms of internalization as are other tools of social construction. In this notion, one can say that in spite of all its efforts, censorship in Iran has not been particularly successful as the explicit prohibition and repressive censorship is still an everyday experience.

Chapter 8

CONCLUSION

In the introduction, I briefly introduced different definitions of censorship and offered a short history of ideas on the subject. I discussed the traditional approach to censorship perceived in its binary opposition to freedom of expression; an idea shared by liberal notions of censorship as an act of repression; being external, coercive, and repressive. I then mentioned the Marxist and neo-Marxist criticism of the liberal conception which, while acknowledging the repressive role of state, are sceptical of the existence of anything as free speech. Gramsci views the hegemony created by social structures hand in hand with direct state censorship and Althusser reduces the role of state as secondary to ideological production and dissemination by the ruling class. New censorship theories inspired mainly by Michel Foucault's theory of power/knowledge question the common perceptions of the relation of ruler–ruled and see censorship as omnipresent and even an incitement to discourse, thus focusing on productive and generative functions of censorship. Pierre Bourdieu also considers state censorship insignificant in comparison with constructive censorship and invisible forms of cultural conditioning aimed at self-censorship. The same as Marxist theorists, Bourdieu stresses the role of social constructions but he goes further to consider linguistic exchanges as relations of power. In his theory, as the structural and impersonal forms of control develop, the need for state censorship diminishes. Thus, the existence of a suppressive censorship regime is itself a testimony of the failure of censorship regime. Judith Butler portrays censorship as a productive form of power claiming that 'censorship seeks to produce subjects according to explicit and implicit norms, and this production of the subject has everything to do with the regulation of speech'.[1] In another relevant argument, she brings the idea of 'linguistic vulnerability' blaming the language itself for offensive speech rather than the speakers. She thereby negates the agency of the speaker arguing that 'the subject is produced within the language through a prior formative exercise of speech'[2]. Nevertheless, Butler makes a slightly different observation which I find useful in forwarding my argument. She views censorship as a 'continuum' which can include overt state repression as well as subtler forms of social construction.

At the end, I discussed criticisms of the new censorship theories which the critics claimed are irresponsive to the experience of those who are subject to censorship. Terry Eagleton called it nothing more than a 'sophistry', 'to claim that, since all speech acts are socially conditioned, no speech is really free'.[3] Beate Müller argued for the significance of political and historical context in censorship debates, and Helen Freshwater called for a redefinition of censorship responsive to the diverse experiences of censorship, and one 'which reflects the socio-historical specificity of instances of control, conditioning or silencing.[…], a definition which is directed by the inclusive logic of "both/and", rather than preserving the censorious modality of either/or'.[4]

In view of the topic at hand, that is, censorship in contemporary Iran, I find Freshwater's approach the most suitable of all. I acknowledge the depth of scholarship in new censorship theories but I think their approach is not helpful in the case of the present study. Although I don't question their legitimacy or theoretical robustness, I think they are problematic in the sense that they portray censorship as a productive force and an unavoidable omnipresent phenomenon widely applied to all forms of social control thereby trivializing the lived experience of Iranian writers who have suffered persecution, imprisonment, and murder and all forms of abuse of power by the state. New censorship theories disproportionately equate the censorship experience of Iranian writers with constructive forms of speech regulation such as editorial reviews or grant refusals. I agree with Freshwater's notion that 'Conclusions about censorship should surely be provisional, rather than fixed; plural rather than singular; time and site-specific, rather than universal'.[5] The complicated new censorship theories therefore, as varied as they are, might be helpful in understanding censorship in Western liberal democracies where direct acts of state censorship are nearly non-existent and have been replaced by indirect forces of economy, education system, canonisation, and the like, but they will not serve me in my discussion of censorship in Iran.

Having established my preferred definition and approach to censorship, I then gave a short history of censorship in Iran from the beginning of press and publication until the 1979 Revolution. In subsequent chapters, I discussed cultural politics and censorship laws and practices in post-Revolutionary Iran. I mentioned the theory of cultural invasion as the backbone of cultural policymaking and the role of the Supreme Leader as the main architect of this theory, and further described the structure and mechanism of censorship apparatus and censors as operators of this system. The changes and variations of censorship practices during different administrations were also mentioned. In Chapter 4, I provided a taxonomy of reasons which can lead to censorship in literature and, through numerous examples, I showed censors at work. More extensive cultural policies were studied under two interrelated sets of reward and punishment, in other words, tokenism and intimidation. The reactions of Iranian writers and poets to censorship were discussed in a separate chapter and the outcome of this troublesome relationship further elaborated. The reader should by now have a rather comprehensive and descriptive image of how censorship works in Iran, who the actors are, and how it influences the corpus of literature produced. It is therefore the time to try and answer the main question of the research: Is censorship in literature good? Insignificant? Or bad?

Views on censorship can be broadly divided into three distinct categories in regard to their answer to the above question. One opinion sees censorship good and even necessary. A second opinion claims to support freedom of expression but doesn't see censorship capable of harming literature. Some of those who subscribe to this opinion believe that literature can even benefit from censorship. The third group defend freedom of expression as a fundamental human right and see no good in censorship whatsoever. As with any other matter of opinion, the boundaries of these categories are not strict and a range of minor differences within each group can be seen as well as some overlaps. However, this division sufficiently covers the major approaches to censorship. I present these opinions briefly and will then analyse them in relation to the censorship experience in contemporary Iran.

Censorship is Not Only Good, it is Necessary

Plato is probably the first recorded thinker to formulate a rationale for intellectual, religious, and artistic censorship. In *The Republic*, he considers it the duty of the state to censor poets, writing: 'It is up to the founders to know the patterns within which the poets must tell stories, and beyond which they are not permitted to go.'[6] In Plato's ideal society, a republic of virtue, there is no place for poets who might imitate things and compose narratives which might harm society. In his view, poets follow their instincts and do not care about the well-being of society, nor do they possess the capacity to judge what is right and what is wrong. He, therefore, believes that the state should protect the people from works of poetry which give way to undesirable feelings and emotions. He adds:

> As for sex and anger, and all the desires and pains and pleasures in the soul which we say follow us in every action, poetic imitation produces effects on us of the same sort. It waters and nurtures them when they ought to be dried up, and establishes them as rulers in us when they ought to be ruled so that we may become better and happier instead of worse and more miserable.[7]

Traditionalist advocates of censorship today follow the same logic. The most recurrent justification is the idea of the harm that freedom of speech inflicts. Censorship of literature in Iran is also justified based on laws which claim to protect cultural values of Iranian society and to prevent harm to these values. The apologists for censorship, however, have not provided any tangible evidence for their claim. No single poem, short story or novel has been named that has led to moral corruption or destabilization of the moral foundations of society. Therefore, their opposition to more openness is usually categorical and based on vague and ambiguous statements.

Some supporters of censorship see it as a balancing force for the social system preventing cultural and social clashes caused by divergent ideas coexisting side by side. They look at censorship as a unifying force which creates a kind of cultural unity or harmony where the dominant culture or discourse can grow and deepen and unite society in the absence of distracting or discordant discourses. Being a multi-ethnic, multi-lingual, and multi-religious country, social cohesion is undoubtedly important in Iran. Some authorities see censorship as a way to prevent cultural disparity or ethnic and religious tensions. Mohammad Hosseini, Minister of Culture and Islamic Guidance during Ahmadinejad's second term in office claims that he supports freedom of expression but doesn't support freedom to insult others and ignore principles and values. Freedom of expression should not lead to an increase in religious or ethnic disputes.[8] There have been cases where a number of publications have been perceived as insulting to some linguistic, religious, or ethnic minority and many officials believe that censorship is one way to ensure such events do not repeat themselves.

On the other hand, some elements within the ruling clergy are in favour of silencing the minority or alternative voices in favour of an assumed dominant voice. They justify the need for the promotion of a dominant culture, namely the Islamic or more specifically the Shia Islam culture, which inevitably involves suppression of alternative cultures. However, censorship is a reflection of the fact that cultural production is not following the ideals and values believed to be dominant and common to all members of the society. The need to censor cultural products shows the failure of the state in the effective use of internal cultural mechanisms. If the dominant culture was truly shared by all, there would be no need for censorship. Resorting to censorship for creating unity and restoring order is a type of deceitful and risky control and may even reduce the possibility of real unity in the society.

Censorship is related to the way the 1979 Revolution is perceived by the authorities. The official discourse sees that upheaval as an Islamic revolution aimed at transforming the entirety of cultural and social life, making society 'Islamic'. In order to achieve this goal, they see it natural to suppress any alternative outlook and promote any literature which may contribute to this goal.

For many of those who believe in censorship, it seems so natural that they don't feel the need to explain their position. The conservative clergy who are largely influential on the control of culture as well as the government officials who implement those controls see the necessity of censorship as self-evident. They live within a discourse which does not question the supremacy of Islamic standards and religious moral codes. Ayatollah Ahmad Jannati, a Friday Prayer Imam of Tehran and the Secretary of Council of Guardians considers some books to be viruses which destroy culture and has urged the government authorities on many occasions not to compromise on Islamic values. He also said that universities, religious seminaries, and the Islamic Revolution Guard Corps have a duty to intervene in this issue: 'The book which is anti-Islamic should not be allowed. The book written by a thoughtless, non-believing and irresponsible writer should not be published.'[9]

Mahmoud Motahharinia is a university lecturer who has worked as a chief censor for a long time. He was Scientific Secretary of the Book Office and thus involved with censorship on a daily basis. He also defends censorship passionately and is against any loosening of its strictures. He actually criticizes the authorities for not being hard enough. According to him, the golden age of *momayyezi* was during Ahmadinejad's administration when the books that passed *momayyezi* were the 'least troublesome'. In his view, *momayyezi* is rooted in the jurisprudential views of Ayatollah Khomeini, in the Qur'an and the Hadith, in the Constitution, and in the guidelines set out by Ayatollah Khomeini and Ayatollah Khamenei. He further believes that there is nowhere on earth where publication is unconditionally free. To support his claim, he gives an example from the United States: *The Professors: The 101 Most Dangerous Academics in America*[10] by David Horowitz. In this book, Horowitz lists 101 professors whose ideas and teachings he labels as un-American and therefore dangerous. Horowitz's book stirred some controversy in the United States and some accused him of threatening academic freedoms by an act reminiscent of McCarthyism. Anyway, Motahharinia uses this example to conclude that even in Western democracies like the United States, you cannot publish everything and if you express unpopular views and cross a line – as some of these professors have done – you will be punished and blacklisted. He also alludes to the conspiracy of enemies. Quoting the then Minister of Intelligence (Heidar Moslehi) he claims that Americans distributed ten million copies of books in the Soviet Union to help bring the system to its knees. In Iran, he says, a hundred million copies of different books have been distributed to weaken the system and some of them have had ten or twenty reruns. 'We still have many books which have no relation to our Islamic principles. Some of them insult Islam. Some of them raise doubt on the foundations of our belief system. Many of the novels spread prostitution and corruption. How can we stop *momayyezi* then?'[11]

There are many other supporters amongst government officials who are less enthusiastic about their restrictive views and prefer not to raise controversy by publicly defending a practice which is in direct contradiction to one of the major promises of the Revolution: freedom. They therefore defend freedom of expression but only as far as it stays within the framework of Islam and the Iranian Constitution.[12] The problem with this conditional support is that there are different and even contradicting views among Muslims and Islamic scholars as to the limits of free speech in Islam. It is therefore unhelpful to restrain freedom of expression to an entity so vast and subject to such diverse interpretations as religion. The Iranian Constitution is not so helpful either because it only demarcates general boundaries and leaves the rest to the ordinary laws which, as we saw in the second chapter of this book, have only added to the confusion.

The belief in the necessity of censorship of literature is deeply rooted in the theory of cultural invasion. According to this theory, the West is using culture as a powerful tool to corrupt the Islamic nation of Iran and to destabilize the system. Censorship is seen, therefore, as one way to fight back and to neutralize the effects of this cultural aggression or colonialism.

Censorship is Bad, but not Always!

There is a second group of thinkers, who believe in freedom of expression as a human right but think that censorship can boost creativity. In their view, the mere experience of censorship gives the censored authors more determination to overcome censorship and to find innovative and creative ways to express themselves. It also encourages poets and writers to see the significance of their functioning within society. As a result, censored authors feel more important and may find more meaning and purpose in their work. A controversy that arises with the censorship systems actually nurtures this idea, since dissident writers are often treated as unimportant by the censorship authorities. At the same time, these 'insignificant' poets and writers are frequently targeted by powerful authorities and become the subject of defamatory books, articles, and even TV programmes. It is in this context that some scholars argue that the challenges and struggles of writing under censorship lead to more creativity. Daniel Grassian, a researcher of Iranian contemporary literature, writes:

> While most Western writers and critics would presumably agree with J.M. Coetzee's claim that state censorship is 'an inherently bad thing', even Coetzee himself suggests that while 'writing does not flourish under censorship[...] there may even be cases where external censorship challenges the writer in interesting ways or spurs creativity'.[13]

Coetzee has written extensively against censorship and this view does not adequately summarize his writings on the subject; but it does show that he also sees some benefit for creativity in the challenges of coping with censorship. Michael Levine expresses a similar idea and views censorship as an impediment, but one whose very resistance makes another, more equivocal and double-edged style of writing possible.[14]

As we saw earlier, an array of new ideas on censorship inspired by Marxist, neo-Marxist, social constructionist, and postmodern thinkers also view censorship as a productive force. Foucault was the first postmodern thinker who analysed how production of discourse requires forms of silencing, discipline, and gatekeeping behaviour.[15] He documents his theory through his analysis of nineteenth-century repression of sexuality where he argues that sex became an object of obsessive attention during this period which, in turn, produced areas of knowledge around this focus of cultural anxiety and broadened the sex discourse.[16]

It is not only theoreticians who have attributed generative force to censorship. The poet Joseph Brodsky also praised the censorship's assumed power of stimulation for metaphorical language.[17] Annabel Patterson holds that internalization of censorship norms is a constitutive feature of creation of literature as a distinct social category. For Patterson, censorship not only contributes to literary qualities such as allusive language, irony, and metaphor, but also for the open-ended experience of the readers' construction of meaning; by making their writings oblique to avoid censorial detection, writers open the door for a greater space of interpretation for readers.[18]

Some Iranian writers follow a similar logic and are optimistic that censorship might actually prove quite fruitful. Masoud Behnoud, a journalist, believes that censorship is not a talent killer and, in some cases – as in 1960s Iran – it actually led to the development and expansion of art and literature. He says: 'Maybe it will have the same effect this time. In the 1960s, no one thought how helpful the closed system would be. The same as now, everyone was trying to get out of the country but it later proved to have been very fruitful.'[19]

There is also a slightly different view – that a writer will write no matter how much external pressure may exist and that he has no duty to worry about publication, as his only duty is to write. Ivan Klima, an author who has first-hand experience of censorship, believes that it is an ineluctable part of modern life, arguing that contemporary society can neither exist in absolute freedom nor in tyranny. He divides freedom into what is external and internal, emphasizing the importance of internal freedom. His thesis is that if you don't have anything to say, you cannot write; but if you have something to convey, you will write it even in the absence of external freedom. As an example, he refers to Russian literature of the nineteenth century which was created in one of the least free empires the world has ever known.[20] Klima questions the significance or effectiveness of censorship. Further, he questions whether it is a good enough excuse simply not to produce a creative work because it will be censored. It seems that many writers who have written without any hope of publication were asking themselves the same question.

Censorship is Destructive and There is No Good in it

Advocates of this idea believe that censorship is a negation of freedom of speech and thereby a breach of human rights. To them, freedom of speech is a universal human right, not a social value specific to a certain culture or a certain political system. Ronald Dworkin, in *A New Map of Censorship* argues that free speech is not simply a right among other rights but that it is the driving force for any change and fulfilment of other rights: 'However democracies may evolve, free speech will remain the right and empowerment without which the struggle for other human rights cannot even be articulated'.[21] According to this constituency, the whole philosophy of censorship is based on a false premise: the assumption that censors are there to protect people and regulate the morals of society. Harry White, author of *Anatomy of Censorship*, argues that moral acts stem from moral opinions, so it is in fact these opinions censors feel they need to protect. But why do opinions need to be protected or enforced at all?

Major reasons repeatedly advanced throughout the history of ideas are that they are divine commands or are necessary for social stability. Nonetheless, White believes that there is a more fundamental reason – the fact that opinions tend to vary. Not only do opinions vary, but also the acceptance or rejection of any opinion tends to vary from one person or group to another because it is in the very nature of opinions to vary. White writes: 'Whatever it may be about, an opinion cannot be convincingly communicated as knowledge from one person or group of believers to another.'[22] There is no reliable way to prove that someone's opinion is right and another's is false. Since people mistake their own opinions for truth, they can resort to violence to impose their opinions on others. Clearly, those who believe their opinions to be true are not happy with others that do not share them. But instead of thinking that their own understanding may not be the universal truth or that something may be wrong with their methods of persuasion and communication, they shift responsibility for the impasse to the other side. It is here that White believes censorship happens.

This shifting of responsibility from the speaker who cannot convincingly demonstrate the truth of his opinions to those who, consequently, do not accept them as true has served through the centuries to establish a hierarchy of belief. It allows the believer to see humanity not as distinguished by the variety of beliefs and opinions men hold, but by the supposed fact that a select and superior few know the truth, by virtue of the special gifts they have been blessed with, and that everyone else does not, due to some flaw within their character.[23]

The theory of harm as the most prevalent justification for censorship has been repeatedly criticized. Opponents of censorship challenge both the question of harm and evidence for it. They argue that no evidence is normally given for the harm and that contradictory evidence is usually ignored. One example is the censorship of indecent expression. According to White, numerous studies in the West to find a relationship between indecent expression and harm have failed to establish such relationship. He maintains:

> To justify censorship for the stated purpose of securing individuals from harm is a bogus claim not only for the reason that there is no evidence that expression can produce actual harm, but because it is not to protect individuals from harm that judges, or preachers, or feminists seek to censor. What they seek is to protect from attack the particular moral system they value and which perhaps is the basis of their power and authority. It is the harm which expression can do to ideas which censorship guards against.[24]

The theory of harm faces a practical difficulty as well: it is unmeasurable. Even if we accept that speech can cause harm, it is practically impossible to weigh that harm against the harm caused by violating the general proscription against censorship.[25] It poses the same old challenge of determining the boundaries of speech rights.

There also seems to be a strong sense of class distinction involved. In White's words, 'Material which the lord of the manor may read with impunity may fall into the hands of the maid or gardener whose minds, unlike his, are presumed to be more open to depraving immoral influences.'[26] The censor does not actually censor the content but its availability to ordinary people. This sense of class distinction is very familiar in the Iranian debates on censorship and is deeply rooted in the mentality of Iranian clergy. Very openly, they divide people into two groups – *khavās* (the elite) and *Avām* (the laymen). Much of the censorship is aimed at protecting the *Avām*, who are perceived to be naïve and inferior. In the case of classical literature, while unabridged original versions are very often published uncensored, simplified selections aimed at wider readership are heavily censored. In the same way, it seems that the ruling class in Iran considers censored material as a way to identify those who are morally weak and corrupt. Therefore, not only is the material censored but if you possess a banned book or movie, this says something about you. It shows that you cannot be trusted and are prone to corruption. This fact places the censorship authorities and their supporters – the ruling clergy – in a paradoxical situation. On the one hand, they consider themselves above corruption. On the other, they act based on their own response to the material they are censoring. For example, they find it necessary that a word such as 'breast' be censored, claiming that it creates sexual arousal in the reader. But how do they know that this word has such an effect? There is no way to know it about others unless we assume that this word gives arousal to these pious men and women themselves.

Earlier I indicated the question of harm as the main pillar on which the defenders of censorship lay their reasoning. The Iranian authorities also claim that they need censorship to protect the social order, Islamic and moral values, the foundations of family, and so on. However, they never give an example of a work of literature which actually damaged any of those values and fail to explain the mechanism by which literature can be so harmful to social and moral values.

Even if one assumes that literature can bring harm, the limited circulation of literature in Iran and the type of readership leave little justification for censoring literature based on the theory of harm. The average circulation of books – excluding educational and academic books – has been decreasing over the past three decades from around 12,000 in 1979–1980 to around 2000 in 2014. The average circulation of literature was 1,332 in 2014[27] which shows a huge decrease from thirty years ago in spite of a doubled population – from 38 million in 1980 to 77 million in 2013. That is why even many of the religious poets and writers and some authorities within the government, especially in cultural organizations, criticize the state of censorship and demand a more relaxed censorship regime. In a more general perspective, one may argue that the lifting of bans on many cultural products during the past thirty years is a clear indication of the futility of censorship. For instance, during the first decade after the Revolution, possession of a music cassette might have put you in jail, as owning a video player could have in the second decade. I remember the 1980s when owning or even renting a video player was a criminal offence punishable by law, the official media was all the time warning against it as a satanic tool which threatens the foundations of family life. Both of these bans have been lifted for years now. One might question the validity of those strongly damning views which were refuted by the same authorities a few years later when they opened thousands of video shops all over the country and launched video production and distribution networks. The development of information, satellite TV, the Internet, and social media makes censoring poetry and literature a futile – if not an absurd – act. In fact, one may claim that censoring literature based on theory of social harm is a lost battle.

In order to understand censorship in Iran, we need to look more closely at the fundamental principles of the Islamic Republic as a form of government based on a religious ideology. We should look deep and wide and consider all manifestations of control of culture and the reasons behind such control. Censorship is not limited to the acts of the censors in crossing out some words and phrases or banning some books. It is present in all cultural, social, political, and economic policies of the state. I understand censorship as a comprehensive set of policies and projects to 'silence, subdue and undermine' alternative discourses in favour of a dominant discourse and I don't even see it limited to culture. Since the early days of the Islamic Republic, the system divided the Iranian population into two major groups: Supporters of the Islamic system and non-supporters. This dichotomy is inherently present in every policy of the state. Government positions, financial incentives, and political advantages 'naturally' belong to those who support the regime. For nearly every position in an adult person's life including entering university or getting a job in the public sector you need to undergo thorough background checks and very often attend political and ideological interviews where your family background, religious knowledge, and political affiliations are scrutinized. You are expected to either prove to support the regime or 'pretend' not to hold nonconformist views. You might find some exceptions to this rule, but exceptions do not invalidate rules. If you oppose the system the least you are expected to do is to 'hide' your opposition and not be vocal about your ideas. All these policies are aimed at 'silencing, suppressing and undermining' alternative discourses and promoting the Islamic discourse and this is what I call 'censorship'. In this outlook, censorship has been the main policy of the Islamic Republic of Iran, the backbone of the system or as Ahmad Shakeri, a pro-regime writer and member of the Book Supervisory Board, calls 'the juice of what the Revolution is pursuing in its ideals'.[28]

It has been argued that censorship stimulates creativity and that authors find innovative ways to express themselves. The use of figurative language, metaphor, and allegory might seem like creative achievements to some scholars. Advocates of this idea seem to be ignoring one major principle in creativity, that is, the freedom to choose a style. To employ euphemism as a literary device is not always an achievement. It can be another tactic at the service of censorship to obscure or sanitize concepts or events. Brodsky's claim that censorship leads to higher quality of literature due to its impetus to the use of Aesopian language faced criticism by a reviewer who perceived his works written 'without the benefit of censorship' [after he left the Soviet Union] were 'superior to his earlier verse, which was the beneficiary of its blessings'.[29] In his study of the use of Aesopian language in modern Russian literature, Lev Lifshitz Losev argues that censorship has long been part of the creative process in Russian literature but warns against the assumption that the writers' reaction to censorship in all circumstances leads to an improved quality of the text, saying

> It is not uncommon for the author[…]to simply eliminate dangerous fragments of the text or to replace passages whose meaning is inescapable with ones broad enough to accommodate many interpretations and ones so stylistically neutral that communication between Author and Reader does not develop on any additional level. It is not unusual for the text to be destroyed in the process, that is, for its overall quality to decline. It is, on the contrary, a daily occurrence in literature under censorship.[30]

The degree of destruction depends on the specific qualities of the censorship regime. So even if we accept Brodsky's judgement, it cannot be generalized or universalized.

And then there is the ethical question: Isn't this whole idea of the use of Aesopian language based on deception? Isn't it the outcome of an unannounced collusion with the censor? Or the pre-emptive surrender to the will of censor without a fight? Matthew d'Ancona, in 'Lexicon of War', writes: 'Euphemism is the subtlest form of censorship.'[31] Employing metaphor by choice is one thing; being forced to overuse it to overcome censorship is quite another. Many Iranian poets have expressed their anger at what they consider to be a sheepish act of cowardice. Alishah Mowlavi, a poet who published his book underground, wrote in a poem dedicated to Simin Behbahani: 'How many metaphors, metaphors, metaphors | those who take refuge in metaphor | grow old with their dreams | they should shout it transparent like you | viva Freedom'.[32] The novelist Tadeusz Konwicki observed that censorship may indeed 'Mobilize a writer to create ways of by-passing censorship, thus [forcing] the writer to employ metaphors which raise the piece of writing to a higher level'.[33] However, in time the hyper subtle forms born out of the game with the censor will themselves become conventions and the 'secret language becomes public, and the censor will ban it too. So newer, subtler forms are devised. And so it goes, on and on, the literature becoming increasingly more obscure, eventually losing all traces of life.'[34] The literature produced by such a web of deception can hardly be considered creative. In Coetzee's words: 'Censors can and often have been outwitted. But the game of slipping Aesopian messages past the censor is ultimately a sterile one, diverting writers from their proper task.'[35]

For those who argue that censorship can help literature flourish and cite the examples of nineteenth-century Russian literature or Eastern European literature under communist regimes, there are some important issues to consider. First of all, those writers who are praised for creating masterpieces under censorship do not support this argument themselves. Eli M. Oboler invites those who argue that the great nineteenth-century Russian literature flourished in spite of and/or as a result of Tsarist censorship to think again:

> The famous case of Tolstoy's unwillingness to write what he feared the Czarist censor might forbid bears repetition at this point. Tolstoy once wrote: 'You would not believe how, from the very commencement of my activity, that horrible censor question has tormented me. I wanted to write what I felt; but at the same time it occurred to me that what I wrote would not be permitted, and involuntarily I had to abandon the work. I abandoned, and went on abandoning, and meanwhile the years passed away.' Who knows what riches for the human spirit have been lost to society through fear of the censor?[36]

People like Ivan Klima, who argued that a writer writes and does not need external freedom, seem to be ignoring the fact that the achievement of some writers in writing good works of literature under some sort of censorship does not rule out the possibility that those same writers might have produced much better works and in greater number in absence of that censorship. There is no way to refute the assumption that nineteenth-century Russia or 1960s Iran could have produced dozens more great writers and hundreds more masterpieces if there had been no censorship. Klima also seems to be over-excited about his own success and that of a few of his peers, and consequently has ignored a larger number who felt sterilized by censorship; those who lived under constant fear or had to suffer humiliation and apologize to dictators when faced with the consequences of their writings. Coetzee uses the term 'alienation' to describe the process Mandelstam went through when he felt the urge to write *Ode to Stalin* in hope of winning mercy from the tyrant.[37] It can well be argued that Mandelstam's experiences of life under censorship prompted him to say, famously: 'I divide all of world literature into authorized and unauthorized works. The former is all trash; the latter, stolen air. I want to spit in the face of every writer who first obtains permission and then writes'.[38]

Although from a completely different standpoint, Ahmad Shakeri uses Klima's argument to deny the destructive role of censorship in contemporary Iranian literature. He blames the secular intellectuals' hostility toward the Islamic regime for portraying censorship as a problem, adding that it is sometimes being manipulated by political factions for political gain. Otherwise, censorship can't be harmful to literary production.

To strengthen his position, he refers to the Iranian diaspora and the works they have published in absence of censorship overseas. He claims that they have had no success in spite of their absolute freedom while those inside the country are complaining that *momayyezi* has prevented the development of literature. He argues that if censorship is really the problem, why haven't the Iranian diaspora writers created great masterpieces and won global awards? He therefore concludes that *momayyezi* cannot be blamed for perceived lack of success of contemporary Iranian literature as the only thing *momayyezi* does is to act as a gatekeeper and thereby secure the minimal standards of a harmless literature.[39] A *Kayhān* newspaper columnist, Pejman Karimi called for boycotting diaspora writers as enemies who accuse Iranian authorities of censorship. He wrote:

> They regularly complain of censorship and ignore the fact that there is no such a thing as censorship in our religious system. What we have is *momayyezi* which is based on rationality, religious and legal, and customary expediency. Can writers who show no shame in their description of some scenes expect a publication licence in a divine system where morality is a pillar of social life? What about poets who ridicule divine values?[40]

He goes on to say that these diaspora writers have had no achievement, are suffering from depression, have petty jobs overseas, or are serving the enemies.[41]

In a debate with Mehdi Yazdani Khorram, a writer and literary journalist, Shakeri said that the pseudo-intellectual movement has turned *momayyezi* into a problem and opposing *momayyezi* is rooted in the opposition toward the rule of *Fiqh* and the support for secularism. '*Momayyezi* is an issue of law and law obedience. Any party who doesn't accept *momayyezi* doesn't accept the rule of law. The root of opposition is opposition to the rule of Sharia law and Shi'a jurisprudence and the support of secular ideas[…]. The pseudo-intellectual movement has been pursuing desacralization and promotion of secularism for the past 40 years.'[42]

He thinks that those who object to censorship are actually objecting to the foundations of the Islamic Republic. There is a tacit threat in this approach which is not unknown to the Iranian cultural scene.

One other important issue to consider is the special characteristics of censorship in present-day Iran and how it compares with other societies around the world. Censorship in Iran is all-inclusive, extensive, amorphous, arbitrary, and unpredictable. It covers all areas of literary activity, as well as the public and private life of authors and readers. Going back to the argument of Ivan Klima and his example of nineteenth-century Russian literature, it should be noted that none of those great works which passed Tsarist censorship would have had any chance of publication in Iran unless they underwent further, more comprehensive censorship. Mohammad Hashem Akbariani wrote: 'They say censorship is universal and exists in all countries. It is true but only a small portion of truth. The larger portion of truth is that the scope of censorship varies considerably from one country to another and this is what really matters.'[43] It is the scope of censorship and the severity of its consequences which makes it such a huge problem – of unimaginable proportions – in Iran. Nadine Gordimer wrote: 'Yet we should not forget that censorship is in many places a matter of life and death, of torture and immense suffering, as a perusal of any issue of the *Index on Censorship* will confirm.'[44]

Lack of clear guidelines allows Iranian censors to use their own discretion and rely on their own interpretation. Consequently, censorship is very confusing and can be disappointing, especially to debut authors. Political factions and security forces can interfere in the process. Books published under one administration may be banned in the next administration. As a result, in many instances censorship goes beyond the books and affects authors in their personal lives. Writers and publishers who repeatedly produce works that do not appeal to the censor come under scrutiny and may be banned, and their records are sometimes handed over to the security authorities. Censorship thus turns into inquisition and writers are prosecuted. Golrokh Ebrahimi Iraee was sentenced to six years in prison allegedly for writing a novel about stoning which she had not published and the manuscript was discovered when the security forces raided her family home to arrest her husband.[45] I was myself interrogated for poetry that I had not published or even read to anyone. As Daniel Grassian observes: 'The Iranian government often acts upon a premise of suspicion and paranoia […]. Literature can then be seen as being either a political tool for the author or something that can have significant political importance.'[46]

The fact that many books never get the opportunity to be published gives an imperfect image of the state of literature in Iran. Fathollah Biniaz, a novelist and literary critic, believes that the best works of Iranian writers never see the light of day: 'The best works never obtain a publication licence. Good works usually receive about 70–80 corrections, most of them disappointing. The third-degree works receive between 30–50 corrections and neutral works of little literary value usually get between 10–15 corrections from the censor.'[47]

As a result of censorship, self-censorship becomes widespread and impacts enormously on creativity. In a critique of Shahriar Mandanipour's novel

Censoring an Iranian Love Story, which he published in exile in the United States, Grassian writes: 'Such self-censorship can and does affect the writing itself. With so much attention placed upon what can and cannot be written, the writer's energy can be dissolved merely in the act of writing a scene. Self-censorship can also disallow a writer from writing what she or he wants to convey to the reader'.[48] Based on what Mandanipour has depicted in his novel, Grassian concludes that 'a contemporary Iranian writer simply cannot write an effective and realistic love story, and that it has become increasingly difficult to establish normal and satisfying relationships under the dictates of the Islamic regime'.[49]

An Iranian author lives in constant fear that his home could be raided and his manuscripts taken away and destroyed, and this permanent worry may have major psychological impact. In his article 'My Temptation', which includes reflections on his life as a dissident writer, Vaclav Havel wrote:

> One of the expressions of the various obsessive neuroses which I suffered from at that time (or perhaps still do) is one that is well known to every dissident: you live in fear for your manuscript. Until such a time as the text which means so much to you is safely stowed somewhere, or distributed in several copies among other people, you live in a state of constant suspense and uncertainty – and as the years go by, surprisingly enough, this does not get easier but, on the contrary, the fear tends to grow into a pathological obsession.[50]

In view of some critics, surrendering to censorship is an immoral act. Akbariani was scathing about it:

> Censorship is changing the text – against your will – in a manner to be acceptable by the censor in exchange for a licence, i.e. the right to publish the book. This is hypocritical, exactly what you do when you change your behaviour to please an employer in exchange for a job or bonus. Surrendering to censorship is the same as surrendering to hypocrisy.[51]

This hypocrisy is reflected very well in the way Iranian fiction depicts Iranian life. According to Amir Hassan Cheheltan, in many Iranian contemporary novels, public space and political life are absent. In an interview with *Frankfurter Algemeine*, he states: 'The life of Iranians in the Iranian novel is a big lie and a distortion of truth'.[52] He considers writing a high-risk profession and believes that under current conditions, Iranian writers are attracted to self-destruction and narcotics or prefer a life in exile over staying in Iran, and that those who stay have no way but to surrender to censorship.[53]

The effects of extreme censorship can be devastating. All techniques adopted by poets and writers to circumvent censorship entail a degree of hypocrisy. The necessity of taking on fake identities impacts upon the development of the writer's identity. Restricting free information can lead to the prevalence of lies. It damages creativity and curtails free imagination. According to Salman Rushdie:

The worst, most insidious effects of censorship is that, in the end, it can deaden the imagination of the people. Where there is no debate, it is hard to go on remembering, every day, that there is a suppressed side to every argument. It becomes almost impossible to conceive of what the suppressed things might be. It becomes easy to think that what has been suppressed was valueless anyway, or so dangerous that it needed to be suppressed. And then the victory of the censor is total.[54]

Direct involvement of the government in literature can send wrong signals to the young and to emerging poets and writers. A special group of poets and writers receive significant publicity and a distinct trend in poetry and fiction is being patronized. It limits the access of young authors to the true variety of literature produced in the country. Even the international reputation of Iranian literature is affected as many books are sponsored for translation into foreign languages by government or semi-government organizations which are merely chosen for their agreeable content rather than their literary merit.

One grave consequence of censorship in Iran is the poor state of literary criticism. The lack of independent literary journals deprives poets and writers of insightful editorials. Literary criticism cannot develop under such conditions. The natural relationship between different generations is cut off or hampered. Emerging authors are denied the benefit of enjoying the experiences of previous generations.

When such conditions last for a generation, they can have disappointing consequences. Seyed Ali Salehi frames the context succinctly: 'We are living in fear of historical censorship. In such conditions, there is rarely anyone who does not lose their aspirations and creativity. Censorship means suffering. It makes creative human beings inactive. Censorship of any form and in any manner is destructive.'[55] The Iranian Writers' Association called the work of censors a slaughtering of 'self-representation and its tools' aimed at 'negating the right of the Iranian people to enjoy avant-garde non-governmental art and literature'.[56] The effect of long-lasting censorship on the creative mind has long been known. Heinrich Heine is quoted to have described his inability to write in absence of censorship during his later years in life. He said: 'Oh, I can't write any more; I can't, because we have no censorship! How can a person write without censorship, if he has always lived under censorship?'[57]

The effects of such censorship can last for as long as the victim of censorship lives. Nadine Gordimer once said: 'Censorship is never over for those who have experienced it. It is a brand on the imagination that affects the individual who has suffered it, forever.'[58]

NOTES

Introduction

1. Vali-ye Asr is a name for the twelfth Shi'ite Imam. After the Revolution, many public institutions changed their names to Islamic names.
2. Matthew Bunn, 'Reimagining Repression: New Censorship Theory and After', *History and Theory* 54, no. 1 (2015): 25–44, 29.
3. Ibid., 30.
4. Ibid., 34.
5. See Antonio Gramsci, *The Gramsci Reader: Selected Writings, 1916–1935* (New York: New York University Press, 2000), 306.
6. Louis Althusser, 'Ideology and Ideological State Apparatuses (Notes towards an Investigation)', in *Lenin and Philosophy and Other Essays*, trans. Ben Brewster (New York: Monthly Review Press, 1971), 127–188.
7. Matthew Bunn, 25
8. Michel Foucault, *Discipline and Punish: The Birth of a Prison*, trans. Alan Sheridan (New York: Vintage Books, Random House, 1995), 194.
9. Michel Foucault, *Power/Knowledge: Selected Interviews and other Writings 1972–1977*, ed. Colin Gordon, trans. Colin Gordon, Leo Marshall, John Mephan, Kate Soper (New York: Pantheon Books, 1980), 98.
10. For a history of censorship and discussions on economic censorship under New Censorship Theory, see Sue Curry Jansen, *The Knot That Binds Power and Knowledge* (New York: Oxford University Press, 1988).
11. Michael Holquist, 'Corrupt Originals: The Paradox of Censorship', *PMLA*, 109, no. 1 (Jan 1994): 14–25.
12. Richard Burt, *Licensed by Authority: Ben Jonson and the Discourse of Censorship* (Ithaca: Cornell University Press, 1993), 12.
13. See Friedrich Nietzsche, *Human, All Too Human: A Book for Free Spirits*, trans. Marion Faber et al. (Cambridge, UK: Cambridge University Press, 1996), 164.
14. Pierre Bourdieu, *Language and Symbolic Power*, ed. John B. Thompson, trans. Gino Raymond and Matthew Adamson (Cambridge, UK: Polity Press, 1991), 138.
15. Ibid., 139.
16. Stanley Fish, *There's No Such Thing as Free Speech* (Oxford: Oxford University Press, 1994), 104.
17. Judith Butler, *Excitable Speech/A Politics of the Performative* (New York: Routledge, 1997), 39.
18. Helen Freshwater 'Towards a Redefinition of Censorship' in *Censorship and Cultural Regulation in the Modern Age*, ed. Beate Müller, (Amsterdam: Rodopi B.V., 2004), 225–245.
19. Foucault, *Discipline and Punish: The Birth of a Prison*, 194.
20. Michel Foucault, *The History of Sexuality, Volume 1: An Introduction*, trans. Robert Hurley (New York: Pantheon Books, 1978), 23.

21 Judith Butler, 'Ruled Out: Vocabularies of the Censor in Censorship' in *Censorship and Silencing, Practices of Cultural Regulation*, ed. Robert C. Post (Los Angeles: The Getty Research Institute, 1998), 247–259.
22 Helen Freshwater, 242.
23 Judith Butler, *Ruled Out*, 249.
24 Beate Müller, 'Mapping the Territory', in *Censorship and Cultural Regulation in the Modern Age*, ed. Beate Müller (Amsterdam: Rodopi B. V., 2004), 1–31.
25 Helen Freshwater, 242.
26 Ibid., 241.
27 Servat, *Iran–Constitution*, trans. International Constitutional Law (Switzerland: Servat, 2010) <http://www.servat.unibe.ch/icl/ir00000_.html> [accessed 18 January 2015].
28 This poster is available to download from many websites including *Asr-e Entezār* website, <http://www.asr-entezar.ir/archives/1618> [accessed 21 October 2016].
29 'Everyone has the right to freedom of opinion and expression; this right includes freedom to hold opinions without interference and to seek, receive, and impart information and ideas through any media and regardless of frontier' *Universal Declaration of Human Rights, Article 19*, United Nations website; <http://www.un.org/en/universal-declaration-human-rights/> [accessed 21 October 2016].
30 Ivan Klima, 'Variation on an Eternal Theme' in *An Embarrassment of Tyrannies: Twenty-Five Years of Index on Censorship*, ed. Webb, W.L. and Rose Bell (London: Victor Gollancz, 1997), 99–103.
31 Salman Rushdie, 'on Censorship', 11 May 2012, *The New Yorker*, <https://www.newyorker.com/books/page-turner/on-censorship> [accessed 2 August 2016].

Chapter 1

1 Mohammad Sadr Hashemi, *Tārikh-e Jarāyed va Majallāt-e Iran* (Isfahan: Kamal Publishers, 1985), 78.
2 Ahmad Karimi Hakkak, 'Censorship', *Encyclopedia Iranica*, http://www.iranicaonline.org/articles/censorship-sansur-in-persia [accessed 17 January 2015].
3 Goel Kohan, *Tārikh-e Sānsur-e Matbuāt-e Iran* (Tehran: Agah Publishers, 1984), Vol. 1: 34–36.
4 Ibid., 50.
5 Hakkak, 'Censorship'.
6 Kohan, Vol. 1: 98.
7 Edward. G. Browne, 'The Persian Press and Persian Journalism, lecture delivered to the Persia Society at 22 Albermale Street, London on Friday 23rd May 1913', published for the Persia Society by John Hogg, London, 11–12.
8 E'temadolsaltaneh, *Almaāser val Āsār*, Chapter 8, 117 (cited in Kohan, Vol. 1: 123).
9 Shireen T. Hunter, *Iran After Khomeini* (New York: The Center for Strategic and International Studies/Praeger Publishers, 1992), 7.
10 Mirza Muhammad Ali Tarbiyat lists 371 which also includes newspapers and other periodical publications published in the aftermath of the Constitutional Declaration in different parts of Iran or abroad. See: Edward G. Browne, *The Press and Poetry of Modern Persia Partly Based on the Manuscript Work of Mirza Muhammad Ali Khan 'Tarbiyat' of Tabriz* (Cambridge, UK: Cambridge University Press, 1914), 27–153.

11 Ervand Abrahamian, *A History of Modern Iran* (New York: Cambridge University Press, 2008), 46.
12 Hakkak, 'Censorship'.
13 Edward G. Browne, *The Persian Revolution of 1905–1909* (London: Frank Cass & Co., 1966), 242.
14 Ibid., 243.
15 *Motammam-e Qanun-e Asāsi-ye Mashruteh*, (Tehran: The Islamic Parliament Research Centre) <http://rc.majlis.ir/fa/law/show/133414> [accessed 14 January 2016]
16 Ibid.
17 Mangol Bayat, *Iran's First Revolution: Shi'ism and the Constitutional Revolution of 1905–1909* (Oxford: Oxford University Press, 1991), 154.
18 Hamid Dabashi, *Iran: A People Interrupted* (New York: The New Press, 2007), 91.
19 Browne, *The Press and Poetry of Modern Persia Partly Based on the Manuscript Work of Mirza Muhammad Ali Khan 'Tarbiyat' of Tabriz*, 17.
20 Ali Gheissari, *Iranian Intellectuals in the 20th Century* (Austin: University of Texas Press, 1998), 16.
21 Hassan Javadi, *Edward Browne va Iran*, 2nd edn (Tehran: Farhang-e Nashr-e Noe, 2017), 424.
22 Dabashi, *Iran: A People Interrupted*, 104.
23 Bayat, *Iran's First Revolution*, 267.
24 Peter Avery, *Modern Iran* (London: Ernest Benn Publishers, 1965), 152.
25 Homa Katouzian, 'Riza Shah's Political Legitimacy and Social Base, 1921–1941', in *The Making of Modern Iran: State and Society under Riza Shah, 1921–1941*, ed. Stephanie Cronin (London: Routledge, 2003), 16.
26 Ibid., 31.
27 Cyrus Ghani, *Iran and the Rise of Reza Shah: From Qajar Collapse to Pahlavi Power* (London: I.B. Tauris, 2000), 328.
28 Fakhreddin Azimi, *The Quest for Democracy in Iran: A Century of Struggle Against Authoritarian Rule* (Cambridge, MA: Harvard University Press, 2008), 27.
29 Ibid.
30 Homa Katouzian, 'Riza Shah's Political Legitimacy and Social Base, 1921–1941', 32.
31 Ibid., 31.
32 Abdulrahim Zakir Hussain, *Adabiyyāt-e Siyāsi-ye Iran dar Asr-e Mashrutiyat, Vol. 1* (Tehran: Elm Publishers, 1998), 63.
33 Rudi Matthee, 'Transforming Dangerous Nomads into Useful Artisans, Technicians, Agriculturalists – Education in the Riza Shah Period', in *The Making of Modern Iran: State and Society under Riza Shah, 1921–1941*, ed. Stephanie Cronin (London: Routledge, 2003), 123.
34 Mehrzad Boroujerdi, 'Triumphs and Travails of Authoritarian Modernization in Iran', in *The Making of Modern Iran: State and Society under Riza Shah, 1921–1941*, ed. Stephanie Cronin (London: Routledge, 2003), 148.
35 Ibid., 150.
36 Ibid., 152.
37 Mohammadreza Shafiei Kadkani, *Advār-e She'r-e Farsi* (Tehran: Tus Publishers, 1980), 50.
38 Edward Posnett, 'Treating His Imperial Majesty's Warts: British Policy towards Iran 1977–79', *Iranian Studies* 45, no. 1 (2012): 119.
39 Simin Fadaee, *Social Movements in Iran: Environmentalism and Civil Society* (London: Routledge, 2012), 45.

40 Tomas B. Phillips, *Queer Sinister Things: The Hidden History of Iran* (Raleigh: Lulu Enterprises Inc, 2012), 72.
41 Ali Asghar Shamim, *Iran in the Reign of His Majesty Mohammad Reza Shah Pahlavi*, trans. Aladin Pazargadi (Self-published: 1965), 10.
42 Ali Gheissari, *Iranian Intellectuals in the 20th Century*.
43 Ibid.
44 Fakhreddin Azimi, *Iran – The Crisis of Democracy: From the Exile of Reza Shah to the Fall of Musaddiq* (London: I. B. Tauris, 1989), 339.
45 Ali Ansari quoted by Simin Fadaee, 45.
46 Fakhreddin Azimi, *Iran – The Crisis of Democracy*, 339.
47 Ibid., 337.
48 Avery, *Modern Iran*, 448–449.
49 Ervand Abrahamian, *Iran Between Two Revolutions* (Princeton: Princeton University Press, 1982), 435.
50 Kamran Talattof, 'Iranian Women's Literature: From Pre-Revolutionary Social Discourse to Post-Revolutionary Feminism', *International Journal of Middle East Studies* 29, no. 4 (November 1997): 531–558.
51 M. R. Ghanoonparvar, *Prophets of Doom: Literature as a Socio-Political Phenomenon in Modern Iran* (Lanham, Maryland: University Press of America, 1984), 80.
52 Mehrzad Boroujerdi, 48–49.
53 Hossein Shahidi, *Journalism in Iran; From Mission to Profession* (London: Routledge, 2007), 3.

Chapter 2

1 Islamic Parliament of Iran, *The Constitution of the Islamic Republic of Iran last amended in 1989* (Tehran: Islamic Parliament of Iran,n.d.) <http://en.parliran.ir/eng/en/Constitution> [accessed 16 November 2016].
2 Ibid.
3 Ibid., article 24.
4 Islamic Parliament Research Centre, *Qānun-e Matbuāt, Art.2* (Tehran: Islamic Parliament Research Centre, 2015) <http://rc.majlis.ir/fa/law/show/91180> [accessed 21 January 2015].
5 Ibid., article 4.
6 Ibid., article 6.
7 Ayatollah Khomeini, '*Payām be Mellat-e Iran, be Monāsebat-e Sāl-e Now*', 21 March 1980, *Sahifeh-ye Nur, Vol.12*, 202–210, Imam Khomeini Comprehensive Website <https://emam.com/posts/view/2299/پیام-به-ملت-ایران،-به-مناسبت-سال-نو‌گانه-به-مسلمانانzwnj%3B%29های-سبزzwnj%3B%26توصیه%26%28> [accessed 30 August 2020].
8 Supreme Council of the Cultural Revolution, *History of Supreme Council of the Cultural Revolution* (Tehran: Supreme Council of the Cultural Revolution) <http://en.farhangoelm.ir/SCCR/History-of-Supreme-Council-of-the-Cultural-Revolut>[accessed 6 July 2016]
9 Ibid.
10 Ibid.

11 Showrā-ye Farhang-e Omumi-ye Keshvar, *Ahdāf, Siyāsathā va Zavābet-e Nashr-e Ketāb* (Tehran: Dabirkhāneh-ye Farhang-e Omumi-ye Keshvar, 1988) <http://pcci.ir/?option=com_content&view=article&id=132:1> [accessed 18 January 2015].
12 Ibid.
13 Ibid.
14 Ayatollah Khomeini, '*Sokhanrāni dar Masjed-e A'zam-e Qom*',15 April 1964, *Sahifeh-ye Nur Vol. 1* (Tehran: Moassesa-ye Tanzim va Nashr-e Āsār-e Imam Khomeini [n.d.]) <http://www.imam-khomeini.ir/fa/books/BooksahifeBody.aspx?id=177> [accessed 23 January 2015].
15 Ibid.
16 Ayatollah Khomeini, '*Towbeh-ye Shāh, Hoquq-e Aqalliyat-hā, Rābeteh-ye Jomhuri-ye Eslāmi ba Gharb: Mosāhebeh ba Die Welt*', 7 November 1978, *Sahifeh-ye Nur, Vol. 4* (Tehran: Moassesa-ye Tanzim va Nashr-e Āsār-e Imam Khomeini [n.d.]) <http://www.imamkhomeini.ir/fa/books/BooksahifeBody.aspx?id=1031> [accessed 23 January 2015].
17 Ibid.
18 Javad Talei, '*Matbuāt-e Iran dar Manganeh-ye do Nezām*' (Germany: DW Persian Online, 6 February 2009) <www.dw.de/مطبوعات-ایران-در-منگنه-دو-نظام۲/a-4008237> [accessed 26 January 2015].
19 Oriana Fallaci, 'An Interview with KHOMEINI', *New York Times*, 7 October 1979. <http://query.nytimes.com/gst/abstract.html?res=9F0DEEDA1438E432A25754C0A9669D946890D6CF> [accessed 23 January 2015].
20 Ibid.
21 Ayatollah Khomeini, '*Sokhanrāni*', 30 August 1986, *Sahifeh-ye Nur, Vol. 20* (Tehran: Moassesa-ye Tanzim va Nashr-e Āsār-e Imam Khomeini, [n.d.]), p. 127 <http://sahifeh.net/?p=7702>[accessed 23 January 2015].
22 Ayatollah Khomeini, '*Hokm, Fatwā-ye Qatl-e Salman Rushdie*', 14 February 1989, *Sahifeh-ye Nur, Vol. 21* (Tehran: Moassesa-ye Tanzim va Nashr-e Āsār-e Imam Khomeini, 1989): 263 <http://www.imam-khomeini.ir/fa/C207_44691/_فتوای_قتل_سلمان_رشدی،_نویسنده_کتاب_کفرآمیز_آیات_شیطانی> [accessed 30 October 2016].
23 Ayatollah Khomeini, *Velāyat-e Faqih* (Tehran: Moassesa-ye Tanzim va Nashr-e Āsār-e Imam Khomeini, 1994), 78.
24 Ayatollah Khamenei, '*Bayānāt pas az Bāzdid az Sāzemān-e Sedā va Simā*', 18 May 2004 (Tehran: Khamenei Portal, 2004) <http://farsi.khamenei.ir/speech-content?id=3232> [accessed 28 January 2015].
25 Ayatollah Khamenei, '*Bayānāt dar Haram-e Motahhar-e Razavi*', 21 March 2014 (Tehran: Khamenei Portal, 2004) <http://farsi.khamenei.ir/speech-content?id=25993> [accessed 28 January 2015].
26 Roxanne Varzi, *Warring Souls: Youth, Media and Martyrdom in Post-Revolution Iran* (USA: Duke University Press, 2006), 40.
27 Ali Mirsepassi, *Democracy in Modern Iran: Islam, Culture, and Political Change* (New York: New York University Press, 2010), 85.
28 Ibid.
29 Some scholars name Ahmad Fardid, a professor of philosophy in Tehran University as the originator of this term. Fardid, nicknamed 'the oral philosopher' – as he wrote very little – had a great impact on some of the most influential figures amongst the hardline and more conservative factions of the Islamic regime. Regardless of the term's origin, it was Al-e Ahmad's book '*Gharbzadegi*' which

brought it into the public domain and fuelled the anti-Western sentiments among the educated youth during the last decade of the Shah's regime.
30 *Shast Daqiqa*, BBC Persian TV, 28 February 2015.
31 Ayatollah Khamenei, '*Bayānāt dar Didār-e Majma'-e Namāyandegān-e Tollāb*', 28 November 1989 (Tehran: Khamenei Portal, 1989) <http://farsi.khamenei.ir/speech-content?id=2228> [accessed 21 April 2015].
32 Ayatollah Khamenei, '*Bayānāt dar Jalaseh-ye Porsesh va Pasokh-e Dāneshjuyān-e Dāneshgāh-e Shahid Beheshti*' 12 May 2003 (Tehran: Khamenei Portal, 2003) <http://farsi.khamenei.ir/speech-content?id=3177> [accessed 2 February 2015].
33 The list is available from the official portal of Ayatollah Khamenei (Tehran: Khamenei Portal, 2015) <http://farsi.khamenei.ir/tag-content?id=1010> [accessed 25 October 2016] New material is being added regularly.
34 Ayatollah Khamenei Portal, '*Tahājom-e Farhangi- Te'dād-e Fish: 102, Te'dād-e Maqāleh: 1*' (Tehran: Khamenei Portal, 2015) <http://farsi.khamenei.ir/keyword-print?id=1010> [accessed 2 February 2015].
35 Ayatollah Khamenei Portal, '*Ettelā' Negāsht: Bish az 200 Sāl Tahājom-e Farhangi*', 9 August 2016 (Tehran: Khamenei Portal, 2016) <http://farsi.khamenei.ir/photo-album?id=33947> [accessed 25 October 2016]
36 Ayatollah Khamenei, '*Bayānāt dar Didār-e Jam'i az Kārgozārān-e Farhangi*', 14 August 1992 (Tehran: Khamenei Portal, 1992) <http://farsi.khamenei.ir/speech-content?id=2630> [accessed 15 April 2015].
37 Ibid.
38 Ayatollah Khamenei quoted by Shahab Esfandiyari, '*Ta'ammoli bar Siyāsat-e Farhangi-ye Ayatollah Khamenei*', 6 April 2016 (Tehran: Khamenei Portal, 2016) <http://farsi.khamenei.ir/others-note?id=32768> [accessed 7 July 2016]
39 Shahab Esfandiyari, '*Ta'ammoli bar Siyāsat-e Farhangi-ye Ayatollah Khamenei*', 6 April 2016 (Tehran: Khamenei Portal, 2016) <http://farsi.khamenei.ir/others-note?id=32768> [accessed 7 July 2016].
40 See, for example; Ayatollah Khamenei, '*Bayānāt dar Didār-e Ra-is va Namāyandegān-e Majles-e Showrā-ye Eslāmi*', 6 June 2016 (Tehran: Khamenei Portal, 2016) <http://farsi.khamenei.ir/speech-content?id=33282> [accessed 7 July 2016].
41 The cultural engineering map can be downloaded from the website of SCCR: *Naqsha-ye Mohandesi-ye Farhangi-ye Keshvar* (Tehran: SCCR Secretariat, 2013) <http://www.sccr.ir/UserFiles/entesharat/%D9%85%D9%87%D9%86%D8%AF%D8%B3_%20%D9%81%D8%B1%D9%87%D9%86%DA%AF__opt.pdf> [accessed 25 October 2016].
42 See for example; '*Chand She'r az Rahbar-e Moazzam-e Enqelāb-e Eslāmi, Hazrat-e Ayatollah Khamenei*' <http://www.tebyan.net/newindex.aspx?pid=934&articleID=412206> [accessed 27 February 2015].
43 Reza Esmaili, *Reza Esmaili dar Goftogu ba Nasim Online* (Iran: Nasim Online, 19 June 2016) <http://nasimonline.ir/Content/Detail/2040759/ان-جوان-همیشه-مدنظر-رهبری< -تقویت-گفتمان-انقلاب-اسلامی-یکی-از-کارکردهای-دیدار-رهبری-با-شاعران-است-شاعر> [accessed 6 July 2016].
44 These meetings are reported in a manner to portray Khamenei as a friendly and approachable father figure to the poets and writers. He is addressed as '*Āghā*', a respectful yet intimate way of addressing seniors – many people address their fathers as *Āghā*. He shows personal interest in the wellbeing of poets and their families and is shown to be aware of new publications. A summary of one such report of a meeting in 2016 as published in ILNA News Agency ('*khodā Konad Haj Ahmad Bargardad*,'

ILNA, 21 June 2016) <http://www.ilna.ir/-حاج-کند-خدا-3/383243-بخش-سیاسی
احمد-برگردد>[accessed 17 September 2016] may shed some light on the atmosphere of such meetings:

It is yet an hour or more to *Azan* and the poetry people are already gathered in the yard [….] The poets are autographing their books to present to *Āghā*. They write "With love and affection", "To the soul of souls", "To the dear leader of the Revolution", and so on. *Āghā* arrives. The crowd move forward to greet the leader. *Āghā* greets them one by one. He asks one of them "Do you feel better? Have you recovered?" *Āghā* is informed of the health and sickness of the men of letters. Reza Borji informs that a Cardinal in Ukraine has converted to *Shi'a* Islam. Ahad Dehbozorgi offers *Āghā* his book. *Āghā* asks: "What is the news in Shiraz?"[….] A poet from Mashhad says he is the messenger of greetings from a poet called "Baghā". "Baghā" is apparently a friend of *Āghā* from his youth. Kafi offers his book, a research into the Islamic Revolution and the Sacred Defence. *Āghā* says such researches are necessary and should be encouraged more [….] Amir Ameli reads from a manuscript: "Put your hand on the sword just for a test, oh Friend/ To see that there are many chests to shield you". *Āghā* says: "Actually, we always have our hand on the sword, Mr Ameli but the battlefield is different today. Today, the battlefield is the field of soft war, political and cultural war." Mohammad Ali Ghasemi has brought a novel. *Āghā* says: "I will read this work. I love novels." Mohammad Ali Mojahedi introduces a thick book in numerous volumes. The Leader asks about his family. We believe someone has visited Mr Mojahedi's mother on behalf of the Leader. Khalil Shafiei comes forward with a few books. He shows one and says: "I collected this book to respond to your concern about religious songs. You said they should be more frequently used in religious festivities." *Āghā* sees Mohammad Kazem Kazemi (Afghan Poet) and greets him. He then says: "I read the *Showkarān dar Sātgin-e Sorkh* (Hemlock in the Red Glass). It is a good novel. I told your President when I saw him recently. He said they found the writer and they are taking care of him."

Kazemi said: "Yes, the writer is Hossein Fakhri. The story is about the time of communists." *Āghā* repeats that he has read the novel. Kazemi thanks *Āghā* for the good developments in regard to Afghan refugees. *Āghā* says: "We like you. We like Afghans and it is not a new thing. When I was young and lived in Mashhad, I used to work with Afghan friends. I liked you since then" […]

The guests say their prayers behind the Leader and then they go inside for *Iftar*. After *Iftar* the poetry readings start. *Āghā* makes jokes when the occasion arises. Qazveh speaks of the powerful poetry movements in *howzeh* (the religious seminaries). Then the poets from neighbouring countries start to read. *Āghā* admires Saeedi's poem and says: "Afghanistan literature is showing its true essence." Dr Naghi Abbas, from India, reads a poem about the Prophet. After every single verse, *Āghā* and the crowd say "Bravo! Bravo!" Seyed Ahmad Hosseini from Pakistan and Nasir Nadim from Balkh read next. Nasir's poem is praised when in some lines he talks about the defenders of the shrines – Iranian-backed fighters in Syria who are [according to the Iranian government] defending the *shi'a* sacred places. Younger poets are next to read. A teenage student, Ruhollah Akbari reads a love ghazal. *Āghā* enquires about his age and the length of time he has been writing poetry. Mohammad Barzegar says: "*Āghā*, I want to read a love poem in Nima's style." When he reads his poem, the Leader of the Revolution says: "This poem is something between Nima's style and free verse. You know that Nima never wrote free verse. Free verse was an invention of Nima's followers." The attendees confirm. He then says: "But I am not sure if this was in Nima's style or in free verse." Then Nasser Feiz reads a satiric poem. After some other poems, the end of reading is announced. It is half past eleven. Then the leader starts his talk. He says that poets are many and the poems are good but he wishes for better. He emphasizes the importance of revolutionary songs and encourages poets to write songs. He gives some examples of the social influence of songs. He continues to say that poets are among the dearest of national treasures and that poetry is like the national development fund. We save poetry so that we might use it someday. He uses this argument to say that poetry should be committed and cannot be indifferent. Even love poetry should carry messages inside it.

He criticises the support for some *velengār* [unprincipled, decadent] artists who do not believe in the Revolution and says: "The authorities should support committed literature." *Āghā* also wants the literature and poetry centres to be sponsored and promoted. He repeats that he has drawn his sword but the battlefield is different today. There is a lot of work to be done in poetry. He then emphasizes the importance of poetry translation and the beauty of diction. He finishes his talk by emphasizing the significance of ritualistic and religious poetry.

As he sits down, poets come close and circle round him. The youngest poet of the circle has his ring blessed at the hand of the Leader[…] Many poets congratulate Moaddab, whose poetry received the leader's admiration. They hug him and praise him. Saeed Biyabanaki says sarcastically: "Moaddab is the next minister of culture."

We step outside! Happy and optimistic about the poetry of this land! Poets are watching the full moon and say: Thanks God!"

45 Ayatollah Khamenei, '*Bayānāt dar Didār bā Shāerān dar Māh-e Mobārak-e Ramadhan*', 16 September 2002 (Tehran: Khamenei Portal, 2008) <http://farsi.khamenei.ir/speech-content?id=4083> [accessed 26 February 2015].
46 Ayatollah Khamenei, '*Bayānāt dar Didār-e Jam'i az Shoarā*', 5 September 2009 (Tehran: Khamenei Portal, 2009) <http://farsi.khamenei.ir/speech-content?id=8001> [accessed 26 February 2015].
47 Ayatollah Khamenei, '*Bayānāt dar Didār-e Dastandarkārān-e Hamāyesh-e Nekudāsht-e Ostād Moshfegh Kashani*', 12 August 2013 (Tehran: Khamenei Portal, 2013) <http://farsi.khamenei.ir/speech-content?id=23500> [accessed 26 February 2015].
48 Ayatollah Khamenei, '*Bayānāt dar Didār-e A'zāy-e Goruh-e Adab va Honar-e Sedāy-e Jomhuri-e Eslami*', 24 February 1992 (Tehran: Khamenei Portal, 1992) <http://farsi.khamenei.ir/speech-content?id=2597> [accessed 26 February 2015].
49 Ayatollah Khamenei, '*Bayānāt dar Didār-e Jam'i az Javānān*', 27 April 1998 (Tehran: Khamenei Portal, 1998) <http://farsi.khamenei.ir/speech-content?id=2884> [accessed 26 February 2015].
50 Ayatollah Khamenei portal '*Enteshār-e Dastneveshtay-e Akhavan Saleth dar Daftar-e Yāddāsht-e Ayatollah Khamenei*',27 August 2014 (Tehran: Khamenei Portal, 2014) <http://farsi.khamenei.ir/news-content?id=27292> [accessed 26 February 2015].
51 Ayatollah Khamenei, '*Bayānāt dar Didār-e Honarmandān va Mas'ulān-e Farhangi-e Keshvar*', 14 October 1994 (Tehran: Khamenei Portal, 1994) <http://farsi.khamenei.ir/speech-content?id=12893> [accessed 26 February 2015].
52 Faraj Sarkoohi,'*Enteqām-e Shāer-e Nāmovafaq az She'r*', (Prague: Radio Farda, 7 July 2010) <http://www.radiofarda.com/content/F7_Commentary_on_Khamenei_Meeting_with_Iranian_Artists/2093557.htm> [accessed 26 February 2015].

53 Ibid.
54 Tasnim News, '*Tavarroqi bar '"Yādestān-e Dust"*', (Tehran: Tasnim News, 22 February 2015) <http://www.tasnimnews.com/Home/Single/661006> [accessed 27 February 2015].
55 Ayatollah Khamenei, '*Bayānāt dar Didār-e Shāerān*', 25 August 2010 (Tehran: Khamenei Portal, 2010) <http://farsi.khamenei.ir/speech-content?id=20753> [accessed 25 January 2015].
56 Fars News: '*Joziyāt-e Khāndani az Motefāvet-tarin Ayādat-e Rahbar-e Enqelāb + Aks*', (Tehran: Fars News Agency, 13 September 2014) <http://www.farsnews.com/newstext.php?nn=13930622000648> [accessed 26 February 2015].
57 Encyclopaedia Iranica, *Etesami, Parvin*, <http://www.iranicaonline.org/articles/etesami-parvin> [accessed 14 February 2017].
58 Ayatollah Khamenei, '*Bayānāt dar Didār-e Honarmandān va Mas'ulān-e Farhangi-e Keshvar*', 13 July 1994 (Tehran: Khamenei Portal, 1994) <http://farsi.khamenei.ir/speech-content?id=12893> [accessed 27 February 2015].
59 Ibid.
60 Ata'ollah Mohajerani, *Mohajerani: Az In Hameh Dorugh Araq-e Sharm bar Chehreh-tān Namineshinad?* (Iran: JARAS, 11 June 2010), <http://www.rahesabz.net/story/17141/> [accessed 13 October 2016]
61 There are hundreds of reports which support the special position of poetry among Iranians. Here is one: Diana Darke, *The Book in every Iranian Home*, 2 November 2014 <https://www.bbc.co.uk/news/magazine-29648166> [accessed 24 July 2018]
62 Edward G. Browne, *The Literature of Persia,* Lecture given at The Persia Society on 26 April 1912, published for the Society by John Hogg, London, 13.
63 Khatereh Sheibani, *The Poetics of Iranian Cinema: Aesthetics, Modernity and Film after the Revolution* (London: I.B. Tauris, 2011), 3.
64 For further information, see: Shamim Doustdar, '*Dah Shab-e Goethe, Revāyat-e Yek Ruydād-e Farhangiy-e Mohem*', *Tamasha*, BBC Persian TV, 17 August 2012 <http://www.bbc.co.uk/persian/arts/2012/08/120817_10nights_tamasha.shtml> [accessed 7 May 2015].
65 Edward G. Browne, *The Literature of Persia*, 12–13.
66 Ibid.
67 Mehdi Aslani, *Kalāgh va Gol-e Sorkh: Khāterat-e Zendān* (Paris: Arash, 2009), 119.

Chapter 3

1 See the website of the Ministry of Culture and Islamic Guidance for more information about the organizational chart and the roles and duties of each division <http://www.farhang.gov.ir/fa/intro> [accessed 8 July 2016].
2 Pre-publication forms are downloadable from the website of the MCIG <http://ketab.farhang.gov.ir/fa/filepool/645/؟فرم-قبل-از-چاپ-مولف-مترجم؟redirectpage=%2ffa%2fforms> [accessed 8 July 2016].
3 Ahmad Rajabzadeh, *Momayyezi-ye Ketāb: Pajuheshi dar 1400 Sanad-e Momayyezi-ye Ketāb dar Sāl-e 1375* (Tehran: Kavir, 2001): 202.
4 Ibid., 60–61.
5 See Chapter 2, 28–29.
6 Blake Atwood, 'Sense and Censorship in the Islamic Republic of Iran', *World Literature Today*, 86, no. 3 (May/June 2012): 38–41.

7 Elaheh Khosravi Yeganeh, *Modir-e Edāreh-ye Ketāb: 'Fe'lan Salāh Namibinim Momayyezān rā Kasi Beshnāsad*' (Tehran: Khabar Online News Agency, 2 March 2014) <http://www.khabaronline.ir/X1Sxxhuflpo0wxofgkqckb42tn1/print/341703/culture/literature?model=PresentationWebUI.Models.Details.DetailsPageViewModel> [accessed 30 October 2016].
8 Mohammad Hossein Papoli Yazdi, *Momayyezi-ye Ketāb va Nāsherān-e Setāreh-dār* (Tehran: Alef News, 30 November 2013) http://old.alef.ir/vdcc4mqix2bqx48.ala2.html?20wml [accessed 10 July 2016].
9 *Sarmomayyez-e Ketāb dar Vezārat-e Farhang va Ershād: Man Hayulā Nistam*, (Tehran: Tabnak News, 26 March 2016) HYPERLINK https://www.tabnak.ir/fa/news/576783/%D8%B3%D8%B1%D9%85%D9%85%DB%8C%D8%B2-%DA%A9%D8%AA%D8%A7%D8%A8E2%80%8C%D9%87%D8%A7-%D8%AF%D8%B1-%D9%88%D8%B2%D8%A7%D8%B1%D8%AA-%D9%81-%D8%B1%D9%87%D9%86%DA%AF-%D9%88 [accessed 10 July 2016].
10 Elaheh Khosravi Yeganeh, *Modir-e Edāreh-ye Ketāb: 'Fe'lan Salāh Namibinim Momayyezān rā Kasi Beshnāsad*'.
11 Ibid.
12 *Sarmomayyez-e Ketāb dar Vezārat-e Farhang va Ershād: Man Hayulā Nistam*.
13 Mahmoud Motahharinia, *Mājerā-ye Enteshār-e Ketāb-e 101 Professor-e Khatarnāk dar America* (Tehran: Mashregh News, 7 October 2013) <http://www.mashreghnews.ir/fa/news/253130/کتاب-انتشار-ماجرای-101-پروفسور-خطرناک-در-آمریکاچرا-مجوز-انتشار-کتب-مخرب-باطل-نمی-شودC%8%80%E2> [accessed 12 July 2016].
14 Ibid.
15 Rajabzadeh, 89.
16 John Milton, *Areopagitica*, ed. J.C. Suffolk (London: University Tutorial Press, 1968), 88.
17 Rajabzadeh, 93.
18 For a discussion on the effects of political factionalism on Iranian cultural policies see: Sussan Siavoshi, 'Cultural Policies and the Islamic Republic: Cinema and Book Publication', *International Journal of the Middle East Studies* 29, no. 4, (November 1997): 509–530.
19 Farrokh Amirfaryar, 'Nashr-e Ketāb dar Sāl-e 1377', *Jahān-e Ketāb*, 87–88 (October 1999): 2.
20 Fatemeh Shams, 'Ideology of Warfare and the Islamic Republic's Poetry of War', *International Journal of Persian Literature*, 1 (2016): 5–58.
21 Amirfaryar, 2.
22 Sussan Siavoshi, 510
23 Amirfaryar, 3.
24 Mohammad Khatami, *Zendagināmeh* (Tehran: Khatami Portal, 2015) <http://www.khatami.ir/biography.html> [accessed 11 February 2015].
25 Amirfaryar, 3.
26 I have personally seen this note. I accompanied Ali Abdollahi to the Book Office and was present when the note was handed to him.
27 Amirfaryar, 3.
28 Christopher de Bellaigue, *The Struggle for Iran* (New York: New York Review of Books, 2007), 7.
29 Amirfaryar, 3.
30 Alireza Mahdiani and Seyed Hassan Mortezavi; *Simā-ye Nashr-e-Ketāb dar Iran tayy-e do Daheh-ye Akhir*, *Rahyāft*, 31 (Autumn and Winter 2003): 29.

31 Mohammad Khatami, *Fardāy-e Behtar barāy-e Iran-e Eslāmi* (Tehran: Salam Newspaper Special Issue, April 1997): 50.
32 Amir Hassan Cheheltan, interviewed by Alireza Gholami, *Tajrobeh* 4, no. 32 (October 2014): 27.
33 Seyed Abolhassan Mokhtabad, '*Negāhi be Tahavvolāt-e Ketāb va Nashr dar Dowrāy-e Mohammad Khatami*' (London: BBC Persian online, 8 August 2005) <http://www.bbc.com/persian/arts/story/2005/08/050808_pm-an-book-khatami.shtml> [accessed 25 July 2018].
34 Ibid.
35 Ibid.
36 Payam Yazdanjoo, '*Sarkub-e Maktub: Dāstan-e ketāb dar dowrān-e Ahmadinejad*' (London: BBC Persian online, 30 June 2013) <http://www.bbc.co.uk/persian/blogs/2013/06/130627_blogfa_l44_nazeran_censorship> [accessed 17 February 2015].
37 Ibid.
38 BBC Persian Online, *Vezārat-e Ershād va Emzāhā-yi ke Zirash Zad; Hasht Sāl Laghv-e Mojavvez-e Ketāb* (London: BBC Persian Online, 31 July 2013) <http://www.bbc.co.uk/persian/arts/2013/07/130724_l41_books_banned_ahmadinejad_list> [accessed 17 February 2015].
39 Bahram Rafiee, *Mahdudiyat-hā-ye Jadid-e Vezārat-e Ershād*, ([n.p.]: Ettelaat Network, [n.d.]) <http://www.ettelaat.net/06-04/news.asp?id=13300> [accessed 17 February 2015].
40 BBC Persian Online, *Monāzereh-ye Bisābeqeh-ye Entekhābāti Mian-e Ahmadinejad va Mousavi*, (London: BBC Persian Online, 3 June 2009) <http://www.bbc.co.uk/persian/iran/2009/06/090603_op_ir88_mousavi_ahmadinejad_debate> [accessed 17 February 2015].
41 Ibid.
42 BBC Persian Online, *Vezārat-e Ershād va Emzāhā-yi ke Zirash Zad; Hasht Sāl Laghv-e Mojavvez-e Ketāb*.
43 BBC Persian Online, *Sālhā-ye Siyāh-e Farhang; Enteqād-e Tond-e Jam'i az Shāerān-e Irani az Dowlat-e Ahmadinejad* (London: BBC Persian Online, 19 September 2013) <http://www.bbc.co.uk/persian/arts/2013/09/130919_l41_book_ershad_advice_poetry_day> [accessed 23 February 2015].
44 Ali Jeihoon, *Hamchenān Zemestān Ast, Negāhi be Sānsur pas az Enqelāb*(London: BBC Persian online, 6 February 2014) <http://www.bbc.co.uk/persian/iran/2014/02/140205_l44_35th_iran_revolution_censorship> [accessed 20 February 2015].
45 Farnaz Amiri, *Goftogu bā Mohsen Parviz dar Bāreh-ye Sānsur va Moāvenat-e Farhangi*, *Āsemān*, 63 (24 September 2013): 102.
46 BBC Persian Online, *Vazir-e Ershād: Dastgāh-hā-ye Amniyati be Barkhi az Modirān-e Farhangi-ye Sabeq Dikta Mikardand* (London: BBC Persian Online, 4 December 2013) <http://www.bbc.co.uk/persian/arts/2013/12/131204_l41_book_jannati_security_comments> [accessed 20 February 2015].
47 Ibid.
48 Alef News, *Rouhani: Naqd-e Rang-e Kafsh va Lebās Naqd Nist* (Tehran: Alef News, 8 February 2015) <http://alef.ir/vdcewo8wpjh8nxi.b9bj.html?259326> [accessed 23 February 2015].
49 BBC Persian Online, *Rouhani az Sharāyet-e Momayyezi-e Ketāb dar Iran Enteqad kard* (London: BBC Persian Online, 8 February 2015) <http://www.bbc.co.uk/persian/iran/2015/02/150208_iran_book_audit_censorship_rouhani> [accessed 23 February 2015].
50 *Kārnāmeh-ye Yeksāleh*, *Andisheh-ye Azād* 3, no. 8 (August 2014): 3–4.

Chapter 4

1 *Sarmomayyez-e Ketāb dar Vezārat-e Farhang va Ershād: Man Hayulā Nistam*, (Tehran: Tabnak News, 26 March 2016). https://www.tabnak.ir/fa/news/ 576783/%D8%B3%D8%B1%D9%85%D9%85%DB%8C%D8%B2- %DA%A9%D8%AA%D8%A7%D8%A8%E2%80%8C%D9%87%D8%A7- %D8%AF%D8%B1-%D9%88%D8%B2%D8%A7%D8%B1%D8%AA-%D9%81- %D8%B1%D9%87%D9%86%DA%AF-%D9%88 [accessed 10 July 2016].
2 Motahharinia. *Mājerā-ye Enteshār-e Ketāb-e 101 Professor-e Khatarnāk dar America*, (Tehran: Mashregh News, 7 October 2013). <http://www.mashreghnews.ir/fa/news/ - 101 - کتاب-انتشار-ماجرای-نمی-باطل-مخرب-کتب E8%80%2C > شود [accessed 12 July 2016].
3 Since the quotations from Rajabzadeh's book are frequent in this chapter, I decided not to reference every individual quote lest it hampers an uninterrupted and comfortable reading experience. Whenever a different source is used, it is referenced in the usual manner. Where a quote is not referenced, the source is: Ahmad Rajabzadeh, *Momayyezi-ye Ketāb: Pajuheshi dar 1400 Sanad-e Momayyezi-ye Ketāb dar Sāl-e 1375* (Tehran: Kavir, 2001): 97–262.
4 Ida Meftahi, *Historicizing Ibtizal as a Counter-Aesthetics Corporeal Criterion*, Forum for the Cultural Studies of Iran (17–19 June 2016), University of St. Andrews <http:// forumfortheculturalstudiesofiran.wp.st-andrews.ac.uk/conferences/abstracts-and- bios/> [accessed 29 October 2016].
5 Lili Golestan, *Goftand Sineh az Dast-e Rad bar Sineh-ash Zad Hazf Shavad*, (Tehran: ISNA, 25 May 2014), <http://www.isna.ir/news/93030401508/ شود-حذف-زد-اش-سینه-بر-رد-دست-از-سینه-گفتند> [accessed 12 July 2016].
6 Author not named in the documents.
7 Author not named in the documents.
8 Author not named in the documents.
9 Author not named in the documents.
10 Author not named in the documents.
11 Masoud Ahmadi, interviewed by Alireza Abiz, 14 August 2012.
12 Alison Flood, 'Man Asian Literary Prize announces longlist', *The Guardian*, 2 November 2011, <http://www.theguardian.com/books/2011/nov/02/man-asian- literary-prize-shortlist> [accessed 23 February 2015].
13 Jan Michalski Foundation, *Edition 2013* (Montricher: Jan Michalski, 2013) <http:// www.fondation-janmichalski.com/en/prix-jan-michalski/edition-2013/> [accessed 23 February 2015].
14 Amir Hakkak, *Mahmoud Dowlatabadi: Barā-ye Ākharin bār be Vezārat-e Ershād Miravam* (London: BBC Persian Online, 8 November 2014) <http://www.bbc.co.uk/ persian/arts/2014/11/141107_l41_book_Dolatabadi> [accessed 23 February 2015].
15 Ibid.
16 Kamran Talattof, *The Politics of Writing in Iran: A History of Modern Persian Literature* (New York: Syracuse University Press, 2000), 6–7.
17 I'm unaware of what the censor means by 'soft text'. It's possible that he is alluding to 'soft war' which the Iranian leader claims the West is waging against Iran.
18 Ahmad Kasravi (1890–1946) was a linguist, lawyer, and a public intellectual. He was a critic of Islam, mainly of Shi'a Clergy. He was assassinated, along with his assistant, by a Shi'a cleric called Navvab Safavi and two of his followers inside the courts of justice in Tehran.
19 Author not named in the documents.
20 Author not named in the documents.

21 Rajabzadeh lists a number of poetry collections censored for no obvious reasons. The list includes *Kabutarān-e Sahar* (The Doves of Dawn) by Taraneh Sohrab, *Nabz-e Ettefāq* (The Pulse of Incident) by Iraj Safshekan, *Sarzamin-e Man, Bānu-ye Man* (My Homeland, My Lady) by Manouchehr Cohen, *Dar Jostoju-ye Ān Loghat-e- Tanhā* (In Search of that Lonely Word) by Yadollah Royaee, *Seksekeh-hā-ye Mard-e Pelāstiki* (Hiccups of the Plastic Man) by Amir Aslani, *Ruzhā-ye Talkh* (Bitter Days) by Afsaneh Afrooz, *Entezār Tanhā Hādeseh Bud* (Waiting Was the Only Accident) by Narguess Esmaili, *Man-o- Nāzi* (Me and Nāzi) by Hossein Panahi, *Az to tā Tarāneh* (From You to the Song) by Mohsen Saeed Sadat, *Sāqi va Jām* (Saqi and the Cup) by Hashemi Gohar, see Rajabzadeh, 229.

22 *Vezārat-e Ershād bar Tabl-e Biqānuni Mikubad* (Tehran: ILNA,27 January 2016) <http://www.ilna.ir/-6/295541-وزارت-ارشاد-بر-طبل-بی-قانونی-می-کوبد-بی-قانونی-ارشاد-بر-طبل-بی-قانونی-می-کوبد-بی-قانونی-> در-کتاب-کودک-تا-کجا-ادامه-دارد [accessed 19 September 2016]

23 Ibid.
24 Ibid.
25 Ibid.

26 *Vazir-e Ershād: Ham Mamnu'olqalam Dāshtim, Ham List-e Siāh* (Tehran: Khabar Online, 13 January 2014) <http://www.khabaronline.ir/detail/332509/culture/book> [accessed 27 October 2016].

27 For example, Hafez Mousavi told RFI (Radio France Internationale) that he had submitted two books of poetry during Ahmadinejad's presidency and had accepted all the corrections demanded by the censorship authorities. Nevertheless, no licence was issued and he was told that the licence for one of his books had been lost. He claims that he followed the case through his publisher and discovered that the authorities from outside the Book Office – security forces – had unofficially blacklisted some writers including himself, as well as a number of publishers. RFI Persian: Jahan-e Ketab (Paris: RFI, 2 January 2014) <http://fa.rfi.fr/گفت20140102-/هنر-و-فرهنگ%8C%80%E2%وگو-با- حافظ-موسوی،-یکی-از-شاعران-ممنوع-القلم-در-ایران> [accessed 19 April 2017].

28 Mohammad Hosseini, *Mamnu'olqalam az kojā Āmad?* Interview (Tehran: Farhangnews, 5 December 2013) <www.farhangnews.ir/content/55250> [accessed 19 April 2017].

29 Seyed Abbas Salehi, quoted by Elaheh Khosravi Yeganeh, *Mamnu'olqalamhā az Sāyeh Birun Āmadand* (Tehran: Khabar Online, 30 December 2013) <www.khabaronline.ir/detail/330096/culture/literature> [accessed 19 April 2017].

30 Sarmomayyez-e Ketāb dar Vezārat-e Farhang va Ershād: Man Hayulā Nistam.

31 Sussan Siavoshi, 'Cultural Policies and the Islamic Republic: Cinema and Book Publication', *International Journal of the Middle East Studies* 29, no. 4, (November 1997): 509–530.

32 Mostafa Khalaji, Bronwen Robertson and Maryam Aghdami, *Cultural Censorship in Iran – Iranian Culture in a State of Emergency* (London: Small Media Foundation, July 2011) <http://smallmedia.org.uk/censorship.pdf> [accessed 27 February 2015].

33 Adel Biabangard Javan (Facebook chat with the author, 26 December 2014).

34 Nasser Zera'ati, *Holul-e Ruh-e Afsar-e Nāzi dar Sansurchiy-e Vezārat-e Ershād* (Amsterdam: Radio Zamaneh, 12 May 2016) <https://www.radiozamaneh.com/277022> [accessed 29 July 2018].

35 This demand is contradictory in itself. If his name is deleted, there will be no need to clarify his status.

36 Alireza Hassani, private chat with the author in Telegram, 26 September 2016.

37 Vladimir Holan, *Selected Poems*, eds Jamila and Ian Milner (Middlesex: Penguin Books, 1971).

Chapter 5

1. Ali Jannati, *Māhvāreh Ham Mesl-e Digar Padideh-hā Paziropteh Shavad* (Tehran: Tabnak News, 25 July 2016) <http://www.tabnak.ir/fa/news/608837/جنتی-ماهواره-هم-مثل-دیگر-پدیده‌هاپذیرفته‌شود%E2%80%8C> [accessed 26 September 2016].
2. Mehdi Ghadimi, Mohammad Hassan Najmi, Masoud Kazemi: *Budjeh-ye Farhangi-ye Keshvar Koja Hazineh Mishavad?*, Shargh, no. 2561 (17 April 2016): 6.
3. Ahmad Karimi-Hakkak, 'Authors and Authorities: Censorship and Literary Communication in the Islamic Republic of Iran' in *Persian Studies in North America: Studies in Honor of Mohammad Ali Jazayery*, ed. Mehdi Marashi (Bethesda, Maryland: Iranbooks, 1994), 311.
4. Ibid.
5. Matthew Bunn, 'Reimagining Repression: New Censorship Theory and After', *History and Theory* 54, no. 1 (2015): 25–44.
6. Dario Fo, 'When they Beat Us, We Suffer', in *An Embarrassment of Tyrannies: Twenty-Five Years of Index on Censorship*, eds W.L. Webb and Rose Bell (London: Victor Gollancz, 1997), 122–125.
7. Website of Golshiri Foundation, <http://www.golshirifoundation.com/award.htm> [accessed 28 February 2015].
8. Alireza Bahrami, *'Ehdā-ye Pesteh bejā-ye Jāyezeh-ye Naqdi'* (Tehran: Asr-e-Iran News, 2013) <http://www.asriran.com/fa/news/262257/%D8%A7%D9%87%D8%AF%D8%A7%DB%8C-%D9%BE%D8%B3%D8%AA%D9%87-%D8%A8%D9%87-%D8%AC%D8%A7%DB%8C-%D8%AC%D8%A7%DB%8C%D8%B2%D9%87-%D9%86%D9%82%D8%AF%DB%8C> [accessed 28 February 2015].
9. Website of Golshiri Foundation <http://www.golshirifoundation.com/award.htm> [accessed 28 February 2015].
10. Website of Tehran Goldsmiths and Jewellers Trade Union, <http://www.tgju.org/> [accessed 15 March 2015].
11. Āl-e Ahmad Award, *Āyinnāmeh-ye Ejrāyi-e Jāyezeh-ye Adabi-ye Jalal Āl-e Ahmad*, (Tehran: Āl-e Ahmad Award, 2015) <http://jalalprize.ir/%D8%A2%D8%A6%DB%8C%D9%86%E2%80%8C%D9%86%D8%A7%D9%85%D9%87%D9%94-%D8%AC%D8%A7%DB%8C%D8%B2%D9%87/> [accessed 28 June 2015].
12. Parvin Award, *Award Bylaws* (Tehran: Parvin Award, 2015) <http://www.parvin.ir/HomePage.aspx?TabID=4501&Site=parvin&Lang=fa-IR> [accessed 28 February 2015].
13. See the website of Fajr Poetry Award, <http://www.fajrpoem.com/fa/index.php#section1> [accessed 28 September 2016].
14. See the Website of Festivals Centre of Art Council, <http://www.artfest.ir/festivals/57> [accessed 28 September 2016].
15. Ibid.
16. Nafiseh Esmaili, *Chand Sekkeh-ye Bahār-e Āzādi dar Dowlat-hā-ye Nohom va Daham e'tā Shod?* (Tehran: Fars News Agency, 29 May 2013) <http://www.farsnews.com/newstext.php?nn=13920307000357> [accessed 17 May 2015].
17. Political Studies and Research Institute, *Negāhi be Jāyezeh-hā-ye Adabi-ye Defā'e Moqaddas az Did-e Kārshenāsān* (Tehran: PSRI, 2015) <http://www.irpsri.com/Show.php?Page=ViewNews&NewsID=4159> [accessed 29 February 2015].
18. Faraj Sarkoohi, *'Ma'nā-ye Jāyezeh-ye Jalal'* (Amsterdam: Radio Zamaneh, 4 December 2014) <http://www.radiozamaneh.com/191456> [accessed 29 February 2015].
19. Masoud Ahmadi, interviewed by Alireza Abiz, 14 August 2012.

20 Tasnim News, *Be Vaqt-e Mahtāb, Dehbashi, Televizion va Montaqedān* (Tehran: Tasnim News, 21 January 2015) <http://www.tasnimnews.com/Home/Single/628344> [accessed 15 May 2015].
21 Gooya News, *Chāp-e Tasvir-e Shāʻer-e Zendeh ruy-e Ketāb Mamnu' Shod, Sarmāyeh* (Gooya News, August 16,2009) <http://news.gooya.com/society/archives/092267.php> [accessed 18 October 2016].
22 Islamic Parliament of Iran, *the Constitution of the Islamic Republic of Iran as amended in 1989, Chapter XII, Article 175* (Tehran: Islamic Parliament of Iran,n.d.) <http://en.parliran.ir/eng/en/Constitution#chapter_13> [accessed 2 February 2015].
23 Islamic Parliament of Iran, *Preamble to the Constitution of the Islamic Republic of Iran* (Tehran: Islamic Parliament of Iran, 2015) <http://en.parliran.ir/index.aspx?fkeyid=&siteid=84&pageid=3054> [accessed 24 February 2015].
24 Website of the *Hoze Honari*, <http://hozehonari.com/Default.aspx?page=20297> [accessed 24 February 2015].
25 Mehdi Ghadimi, Mohammad Hassan Najmi, Masoud Kazemi.
26 Website of the *Hoze Honari*: <http://hozehonari.com/Default.aspx?page=20501> [accessed 26 September 2016]
27 Sooremehr Publishers Website, '*Fazel Nazari- Zendagināmeh*', <http://www.sooremehr.ir/fa/author/972> [accessed 13 October 2016].
28 Mohammadreza Rostami, '*Sahm-e Vezārat-e Ershād az Budjeh-ye Farhangi Cheqadr Ast? Fehrest-e Nehād-hā-yi ke Barā-ye Kār-e Farhangi Budjeh Migirand*' (Tehran: Khabar Online News Agency, 5 May 2014) <http://www.khabaronline.ir/detail/353289/culture/5519> [accessed 26 February 2015].
29 Website of the Tehran Municipality Cultural-Art Organization, <http://www.farhangsara.ir/%D9%81%D8%B1%D9%87%D9%86%DA%AF%D8%B3%D8%B1%D8%A7%D9%87%D8%A7.aspx> [accessed 26 February 2015].
30 Website of Tabriz Municipality Cultural-Art Organization, <http://honar.tabriz.ir/#جشنواره کتاب سال تبریز> [accessed 26 February 2015].
31 Hossein Noushabadi, *Barkhord-e Jeddi-ye Vezārat-e Ershād Bā Chāp-e Ketāb-hā-ye Bedun-e Mojavvez* (Tehran: IBNA, 7 April 2015) <http://www.ibna.ir/fa/doc/report/220671/برخورد-جدی-وزارت-ارشاد-چاپ-کتاب-های-بدون-مجوز-ورود-کتاب-صورت-قاچاق> [accessed 18 October 2016].
32 Website of Anjoman-e Qalam-e Iran, <http://www.anjomanghalam.ir/?page_id=5> [accessed 26 February 2015].
33 Faraj Sarkoohi, *Anjoman-e Qalam-e Irani va Jahāni, Hamnām va Bishebāhat* (London: BBC Persian Online, 20 December 2011) <http://www.bbc.co.uk/persian/arts/2011/12/111219_l41_book_international_pen_vs_ghalam.shtml> [accessed 26 February 2015].
34 Website of Khāneh-ye Shāerān-e Iran, <http://poetry.ir/?sn=abouts&lang> [accessed 26 February 2015].
35 Khāneh-ye Shāerān-e Iran, *Farākhān-e Ozviyat-e Daftar-e She'r-e Javān* (Tehran: Khāneh-ye Shāerān-e Iran Website, 16 October 2014) <http://poetry.ir/?sn=news&pt=full&lang=&id=daftarsherejavan> [accessed 26 February 2015].
36 Website of Kānun-e Adabiyyāt-e Iran, <http://kanonweb.blogfa.com/> [accessed 26 February 2015].
37 Website of Bonyād-e She'r va Adabiyyāt-e Dāstāni-ye Irāniān, <http://www.adabiatirani.com/fa/> [accessed 26 September 2016].
38 At a conference, Ali Tabibnia, Minister of Commerce and Financial Affairs stated that government's share in the Iranian economy had reached around 90 percent. See

Ali Tabibnia, '*Sahm-e Dowlat az Eqtesād-e Melli Taqriban be 90 Darsad Rasideh-ast*', (Iran: Tabnak News, 28 October 2015) <http://www.tabnak.ir/fa/news/353928/ سهم-دولت-از-اقتصاد-ملی-تقریباً-به-90-در صد-رسیده-است> [accessed 27 September 2016].

39 Mehrangiz Kar, *Sānsur: Si Sāl Hamrāhi bā Enqelāb* (Washington DC: Gozaar, 2 June 2010) <http://www.gozaar.org/persian/articles-fa/4167.html> [accessed 10 March 2015].

40 Sayeh Fathi, '*Rotbeh-bandi-ye Ruznāmeh-hā*', *Tejārat-e Fardā*, June 2014 <http://tejarat.donya-e-eqtesad.com/fa/packagestories/details?story=ddfc7407-68ce-4493-a285-907acccf8aab> [accessed 10 March 2015].

41 Amir Rostagh, *Dah Rokhdād-e Mohemm-e Arseh-ye Ketāb va Nashr dar Sāl-e 93* (London: BBC Persian Online, 23 March 2015) <http://www.bbc.co.uk/persian/arts/2015/03/150323_l51_yearender_93_books> [accessed 29 March 2015].

42 Nehād-e Ketābkhāneh-hā-ye Omumi-ye Keshvar, *Shiveh-hā-ye Kharid-e Manābe' dar Nehād-e Ketābkhāneh-hā-ye Omumi-ye Keshvar* (Tehran: Nehād-e Ketābkhāneh-hā-ye Omumi-ye Keshvar, 2012) <http://www.iranpl.ir/portal/Home/Default.aspx?CategoryID=d2bbc618-ff69-45db-88dd-710b2bd2d281> [accessed 19 March 2015].

43 Statistics from the portal of Tehran International Book Fair, for example, <http://www.tibf.ir/page/535619014c00003f0815368d> [accessed 21 March 2015].

44 One example is a report by Saeed Kamali Dehghan, 'Tehran International Book Fair launches crackdown on "harmful" titles', *The Guardian*, 2 May 2012 <http://www.theguardian.com/world/2012/may/02/tehran-international-book-fair-crackdown> [accessed 17 February 2015].

45 Reza Baraheni, '*Goftogu-ye Hassan Zerehi bā Reza Baraheni*' (Iranian Writers' Association (in Exile)), 4 January 2015) <http://iwae.info/1393/10/14/%DA%AF%D9%81%D8%AA%DA%AF%D9%88%DB%8C-%D8%A2%D9%82%D8%A7%DB%8C-%D8%AD%D8%B3%D9%86-%D8%B2%D8%B1%D9%87%DB%8C-%D8%A8%D8%A7-%D8%AF%DA%A9%D8%AA%D8%B1-%D8%B1%D8%B6%D8%A7-%D8%A8%D8%B1%D8%A7%D9%87%D9%86%DB%8C [accessed 10 March 2015].

46 Mansour Kooshan, *Tabassom-hā va Taa'ssof-hā* (London: H&S Media, 2013), 282.

47 Vahid Pourostad, *Mohākemeh-ye Ādineh* (Tehran: Rooznegār, 2002), 31.

48 Ibid., 46.

49 Not to be mistaken for Lebanese Hezbollah. *Hezbollah* or *Hezbollahi* is a general name for hardline supporters of the Iranian regime. It is used in the same meaning throughout this book.

50 Farnoosh Amirshahi, *Janjāl-hā-ye Kārikāturi*, (London: BBC Persian Online, 30 September 2012) <http://www.bbc.co.uk/persian/iran/2012/09/120930_l42_ir_caricature.shtml> [accessed 10 March 2015].

51 Ibid.

52 BBC Persian Online, '*Māhnāmeh-ye Adabi-ye Kārnāmeh Towqif Shod*' (London: BBC Persian Online, 7 April 2005) <http://www.bbc.co.uk/persian/arts/story/2005/04/050407_pm-karnameh-suspended.shtml> [accessed 10 March 2015].

53 Rebecca Knuth, *Libricide: The Regime-Sponsored Destruction of Books and Libraries in the Twentieth Century* (Westport: Praeger, 2003), 50.

54 Radio Zamaneh, '*Rasāneh-hā-yi ke Madfun Shodand*' (Amsterdam: Radio Zamaneh, 13 February 2008) <http://zamaaneh.com/movie/2008/02/post_77.html> [accessed 15 March 2015].

55 Faraj Sarkoohi, *Yās va Dās* (Sweden: Baran, 2002), 94.

56 Masoud Noghrehkar, '*Tāvān-e Dādkhāhi*' ([n.p]: Asr-e Nou, 29 October 2007) <http://asre-nou.net/1386/aban/7/m-noghrekar.html> [accessed 10 March 2015].

57 Aliasghar Ramezanpour, '*Guneh-yi Naslkoshi-ye Farhangi dar Jariyān Ast*' (interviewed by Payam Ghasemi) (Washington DC: Gozaar, 23 April 2008) <http://www.gozaar.org/persian/interview-fa/3532.html> [accessed 19 March 2015].
58 Sarkoohi, *Yās va Dās*, 102.
59 '*Saeed Emami Pishnehād-e Eslāh-e Qanun-e Matbuāt rā Dadeh Ast*', *Salam* (6 July 1999): 1.
60 Sarkoohi, *Yās va Dās*, 129.
61 In a 'Chicken Kebab', the victim's legs are tied together, their hands are cuffed and they are hung from a rod like a chicken on a roller grill.
62 Ibid.
63 Seyed Ali Salehi, *Chenān ketāb rā bar Gardanam Kubidand ke Taādolam rā az Dast Dādam* (interviewed by Hadi Hosseininejad), ILNA, 17 July 2013) (Tehran: Shahrwandan, 2013) <http://www.shahrwandan.ir/news/12749> [accessed 19 March 2015].
64 Sarkoohi, *Yās va Dās*, 129.
65 Akbar Ganji, *Qatlhā-ye Zanjireh-yi Prozheh-ye Hokumat Bud* (interviewed by Jamshid Barzegar) (London: BBC Persian Online, 7 December 2010) <http://www.bbc.co.uk/persian/iran/2010/12/101207_ganji_serial_murders.shtml>[accessed 23 March 2015].
66 Sarkoohi, *Yās va Dās*, 175.
67 Amir Farshad Ebrahimi, *Barā-ye Mordanash Hanuz Zud Bud* ([n.p.]: Iran Human Rights, [n.d.]) <http://www.irhumanrights.com/sirjani.htm> [accessed 8 April 2015].)
68 Akbar Ganji, *Ālijenāb-e Sorkhpush va Ālijenābān-e Khākestari* (Tehran: Tarh-e Now, 2000), 6.
69 Ganji, interview by Jamshid Barzgar.
70 Sarkoohi, *Yās va Dās*, 154.
71 Ibid., 150.
72 *List-e Terror-e Sepāh-e Sarboland-e Mohammad*, 23 April 2004 <http://news.gooya.com/politics/archives/009574.php> [accessed 23 March 2015].

The letter reads as follows:

Now that we see the devilish scribblers are using their dark and satanic pens to target the Islamic culture and annihilate the righteous principles of Muhammad's religion, following the revolutionary executions of the corrupt and worthless enemy in 1998, we are fully prepared to dry out the seed of corruption in this land. We are ready to send the kaffirs who have surrendered themselves to Satan to hell with the help of the Qur'an and as any truthful free man should do. When our divine country, Iran, is being destroyed at the hand of a bunch of worthless scribblers, no patience is allowed. The punishment of kaffirs who oppose Islam will continue until they are completely uprooted. We, the Proud Army of Muhammad – seeking help from the Almighty and under the shadow of the Holy Qur'an – will wipe out all signs of infidelity and corruption from this land and promise the Muslim and suppressed people of Iran and the families of the martyrs that a better day will arrive. Now that the divine decree is being enforced by the flash of swords of the Proud Army of Muhammad, we request the noble people to pray to God to dry out the dark pens of infidelity. Amen.

In their first revolutionary act, the Proud Army of Muhammad will wash the terrain of Islamic Iran with the corrupt blood of the following group of Corrupters of the Earth:

Mahmoud Dowlatabadi, Ali Ashraf Darvishian, Simin Behbahani, Fariborz Raeis Dana, Seyed Ali Salehi, Mohammad Mohammad Ali, Akbar Masoumbeigi, Ali Sedaghati Khayyat, Changiz Pahlavan, Gholamhossein Salemi, Mohammad Ali Sepanlou, Amir Hassan Cheheltan, Mohammad Khalili, Moniroo Ravanipour, Shirin Ebadi, Javad Mojabi, Abbas Mokhber, Kaveh Goharin, Iraj Kaboli, Mehrangiz Kar, Sayer Mohammadi, Hafez Mousavi, Nastaran Mousavi, Nasser Vahdati, Sadegh

Homayouni, Nahid Foroughan, Pouran Farrokhzad, Mahin Khadivi, Aboutorab Khosravi, Maryam Khorasani, Reza Khandan Mahabadi, Mohammad Ali Shakeri Yekta, Jahed Jahanshahi, Nahid Tavassoli, Alireza Panjaei, Alireza Babayi, Farkhondeh Aqayi, M. Ravanshid, Abdolhamid Abolhamd, Shiva Arastouyi, Majid Amin Moayed, Ali Babachahi, Yarali Pourmoghadam, Changiz Pahlavan, Alireza Jabbari, Reza Chaychi, Aliasghar Rashedan, Moniroo Ravanipour, Nasser Zarafshan, Reza Abed, Farzaneh Taheri, Emran Salahi, Shams Langroodi, Javad Shojaeifard, Faramarz Sedehi, Hossein Sanapour, Esmail Raha, Ghasem Roubin, Jalal Bayram, Firouz Gouran, Hossein Atashparvar, Asghar Elahi, Alireza Abiz, Hashem Banapour, Ghasem Roubin, Farideh Razi, Farzaneh Karampoor, Maryam Khorasani, Iraj Ziayi, Aboutorab Khosravi, Fariba Vafi, Farkhonda Hajizadeh.

[Signed] The Proud Army of Muhammad.

Remarks by the author: some names are repeated in the list.

73 Sarkoohi, *Yās va Dās*, 94.
74 Ganji, *Ālijenāb-e Sorkhpush va Ālijenābān-e Khākestari*, 110.
75 Sarkoohi, *Yās va Dās,* 139.
76 Ibid., 95.
77 Some of the subtitles include 'The Secret Army of Intellectuals', 'The Cavaliers of Cultural NATO', 'Documented Untold Secrets on the 20-year Activity of the Intellectuals', 'The Face of Agents in Culture and Politics: Vol. 8, Daryoush Shayegan, Gholamhossein Saedi, Ahmad Shamlou, Ali Dashti', 'The Face of Agents in Culture and Politics: Vol. 7; Bagher Momeni, Sadegh Hedayat, Simin Behbahani, Abbas Pahlavan, Farrokh Ghaffari, Jafar Rayed'. According to the Keyhan Institute, fifty-three volumes of 'The Hidden Half' have been published so far (April 2015). For further information, see the Keyhān Institute website <http://www.keyhanbook.ir/?cat=4&paged=8> [accessed 12 April 2015].
78 Kalemeh News, *Khātereh-ye Pournejati az Barnameh-ye Hoviyat va Dr. Zarrinkoob* (Tehran: Kalemeh News, 19 September 2013) <http://www.kaleme.com/1392/06/28/klm-158702/> [accessed 2 April 2015].
79 Faraj Sarkoohi, *Ta'qib, Robāyesh, Takzib; an interview with Faraj Sarkoohi* ([n. p.]: Khat-e Solh Monthly, 20 February 2014) <http://www.peace-mark.org/taghib-robayesh-takzib> [accessed 1 April 2015].
80 Ibid.
81 Irena Maryniak 'The Lubianka's Hidden Treasure – An Interview with Vitaly Shentalinsky', in *An Embarrassment of Tyrannies: Twenty-Five Years of Index on Censorship*, ed. by W.L. Webb and Rose Bell (London: Victor Gollancz, 1997), 177–181.
82 Mehrdad Aalikhani, pages from interrogations (unconfirmed), different online sources including <http://freedomvatan.blogspot.co.uk/2009/01/blog-post_06.html> [accessed 14 April 2015].
83 M. Ravanshid, *Bejā-ye Hameh-ye Ānhā ke Gom Shodand: Goftogu bā Hei'at Dabirān-e Kānun-e Nevisandegān-e Iran* (Sweden: Ketāb-e Arzān, 2014), 63.
84 Alireza Jabbari, *Atashi Hargez khāmush Nakhāhad Shod* ([n.p.]: Gooya News, 25 November 2005) <http://news.gooya.com/culture/archives/039920.php> [accessed 13 April 2015].
85 Asr-e Nou News, *'Simin Behbahani: M. Azad bi Ejāzeh Motevalled Shod va bi Ejāzeh ham Dafn Shod'* quoting from ILNA (Asr-e Nou, [n.d.]) <http://asre-nou.net/1384/bahman/12/m-azad.html> [accessed 13 April 2015]. The name 'Azad' means free.

86 Radio Zamaneh, *Raeis Dana: Kānun dar Marasem-e Tashyi'e Simin Behbahani Sherkat Namikonad* (Amsterdam: Radio Zamaneh, 21 August 2014) <http://www.radiozamaneh.com/170851> [accessed 13 April 2015].
87 Ezzatollah Fouladvand, *Az Shekastan-e Sang-e Mazār-e Shamlou tā Āhang-e Veirāni-ye Maqbareh-ye Hafez'*, *Hafiz*, 76 (November 2010): 53.
88 Eghtesad News; *Serial-e Ettefāqāt-e Ajib dar Behesht-e Zahra* (Tehran: Eghtesad News, 8 October 2016) <http://www.eghtesadonline.com/-سریال-30/150533-بخش-عمومی/اتفاقات-عجیب-در-بهشت-زهرا> [accessed 12 October 2016].
89 ISNA, *Ettefāq va E'terāzi Digar dar Bāreh-ye Sang-e Qabr-e Sepanlou* (Tehran: ISNA, 17 October 2016) <http://www.isna.ir/news/95072615144/اتفاق-و-اعتراضی-دیگر-درباره-سنگ-قبر-سپانلو> [accessed 18 October 2016].

Chapter 6

1 Ervand Abrahamian, *Iran between Two Revolutions*, Princeton: Princeton University Press, 1982, 502.
2 'The Declaration of 134 Iranian Writers, 1994', quoted from Mozaffari, Nahid and Ahmad Karimi Hakkak, eds *Strange Times in Persia, an Anthology of Contemporary Iranian Literature*, London: I.B. Tauris, 2009, xv.
3 Ravanshid, M., *Bejā-ye Hameh-ye Ānhā ke Gom Shodand: Goftogu bā Hei'at Dabirān-e Kānun-e Nevisandegān-e Iran*, Sweden: Ketāb-e Arzān, 2014. 32.
4 *'Mojavvez-e Chāp-e Ketāb rā Laghv Konid, Andisheh-ye Āzād*, 3, no. 6 (August 2013): 31.
5 Amir Hassan Cheheltan, interviewed by Alireza Gholami, Tajrobeh 4, no.32 (October 2014): 27.
6 *Andisheh-ye Āzād*, 3, no. 6 (August 2013): 53.
7 For more information, see the website at <http://www.iran-pen.com/english/home.html> [accessed 9 April 2015].
8 For more information, see the website at <http://www.thofs.org> [accessed 12 January 2015].
9 Saeedeh Hassani, *Sānsur Mikonam pas Hastam*, quoted from Qanun <http://sobbekheir.com/entertainment/طنز-سانسور-می%8C%80%E2کنم-پس-هستم> [accessed 12 October 2016].
10 Mehrshad Mortezavi, *Tanz/Sānsur-e Kalameh-ye Sharāb az Ash'ār-e Bozorgān* quoted from Qanun (Tehran: ISNA, January 19, 2016) <http://www.isna.ir/news/94102917402/طنز-سانسور-سی-مملکت-بارش-از-اشعار-بزرگان> [accessed 12 October 2016].
11 Hadi Jamali, *'Ay Delbar-e Man, Ay Qad-o Bālāt Senoqta*, available in many online places, for example, <http://www.cloob.com/u/1saman1/114282193/%D8%A7%DB%8C_%D8%AF%D9%84%D8%A8%D8%B1_%D9%85%D9%86_%D8%A7%DB%8C_%D9%82%D8%AF_%D9%88_%D8%A8%D8%A7%D9%84%D8%A7%D8%AA_%D8%B3%D9%87_%D9%86%D9%82%D8%B7%D9%877> [accessed 12 April 2015].
12 Abdolhossein Azarang, *Nashr-e Makhfi bā Horuf-e Riz*, *Andisheh-ye Puyā*, 23 (January–February 2015), Centre for the Great Islamic Encyclopaedia <http://www.cgie.org.ir/fa/news/27439> [accessed 12 April 2015].
13 DW Persian, *Zakhm-e bāz-e Parvandeh-ye Qatlhā-ye Zanjireh-yi* (Germany: DW Persian, 2 December 2013) <http://www.dw.com/fa-ir/زخم-باز-پرونده-قتلهای-زنجیره/a-17265915> [accessed 4 October 2016].
14 A. M. 'Nush-e Jān-e Shān', *Andisheh-ye Āzād* 3, no. 1 (Spring 2011): 16.

15 *Andisheh-ye Āzād* 3, no. 6 (August 2013): 20.
16 '*Akhbār-e Ahl-e Qalam*', *Andisheh-ye Āzād* 3, no. 4 (September 2012): 14–15.
17 Hossein Noushabadi, *Barkhord-e Jeddi-ye Vezārat-e Ershād Bā Chāp-e Ketāb-hā-ye Bedun-e Mojavvez* (Tehran: IBNA, 7 April 2015) <http://www.ibna.ir/fa/doc/report/ 220671/ صورت-قاچاق-های-بدون-مجوز-ورود-کتاب‌برخورد-جدی-وزارت-ارشاد-چاپ-کتاب-> [accessed 18 October 2016].
18 Entekhab News, *Jam'āvari-ye Ketāb-hā-ye Bedun-e Mojavvez az Namāyeshgāh-e Ketāb* (Tehran: Entekhab, 1 May 2014) <http://www.entekhab.ir/fa/news/159363/ های-بدون-مجوز-از-نمایشگاه-کتاب%E2%80%8Cآوری-کتاب%E2%80%8Cجمع> [accessed 4 October 2016].
19 Nasim News Agency, *Ershād dar Barzakh* (Tehran: Nasim, 28 January 2015) <http:// nasimonline.ir/Content/Detail/974694/ارشاد-در-برزخ> [accessed 4 October 2016].
20 SNN, *Hayulā-yi ke az Vitrin-e Ketābforushi-hā-ye Tehran Sar Dar Āvard* (Tehran: SNN, 27 March 2015) <http://www.snn.ir/print/398319> [accessed 4 October 2016].
21 Sayer Mohammadi, '*Bāzār Siyāh-e Ketāb-hā-ye Jeld Sefid*', *Iran* (27 April 2014): 12.
22 Sepideh Zarrinpanah, *Dar Jostoju-ye Hall-e Moshkel-e Nashr-e Farsi dar khārej-e Keshvar* (London: BBC Persian Online, 30 June 2011) <http://www.bbc.co.uk/persian/ arts/2011/06/110630_l41_book_farsi_publication_abroad.shtml> [accessed 8 April 2015].
23 Nogaam Website <http://nogaam.com/books/published/> [accessed 12 October 2016].
24 H&S Media website <http://www.hands.media/books/> [accessed 12 October 2016].
25 Persian was the third language after English and Portugese according to a report in 2003 <http://web.archive.org/web/20031202022722/http://www.blogcensus. net/?page=lang> [accessed 30 October 2016].
26 Lourent Giacobini et al. *Whither Blogestan: Evaluating Shifts in Persian Cyberspace*, (Iran Media Program, University of Pennsylvania, March 2014) <http://www. iranmediaresearch.org/en/research/download/1607> [accessed 30 September 2016], 5.
27 Parisa Tonekaboni, *Weblogistān-e Fārsi be Kodām Su Miravad* (Germany: Goethe Institute, May 2015) <http://www.goethe.de/ges/phi/prj/ffs/the/103/fa14587618.htm> [accessed 30 September 2016].
28 Lourent Giacobini et al., 15.
29 Ibid., 5.
30 Ibid., 5.
31 Mehdi Jami, *Weblogistān Hāfezeh-ye Jam'i-ye Māst* (Sibestaan blog, 8 September 2015) <http://sibestaan.malakut.org/4120> [accessed 31 October 2016].
32 Some popular websites include: <https://azadieiran2.wordpress.com/>, <http://ketabnak.com/>, <http://www.takbook.com/>, <http://www.parsbook.org/>, <http://www.irebooks.com/>. An example of a book-sharing club in social media is <https://www.facebook.com/groups/BashgaheKetab/>.
33 Lev Loseff, *On the Beneficence of Censorship: Aesopian Language in Modern Russian Literature* (Munchen: Sanger, 1984), x.
34 Ibid., pages 86–124 contain a description of poetics of Aesopian language and different tools used for that purpose.
35 *Little Black Fish* and *24 Hours Between Dream and Reality* by Behrangi are good examples of political allegory disguised as children's stories.
36 Joseph Brodsky, quoted in *On the Beneficence of Censorship: Aesopian Language in Modern Russian Literature* by Lev Loseff (Munchen: Sagner, 1984), 12.

37 Lev Lifshitz-Losev, 'What it means to be censored', trans. Joseph Deney, *The New York Review of Books*, 29 June 1978, <https://www.nybooks.com/articles/1978/06/29/what-it-means-to-be-censored/> [accessed 20 July 2017].
38 See, for example, his novels '*Sou-e Qasd be Zāt-e Homāyuni*' set in Qajar era, '*Yek Parvanday-e Kohneh*' set in the Pahlavi era, *Simāb va Kimiyāy-e Jān*' set during the Mongol invasion of Asia.
39 None of the major works by Khosravi including his three novels, '*Rood-e Rāvi*', 'Asfār-e Kātebān', and '*Malakān-e Azāb*' reveal the setting of the story.
40 Mohammadreza Pourjafari (in conversation with Alireza Abiz, 23 March 2012).
41 Mohammad Ali Sepanlou, Interview, *Mardomsālāri*, 3602 (23 October 2014): 6.

Chapter 7

1 Fatemeh Shams, 'The Dialectic of Poetry and Power in Iran', *Dirasat* (published by King Faisal Center for Research and Islamic Studies), no. 3 (February 2015): 18.
2 Ahmad Karimi-Hakkak, 'Authors and Authorities: Censorship and Literary Communication in the Islamic Republic of Iran' in *Persian Studies in North America: Studies in Honor of Mohammad Ali Jazayery*, ed. Mehdi Marashi (Bethesda, Maryland: Iranbooks, 1994), 314.
3 Fatemeh Shams, The Dialectic of Poetry and Power in Iran, 19.
4 Ibid., 29–30.
5 Mehdi Moosavi, Fatemeh Ekhtesari, and Mohammadreza Haji Rostam Begloo are three examples of poets who call themselves progressive or postmodern ghazal writers. All three were forced into exile after spending some time in jail for poetry-related offences.
6 '*She'r-e Daheh-ye Haftād dar Goftogu-ye Ekhtesāsi bā Houshyar Ansarifar, Tamasha*, BBC Persian TV, 4 November 2014 <http://www.bbc.com/persian/arts/2014/11/141104_l42_vid_tamasha_houshyar_ansarifard> [accessed 21 February 2015].
7 Alice Nakhimovsky. 'Review of "On the Beneficence of Censorship: Aesopian Language in Modern Russian Literature" by Lev Loseff', *The Slavic and East European Journal* 30 (Autumn 1986): 453–455.
8 Ahmad Karimi-Hakkak. Authors and Authorities: Censorship and Literary Communication in the Islamic Republic of Iran, 309.
9 Beate Müller, 'Mapping the Territory' in *Censorship and Cultural Regulation in the Modern Age*, ed. Beate Müller (Amsterdam: Rodopi B.V., 2004), 1–31, 16.
10 See the part on Punishment in Chapter 5.
11 Fanoos Bahadorvand '*Āncheh be Nām-e Momayyezi dar Edāreh-ye Arzeshyābi-ye ketāb-e Vezārat-e Ershād Rokh Midahad*', *Andisheh-ye Āzād* 3, no. 4 (September 2012): 16.
12 Reza Jolayi, interviewed by Alireza Gholami, *Tajrobeh* 3, no. 22 (August 2013): 57.
13 Christopher de Bellaigue, *The Struggle for Iran* (New York: New York Review of Books, 2007), 205.
14 Mansour Khalaj, interviewed by *Namāyeshnāmeh Quarterly*, nos. 2 and 3 (Summer and Autumn 2011): 42.
15 M. Ravanshid, *Bejā-ye Hameh-ye Ānhā ke Gom Shodand: Goftogu bā Hei'at Dabirān-e Kānun-e Nevisandegān-e Iran* (Sweden: Ketāb-e Arzān, 2014), 54-56.
16 Ahmad Mahmoud, *Memoirs*, published posthumously on Persian Contemporary Fiction Channel in Telegram, 31 October 2016.

17 Masoud Ahmadi, interviewed by Alireza Abiz, 14 August 2012.
18 Philip Roth, 'In Prague', *The New Yorker* (3 May 2013) <http://www.newyorker.com/books/page-turner/in-prague> [accessed 18 June 2015].
19 Ketabenaab Website, *Negāhi be Hāshiyeh-hā-ye Romān-e 'Davāzdahom'-e Moazzeni; Daghdagheh-hā-ye Dini yā Siāsikāri?/ Enfe'āl-e Sāderkonandegān-e Mojavvez* <http://ketabenaab.ir/1393/05/10/%D9%86%DA%AF%D8%A7%D9%87%DB%8C-%D8%A8%D9%87-%D8%AD%D8%A7%D8%B4%DB%8C%D9%87%E2%80%8C%D9%87%D8%A7%DB%8C-%D8%B1%D9%85%D8%A7%D9%86-%D8%AF%D9%88%D8%A7%D8%B2%D8%AF%D9%87%D9%85-%D9%85%D9%88%D8%B0/> [accessed 20 April 2015].
20 Mehr News Agency; *Shāhnāmeh-e Dovvom Cheguneh Khalq Shod*, (Tehran: Mehr News Agency, 6 May 2015) <http://www.mehrnews.com/news/2569660/شاهنامه-دوم-چگونه-خلق-شد-کاملترین-شرح-منظوم-زندگی-امام-علی-ع> [accessed 29 October 2016].
21 Shabnam News, *Budjeh-ye Āfarinesh va Pazhuhesh dar Bonyād Kamtar az Dastmozd-e yek Fasl-e Bāzikon-e Football Ast* (Tehran: Shabnam News, 23 April 2014) <http://www.shabnamnews.com/news/14479> [accessed 21 April 2015].
22 Kaveh Mirabbasi, *Adabiyyāt-e Āpārtemāni Ravāj Peidā Kardeh-ast* (Tehran: IBNA, 6 August 2008) <http://www.ibna.ir/fa/doc/tolidi/23731/میر-عباسی-ادبیات-آپارتمانی-رواج-پیدا-کرده> [accessed 13 October 2016].
23 Ata'tollah Mohajerani, *Mohajerani: Az In Hameh Dorugh Araq-e Sharm bar Chehrehtān Namineshinad?* (Iran: JARAS, 11 June 2010), <http://www.rahesabz.net/story/17141/> [accessed 13 October 2016].
24 Hassan Mahmoudi, *Momayezzi be Romān-e Man Zarbeh Zad* (Tehran: Khabar Online, 22 August 2014) <http://www.khabaronline.ir/detail/371300/culture/literature> [accessed 12 October 2016].
25 Asr-e Iran, *Taqdir-e Rahbar-e Enqelāb az Rāvi va Nevisandeh-ye Ketab-e Dā* (Tehran: Asr-e Iran, 10 May 2010) <http://www.asriran.com/fa/news/113741/تقدیر-رهبر-انقلاب-از-راوی-و-نویسنده-کتاب-دا> [accessed 13 October 2016]
26 Ibid.
27 Sooremehr Website; *ketāb-e Dā* (Tehran: Sooremehr Website) <http://www.sooremehr.ir/fa/book/2235/کتاب-دا> [accessed 13 October 2016].
28 Link to the book's page in publisher's website: <http://www.mazdapublishers.com/book/one-womans-war> [accessed 13 October 2016].
29 Alireza Kamari, *Dā Māhiyati Goftār Nevesht Dārad, Romān Nist* (Tehran: IBNA, 29 May 2009) <http://www.ibna.ir/fa/doc/report/38756/دا-ماهیتی-گفتار-نوشت-رمان-نیست> [accessed 13 October 2016].
30 Amir Hassan Cheheltan, *Mikhāhand Romāni Benevisam ke dar Ān Zendagi-e Irani ra Tahrif Karda Bāsham* (Tehran: ILNA, 21 June 2016) <http://www.ilna.ir/می-379387/6-خواهند-رمانی-بنویسم-که-در-آن-زندگی-ایرانی-را-تحریف-کرده-باشم> [accessed 13 October 2016].
31 Ibid.
32 Faraj Sarkoohi, '*Haft ruz-e ketāb* (London: BBC Persian Online, 1 September 2011) <http://www.bbc.co.uk/persian/arts/2011/09/110901_l41_books_7_days_1sep_11> [accessed 14 April 2015].
33 Mohammad Hashem Akbariani, '*Yādhā-yi az Sālhā-ye Dur va Nazdik*', E'temād (16 April 2015): 16. <http://www.etemaad.ir/Default.aspx?NPN_Id=125&PageNO=16#> [accessed 20 April 2015].
34 Cheheltan, 40.
35 Ibid., 37.

36 Masoud Ahmadi.
37 Aamout Publishers, '*Porforushtarinhā*' (Tehran: Aamout Publishers, 19 March 2015) <http://www.aamout.com/search/label/alireza-roshan> [accessed 22 April 2015].
38 For information about their arrest, see Harriet Staff 'Iranian Poets Fateme Ekhtesari and Mehdi Moosavi Imprisoned', <http://www.poetryfoundation.org/harriet/2013/12/iranian-poets-fateme-ekhtesari-and-mehdi-moosavi-imprisoned/> [accessed 22 April 2015].
39 Wole Soyinka, 'Jihad for Freedom', *Index on Censorship* 18, no. 5 (1989): 20–21.
40 Breyten Breytenbach, *End Papers* (London: Faber & Faber, 1986), 134.
41 Ibid., 109.
42 Effim Etkind, *Notes of a Non-conspirator*, trans. Peter France (Oxford: Oxford University Press, 1978), 174–175.
43 Ahmad Karimi-Hakkak, Authors and Authorities: Censorship and Literary Communication in the Islamic Republic of Iran, 310.
44 Nasser Taghvayi, interviewed by Mehdi Yazdani Khorram and Alireza Gholami, *Tajrobeh* 3, no. 22 (August 2013): 28.
45 Akbariani, *Yādhā-yi az Sālhā-ye Dur va Nazdik*.
46 Abduljabbar Kakayi, interviewed by Mohammad Tangestani (Iran Wire: 21 June 2016) <https://iranwire.com/fa/blogs/3512/7758> [accessed 13 October 2016].
47 Ibid.
48 Ibid.
49 Ibid.
50 Pierre Bourdieu, *Language and Symbolic Power*, ed. John B. Thompson, trans. Gino Raymond and Matthew Adamson (Cambridge, UK: Polity Press, 1991), 230.

Chapter 8

1 Judith Butler, 'Ruled Out: Vocabularies of the Censor in Censorship' in *Censorship and Silencing, Practices of Cultural Regulation*, ed. Robert C. Post (Los Angeles: The Getty Research Institute, 1998), 252.
2 Judith Butler, *Excitable Speech/A Politics of the Performative* (New York: Routledge, 1997), 39.
3 Terry Eagleton, *Figures of Dissent, Critical Essays on Fish, Spivak, Zizek and Others* (London: Verso, 2005), 176.
4 Helen Freshwater 'Towards a Redefinition of Censorship' in *Censorship and Cultural Regulation in the Modern Age*, ed. Beate Müller, (Amsterdam: Rodopi B.V., 2004), 225.
5 Ibid., 242.
6 Plato, *The Republic*, trans. R. E. Allen (New Haven: Yale University Press, 2006), 63.
7 Ibid., 341.
8 Mohammad Hosseini, *Mamnu'olqalam az kojā Āmad?*, Interview *(Tehran:* Farhangnews, 5 December 2013) <http://www.farhangnews.ir/content/55250> [accessed 17 April 2017].
9 Ahmad Jannati: *Nabāyad be Ketāb-e Nevisandeh-ye Bi-e'teqād Mojavvez Dād* (London: BBC Persian Online, 2 May 2014) <http://www.bbc.com/persian/arts/2014/05/140419_l45_jannati_books_critique)> [accessed 12 July 2016].
10 For more information, see David Horowitz, *The Professors: The 101 Most Dangerous Academics in America* (Washington, DC: Regency Publishing, 2006).

11 Mahmoud Motahharinia, *Mājerā-ye Enteshār-e Ketāb-e 101 Professor-e Khatarnāk dar America* (Tehran: Mashregh News, 7 October 2013) <http://www.mashreghnews.ir/fa/news/-101-کتاب-انتشار-ماجرای / 253130%انتشار-مجوز-آمریکاچرا-در-خطرناک-پروفسور-شود <E2%80%8C کتب-مخرب-باطل-نمی> [accessed 12 July 2016].
12 For example, see the Memorandum of Association of *Anjoman-e Qalam-e Iran* (Iran: Anjoman-e Qalam-e Iran, 2015) <http://www.anjomanQalam.ir/> [accessed 15 February 2015].
13 Daniel Grassian, *Iranian and Diasporic Literature in the 21st Century: A Critical Study* (Jefferson, North Carolina: McFarland & Co Inc., 2013), 169.
14 Michael Levine, *Writing Through Repression: Literature, Censorship, Psychoanalysis* (Baltimore: The Johns Hopkins University Press, 1994), 2.
15 Michel Foucault, *The History of Sexuality, Volume I: An Introduction*, trans. Robert Hurley (New York: Pantheon Books, 1978), 84.
16 Ibid., 15–35 (The Repression Hypothesis).
17 Joseph Brodsky, quoted in *On the Beneficence of Censorship: Aesopian Language in Modern Russian Literature* by Lev Loseff (Munchen: Sagner, 1984), 12.
18 Annabel M. Patterson, *Censorship and Interpretation: The Conditions of Writing and Reading in Early Modern England* (Madison: University of Wisconsin Press, 1984), 18.
19 Masoud Behnoud, interviewed by Reyhaneh Zahiri in *Az Tehran ta Nākojā* (London: H&S Media, 2016), 32.
20 Ivan Klima, 'Variation on an Eternal Theme' in *An Embarrassment of Tyrannies: Twenty-Five Years of Index on Censorship*, ed. Webb, W.L. and Rose Bell (London: Victor Gollancz, 1997), 99–103.
21 Ronald Dworkin, 'A New Map of Censorship', *Index of Censorship* 23, nos. 1–2, (1994): 9–15.
22 Harry White, *Anatomy of Censorship: Why the Censors Have it Wrong* (Lanham: University Press of America Inc, 1997), 101.
23 Ibid., 104.
24 Ibid., 100.
25 Abigail Levin, quoted in Matthew Bunn, 'Reimagining Repression: New Censorship Theory and After', *History and Theory 54*, no. 1 (2015): 25–44.
26 Ibid., 22.
27 ILNA, *Sahm-e Khānavār-hā-ye Irāni az Ketāb Cheqadr Ast* (Iran: ILNA, 4 March 2015) <http://www.ilna.ir/-هنر-فرهنگ-بخش-6/257281-است-چقدر-کتاب-از-ایرانی-های-خانوار-سهم> [accessed 10 October 2016].
28 BBC Persian Online, *Ozv-e Hei'at-e Nezārat bar Ketāb: 'Momayyezi' Osāreh-ye Ārmānhā-ye Enqelāb Ast* (London: BBC Persian Online, 8 June 2011) <http://www.bbc.co.uk/persian/arts/2011/06/110608_l41_book_ahmad_shakeri_int.shtml> [accessed 20 April 2015].
29 Alice Nakhimovsky, 'Review of "On the Beneficence of Censorship: Aesopian Language in Modern Russian Literature" by Lev Loseff', *The Slavic and East European Journal* 30, no. 3 (Autumn, 1986): 453–455.
30 Lev Loseff, *On the Beneficence of Censorship: Aesopian Language in Modern Russian Literature*, 143.
31 Matthew Ancona, 'Lexicon of War', in *An Embarrassment of Tyrannies: Twenty-Five Years of Index on Censorship*, ed. W. L. Webb and Rose Bell (London: Victor Gollancz, 1997), 167.

32 Alishah Mowlavi, '*Kāmelan Khosusi barā-ye Āgāhi-ye Omum*' (Iran: Underground, 2012), 10.
33 Tadeusz Konwicki, 'Delights of Writing under Censorship (Poland): Interview with one of Poland's best-known writers, whose novels are banned', *Index on Censorship* 15, no. 3 (March 1968): 30.
34 Tadeusz Konwicki, quoted in *On Cultural Freedom: An Exploration of Public Life in Poland and America*, by Jeffery C. Goldfarb (Chicago: University of Chicago Press, 1982), 90.
35 J.M. Coetzee, *Giving Offense, Essays on Censorship* (Chicago: The University of Chicago Press, 1996), VIII.
36 Eli M. Oboler, *The Fear of the Word: Censorship and Sex* (New Jersey: The Scarecrow Press, 1974), 138 (quoting from *The Great Society*, by Graham Wallas (New York: Macmillan, 1923)), 196–197.
37 J.M. Coetzee, 'Osip Mandelstam and the Ode to Stalin', in *Giving Offense, Essays on Censorship*, by J. M. Coetzee (Chicago: The University of Chicago Press, 1996), 109.
38 Osip Mandelstam, *The Collected Critical Prose and Letters*, ed. and trans. Jane Gary Harris (London: Collins Harvill, 1991), 316.
39 Fars News Agency, *Monāzereh dar bāreh-ye Momayyezi dar Howzeh-ye Nashr'* (Iran: Fars News Agency, 8 June 2011) <http://www.farsnews.com/newstext.php?nn=13950409001085> [accessed 06 July 2016].
40 Pejman Karimi, *Tahrim Konim*, (Tehran: Kayhan, 22 October 2016) <http://kayhan.ir/fa/print/88364> [accessed 29 October 2016].
41 Ibid.
42 Fars News Agency, *Monāzereh dar bāreh-ye Momayyezi dar Howzeh-ye Nashr'*.
43 Akbariani, Mohammad H., '*Yādhāyi az Sālhā-ye Dur va Nazdik*', *E'temād*, 2015, 16 <http://etemadnewspaper.ir/?News_Id=12880> [accessed 20 April 2015].
44 Nadine Gordimer, quoted in *Literature and Censorship*, ed. Nigel Smith (Cambridge, UK: D.S. Brower, 1993), IX.
45 BBC Persian Online, *Afv-e Beinolmelal Khāstār-e Āzādi-ye Nāmashrut-e Golrokh Ebrahimi Shod* (London: BBC Persian Online, 24 October 2016) <http://www.bbc.com/persian/iran-37758360> [accessed 29 October 2016].
46 Daniel Grassian, *Iranian and Diasporic Literature in the 21st Century: A Critical Study*, 168.
47 Fathollah Biniaz, *Interviewed by Sepideh Jodayri* (Canada: Shahrgon, 25 April 2015) <http://shahrgon.com/fa/2015/04/25/%DA%AF%D9%81%D8%AA%E2%80%8C%D9%88%DA%AF%D9%88-%D8%A8%D8%A7-%D9%81%D8%AA%D8%AD%E2%80%8C%D8%A7%D9%84%D9%84%D9%87-%D8%A8%DB%8C%E2%80%8C%D9%86%DB%8C%D8%A7%D8%B2/> [accessed 27 April 2015].
48 Daniel Grassian, *Iranian and Diasporic Literature in the 21st Century: A Critical Study*, 177.
49 Ibid., 186.
50 Vaclav Havel, 'My Temptation', in *An Embarrassment of Tyrannies: Twenty-Five Years of Index on Censorship*, ed. W. L. Webb and Rose Bell (London: Victor Gollancz, 1997), 134–138.
51 Akbariani, *Yādhā-yi az Sālhā-ye Dur va Nazdik*.
52 Amir Hassan Cheheltan, 'Zensur im Iran', *Frankfurter Algemeine*, 7 April 2015 <http://www.faz.net/aktuell/feuilleton/debatten/amir-hassan-cheheltan-ueber-romanzensur-in-iran-13524175.html?printPagedArticle=true#pageIndex_2> [accessed 3 May 2015].

53 Ibid.
54 Salman Rushdie, 'Last Chance?', in *An Embarrassment of Tyrannies: Twenty-Five Years of Index on Censorship*, ed. W. L. Webb and Rose Bell (London: Victor Gollancz, 1997), 115–118.
55 Seyed Ali Salehi, *Chenān ketāb rā bar Gardanam Kubidand ke Taādolam rā az Dast Dādam* (Interviewed by Hadi Hosseininejad,) *ILNA* (Tehran: ILNA, 17 July 2013) <http://www.shahrwandan.ir/news/12749> [accessed 20 April 2015].
56 Statement of the Iranian Writers' Association, 13 November 2008 (emailed to Alireza Abiz).
57 Fanny Lewald, *A Year of Revolutions: Fanny Lewald's Recollections of 1848*, trans., edited and annotated by Hanna Ballin Lewis, (Providence: Berghahn, 1977), 52.
58 Telegraph Books, 'Nadine Gordimer: Ten inspiring quotes', *The Telegraph*, 15 July 2014, <http://www.telegraph.co.uk/culture/books/10967194/Nadine-Gordimer-Ten-inspiring-quotes.html> [accessed 1 April 2015].

BIBLIOGRAPHY

Books

Abiz, Alireza, *Az Miz-e Man Sedā-ye Derakhti Mi-āyad*, Tehran: Negāh, 2013.
Abiz, Alireza, *Negahdār Bāyad Piyādeh Shavim*, Tehran: Nārenj, 1998.
Abiz, Alireza, *Spāgeti bā Sos-e Mekziki*, Tehran: Saleth, 2004.
Abrahamian, Ervand, *A History of Modern Iran*, New York: Cambridge University Press, 2008.
Abrahamian, Ervand, *Iran between Two Revolutions*, Princeton: Princeton University Press, 1982.
Afary, Janet, ed. *the Iranian Constitutional Revolution, 1906–1911: Grassroots Democracy, Social Democracy, & the Origins of Feminism*, New York: Columbia University Press, 1996.
Althusser, Louis, 'Ideology and Ideological State Apparatuses, Notes Towards an Investigation', in *Lenin and Philosophy and Other Essays*, trans. Ben Brewster, 127–186. New York: Monthly Review Press, 1971.
Aslani, Mehdi, *Kalāgh va Gol-e Sorkh: Khāterat-e Zendān*, Paris: Arash, 2009.
Avery, Peter, *Modern Iran*, London: Ernest Benn, 1965.
Azimi, Fakhreddin, *Iran – The Crisis of Democracy: From the Exile of Reza Shah to the Fall of Musaddiq*, London: I.B. Tauris, 1989.
Azimi, Fakhreddin, *The Quest for Democracy in Iran: A Century of Struggle Against Authoritarian Rule*, Cambridge, MA: Harvard University Press, 2008.
Bayat, Mangol, *Iran's First Revolution. Shi'ism and the Constitutional Revolution of 1905–1909*, Oxford: Oxford University Press, 1991.
Behnam, M. R., *Cultural Foundations of Iranian Politics*, Salt Lake City: University of Utah Press, 1986.
Behnoud, Masoud, interviewed by Reyhaneh Zahiri, *Az Tehran ta Nākojā*, London: H&S Media, 2016.
Boroujerdi, Mehrzad, 'Triumphs and Travails of Authoritarian Modernization in Iran', in *The Making of Modern Iran: State and Society under Riza Shah, 1921–1941*, edited by Stephanie Cronin, 145–154. London: Routledge, 2003.
Bourdieu, Pierre, *Language and Symbolic Power*, ed. John B. Thompson, trans. Gino Raymond and Matthew Adamson, Cambridge, UK: Polity Press, 1991.
Breytenbach, Breyten, *End Papers*, London: Faber & Faber, 1986.
Brodsky, Joseph, quoted in *On the Beneficence of Censorship: Aesopian Language in Modern Russian Literature* by Lev Loseff, Munchen: Sagner, 1984.
Browne, Edward G., *The Literature of Persia, Lecture given at The Persia Society on Friday April 26th 1912 at 5 p.m.*, published for the Society by John Hogg, London.
Browne, Edward G., *The Persian Revolution of 1905–1909*, London: Frank Cass & Co., 1966.
Browne, Edward G., *The Press and Poetry of Modern Persia Partly Based on the Manuscript Work of Mirza Muhammad Ali Khan "Tarbiyat" of Tabriz*, Cambridge, UK: Cambridge University Press, 1914.

Burt, Richard, *Licensed by Authority: Ben Jonson and the Discourse of Censorship*, Ithaca: Cornell University Press, 1993.
Burt, Richard, *The Administration of Aesthetics/ Censorship,Political Criticism, and the Public Sphere*, Minneapolis: University of Minnesota Press, 1994.
Butler, Judith, *Excitable Speech/A Politics of the Performative*, New York: Routledge, 1997.
Butler, Judith, 'Ruled Out: Vocabularies of the Censor in Censorship', in *Censorship and Silencing, Practices of Cultural Regulation*, edited by Robert C. Post, 247–259. Los Angeles: The Getty Research Institutue, 1998.
Chehabi, H. E. and Vanessa Martin, eds *Iran's Constitutional Revolution: Popular Politics, Cultural Transformations and Transnational Connections*, London: I.B. Tauris, 2010.
Coetzee, J. M., *Giving Offense: Essays on Censorship*, Chicago: The University of Chicago Press, 1996.
Dabashi, Hamid, *Iran: A People Interrupted*, New York: New Press, 2007.
D'Ancona, Matthew, 'Lexicon of War', in *An Embarrassment of Tyrannies: Twenty-Five Years of Index on Censorship*, edited by Webb, W.L. and Rose Bell, 167–169. London: Victor Gollancz, 1997.
Darnton, Robert, *Censors at Work: How States shaped Literature*, New York: W.W. Norton & Company, 2014.
Daryabandari, Najaf, 'Akhavan, Shāer-e Shekast', in *Bāgh-e Bibargi: Yādnāmeh-ye Mehdi Akhavan Saleth*, edited by Morteza Kakhi, 241–250. Tehran: Zemestan, 1991.
De Bellaigue, Christopher, *The Struggle for Iran*, New York: New York Review of Books, 2007.
Devos, Bianca and Christoph Werner, eds *Culture and Cultural Politics Under Reza Shah: The Pahlavi State, New Bourgeoisie and the Creation of a Modern Society in Iran*, London: Routledge, 2014.
Eagleton, Terry, *Figures of Dissent, Critical Essays on Fish, Spivak, Zizek and Others*, London: Verso, 2005.
Etkind, Effim, *Notes of a Non-conspirator*, trans. Peter France, Oxford: Oxford University Press, 1978.
Fadaee, Simin, *Social Movements in Iran: Environmentalism and Civil Society*, London: Routledge, 2012.
Farahati, H., *Az Ān Sālhā va Sālhā-ye Digar*, Germany: Forough, 2006.
Fardoust, Hossein, *Zohur va Soqut-e Saltanat-e Pahlavi*, Tehran: Ettelā'āt, 1991.
Fish, Stanley, *There's No Such Thing as Free Speech*, Oxford: Oxford University Press, 1994.
Fo, Dario, 'When they Beat Us, we Suffer', in *An Embarrassment of Tyrannies: Twenty-Five Years of Index on Censorship*, edited by Webb, W.L. and Rose Bell, 122–125. London: Victor Gollancz, 1997.
Foucault, Michel, *Discipline and Punish: The Birth of a Prison*, trans. Alan Sheridan, New York: Vintage Books, 1995.
Foucault, Michel, *Power/Knowledge: Selected Interviews and other Writings 1972–1977*, ed. Colin Gordon, trans. Colin Gordon, Leo Marshall, John Mephan, Kate Soper, New York: Pantheon Books, 1980.
Foucault, Michel, *The History of Sexuality, Volume I: An Introduction*, trans. Robert Hurley, New York: Pantheon Books, 1978.
Freshwater, Helen, 'Towards a Redefinition of Censorship', in *Censorship and Cultural Regulation in the Modern Age*, edited by Beate Müller, 225–245. Amsterdam: Rodopi B.V., 2004.
Ganji, Akbar, *Ālijenāb-e Sorkhpush va Ālijenābān-e Khākestari*, Tehran: Tarh-e Now, 2000.
Ghani, Cyrus, *Iran and the Rise of the Reza Shah: From Qajar Collapse to Pahlavi Power*, London: I.B. Tauris, 2000.

Ghanoonparvar, M. R., *Prophets of Doom: Literature as a Socio-Political Phenomenon in Modern Iran*, New York: University Press of America, 1984.
Gheissari, Ali, *Iranian Intellectuals in the 20th Century*, Austin: University of Texas Press, 1998.
Ghods, M. R., *Iran in the Twentieth Century: A Political History*, London: Adamantine Press, 1989.
Gilbert, Nora, *Better Left Unsaid: Victorian Novels, Hays Code Films, and the Benefits of Censorship*, Stanford: Stanford University Press, 2013.
Goldfarb, Jeffery C., *On Cultural Freedom: An Exploration of Public Life in Poland and America*, Chicago: University of Chicago Press, 1982.
Gordon, Daniel, ed. *Postmodernism and the Enlightenment/New Perspectives in Eighteenth-Century French Intellectual History*, New York: Routledge, 2001.
Gramsci, Antonio, *The Gramsci Reader: Selected Writings*, 1916–1935, New York: New York University Press, 2000.
Grassian, Daniel, *Iranian and Diasporic Literature in the 21st Century: A Critical Study*, Jefferson, North Carolina: McFarland & Co Inc., 2013.
Hand, Sean, *The Levinas Reader*, Oxford: Blackwell, 1989.
Havel, Vaclav, 'My Temptation', in *An Embarrassment of Tyrannies: Twenty-Five Years of Index on Censorship*, edited by W.L. Webb and Rose Bell, 134–138. London: Victor Gollancz, 1997.
Hiro, Dilip, *The Iranian Labyrinth, Journeys Through Theocratic Iran and its Furies*, New York: Nation Books, 2005.
Holan, Vladimir, *Selected Poems*, trans. Jamila and Ian Milner, Middlesex: Penguin Books, 1971.
Horowitz, David, *The Professors: The 101 Most Dangerous Academics in America*, Washington, DC: Regency Publishing, 2006.
Hunter, Shireen T., *Iran After Khomeini*, New York: The Center for Strategic and International Studies/Praeger, 1992.
Hussain, Abdulrahim Zakir, *Adabiyyāt-e Siyāsi-ye Iran dar Asr-e Mashrutiyat, Vol. 1*, Tehran: Elm, 1998.
Jansen, Sue Curry, *The Knot That Binds Power and Knowledge*, New York: Oxford University Press, 1988.
Javadi, Hassan, *Edward Browne va Iran*, 2nd edn, Tehran: Farhang-e Nashr-e Noe, 2017.
Kamrava, Mehran, *Revolution in Iran: The Roots of Turmoil*, London: Routledge, 1990.
Kasravi, Ahmad, *History of the Iranian Constitutional Revolution, Vol. 1*, trans. Evan Siegel, Costa Mesa: Mazda, 2006.
Karimi-Hakkak, Ahmad, 'Authors and Authorities: Censorship and Literary Communication in the Islamic Republic of Iran', in *Persian Studies in North America: Studies in Honor of Mohammad Ali Jazayery*, edited by Mehdi Marashi, 307–338. Bethesda, Maryland: Iranbooks, 1994.
Katouzian, Homa, *Musaddiq and the Struggle for Power in Iran*, London: I.B. Tauris, 1990.
Katouzian, Homa, 'Riza Shah's Political Legitimacy and Social Base, 1921–1941', in *The Making of Modern Iran: State and Society under Riza Shah, 1921–1941*, edited by Stephanie Cronin, 15–36. London: Routledge, 2003.
Keddie, Nikki R., *Qajar Iran and the Rise of Reza Khan 1796–1925*, Costa Mesa: Mazda, 1999.
Keddie, Nikki R., *Roots of Revolution: An Interpretive History of Modern Iran with a Section by Yann Richard*, New Haven; London: Yale University Press, 1981.
Khomeini, Ayatollah, *Mahram-e Rāz*, Tehran: Moassesa-ye Tanzim va Nashr-e Āsār-e Imam Khomeini, 1990.

Khomeini, Ayatollah, *Velāyat-e Faqih*, Tehran: Moassesa-ye Tanzim va Nashr-e Āsār-e Imam Khomeini, 1994.
Khosravi, Fariborz, *Sānsur dar Āyineh: Nazarāt-e Momayyezān-e Ketāb dar Dowrān-e Pahlavi-ye Dovvom*, Tehran: Ketābkhāneh-ye Melli-ye Jomhuri-ye Eslāmi, 2002.
Klima, Ivan, 'Variation on an Eternal Theme', in *An Embarrassment of Tyrannies: Twenty-Five Years of Index on Censorship*, edited by W.L. Webb and Rose Bell, 99–103. London: Victor Gollancz, 1997.
Knuth, Rebecca, *Libricide: The Regime-Sponsored Destruction of Books and Libraries in the Twentieth Century*, Westport: Praeger, 2003.
Kohan, Goel, *Tārikh-e Sānsur-e Matbuāt-e Iran*, Tehran: Agah, 1984.
Kooshan, Mansour, *Tabassom-hā va Ta'ssof-hā*, London: H&S Media, 2013.
Laclau, Ernesto and Mouffe, Chantal, *Hegemony and Socialist Strategy: Towards a Radical Democratic Politics*, London: Verso, 1985.
Levin, Abigail, *The Cost of Free Speech: Pornography, Hate Speech and their Challenges to Liberalism*, London: Palgrave Macmillan, 2010.
Levine, Michael G., *Writing through Repression: Literature, Censorship, Psychoanalysis*, Baltimore: The John Hopkins Press, 1994.
Lewald, Fanny, *A Year of Revolutions: Fanny Lewald's Recollections of 1848*, ed., trans., and annotated by Hanna Ballin Lewis, Providence: Berghahn, 1977.
Loseff, Lev, *On the Beneficence of Censorship: Aesopian Language in Modern Russian Literature*, Munchen: Sanger, 1984.
Majd, Mohammad G., *From Qajar to Pahlavi Iran, 1919–1930*, Lanham: University Press of America, 2008.
Majd, Mohammad G., *Great Britain & Reza Shah: The Plunder of Iran, 1921–1941*, Gainesville: University Press of Florida, 2001.
Mandelstam, Osip, *The Collected Critical Prose and Letters*, ed. and trans. Jane Gary Harris, London: Collins Harvill, 1991.
Martin, Vanessa, *Iran between Islamic Nationalism and Secularism: The Constitutional Revolution of 1906*, London: I.B. Tauris, 2013.
Maryniak, Irena, 'The Lubianka's Hidden Treasure – An Interview with Vitaly Shentalinsky', in *An Embarrassment of Tyrannies: Twenty-Five Years of Index on Censorship*, edited by W. L. Webb and Rose Bell, 177–181. London: Victor Gollancz, 1997.
Matin, Kamran, ed. *Recasting Iranian Modernity: International Relations and Social Change*, New York: Routledge, 2013.
Matthee, Rudi, 'Transforming Dangerous Nomads into Useful Artisans, Technicians, Agriculturalists – Education in the Riza Shah Period', in *The Making of Modern Iran: State and Society under Riza Shah, 1921–1941*, edited by Stephanie Cronin, 123–144. London: Routledge, 2003.
Milani, Abbas, *The Shah*, New York: Palgrave Macmillan, 2011.
Milani, Mohsen M., *The Making of Iran's Islamic Revolution: From Monarchy to Islamic Republic*, 2nd edn, Boulder: Westview Press, 1994.
Milton, John, *Areopagitica*, ed. J. C. Suffolk, London: University Tutorial Press, 1968.
Mirsepassi, Ali, *Democracy in Modern Iran: Islam, Culture, and Political Change*, New York: New York University Press, 2010.
Moaveni, Azadeh, *Lipstick Jihad: A Memoir of Growing up Iranian in America and American in Iran*, New York: Public Affairs, 2006.
Moazami, Behrooz, *State, Religion, and Revolution in Iran, 1796 to the Present*, New York: Palgrave Macmillan, 2013.
Mostyn, Trevor, *Censorship in Islamic Societies*, London: Saqi, 2002.
Mowlavi, Alishah, *Kāmelan Khosusi barā-ye Āgāhi-ye Omum*, Iran: Underground, 2012.

Mozaffari, Nahid and Ahmad Karimi Hakkak, eds *Strange Times in Persia, an Anthology of Contemporary Iranian Literature*, London: I.B. Tauris, 2009.
Müller, Beate, 'Censorship and Cultural Regulation: Mapping the Territory', in *Censorship and Cultural Regulation in the Modern Age*, edited by Beate Müller, 1–32. Amsterdam: Rodopi B. V., 2004.
Naficy, Hamid, *A Social History of Iranian Cinema, Volume 4 – the Globalizing Era, 1984–2010*, Durham, N.C Duke University Press, 2012.
Nafisi, Azar, *Reading Lolita in Tehran*, New York: Random House, 2003.
Nietzche, Friedrich, *Human, All Too Human: A Book for Free Spirits*, trans. Marion Faber et al., Cambridge, UK: Cambridge University Press, 1996.
Oboler, Eli M., *The Fear of the Word: Censorship and Sex*, New Jersey: The Scarecrow Press, 1974.
Patterson, Annabel M., *Censorship and Interpretation: The Conditions of Writing and Reading in Early Modern England*, Madison: University of Wisconsin Press, 1984.
Phillips, Tomas B., *Queer Sinister Things: The Hidden History of Iran*, Raleigh: Lulu Enterprises Inc, 2012.
Plato, *The Republic*, trans. R. E. Allen, New Haven: Yale University Press, 2006.
Post, Robert, ed. *Censorship and Silencing: Practices of Cultural Regulation*, Los Angeles: Getty Research Institute for the History of Art and the Humanities, 1998.
Pourostad, Vahid, *Mohākemeh-ye Ādineh*, Tehran: Ruznegār, 2002.
Qaed, Mohammad, *Eshqi: Simā-ye Najib-e Yek Ānārshist*, Tehran: Tarh-e-Now, 2001.
Rajabzadeh, Ahmad, *Momayyezi-ye Ketāb: Pajuheshi dar 1400 Sanad-e Momayyezi-ye Ketāb dar Sāl-e 1375*, Tehran: Kavir, 2001.
Ravanshid, M., *Bejā-ye Hameh-ye Ānhā ke Gom Shodand: Goftogu bā Hei'at Dabirān-e Kānun-e Nevisandegān-e Iran*, Sweden: Ketāb-e Arzān, 2014.
Rosenfeld, Sophia, 'Writing the History of Censorship in the Age of Enlightenment', in *Postmodernism and the Enlightenment/New Perspectives in Eighteenth-Century French Intellectual History*, edited by Daniel Gordon, 117–145. New York: Routledge, 2001.
Rushdie, Salman, 'Last Chance?' in *An Embarrassment of Tyrannies: Twenty-Five Years of Index on Censorship*, edited by W. L. Webb and Rose Bell, 115–118. London: Victor Gollancz, 1997.
Sadr Hashemi, Mohammad, *Tārikh-e Jarāyed va Majallāt-e Iran*, Isfahan: Kamal, 1985.
Sarkoohi, Faraj, *Yās va Dās*, Sweden: Baran, 2002.
Sarkoohi, Faraj, *Shab-e Dardmand-e Ārezumandi*, Stockholm: Baran, 1999.
Shafiei Kadkani, Mohammadreza, *Advār-e She'r-e Farsi*, Tehran: Tus, 1980.
Shahidi, Hossein, *Journalism in Iran; From Mission to Profession*, London: Routledge, 2007.
Shamim, Ali Asghar, *Iran in the Reign of His Majesty Mohammad Reza Shah Pahlavi*, trans. Aladin Pazargadi: self-published, 1965.
Sheibani, Khatereh, *The Poetics of Iranian Cinema: Aesthetics, Modernity and Film after the Revolution*, London: I.B. Tauris, 2011.
Smith, Nigel, ed. *Literature and Censorship*, Cambridge, UK: D.S.Brewer, 1993.
Tadeusz, Konwicki, quoted in *On Cultural Freedom: An Exploration of Public Life in Poland and America*, by Jeffery C. Goldfarb, Chicago: University of Chicago Press (1982), 90.
Taheri, Amir, *The Unknown Life of the Shah*, London: Hutchinson, 1991.
Talattof, Kamran, *The Politics of Writing in Iran: A History of Modern Persian Literature*, New York: Syracuse University Press, 2000.
Thompson, Elizabeth F., *Justice Interrupted: The Struggle for Constitutional Government in the Middle East*, Cambridge, MA: Harvard University Press, 2013.

Varzi, Roxanne, *Warring Souls: Youth, Media and Martyrdom in Post-Revolution Iran*, Durham, NC: Duke University Press, 2006.
Wallas, Graham, *The Great Society*, New York: Macmillan, 1923.
White, Harry, *Anatomy of Censorship: Why the Censors have it Wrong*, Lanham: University Press of America, 1997.
Zabih, Sepehr, *The Mossadegh Era: Roots of the Iranian Revolution*, Chicago: Lake View Press, 1982.

Journals and Periodicals

Ahmadi, Ahmadreza, '*Goftogu-ye Abdolhossein Azarang Va Ali Dehbashi Ba Ahmadreza Ahmadi*', *Bokhārā*, 18, 2001, 181–204.
Akbariani, Mohammad H., '*Yādhāyi az Sālhā-ye Dur va Nazdik*', *E'temād*, 2015, 16 <http://etemadnewspaper.ir/?News_Id=12880> [accessed 20 April 2015].
'*Akhbār-e Ahl-e Qalam*', *Andisheh-ye Āzād*, 3.4, 2012, 14–15.
Amirfaryar, Farrokh, '*Nashr-e Ketāb dar Sāl-e 1377*', *Jahān-e Ketāb*, 87–88, (1999): 2–3.
Amiri, Farnaz, '*Goftogu bā Mohsen Parviz dar Bāreh-ye Sānsur va Moāvenat-e Farhangi*', *Āsemān*, 63 (2013): 102–3.
Atwood, Blake, 'Sense and Censorship in the Islamic Republic of Iran', *World Literature Today*, 86, no. 3 (May/June 2012): 38–41.
Azarang, Abdolhossein, *Nashr-e Makhfi bā Horuf-e Riz*, *Andisheh-ye Puyā*, January-February 2015, Centre for the Great Islamic Encyclopaedia <http://www.cgie.org.ir/fa/news/27439> [accessed 12 April 2015].
Bahadorvand, Fanoos, '*Āncheh be Nām-e Momayyezi dar Edāreh-ye Arzeshyābi-ye Ketāb-e Vezārat-e Ershād Rokh Midahad*', *Andisheh-ye Āzād*, 3, no. 4 (2012): 16.
Bunn, Matthew, 'Reimagining Repression: New Censorship Theory and After', *History and Theory*, 54, no. 1 (2015): 25–44.
Cheheltan, Amir H., 'Interviewed by Alireza Gholami', *Tajrobeh*, 4, no. 32 (2014): 26–40.
Cheheltan, Amir H., 'Zensur Im Iran', *Frankfurter Algemeine*, (2015) <http://www.faz.net/aktuell/feuilleton/debatten/amir-hassan-cheheltan-ueber-romanzensur-in-iran-13524175.html?printPagedArticle=true#pageIndex_2> [accessed 3 May 2015].
Dayyani, Mohammad Hossein and Nasrin Tajaddod, '*Didgāh-e Nāsherān dar bāreh-ye Sobāt-e Siāsi va Eqtesādi-ye Hākem bar Nashr-e Ketāb tayy-e Sālhā-ye 1376 tā 1383*', *Ketābdāri va Etteālā'rasāni*, 33 (2006): 22–41.
Delgado, Richard, 'First Amendment Formalism is Giving Way to First Amendment Legal Realism', *Harvard Civil Rights – Civil Liberties Law Review*, 29 (1994): 169–170.
Dworkin, Ronal, 'A New Map of Censorship', *Index of Censorship*, 1–2 (1994): 9–15.
Enteshār-e 'Ān ke Nevesht', *Andisheh-ye Āzād*, 3, no. 6 (2013): 20.
Fallaci, Oriana, 'An Interview with KHOMEINI', *New York Times*, (1979) <http://query.nytimes.com/gst/abstract.html?res=9F0DEEDA1438E432A25754C0A9669D946890D6CF> [accessed 23 January 2015].
Fouladvand, Ezzatollah, '*Az Shekastan-e Sang-e Mazār-e Shamlou tā Āhang-e Veirāni-ye Maqbareh-ye Hafiz*', *Hafiz*, 76 (2010): 45–53.
Gey, Steven G., 'The Case Against Postmodern Censorship Theory', *University of Pennsylvania Law Review*, (December 1996): 193–297.
Ghadimi, Mehdi et al., '*Budjeh-ye Farhangi-ye Keshvar Koja Hazineh Mishavad?*, *Shargh*, 2561 (17 April 2016): 6.

Holquist, Michael, 'Corrupt Originals: The Paradox of Censorship', *PMLA*, 109, no. 1 (January 1994): 14–25.
Jansen, Sue Curry, 'Ambiguities and Imperatives of Market Censorship, the Brief History of a Critical Concept', *Westminster Papers in Communication and Culture*, 7, no. 2 (2010): 12–30.
Jolayi, Reza, 'interviewed by Alireza Gholami', *Tajrobeh*, 3, no. 22 (2013): 56–7.
Kamali Dehghan, Saeed, 'Tehran International Book Fair Launches Crackdown on "harmful" Titles', *The Guardian* (2012) <http://www.theguardian.com/world/2012/may/02/tehran-international-book-fair-crackdown> [accessed 17 February 2015].
'Kārnāmeh-ye Yeksāleh', *Andisheh-ye Āzād*, 3.8 (2014): 3–4.
Khalaj, Mansour, 'interviewed by *Namāyeshnāmeh Quarterly*, 2 and 3 (Summer and Autumn 2011): 42.
Konwicki, Tadeusz, 'Delights of Writing under Censorship (Poland): Interview with one of Poland's best-known writers, whose novels are banned', *Index on Censorship*, 15, no. 3 (1968): 30–32.
Lifshitz-Losev, Lev, trans. Joseph Deney, 'What it Means to be Censored', The New York Review of Books, June 29, 1978, <https://www.nybooks.com/articles/1978/06/29/what-it-means-to-be-censored/> [accessed 20 July 2017].
Mahdiani, Alireza, and Seyed Hassan Mortazavi, 'Simā-ye Nashr-e Ketāb dar Iran tayy-e do Daheh-ye Akhir', *Rahyāft*, 31 (2003): 24–31.
M.A. 'Nush-e Jān-e Shān', *Andisheh-ye Āzād*, 3, no. 1 (2011): 16.
Mohammadi, Sayer, 'Bāzār Siyāh-e Ketābhā-ye Jeld Sefid', *Iran*, (2014): 12.
'Mojavvez-e Chāp-e Ketāb rā Laghv Konid', *Andisheh-ye Āzād*, 3.6 (2013): 31–32.
Mondry, Henrietta, 'Is the End of Censorship in the Former Soviet Union a Good Thing? The Case of Vasily Rosanov', *East European Jewish Affairs*, 32, no. 2 (Winter 2002): 114–120.
Nakhimovsky, Alice, 'Review of "On the Beneficence of Censorship: Aesopian Language in Modern Russian Literature"' by Lev Loseff, *The Slavic and East European Journal*, 30 (Autumn 1986): 453–455.
Posnett, Edward, 'Treating His Imperial Majesty's Warts: British Policy towards Iran 1977–79', *Iranian Studies*, 45, no. 1 (2012): 119–137.
Roth, Philip, 'In Prague', *The New Yorker* (2013), <http://www.newyorker.com/books/page-turner/in-prague> [accessed 18 June 2015].
Saeed Emami Pishnehād-e Eslāh-e Qanun-e Matbuāt rā Dadeh Ast, Salam, (1999): 1.
Sangari, Mohammadreza, 'Kholāseh-ye Neshast-e "Barrasi-ye She'r-e Enqelāb-e Eslāmi va Yādkard-e Doctor Qeysar Aminpour"', *Ketāb-e Māh: Adabiyyāt va Falsafa*, 13 (2008): 15–23.
Sepanlou, Mohammad Ali, 'Interview', *Mardomsālāri*, 3602 (23 October 2014): 6.
Shams, Fatemeh, 'Ideology of Warfare and the Islamic Republic's Poetry of War', *International Journal of Persian Literature*, 1 (2016): 5–58.
Shams, Fatemeh, 'The Dialectic of Poetry and Power in Iran', *Dirasat (published by King Faisal Center for Research and Islamic Studies)*, no. 3 (February 2015).
Siavoshi, Sussan, 'Cultural Policies and the Islamic Republic: Cinema and Book Publication', *International Journal of the Middle East Studies*, 29, no. 4 (November 1997): 509–530.
Soyinka, Wole, 'Jihad for Freedom', *Index on Censorship*, 18, no. 5 (1989): 20–30.
Talattof, Kamran, 'Iranian Women's Literature: From Pre-Revolutionary Social Discourse to Post-Revolutionary Feminism', *International Journal of Middle East Studies*, 29, no. 4 (November 1997): 531–558.

Taghvayi, Nasser, 'interviewed by Mehdi Yazdani Khorram and Alireza Gholami', *Tajrobeh*, 3, no. 22 (2013): 22–30.
Telegraph Books, 'Nadine Gordimer: Ten Inspiring Quotes', *The Telegraph*, (2014) <http://www.telegraph.co.uk/culture/books/10967194/Nadine-Gordimer-Ten-inspiringquotes.html> [accessed 1 April 2015].

Online Sources

Aalikhani, Mehrdad, *pages from interrogations* (unverified) <http://freedomvatan.blogspot.co.uk/2009/01/blog-post_06.html> [accessed 14 April 2015].
Aamout Publishers, *Porforushtarin-hā* (Tehran: Aamout Publishers, 19 March 2015) <http://www.aamout.com/search/label/alireza-roshan> [accessed 22 April 2015].
Āftāb News, *Rahmandoost: Mathnavi ham Momayyezi Shoda Ast* (Iran: Āftāb News Network, 19 August 2011) <http://aftabnews.ir/vdcd5x0fkyt0sj6.2a2y.html> [accessed 20 February 2015].
Āl-e Ahmad Award, *Āyinnāmeh-ye Ejrāyi-e Jāyezeh-ye Adabi-ye Jalal Āl-e Ahmad* (Tehran: Āl-e Ahmad Award, 2015) <http://jalalprize.ir/%D8%A2%D8%A6%DB%8C%D9%86%E2%80%8C%D9%86%D8%A7%D9%85%D9%87%D9%94%D8%AC%D8%A7%DB%8C%D8%B2%D9%87/> [accessed 28 June 2015].
Alef News, *Rouhani: Naqd-e Rang-e Kafsh va Lebās Naqd Nist* (Tehran: Alef News, 8 February 2015) <http://alef.ir/vdcewo8wpjh8nxi.b9bj.html?259326> [accessed 23 February 2015].
Amirshahi, Farnoosh, *Janjālhā-ye Kārikāturi* (London: BBC Persian Online, 30 September 2012) <http://www.bbc.co.uk/persian/iran/2012/09/120930_l42_ir_caricature.shtml> [accessed 10 March 2015].
Anjoman-e Qalam-e Iran, *The Memorandum of Association of Anjoman-e Qalam-e Iran* (Iran: Anjoman-e Qalam-e Iran, 2015) <http://www.anjomanQalam.ir/> [accessed 15 February 2015].
Ansarifar, Houshyar, *She'r-e Daheh-ye Haftād dar Goftogu-ye Ekhtesāsi bā Houshyar Ansarifar*, Tamasha: BBC Persian TV, 4 November 2014, <http://www.bbc.com/persian/arts/2014/11/141104_l42_vid_tamasha_houshyar_ansarifard> [accessed 21 February 2015].
Asr-e Iran, *Taqdir-e Rahbar-e Enqelāb az Rāvi va Nevisandeh-ye Ketab-e Dā* (Tehran: Asr-e Iran, 10 May 2010) <http://www.asriran.com/fa/news/113741/تقدیر-رهبر-انقلاب-از-راوی-و-نویسنده-کتاب-دا> [accessed 13 October 2016].
Asr-e Nou News, *Simin Behbahani: M. Azad bi Ejāzeh Motevalled Shod va bi Ejāzeh ham Dafn Shod* ([n.p.]: Asr-e Nou, [n.d.]) <http://asre-nou.net/1384/bahman/12/m-azad.html> [accessed 13 April 2015].
Ayatollah Khamenei Portal, *Enteshār-e Dastneveshteh-ye Akhavan Saleth dar Daftar-e Yāddāsht-e Ayatollah Khamenei*, 27 August 2014 (Tehran: Khamenei Portal, 2014) <http://farsi.khamenei.ir/news-content?id=27292> [accessed 26 February 2015].
Ayatollah Khamenei Portal, *Ettelā' Negāsht: Bish az 200 Sāl Tahājom-e Farhangi*, 9 August 2016 (Tehran: Khamenei Portal, 2016) <http://farsi.khamenei.ir/photo-album?id=33947> [accessed 25 October 2016].
Ayatollah Khamenei Portal, *Tahājom-e Farhangi- Te'dād-e Fish: 102, Te'dād-e Maqāleh: 1* (Tehran: Khamenei Portal, 2015) <http://farsi.khamenei.ir/keyword-print?id=1010> [accessed 2 February 2015].

Bahrami, Alireza, *Ehdā-ye Pesteh Bejā-ye Jāyezeh-ye Naqdi* (Tehran: Asr-e-Iran News, 2013) <http://www.asriran.com/fa/news/262257/%D8%A7%D9%87%D8%AF% D8%A7%DB%8C-%D9%BE%D8%B3%D8%AA%D9%87-%D8%A8%D9%87- %D8%AC%D8%A7%DB%8C-%D8%AC%D8%A7%DB%8C%D8%B2%D9%87- %D9%86%D9%82%D8%AF%DB%8C> [accessed 28 February 2015].

Baraheni, Reza, *Goftogu-ye Hassan Zerehi bā Reza Baraheni* (Iranian Writers' Association (in Exile), 4 January 2015) <http://iwae.info/1393/10/14/%DA%AF%D9%81%D8% AA%DA%AF%D9%88%DB%8C-%D8%A2%D9%82%D8%A7%DB%8C-%D8%AD% D8%B3%D9%86-%D8%B2%D8%B1%D9%87%DB%8C-%D8%A8%D8%A7-%D8% AF%DA%A9%D8%AA%D8%B1-%D8%B1%D8%B6%D8%A7-%D8%A8%D8%B1% D8%A7%D9%87%D9%86%DB%8C/> [accessed 10 March 2015].

BBC Persian Online, *Afv-e Beinolmelal Khāstār-e Āzādi-ye Nāmashrut-e Golrokh Ebrahimi Shod* (London: BBC Persian Online, 24 October 2016) <http://www.bbc.com/persian/ iran-37758360> [accessed 29 October 2016].

BBC Persian Online, *Māhnāmeh-ye Adabi-ye Kārnāmeh Towqif Shod* (London: BBC Persian Online, 7 April 2005) <http://www.bbc.co.uk/persian/arts/ story/2005/04/050407_pm-karnameh-suspended.shtml> [accessed 10 March 2015].

BBC Persian Online, *Monāzereh-ye Bisābeqeh-ye Entekhābāti Mian-e Ahmadinejad va Mousavi* (London: BBC Persian Online, 3 June 2009) <http://www.bbc.co.uk/persian/iran/ 2009/06/090603_op_ir88_mousavi_ahmadinejad_debate> [accessed 17 February 2015].

BBC Persian Online, *Ozv-e Hei'at-e Nezārat bar Ketāb: 'Momayyezi' Osāreh-ye Ārmānhā-ye Enqelāb Ast* (London: BBC Persian Online, 8 June 2011) <http://www.bbc.co.uk/persian/ arts/2011/06/110608_l41_book_ahmad_shakeri_int.shtml> [accessed 20 April 2015].

BBC Persian Online, *Rouhani az Sharāyet-e Momayyezi-e Ketāb dar Iran Enteqad kard* (London: BBC Persian Online, 8 February 2015) <http://www.bbc.co.uk/persian/iran/ 2015/02/150208_iran_book_audit_censorship_rouhani> [accessed 23 February 2015].

BBC Persian Online, *Sālhāy-e Siāh-e Farhang; Enteqād-e Tond-e Jam'i az Shāeran-e Irani az Dowlat-e Ahmadinejad* (London: BBC Persian Online, 19 September 2013) <http:// www.bbc.co.uk/persian/arts/2013/09/130919_l41_book_ershad_advice_poetry_day> [accessed 23 February 2015].

BBC Persian Online, *Vazir-e Ershād: Dastgāh-ha-ye Amniati be Barkhi az Modirān-e Farhangi-ye Sabeq Dikta Mikardand* (London: BBC Persian Online, 4 December 2013) <http://www.bbc.co.uk/persian/arts/2013/12/131204_l41_book_jannati_security_ comments> [accessed 20 February 2015].

BBC Persian Online, *Vezārat-e Ershād va Emzāhā-yi ke Zirash Zad; Hasht Sāl Laghv-e Mojavvez-e Ketāb* (London: BBc Persian Online, 31 July 2013) <http://www.bbc. co.uk/persian/arts/2013/07/130724_l41_books_banned_ahmadinejad_list> [accessed 17 February 2015].

BBC Persian TV, *Shast Daqiqa*, BBC Persian TV, 28 February 2015.

Biniaz, Fathollah, *interviewed by Sepideh Jodeyri* (Canada: Shahrgon, 25 April 2015) <http://shahrgon.com/fa/2015/04/25/%DA%AF%D9%81%D8%AA%E2%80%8C %D9%88%DA%AF%D9%88-%D8%A8%D8%A7-%D9%81%D8%AA%D8%AD% E2%80%8C%D8%A7%D9%84%D9%84%D9%87-%D8%A8%DB%8C%E2%80%8- C%D9%86%DB%8C%D8%A7%D8%B2/> [accessed 27 April 2015].

Cheheltan, Amir Hassan, *Mikhāhand Romāni Benevisam ke dar Ān Zendagi-e Irani ra Tahrif Karda Bāsham* (Tehran: ILNA, 21 June 2016) <http://www.ilna.ir/-379387/6- می‌خواهند-رمانی-بنویسم-که-در-آن-زندگی-ایرانی-را-تحریف-کرده-باشم‌بخش-فرهنگ-هنر> [accessed 13 October 2016].

Darke, Diana, *The Book in every Iranian Home*, (UK: BBC, 2 November 2014) <https://www.bbc.co.uk/news/magazine-29648166> [accessed 24 July 2018].

Dehkhoda, Aliakbar and others, *Loghatnāmeh* (Iran: Parsi Open Wiki Dictionary, 2015) <http://www.loghatnaameh.org/dehkhodasearchresult-fa.html?searchtype=0&word=2YXZhduM2LLbjA%3d%3d> [accessed 26 January 2015].

Doustdar, Shamim, *Dah Shab-e Goethe, Revāyat-e Yek Ruydād-e Farhangi-ye Mohem*, Tamasha, BBC Persian TV, 17 August 2012 <http://www.bbc.co.uk/persian/arts/2012/08/120817_10nights_tamasha.shtml> [accessed 7 May 2015].

DW Persian, *Zakhm-e bāz-e Parvandeh-ye Qatlhā-ye Zanjireh-yi*, (Germany: DW Persian, 2 December 2013) <http://www.dw.com/fa-ir/زخم-باز-پرونده-قتلهای-زنجیرهای/a-17265915> [accessed 4 October 2016].

Ebrahimi, Amir F., *Barā-ye Mordanash Hanuz Zud Bud* ([n.p.]: Iran Human Rights, [n.d.]) <http://www.irhumanrights.com/sirjani.htm> [accessed 8 April 2015].

Eghtesad News; *Serial-e Ettefāqāt-e Ajib dar Behesht-e Zahra* (Tehran: Eghtesad News, 8 October 8, 2016) <http://www.eghtesadonline.com/بخش-عمومی-150533/30-سریال-اتفاقات-عجیب-در-بهشت-زهرا> [accessed 12 October 2016]

Encyclopedia Iranica, *Etesami, Parvin*, <http://www.iranicaonline.org/articles/etesami-parvin> [accessed 14 February 2017].

Entekhab News, *Jam'āvari-ye Ketāb-hā-ye Bedun-e Mojavvez az Namāyeshgāh-e Ketāb* (Tehran: Entekhab, 1 May 2014) <http://www.entekhab.ir/fa/news/159363/جمع%E2%80%8Cآوری-کتاب%E2%80%8Cهای-بدون-مجوز-از-نمایشگاه-کتاب%E2%80%8C> [accessed 4 October 2016].

Esfandiyari, Shahab, *Ta'ammoli bar Siyāsat-e Farhangi-ye Ayatollah Khamenei*, 6 April 2016 (Tehran: Khamenei Portal, 2016) <http://farsi.khamenei.ir/others-note?id=32768> [accessed 7 July 2016].

Esmaili, Nafiseh, *Chand Sekkeh-ye Bahār-e Āzādi dar Dowlat-hā-ye Nohom va Dahom E'tā Shod?* (Tehran: Fars News Agency, 29 May 2013) <http://www.farsnews.com/newstext.php?nn=13920307000357> [accessed 17 May 2015].

Esmaili, Reza, *Reza Esmaili dar Goftogu ba Nasim Online* (Iran: Nasim Online, 19 June 2016) <http://nasimonline.ir/Content/Detail/2040759/تقویت-گفتمان-انقلاب-اسلامی-یکی-از-کارکردهای-دیدار-رهبری-با-شاعران-است-شاعران-جوان-همیشه-مدنظر-رهبری> [accessed 6 July 2016].

Fars News, *Joziyāt-e Khāndani az Motefāvet-tarin Ayādāt-e Rahbar-e Enqelāb + Aks* (Tehran: Fars News Agency, 13 September 2014) <http://www.farsnews.com/newstext.php?nn=13930622000648> [accessed 26 February 2015].

Fars News, *Monāzereh dar bāreh-ye Momayyezi dar Howzeh-ye Nashr* (Iran: Fars News Agency, 8 June 2011) <http://www.farsnews.com/newstext.php?nn=13950409001085> [accessed 06 July 2016].

Fathi, Sayeh, 'Rotbeh-bandi-ye Ruznāmeh-hā', Tejārat-e Fardā, June 2014 <http://tejarat.donya-e-eqtesad.com/fa/packagestories/details?story=ddfc7407-68ce-4493-a285-907acccf8aab> [accessed 10 March 2015].

Flood, Alison, 'Man Asian Literary Prize announces longlist', *The Guardian*, 2 November 2011, <http://www.theguardian.com/books/2011/nov/02/man-asian-literary-prize-shortlit> [accessed 23 February 2015].

Ganji, Akbar, *Qatlhā-ye Zanjireh-yi Prozheh-ye Hokumat Bud* (interviewed by Jamshid Barzegar) (London: BBC Persian Online, 7 December 2010) <http://www.bbc.co.uk/persian/iran/2010/12/101207_ganji_serial_murders.shtml> [accessed 23 March 2015].

Giacobini, Lourent et al., *Whither Blogestan: Evaluating Shifts in Persian Cyberspace* (Iran Media Program, University of Pennsylvania, March 2014) <http://www.iranmediaresearch.org/en/research/download/1607> [accessed 30 September 2016].

Golestan, Lili, *Goftand Sineh az Dast-e Rad bar Sineh-ash Zad Hazf Shavad*, (Tehran: ISNA, 25 May 2014) <http://www.isna.ir/news/93030401508/ گفتند-سینه-از-دست-رد-بر-سینه-اش-زد-حذف-شود> [accessed 12 July 2016].

Gooya News, *Chāp-e Tasvir-e Shāʻer-e Zendeh ruy-e Ketāb Mamnuʻ Shod, Sarmāyeh* (Gooya News, August 16, 2009) <http://news.gooya.com/society/archives/092267.php> [accessed 18 October 2016].

Hakkak, Amir, *Mahmoud Dowlatabadi: Barā-ye Ākharin bār be Vezārat-e Ershād Miravam* (London: BBC Persian Online, 8 November 2014) <http://www.bbc.co.uk/persian/arts/2014/11/141107_l41_book_Dolatabadi> [accessed 23 February 2015].

Hassani, Saeedeh, *Sānsur Mikonam pas Hastam*, quoted from Qanun, http://sobbekheir.com/entertainment/طنز-سانسور-می%8C%80%E2شوم،-پس-هستم> [accessed 12 October 2016].

Hosseini, Mohammad, *Mamnuʻolqalam az kojā Āmad?*, interview (Tehran: Farhangnews, 5 December 2013) www.farhangnews.ir/content/55250 [accessed 19 April 2017].

Ian Michalski Foundation, *Edition 2013* (Montricher: Jan Michalski Foundation, 2013) <http://www.fondation-janmichalski.com/en/prix-jan-michalski/edition-2013/> [accessed 23 February 2015].

Iranian Labor News Agency, *Ali Jannati: Agar Qurʻan Vahy-e Monzal Nabud, Momayyezān ān rā ham rad Mikardand* (Tehran: ILNA, 8 October 2013) <http://www.ilna.ir/news/news.cfm?id=111441> [accessed 20 February 2015].

Iranian Labor News Agency, *khodā Konad Haj Ahmad Bargardad* (Tehran: ILNA, 21 June 2016) <http://www.ilna.ir/-احمد-حاج-کند-خدا-3/383243-بخش-سیاسی-برگردد> [accessed 17 September 2016].

Iranian Labor News Agency, *Sahm-e Khānavār-hā-ye Irāni az Ketāb Cheqadr Ast* (Tehran: ILNA, 4 March 2015) <http://www.ilna.ir/-سهم-6/257281-هنر-فرهنگ-بخش خانوارهای-ایرانی-از-کتاب-چقدر-است> [accessed 10 October 2016].

Iranian Labor News Agency, *Vezārat-e Ershād bar Tabl-e Biqānuni Mikubad* (Tehran: ILNA, 27 January 2016) <http://www.ilna.ir/-بی-طبل-بر-ارشاد-وزارت-6/295541-هنر-فرهنگ-بخش قانونی-می-کوبد-بی-قانونی-در-کتاب-کودک-تا-کجا-ادامه-دارد> [accessed 19 September 2016].

Islamic Parliament of Iran, *the Constitution of the Islamic Republic of Iran as amended in 1989, Chapter XII, Article 175* (Tehran: Islamic Parliament of Iran,n.d.) <http://en.parliran.ir/eng/en/Constitution#chapter_13> [accessed 2 February 2015].

Islamic Parliament of Iran, *Preamble to the Constitution of the Islamic Republic of Iran* (Tehran: Islamic Parliament of Iran, 2015) <http://en.parliran.ir/index.aspx?fkeyid=&siteid=84&pageid=3054> [accessed 24 February 2015].

Islamic Parliament Research Center, *Qānun-e Matbuʻāt, Art.2* (Tehran: Islamic Parliament Research Centre, 2015) <http://rc.majlis.ir/fa/law/show/91180> [accessed 21 January 2015].

ISNA, *Ettefāq va Eʻterāzi Digar dar Bāreh-ye Sang-e Qabr-e Sepanlou* (Tehran: ISNA, 17 October 2016) <http://www.isna.ir/news/95072615144/-درباره-دیگر-اعتراضی-و-اتفاق سنگ-قبر-سپانلو> [accessed 18 October 2016].

Jabbari, Alireza, *Atashi Hargez khāmush Nakhāhad Shod* (Gooya News, 25 November 2005) <http://news.gooya.com/culture/archives/039920.php> [accessed 13 April 2015].

Jamali, Hadi, *Ay Delbar-e Man, Ay Qad-o Bālāt Senoqteh*, <http://www.cloob.com/u/1saman1/114282193/%D8%A7%DB%8C_%D8%AF%D9%84%D8%A8%D8%B1_%D9%85%D9%86_%D8%A7%DB%8C_%D9%82%D8%AF_%D9%88_%D8%A8%D8%A7%D

9%84%D8%A7%D8%AA_%D8%B3%D9%87_%D9%86%D9%82%D8%B7%D9%87> [accessed 12 April 2015].

Jami, Mehdi, *Weblogistān Hāfezeh-ye Jam'i-ye Māst*, (Sibestaan blog, 8 September 2015) <http://sibestaan.malakut.org/4120> [accessed 31 October 2016].

Jannati, Ahmad, *Nabāyad be Ketāb-e Nevisandeh-ye Bi-e'teqād Mojavvez Dād* (London: BBC Persian Online, 2 May 2014) <http://www.bbc.com/persian/arts/2014/05/140419_ l45_jannati_books_critique> [accessed 12 July 2016].

Jannati, Ali, *Māhvāreh Ham Mesl-e Digar Padideh-hā Paziroteh Shavad* (Tehran: Tabnak News, 25 July 2016) <http://www.tabnak.ir/fa/news/608837/-جنتی-ماهواره-هم-مثل-دیگر-پدیده%E2%80%8Cشود-فته-شود-پذیر-ها> [accessed 26 September 2016].

Jeihoon, Ali, *Hamchenān Zemestān Ast, Negāhi be Sānsur pas az Enqelāb* (London: BBC Persian online, 6 February 2014) <http://www.bbc.co.uk/persian/ iran/2014/02/140205_l44_35th_iran_revolution_censorship> [accessed 20 February 2015].

Kakayi, Abduljabbar, *interviewed by Mohammad Tangestani* (Iran Wire: 21 June 2016) <https://iranwire.com/fa/blogs/3512/7758> [accessed 13 October 2016].

Kalemeh News, *Khātereh-ye Pournejati az Barnameh-ye Hoviyat va Dr. Zarrinkoob* (Tehran: Kalemeh News, 19 September 2013) <http://www.kaleme.com/1392/06/28/ klm-158702/> [accessed 2 April 2015].

Kalemeh News, Seyed Ali Salehi: *She'r Ya'ni Ro'yā-hā-ye yek Mellat, Ro'yā-hā rā Namitavān Sānsur kard* (Tehran: Kalemeh, 30 December 2014) <http://www.kaleme. com/1393/10/09/klm-206224/> [accessed 15 April 2015].

Kamari, Alireza, *Dā Māhiyati Goftār Nevesht Dārad, Romān Nist* (Tehran: IBNA 29 May 2009) <http://www.ibna.ir/fa/doc/report/38756/دا-ماهيتي-گفتار-نوشت-رمان-نیست> [accessed 13 October 2016].

Kar, Mehrangiz, *Sānsur: Si Sāl Hamrāhi bā Enqelāb* (Washington, DC: Gozaar, 2 June 2010) <http://www.gozaar.org/persian/articles-fa/4167.html> [accessed 10 March 2015].

Karimi Hakkak, Ahmad '*Censorship*', *Encyclopedia Iranica* <http://www.iranicaonline.org/ articles/censorship-sansur-in-persia> [accessed 17 January 2015].

Karimi, Pejman, *Tahrim Konim* (Tehran: Kayhan, 22 October 2016) <http://kayhan.ir/fa/ print/88364> [accessed 29 October 2016].

ketāb-e Dā (Tehran: Sooremehr Website) <http://www.sooremehr.ir/fa/book/2235/دا-کتاب> [accessed 13 October 2016].

Ketabennab, *Negāhi be Hāshiyeh-hā-ye Romān-e 'Davāzdahom'-e Moazzeni; Daghdagheh-hā-ye Dini yā Siāsikāri?/Enfe'āl-e Sāderkonandegān-e Mojavvez!* <http://ketabenaab.ir/ 1393/05/10/%D9%86%DA%AF%D8%A7%D9%87%DB%8C-%D8%A8%D9%87-%D8 %AD%D8%A7%D8%B4%DB%8C%D9%87%E2%80%8C%D9%87%D8%A7%DB% 8C-%D8%B1%D9%85%D8%A7%D9%86-%D8%AF%D9%88%D8%A7%D8%B2%D8 %AF%D9%87%D9%85-%D9%85%D9%88%D8%B0/> [accessed 20 April 2015].

Khabar Online, *Vazir-e Ershād: Ham Mamnu'olqalam Dāshtim, Ham List-e Siāh* (Tehran: Khabar Online, 13 January 2014) <http://www.khabaronline.ir/detail/332509/culture/ book> [accessed 27 October 2016].

Khalaji, Mostafa, Bronwen Robertson and Maryam Aghdami, *Cultural Censorship in Iran – Iranian Culture in a State of Emergency* (London: Small Media Foundation, July 2011) <http://smallmedia.org.uk/censorship.pdf> [accessed 27 February 2015].

Khamenei, Ayatollah, *Bayānāt dar Didār-e A'zā-ye Goruh-e Adab va Honar-e Sedā-ye Jomhuri-e Eslami*, 24 February 1992 (Tehran: Khamenei Portal, 1992) <http://farsi. khamenei.ir/speech-content?id=2597> [accessed 26 February 2015].

Khamenei, Ayatollah, *Bayānāt dar Didār bā Shāerān dar Māh-e Mobārak-e Ramadhan*, 16 September 2002 (Tehran: Khamenei Portal, 2008) <http://farsi.khamenei.ir/speech-content?id=4083> [accessed 26 February 2015].

Khamenei, Ayatollah, *Bayānāt dar Didār-e Dast-andarkārān-e Hamāyesh-e Nekudāsht-e Ostād Moshfegh Kashani*, 12 August 2013 (Tehran: Khamenei Portal, 2013) <http://farsi.khamenei.ir/speech-content?id=23500> [accessed 26 February 2015].

Khamenei, Ayatollah, *Bayānāt dar Didār-e Honarmandān va Mas'ulān-e Farhangi-ye Keshvar*, 13 July 1994 (Tehran: Khamenei Portal, 1994) <http://farsi.khamenei.ir/speech-content?id=12893> [accessed 27 February 2015].

Khamenei, Ayatollah, *Bayānāt dar Didār-e Honarmandān va Mas'ulān-e Farhangi-e Keshvar*, 14 October 1994 (Tehran: Khamenei Portal, 1994) <http://farsi.khamenei.ir/speech-content?id=12893> [accessed 26 February 2015].

Khamenei, Ayatollah, *Bayānāt dar Didār-e Jam'i az Javānān*, 27 April 1998 (Tehran: Khamenei Portal, 1998) <http://farsi.khamenei.ir/speech-content?id=2884> [accessed 26 February 2015].

Khamenei, Ayatollah, *Bayānāt dar Didār-e Jam'i az Kārgozārān-e Farhangi*, 14 August 1992 (Tehran: Khamenei Portal, 1992) <http://farsi.khamenei.ir/speech-content?id=2630> [accessed 15 April 2015].

Khamenei, Ayatollah, *Bayānāt dar Didār-e Jam'i az Shoarā*, 5 September 2009 (Tehran: Khamenei Portal, 2009) <http://farsi.khamenei.ir/speech-content?id=8001> [accessed 26 February 2015].

Khamenei, Ayatollah, *Bayānāt dar Didār-e Majma'-e Namāyandegān-e Tollāb*, 28 November 1989 (Tehran: Khamenei Portal, 1989) <http://farsi.khamenei.ir/speech-content?id=2228> [accessed 21 April 2015].

Khamenei, Ayatollah, *Bayānāt dar Didār-e Ra-is va Namāyandegān-e Majles-e Showrā-ye Eslāmi'*, 6 June 2016 (Tehran: Khamenei Portal, 2016) <http://farsi.khamenei.ir/speech-content?id=33282> [accessed 7 July 2016].

Khamenei, Ayatollah, *Bayānāt dar Didār-e Shāerān*, 25 August 2010 (Tehran: Khamenei Portal, 2010) <http://farsi.khamenei.ir/speech-content?id=20753> [accessed 25 January 2015].

Khamenei, Ayatollah, *Bayānāt dar Haram-e Motahhar-e Razavi*, 21 March 2014 (Tehran: Khamenei Portal, 2014) <http://farsi.khamenei.ir/speech-content?id=25993> [accessed 28 January 2015].

Khamenei, Ayatollah, *Bayānāt dar Jalaseh-ye Porsesh va Pasokh-e Dāneshjuyān-e Dāneshgāh-e Shahid Beheshti*, 12 May 2003 (Tehran: Khamenei Portal, 2003) <http://farsi.khamenei.ir/speech-content?id=3177> [accessed 2 February 2015].

Khamenei, Ayatollah, *Bayānāt pas az Bāzdid az Sāzemān-e Sedā va Simā*, 18 May 2004 (Tehran: Khamenei Portal, 2004) <http://farsi.khamenei.ir/speech-content?id=3232> [accessed 28 January 2015].

Khamenei, Ayatollah, *Chand She'r az Rahbar-e Moazzam-e Enqelāb-e Eslāmi, Hazrat-e Ayatollah Khamenei* <http://www.tebyan.net/newindex.aspx?pid=934&articleID=412206> [accessed 27 February 2015].

Khāneh-ye Shāerān-e Iran, Farākhān-e Ozviyat-e Daftar-e She'r-e Javān (Tehran: Khāneh-ye Shāerān-e Iran Website, 16 October 2014) <http://poetry.ir/?sn=news&pt=full&lang=&id=daftarsherejavan> [accessed 26 February 2015].

Khatami, Mohammad, *Zendagināmeh* (Tehran: Khatami Portal, 2015) <http://www.khatami.ir/biography.html> [accessed 11 February 2015].

Khomeini, Ayatollah, 'Payām be Mellat-e Iran, be Monāsebat-e Sāl-e Now', 21 March 1980, *Sahifeh-ye Nur*, 12: 202-210, Imam Khomeini Comprehensive Website [n.d.]

28%--ون-ل-اس-ت-ع-ب-س-ان-م-ہب-،ن-اری-ا-ت-ل-م-ہب-پیام/2299/view/posts/com.emam://https>
<29% >مسلمانان-به - گانه zwnj%3B 26% سیزده- های zwnj%3Bتوصیه%26 [accessed 30 August 2020]

Khomeini, Ayatollah, '*Hokm, Fatwā-ye Qatl-e Salman Rushdie*', 14 February 1989, Sahifeh-ye Nur, Vol. 21 (Tehran: Moassesa-ye Tanzim va Nashr-e Āsār-e Imam Khomeini, 1989), 263 <http://www.imam-khomeini.ir/fa/C207_44691/_ فتوای_قتل_سلمان_رشدی،_نویسنده_کتاب_کفرآمیز_آیات_شیطانی> [accessed 30 October 2016].

Khomeini, Ayatollah, *Sokhanrāni*, 30 August 1986, Sahifeh-ye Nur, Vol. 20 (Tehran: Moassesa-ye Tanzim va Nashr-e Āsār-e Imam Khomeini, [n.d.]), 127 <http://sahifeh.net/?p=7702> [accessed 23 January 2015].

Khomeini, Ayatollah, *Sokhanrāni dar Masjed-e A'zam-e Qom*, 15 April 1964, Sahifeh-ye Nur, Vol. 1 (Tehran: Moassesa-ye Tanzim va Nashr-e Āsār-e Imam Khomeini [n.d.]) <http://www.imam-khomeini.ir/fa/books/BooksahifeBody.aspx?id=177> [accessed 23 January 2015].

Khomeini, Ayatollah, *Towbeh-ye Shāh, Hoquq-e Aqalliyat-hā, Rābeteh-ye Jomhuri-ye Eslāmi ba Gharb: Mosāhebeh ba Die Welt*, 7 November 1978, Sahifeh-ye Nur, Vol. 4 (Tehran: Moassesa-ye Tanzim va Nashr-e Āsār-e Imam Khomeini [n.d.]) <http://www.imamkhomeini.ir/fa/books/BooksahifeBody.aspx?id=1031> [accessed 23 January 2015].

Khosravi Yeganeh, Elaheh, *Modir-e Edāreh-ye Ketāb: 'Fe'lan Salāh Namibinim Momayyezān rā Kasi Beshnāsad'* (Tehran: Khabar Online News Agency, 02 March 2014) <http://www.khabaronline.ir/X1Sxxhuflpo0wxofgkqckb42tn1/print/341703/culture/literature?model=PresentationWebUI.Models.Details.DetailsPageViewModel> [accessed 30 October 2016].

List-e Terror-e Sepāh-e Sarboland-e Mohammad, 23 April 2004 <http://news.gooya.com/politics/archives/009574.php> [accessed 23 March 2015].

Mahmoudi, Hassan, *Momayezzi be Romān-e Man Zarbeh Zad* (Tehran: Khabar Online, 22 August 2014) <http://www.khabaronline.ir/detail/371300/culture/literature> [accessed 12 October 2016].

Meftahi, Ida, *Historicizing Ibtizal as a Counter-Aesthetics Corporeal Criterion*, St Andrews: Forum for the Cultural Studies of Iran (17–19 June 2016), University of St. Andrews, <http://forumfortheculturalstudiesofiran.wp.st-andrews.ac.uk/conferences/abstracts-and-bios/> [accessed 29 October 2016].

Mehr News Agency; *Shāhnāmeh-e Dovvom Cheguneh Khalq Shod*, (Tehran: Mehr News Agency, 6 May 2015) <http://www.mehrnews.com/news/2569660/ شاهنامه-دوم-چگونه-خلق-شد-کاملترین-شرح-منظوم-زندگی-امام-علی-ع> [accessed 29 October 2016].

Mirabbasi, Kaveh, *Adabiyyāt-e Āpārtemāni Ravāj Peidā Kardeh-ast* (Tehran: IBNA 6 August 2008) <http://www.ibna.ir/fa/doc/tolidi/23731/میر عباسی-ادبیات-آپارتمانی-رواج-پیدا-کرده> [accessed 13 October 2016].

Mohajerani, Ata'ollah, *Mohajerani: Az In Hameh Dorugh Araq-e Sharm bar Chehreh-tān Namineshinad?* (Iran: JARAS, 11.06.2010) <http://www.rahesbz.net/story/17141/> [accessed 13 October 2016].

Mokhtabad, Seyed Abolhassan, '*Negāhi be Tahavvolāt-e Ketāb va Nashr dar Dowrāy-e Mohammad Khatami*' (London: BBC Persian Online, 8 August 2005) <http://www.bbc.com/persian/arts/story/2005/08/050808_pm-an-book-khatami.shtml> [accessed 25 July 2018].

Mortezavi, Mehrshad, *Tanz/Sānsur-e Kalameh-ye Sharāb az Ash'ār-e Bozorgān* quoted from Qanun (Tehran: ISNA, January 19, 2016) <http://www.isna.ir/news/94102917402/ طنز-سانسور-کلمه-شراب-از-اشعار-بزرگان> [accessed 12 October 2016].

Motahharinia, Mahmoud, *Mājerā-ye Enteshār-e Ketāb-e 101 Professor-e Khatarnāk dar America* (Tehran: Mashregh News, 7 October 2013) <http://www.mashreghnews.ir/fa/news/253130/ماجرای-انتشار-کتاب-101-پروفسور-خطرناک-در-آمریکاچرا-مجوز-انتشار-کتب-مخرب-باطل-نمی%E2%80%8Cشود> [accessed 12 July 2016].

Motammam-e Qanun-e Asāsi-ye Mashruteh (Tehran: The Islamic Parliament Research Centre) <http://rc.majlis.ir/fa/law/show/133414> [accessed 14 January 2016].

Nasim News Agency, *Ershād dar Barzakh* (Tehran: Nasim, 28 January 2015) <http://nasimonline.ir/Content/Detail/974694/ارشاد-در-برزخ> [accessed 4 October 2016].

Nazari, Fazel, '*Zendagināmeh*' (Tehran: Sooremehr Publishers Website) <http://www.sooremehr.ir/fa/author/972> [accessed 13 October 2016].

Nehād-e Ketābkhāneh-hā-ye Omumi-ye Keshvar, *Shiveh-hā-ye Kharid-e Manābe' dar Nehād-e Ketābkhāneh-hā-ye Omumi-ye Keshvar* (Tehran: Nehād-e Ketābkhāneh-hā-ye Omumi-ye Keshvar, 2012) <http://www.iranpl.ir/portal/Home/Default.aspx?CategoryID=d2bbc618-ff69-45db-88dd-710b2bd2d281> [accessed 19 March 2015].

Noghrehkar, Masoud, *Tāvān-e Dādkhāhi* ([n.p.]: Asr-e Nou, 29 October 2007) <http://asre-nou.net/1386/aban/7/m-noghrekar.html> [accessed 10 March 2015].

Noushabadi, Hossein, *Barkhord-e Jeddi-ye Vezārat-e Ershād Bā Chāp-e Ketāb-hā-ye Bedun-e Mojavvez* (Tehran: IBNA, 7 April 2015) <http://www.ibna.ir/fa/doc/report/220671/برخورد-جدی-وزارت-ارشاد-چاپ-کتاب-های-بدون-مجوز-ورود-کتاب-صورت-قاچاق> [accessed 18 October 2016].

Papoli Yazdi, Mohammad Hosein, *Momayyezi-ye Ketāb va Nāsherān-e Setāreh-dār* (Tehran: Alef News, 30 November 2013) [accessed 10 July 2016].

Parvin Award, *Parvin Award Bylaws* (Tehran: Parvin Award, 2015) <http://www.parvin.ir/HomePage.aspx?TabID=4501&Site=parvin&Lang=fa-IR> [accessed 28 February 2015].

Payvandsaraa, *Emtenā' az Paziroftan-e Jayezeh-ye Dowlati-ye She'r-e Fajr* ([n.p.]: Payvandsaraa website, 12 March 2015) <http://payvandsaraa.blogspot.co.uk/2015/03/blog-post_76.html> [accessed 15 April 2015].

Political Studies and Research Institute, *Negāhi be Jāyezeh-hā-ye Adabi-ye Defā'e Moqaddas az Did-e Kārshenāsān* (Tehran: Political Studies and Research Institute, 2015) <http://www.irpsri.com/Show.php?Page=ViewNews&NewsID=4159> [accessed 29 February 2015].

Radio Zamaneh, *Raeis Dana: Kānun dar Marāsem-e Tashyi'e Simin Behbahani Sherkat Namikonad* (Amsterdam: Radio Zamaneh, 21 August 2014) <http://www.radiozamaneh.com/170851> [accessed 13 April 2015].

Radio Zamaneh, *Rasāneh-hā-yi ke Madfun Shodand* (Amsterdam: Radio Zamaneh, 13 February 2008) <http://zamaaneh.com/movie/2008/02/post_77.html> [accessed 15 March 2015].

Rafiee, Bahram, *Mahdudiyat-hā-ye Jadid-e Vezārat-e Ershād* ([n.p.]: Ettelaat Network, [n.d.]) <http://www.ettelaat.net/06-04/news.asp?id=13300> [accessed 17 February 2015].

Ramezanpour, Aliasghar, *Guneh-yi Naslkoshi-ye Farhangi dar Jariyān Ast* (interviewed by Payam Ghasemi) (Washington, DC: Gozaar, 23 April 2008) <http://www.gozaar.org/persian/interview-fa/3532.html> [accessed 19 March 2015].

RFI Persian *Jahān-e Ketāb* (Paris, RFI, 2 January 2014) <http://fa.rfi.fr/گفت-و-گو-با-حافظ-موسوی،-یکی-از-شاعران-ممنوع-القلم-در-ایران-هنر%E2%80%8C-20140102/> [accessed 19 April 2017].

Rostagh, Amir, *Dah Rokhdād-e Mohemm-e Arseh-ye Ketāb va Nashr dar Sāl-e 93* (London: BBC Persian Online, 23 March 2015) <http://www.bbc.co.uk/persian/arts/2015/03/150323_l51_yearender_93_books> [accessed 29 March 2015].

Rostami, M. R., *Sahm-e Vezārat-e Ershād az Budjeh-ye Farhangi Cheqadr Ast? Fehrest-e Nehād-hā-yi ke Barā-ye Kār-e Farhangi Budjeh Migirand* (Tehran: Khabar Online News Agency, 5 May 2014) <http://www.khabaronline.ir/detail/353289/culture/5519> [accessed 26 February 2015].

Salehi, Seyed A., *Chenān ketāb rā bar Gardanam Kubidand ke Ta'ādolam rā az Dast Dādam* (interviewed byHadi Hosseininejad), ILNA, 17 July 2013) (Tehran: Shahrwandan, 2013) <http://www.shahrwandan.ir/news/12749> [accessed 19 March 2015].

Salehi, Seyed Abbas, cited in Elaheh Khosravi Yeganeh, *Mamnu'olqalamhā az Sāyeh Birun Āmadand* (Tehran: Khabar Online, 30 December 2013) <www.khabaronline.ir/detail/330096/culture/literature> [accessed 19 April 2017].

Sarkoohi, Faraj, *Anjoman-e Qalam-e Irani va Jahāni, Hamnām va Bishebāhat* (London: BBC Persian Online, 20 December 2011) <http://www.bbc.co.uk/persian/arts/2011/12/111219_l41_book_international_pen_vs_ghalam.shtml> [accessed 26 February 2015].

Sarkoohi, Faraj, *Enteqām-e Shāer-e Nāmovaffaq az She'r* (Prague: Radio Farda, 7 July 2010) <http://www.radiofarda.com/content/F7_Commentary_on_Khamenei_Meeting_with_Iranian_Artists/2093557.htm> [accessed 26 February 2015].

Sarkoohi, Faraj, *Haft ruz-e ketāb* (London: BBC Persian Online, 1 September 2011) <http://www.bbc.co.uk/persian/arts/2011/09/110901_l41_books_7_days_1sep_11> [accessed 14 April 2015].

Sarkoohi, Faraj, *Ma'nā-ye Jāyezeh-ye Jalal* (Amsterdam: Radio Zamaneh, 4 December 2014) <http://www.radiozamaneh.com/191456> [accessed 29 February 2015].

Sarkoohi, Faraj, *Nevisandegān-e Khodi va Gheir-e Khodi* (London: BBC Persian Online, 20 December 2011) <http://www.bbc.co.uk/persian/arts/2011/12/111219_l41_book_international_pen_vs_Qalam.shtml> [accessed 14 April 2015].

Sarkoohi, Faraj, *Ta'qib, Robāyesh, Takzib; an interview with Faraj Sarkoohi* ([n.p.].: Khat-e Solh Monthly, 20 February 2014) <http://www.peace-mark.org/taghib-robayesh-takzib> [accessed 1 April 2015].

Shabnam News, *Budjeh-ye Āfarinesh va Pazhuhesh dar Bonyād Kamtar az Dastmozd-e yek Fasl-e Bāzikon-e Football Ast* (Tehran: Shabnam News, 23 April 2014) <http://www.shabnamnews.com/news/14479> [accessed 21 April 2015].

Shohadā-ye Iran News, *Hayulā-ye Mostahjan-e Adabiyyāt dar Vitrin-e Ketābforushi-hā* (Tehran: Shohadā-ye Iran News Site, 23 February 2015) <http://shohadayeiran.com/fa/news/67052/%D9%87%DB%8C%D9%88%D9%84%D8%A7%DB%8C-%D9%85%D8%B3%D8%AA%D9%87%D8%AC%D9%86-%D8%A7%D8%AF%D8%A8%DB%8C%D8%A7%D8%AA-%D8%AF%D8%B1-%D9%88%DB%8C%D8%AA%D8%B1%DB%8C%D9%86%E2%80%8C-%DA%A9%D8%AA%D8%A7%D8%A8%E2%80%8C%D9%81%D8%B1%D9%88%D8%B4%DB%8C%E2%80%8C%D9%87%D8%A7> [accessed 23 March 2015].

Showrā-ye Farhang-e Omumi-ye Keshvar, *Ahdāf, Siyāsathā va Zavābet-e Nashr-e Ketāb* (Tehran: Dabirkhāneh-ye Farhang-e Omumi-ye Keshvar, 1988) <http://pcci.ir/?option=com_content&view=article&id=132:1> [accessed 18 January 2015].

SNN, *Hayulā-yi ke az Vitrin-e Ketābforushi-hā-ye Tehran Sar Dar Āvard* (Tehran: SNN, 27 March 2015) <http://www.snn.ir/print/398319> [accessed 4 October 2016].

Staff, Harriet, 'Iranian Poets Fateme Ekhtesari and Mehdi Moosavi Imprisoned' <http://www.poetryfoundation.org/harriet/2013/12/iranian-poets-fateme-ekhtesari-and-mehdi-moosavi-imprisoned/> [accessed 22 April 2015].

Supreme Council of the Cultural Revolution, *History of Supreme Council of the Cultural Revolution* (Tehran: SCCR website) <http://en.farhangoelm.ir/SCCR/History-of-Supreme-Council-of-the-Cultural-Revolut> [accessed 6 July 2016].

Supreme Council of the Cultural Revolution, *Naqsha-ye Mohandesi-ye Farhangi-ye Keshvar* (Tehran: SCCR Secretariat, 2013) <http://www.sccr.ir/UserFiles/entesharat/%D9%85%D9%87%D9%86%D8%AF%D8%B3_%20%D9%81%D8%B1%D9%87%D9%86%DA%AF__opt.pdf> [accessed 25 October 2016].

Tabibnia, Ali *Sahm-e Dowlat az Eqtesād-e Melli Taqriban be 90 Darsad Rasideh-ast*, (Iran: Tabnak News, 28 October 2015) <http://www.tabnak.ir/fa/news/353928/-سهم-دولت-از-اقتصاد-ملی-تقریباً-به-90-درصد-رسیده-است> [accessed 27 September 2016].

Tabnak News, *Sarmomayyez-e Ketāb dar Vezārat-e Farhang va Ershād: Man Hayulā Nistam* (Tehran: Tabnak News, 26 March 2016) https://www.tabnak.ir/fa/news/576783/%D8%B3%D8%B1%D9%85%D9%85%DB%8C%D8%B2-%DA%A9%D8%AA%D8%A7%D8%A8%E2%80%8C%D9%87%D8%A7-%D8%AF%D8%B1-%D9%88%D8%B2%D8%A7%D8%B1%D8%AA-%D9%81-%D8%B1%D9%87%D9%86%DA%AF-%D9%88 [accessed 10 July 2016].

Talei, Javad, *Matbuāt-e Iran dar Manganeh-ye do Nezām* (Germany: DW Persian Online, 6 February 2009) <www.dw.de/مطبوعات-ایران-در-منگنه-دو-نظام٢/a-4008237> [accessed 26 January 2015].

Tasnim News, *Be Vaqt-e Mahtāb, Dehbashi, Televizion va Montaqedān* (Tehran: Tasnim News, 21 January 2015) <http://www.tasnimnews.com/Home/Single/628344> [accessed 15 May 2015].

Tasnim News, *Tavarroqi bar "Yādestān-e Dust"*, (Tehran: Tasnim News, 22 February 2015) <http://www.tasnimnews.com/Home/Single/661006> [accessed 27 February 2015].

Tonekaboni, Parisa, *Weblogistān-e Fārsi be Kodām Su Miravad* (Germany: Goethe Institute, May 2015) <http://www.goethe.de/ges/phi/prj/ffs/the/103/fa14587618.htm> [accessed 30 September 2016].

United Nations Website, *Universal Declaration of Human Rights, Article 19*, <http://www.un.org/en/universal-declaration-human-rights/> [accessed 21 October 2016].

Yazdanjoo, Payam, *Sarkub-e Maktub: Dāstan-e ketāb dar dowrān-e Ahmadinejad* (London: BBC Persian Online, 30 June 2013) <http://www.bbc.co.uk/persian/blogs/2013/06/130627_blogfa_l44_nazeran_censorship> [accessed 17 February 2015].

Zarrinpanah, Sepideh, *Dar Jostoju-ye Hall-e Moshkel-e Nashr-e Farsi dar khārej-e Keshvar* (London: BBC Persian Online, 30 June 2011) <http://www.bbc.co.uk/persian/arts/2011/06/110630_l41_book_farsi_publication_abroad.shtml> [accessed 8 April 2015].

Websites Consulted

Anjoman-e Qalam-e Iran, <http://www.anjomanghalam.ir/?page_id=5> [accessed 26 February 2015].

Asr-e Entezār Website, <http://www.asr-entezar.ir/archives/1618> [accessed 21 October 2016].

Ayatollah Khamenei Portal, <http://farsi.khamenei.ir/tag-content?id=1010> [accessed 2 February 2015].

Blog Census, <http://web.archive.org/web/20031202022722/http://www.blogcensus.net/?page=lang> [accessed 30 October 2016].

Bonyād-e She'r va Adabiyyāt-e Dāstāni-ye Irāniān, <http://www.adabiatirani.com/fa/> [accessed 26 September 2016].

Golshiri Foundation, <http://www.golshirifoundation.com/award.htm> [accessed 28 February 2015].
Fajr Poetry Award, <http://www.fajrpoem.com/fa/index.php#section1> [accessed 28 September 2016].
Festivals Centre of the Art Council, <http://www.artfest.ir/festivals/57> [accessed 28 September 2016].
H&S Media, <http://www.hands.media/books/> [accessed 8 April 2015].
The House of Free Speech, <http://www.thofs.org> [accessed 12 January 2015].
Hoze Honari, <http://hozehonari.com/Default.aspx?page=20297> [accessed 24 February 2015].
Iranian PEN Centre in Exile, <http://www.iran-pen.com/english/home.html> [accessed 9 April 2015].
Kānun-e Adabiyyāt-e Iran, <http://kanonweb.blogfa.com/> [accessed 26 February 2015].
Keyhān Institute, <http://www.keyhanbook.ir/?cat=4&paged=8> [accessed 12 April 2015].
Khāneh-ye Shāerān-e Iran, <http://poetry.ir/?sn=abouts&lang> [accessed 26 February 2015].
Mazda Publishers, <http://www.mazdapublishers.com/book/one-womans-war> [accessed 13 October 2016].
Ministry of Culture and Islamic Guidance, <http://www.farhang.gov.ir/fa/intro> [accessed 8 July 2016].
Naakojaa Publishers, <http://www.naakojaa.com/> [accessed 25 March 2015].
Nogaam Publishers, <http://www.nogaam.com/> [accessed 25 March 2015].
Tabriz Municipality Cultural-Art Organization, <http://honar.tabriz.ir/#سال جشنواره کتاب تبریز> [accessed 26 February 2015].
Tehran Goldsmiths and Jewellers Trade Union, <http://www.tgju.org/> [accessed 15 March 2015].
Tehran International Book Fair, <http://www.tibf.ir/page/535619014c00003f0815368d> [accessed 21 March 2015].
Tehran Municipality Cultural-Art Organization, <http://www.farhangsara.ir/%D9%81%D8%B1%D9%87%D9%86%DA%AF%D8%B3%D8%B1%D8%A7%D9%87%D8%A7.aspx> [accessed 26 February 2015].

Other Sources

Abdollahi, Ali, *interviewed by Alireza Abiz* (2012).
Ahmadi, Masoud, *Interviewed by Alireza Abiz* (2012).
Biabangard Javan, Adel, *Facebook chat with Alireza Abiz* (2014).
Hassani, Alireza, *Private chat with Alireza Abiz in Telegram* (2016).
Iranian Writers Association, *Statement dated 13 November 2008, Email to Alireza Abiz* (2008).
Iravani, Azadeh, *Email to Alireza Abiz* (2015).
Mahmoud, Ahmad, *Memoirs*, published posthumously in Persian Contemporary Fiction Channel in Telegram (31 October 2016).
Pourjafari, Mohammadreza, *Conversation with Alireza Abiz* (2012).
Ravanshid, M., *Interviewed by Alireza Abiz* (2012).

INDEX

Abrahamian, Ervand 19, 25, 123, 135
addiction/drug references 47, 82, 90
Ādineh literary journal 115, 116
advertisements 54, 114
Aesopian language 14, 100, 131, 154–5
Āghā, use of term 69–70, 165–6 n.44
Ahmadinejad, Mahmoud 12, 56, 57, 58, 91, 109, 148
Akbariani, Mohammad Hashem 141, 143, 157, 158
Akhavan Saleth, Mehdi 37, 84, 93
alcohol references 47, 48, 81, 100, 132
Al-e Ahmad, Jalal 32, 108, 164 n.29
aliases 128, 129
allegory, *see* Aesopian language; figurative language
Althusser, Louis 4, 145
Amini, Ismail (Dr) 95–6
Amirfaryar, Farrokh 53–5
animal references 48, 81, 83, 86, 90
Anjoman-e Qalam-e Iran (Iran Pen Association) 112, 113
annual poetry meetings 36, 165–7 n.44
anonymity
    authors 128, 129
    censors 44, 48–50
Ānsār-e Hezbollah 117, 120
'anti-revolutionary' writing, state perceptions 34, 68–9, 92
appraisal, *see momayyezi*
Arabic versus Persian words 88–9, 142
Arabs, ethnic and minority issues 71
arbitrary nature of censorship 57, 141, 143, 157 *see also* unpredictability of censors
Art Council (*Hoze Honari*) 31, 111
Asadzadeh, Mohammadreza 127
Atashi, Manouchehr 40, 120
auditing, *see momayyezi*
Ayatollahs
    use of term in literature 74 *see also* Jannati; Khamenei; Khomeini

Bahar, Malekolshoara 21, 37
Bahar, Mohammad Taghi 22, 23, 45
barrasi (valuation), euphemism for censorship 12, 44, 50
beauty, descriptions censored 65–6, 88
Behbahani, Simin 38, 40, 93, 121, 155
benefits of censorship 6–7, 14, 147–51, 154
blacklisted writers and publishers 57, 61, 91, 172 n.27
blasphemy 28, 76–8
blogging/Blogistan 128–30
Bonyād-e She'r va Adabiyyāt-e Dāstani-ye Irāniān (Iranian foundation for Poetry and Fiction) 112–13
book fairs 57, 114, 127, 175 n.44
Book Office (MCIG Department General of Book and Reading) 12, 29, 43–5, 48–58
bookshops 71, 116, 127
Bourdieu, Pierre 5–6, 144, 145
breast(s) 63–4, 90, 102, 153
bribery of censors 50, 132
bribery of writers 106
Brodsky, Joseph 131, 150, 154
Budan Asan Nist ("To Be is not Easy") by Vladimir Holan 101–4
Bunn, Matthew 4, 106
Burgess, Edward 17–18
Butler, Judith 6, 7, 145

card games/playing cards 82, 90
CDs of books, word searching 57
'censorship', avoiding use of word in Iran 12, 44
"Censorship of Books: Research on 1400 Documents of Book Censorship in Year 1375" by Rajabzadeh 12, 44–5, 51–2, 60, 61, 67, 86
Censorship Department (19th century) 19
censors (*momayyezes* or *barrases*)
    education and training 49, 50, 51, 52
    job titles 12, 43–4, 50

payment 50–1
process of assessment 44, 59–104
relationship with writers 49, 55, 95–6
secrecy of identity 44, 48–50
team leaders/senior censors 44, 51
Centre for Literary Creativities 111
chador 73, 75–6
chain murders 117, 119–20
changes over time in the censor machine 52–8
chief censor (unidentified), interviews 49, 50, 51, 59, 91
children
    censorship of children's literature 83, 89–90
    exposure to literature 1–2, 133–4
Children and Young Adults Intellectual Development centres 111, 133
Christianity 47, 77, 78, 90
cinema/film-makers 14, 40, 89, 99
classical literature 62
classical poetry 45, 66–7, 84, 134–5
clothing
    Islamic dress 73, 74, 75–6
    Western/immodest 48, 60, 64
coercive control of expression, *see* punishment; repressive censorship
Coetzee, J.M. 150, 155, 156
communism
    views of 29, 32, 71–2, 91, 93, 94 *see also* leftist movements and ideology; Soviet Union
conditional authorization for publication 44, 45, 59
Constitutional Revolution (1905–1911) 10, 19–21
Constitution of Iran
    constitutional monarchy 19–20, 24, 29
    Islamic Republic 10–11, 27, 110, 149
constructive nature of censorship 6–7, 14, 150–1 *see also* creativity
contemporary theory, *see* new (postmodern) censorship theories
copyleft, free distribution of literature 130
copyright issues, illegal distribution of literature accepted by authors 126, 130
coup d'états
    1908 21
    1921 22
    1953 10, 17, 24–5, 26

creativity
    stimulated by censorship 6–7, 14, 149–51, 154
    suppressed by censorship 154, 155–6, 157–9
cultural control, beyond direct censorship 13, 105–6
Cultural Engineering Map project 28, 35
cultural institutions, state control 105, 110–13
cultural invasion theory 11, 31–5, 51, 117, 118, 146, 149
Cultural Revolution, origin and aims 11, 28, 30–1
Cultural Revolution Headquarters establishment 28
    see also Supreme Council of Cultural Revolution
cultural/social/lifestyle issues, reasons for censorship 47, 48, 60–1, 80–8, 149
cultural unity, role of censorship 147–8

Daftar-e She'r-e Javān (Young Poetry Office) 112
dancing references 48, 62, 80, 84, 90
Dastan-e Enqelab (Revolution's Story) international festival 108–9
deception/distortion of truth, surrendering to censorship 15, 155, 158
defence of censorship 6–7, 14, 147–51, 154
definitions of censorship 3–4, 7, 9, 145–6
degarandish writers 35, 39
Department of Government Press (19th century) 18
desecration of graves 121
destruction of books 2, 116
diaspora, *see* exiled writers and intellectuals
divorce references 83, 90
dog references 48, 81, 83, 90, 103
dots (ellipses) for censored words 84, 103, 125, 132
Dowlatabadi, Mahmoud 40, 65, 67–8, 120, 137
dowlati (State) writers 39
drug/addiction references 47, 82, 90

economic relations
    economic censorship 13, 106, 113–15, 137–8

independent literary awards 107–8
market forces 3–4, 5, 6, 9, 106
education 4, 28, 31
educational books 90
effects of censorship on literature 133–44, 149–51, 154
effects of censorship on writers 136, 142–3
Ekhtesari, Fatemeh 142, 180 n.5
electronic books by exiled Iranians 128
ellipses (three dots) for censored words 84, 103, 125, 132
Emami, Saeed 116, 117, 118, 120
erotic content, *see* sexual references
E'temad interviews 49, 50, 51, 59, 91
E'temadolsaltaneh 18–19
E'tesami, Pavin 38
ethical and moral issues
   principles of Press Law 27
   surrendering to censorship 15, 155, 158
ethnic and minority issues 71
euphemisms
   for 'censorship' 12, 43–4, 50, 156
   censorship effects on literature 154, 155 *see also* Aesopian language
exiled writers and intellectuals (Iranian diaspora)
   Ahmad Shakeri's view of 156
   Asadipour 92
   choosing a life in exile 13, 15, 18, 113, 158
   Hejazi 107
   Internet contact with Iran 129
   Iranian Pen in Exile 125
   Kasrayi 120
   Mohajerani 39–40
   publishing abroad 128
experience of censorship, subjective/lived experience 7, 8–9, 106, 133, 146
'external, coercive and repressive' censorship 3–4, 8, 113
   see also punishment; repressive censorship
extrajudicial killings 117
   see also murders
extratextual censorship 91–5

Fajr International Poetry Festival 108
fame of writers 36, 106, 107, 110, 142
Fardid, Ahmad 164 n.29
Farrokhzad, Forough 38, 94–5
fatwa against Salman Rushdie 30, 92, 142
'Festival of 20 Years of Iranian Fiction' (1997) 39
festivals 39–40, 108–9, 111, 112, 113
fiction
   anti-war novels 40, 139–40
   censorship figures 45
   crime novels 83
   historical 84–5, 132
   political themes 67–8
   problem for censors 59–60
   'sexual' content 62–3
figurative language
   assumed to be problematic 77
   to avoid censorship 26, 59, 63, 131, 132, 135, 150, 154
film-makers/cinema 14, 40, 89, 99
financial pressures, *see* economic relations
Firoozkoohi, Amiri 37, 38
First World War 22
Foucault, Michel 5, 6–7, 145, 150
freedom of expression/free speech
   Ayatollah Khomeini's stated views 29, 30
   as basic human right 14, 147, 151
   binary opposition to censorship 3
   as a concept 4, 6
   Constitution and laws of Iran 10–11
   defended by supporters of censorship 149–50
   importance in Iran 14
   theoretical impossibility 5, 6
freedom of the press, constitutional restrictions 10–11, 27–8
Freshwater, Helen 6, 7, 8, 146
funding of censorship 50–1
funerals 40, 106, 120–1

gambling references 48, 80, 81, 82
Ganji, Akbar 117, 118
Gardun literary journal 115
generative/productive force of censorship 6–7, 14, 150–1
Ghaffari, Parvin 66
gharbzadegi (Westoxification) 32, 164 n.29
ghazal style poetry 36, 111, 134, 135
gheir-e khodi (outsider) concept 39
'God', use of word 75, 77–8
Golshiri Foundation/Golshiri Award 107, 108

Golshiri, Houshang 75, 92, 120, 128
Gramsci, Antonio 4, 145
Guardian Council 27
guidelines on censorship 27–9, 46

Haji, problematic usage 69–70, 94
Hajv poetry 84
Hakkak, Ahmad Karimi 17, 18, 20, 105, 134, 136
Harandi, Saffar 56
harms, justification for censorship 3, 27–8, 147–9, 152–3
Hassani, Alireza 101–4
Hedayat, Sadiq 25, 93, 94, 107
Hejazi, Arash 92
heroes, persecuted writers 142
Hezbollah (hardline regime supporters) 115, 116, 117, 120, 175 n.49
hierarchy of belief 152
hijab 73, 75, 94, 115, 144
historical figures, out of favour 71, 79
historical references, views of censors 47, 79–80, 84–5, 132
historical works, referencing problematic writers 94–5
history
    censorship before the Cultural Revolution 10, 17–26
    censorship since ancient times 9–10
    cultural invasion theory 32
    Victorian censorship 7
Holan, Vladimir 101–4
Hosseini, Ali 70, 76
Hosseini, Mohammad 57, 91, 148
Hoze Honari (The Art Council) 31, 111
human rights
    freedom of expression 3, 14, 147, 151, 161 n.29
    violations as punishment 113, 117–19
humiliation tactics 118–19, 137–8, 156
hypocrisy, surrendering to censorship 15, 158

IBNA, *see* Iranian Book News Agency
ICA, *see* Islamic Consultative Assembly
identity hiding, *see* anonymity
idioms, taken out of context 64, 76, 81, 83
"I Hear a Tree From My Desk" by Alireza Abiz 96–101

illegal sales of banned books 125–8
illustrations in books 47, 83, 88, 90
image of society distorted by censorship 139–42
Imamzadeh Taher Cemetery 120–1
immorality, *see* ethical and moral issues; sexual references
imprisonment 116, 117, 123, 136, 142, 157
independent literary awards 107–8
indirect forces of censorship 4, 5, 145
inquisition 19, 93, 157
insider/outsider concept 39
integrity of writers 109–10
intellectual aggression, *see* cultural invasion theory
intellectuals
    Ayatollah Khomeini's view 34–5
    blamed for making censorship a problem 156
intergenerational relationship of writers 13, 129, 159
internal freedom, writing in spite of censorship 151
International literary festivals 108
Internet
    blogging 128–30
    censorship and control 129–30
    other uses by writers 128, 130
    rendering censorship futile 153
interrogation 41, 117, 119–20, 138, 157
intimidation 13, 106, 129–30, 146
"Into Darkness … Trapped by the Shah" (*Ta Siyahi … Dar Dam-e Shah*) by Parvin Ghaffari 66
Iranian Book News Agency (IBNA) 127
Iranian diaspora, *see* exiled writers and intellectuals
Iranian foundation for Poetry and Fiction (*Bonyād-e She'r va Adabiyyāt-e Dāstani-ye Irāniān*) 112–13
Iranian Poetry Today, award enterprise of *Kārnāmeh* journal 108
Iranian Poets Society (*Khaneh-ye Shaeran-e Iran*) 112, 113
Iranian Writers Association (*Kānun-e Nevisandegān-e Iran*) 26, 56, 58, 94, 112, 120, 121, 159
Iran Literary Centre (*Kānun-e Adabiyyāt-e Iran*) 112

Iran Pen Association (*Anjoman-e Qalam-e Iran*) 112, 113
Iraq–Iran war 30, 33–4, 53, 54, 70, 109, 127, 139–40
Islamic Consultative Assembly (ICA) 27, 28
Islamic culture
  justification for censorship 148
  promotion by cultural organizations 105, 110–12
  propagation by press 27
Islamic dress 73, 74, 75–6
Islamic ideology
  in conflict with Iranian identity/culture 62, 73
  Cultural Revolution 31
  need to silence/subdue/undermine alternative discourses 148, 153–4
  principles 11, 19, 27, 28, 77, 149
  rule of law 156
  values seen as self-evidently right 148
  versus nationalistic sentiments 19, 23, 71, 85, 89
  see also religious references
Islamic Propagation Organization (*Sazeman-e Tabliqat-e Eslami*) 31, 39, 111, 139
Islamic Republic of Iran Broadcasting (IRIB) 105, 110–11, 119

Jalal-e Al-e Ahmad Awards 108
Jannati, Ahmad (Ayatollah) 148
Jannati, Ali 57, 91
journals, closed down 115
justification for censorship 147–53

Kakayi, Abduljabbar 143–4
Kānun-e Adabiyyāt-e Iran (Iran Literary Centre) 112
Kānun-e Nevisandegān-e Iran (Iranian Writers' Association/*Kānun*) 26, 56, 58, 94, 112, 120, 121, 123–5, 159
Karimi Hakkak, Ahmed 17, 18, 20, 105, 134, 136
Kārnāmeh literary journal 115
Kasravi, Ahmad 77, 95, 171 n.18
Keyhān (Pro-government newspaper and books of articles) 118, 119, 177 n.77

Khamenei, Sayyid Ali Hosseini (Grand Ayatollah)
  annual poetry meetings 36, 134–5, 165–7 n.44
  called *Āghā* 70
  changes to SCCR 28
  cultural invasion 32–4
  importance of culture 11, 31
  poet and critic 36–40
  relationship with poetry and literature 11, 35, 36, 40, 41
  views on war literature 139, 140
  see also Supreme Leader
Khaneh-ye Shaeran-e Iran (Iranian Poets Society) 112
Khatami, Mohammad 12, 39, 44, 54–8, 95, 107, 118, 124
khodi (insider) concept 39
Khomeini, Sayyid Ruhollah (Grand Ayatollah)
  confusion of opinions on freedom of expression 11, 29, 30
  Cultural Revolution 28, 30–1
  Fatwa against Rushdie 30, 92, 142
  importance of culture 11
  interest and views on poetry 36, 41, 134
  threats from East and West 32
  see also Supreme Leader
kissing references 63, 65
Klima, Ivan 14, 138, 151, 155–6
Kown/Kun ambiguity 84

language
  abusive/indecent/slang 83–4
  idioms taken out of context 64, 76, 81, 83
  Persian language 88–9, 141–2
  see also Aesopian language; euphemisms; figurative language
Larijani, Ali 12, 54, 112, 119
lasting effects of censorship 159
leftist movements and ideology 32, 61, 68
  see also communism; Marxist theory/approach
legal issues
  laws and policies 10–11, 20, 27–41, 43, 116
  Sharia law 56, 156

Index

legislation
   confusion and ambiguity 11, 30
   ICA as law maker 27–8
   role of SCCR 28
Lesser Despotism period 20
'letter of 134 Writers' (1994) 115, 123–4
letters condemning independent writers 116, 118, 176 n.72
letters of protest against censorship 39–40, 49, 92, 115, 123–4
libraries 1–2, 55, 112, 114, 115–16, 133–4
licencing requirements and process 29, 43–5, 54, 55, 56
lifestyle/cultural/social references, reasons for censorship 47, 48, 60–1, 80–8, 149
literary awards 39–40, 56, 105, 107–13, 124, 134
literary books (history/anthologies/criticism and commentary) 45, 60
literary criticism
   lacking in Iran 159
   role of censors 84–9
literary journals 115
lived experience of feeling censored 7, 8–9, 106, 133, 146
"Lolita" by Vladimir Nabokov 127
love, references censored 47, 63, 65–6, 67, 89–90
lyricism, conflation with eroticism 60, 62, 66–7
lyric poetry 41, 60, 66–7

magazines, *see* literary journals; newspapers and periodicals
map project, Cultural Engineering 28, 35
market forces role in censorship 3–4, 5, 6, 9, 106
Marxist theory/approach 4, 47, 145, 150
mass communication media
   diffusing Islamic culture 27
   see also Internet; newspapers and periodicals; television and radio
Mathnavi poem by Jalal al-Din Muhammad Balkhi 62
MCIG, *see* Ministry of Culture and Islamic Guidance
Mehregan-e Adab Award 107
memorial services 106, 120

metaphorical language 131, 150, 155
   see also figurative language
Ministry of Culture and Islamic Guidance (MCIG)
   authority change effects 53, 54
   Department General of Book and Reading (Book Office) 12, 29, 43–5, 48–58
   Khatami as minister 12, 44, 54, 58
   limits to influence 105
   literary awards 108
   other ministers 12, 56–7
   responsibilities and duties 43
Mirsalim, Mostafa 12, 54–5
mobtazal
   use of term 61–2, 63, 67, 85, 92
   see also sexual references
Mohajerani, Ata'ollah 32, 39–40, 56
Mohammad Reza Shah 10, 23–4
Mokhtari, Mohammad 120, 125
Molavi, Alishah 127
momayyezi (auditing/appraisal), euphemism for censorship 12, 43–4, 50, 156
Momayyezi-ye Ketāb: Pajuheshi dar 1400 Sanad-e Momayyezi-ye Ketāb dar Sāl-e 1375 (Censorship of Books: Research on 1400 Documents of Book Censorship in Year 1375) by Ahmad Rajabzadeh 12, 44–5, 60–1
monarchy
   constitutional 19–20, 24, 29
   preconstitutional 17–20
moral issues, *see* ethical and moral issues
moral restraint, self-censorship 143–4
moral weakness, shown by possession of banned material 152–3
Mosaddeq, Mohammad (Dr) 10, 24, 25, 26, 71
Motahharinia, Mahmoud (Dr) 50–1, 59–60, 148–9
Mousavi, Hafez 88, 172 n.27
Mousavi, Mehdi 142
Mousavi, Mir Hossein 57, 113
Mozaffar al-Din Shah 19–20
Muhammad Ali Shah 20
mullah/Mullah, usage criticised 73, 74, 79–80
Muller, Beate 7–8, 136
murders 92, 116, 117–18, 119–20, 125, 136
music 47, 134

names
  authors concealing 128, 129
  censors concealing 44, 48–50
  changed or criticised by censors 69–71, 73, 74–5, 86
  Khamenei avoiding naming poets 37, 38
  perceived insults to 88
Nāser al-Din Shah 17–19
nationalism/nationalistic sentiments 19, 21, 23, 71, 85, 89
National Radio and Television, *see* Islamic Republic of Iran Broadcasting
Nazari, Fazel 111
need for censorship 144, 147–9
'Neither the East, Nor the West / Islamic Republic', Khomeini 32
new (postmodern) censorship theories 4, 5, 8, 145–6, 150–1
newspapers and periodicals
  circulation in Iran 55
  closed down 29–30, 115
  history 17–19
  interviews with censorship officials 49, 50, 51, 59, 91
  official advertisements 114

"Objectives, Policies, Rules and Regulations for Publishing Books" (document ratified by SCCR 1988) 28–9, 46
online publication 128–9
  see also blogging; Internet
open protests to censorship 123–5
opinions, variation and beliefs 151–2
outwitting censors 130–2
  see also Aesopian language; figurative language

Pahlavi dynasty 22–6, 33, 79
paper supply for publishers, state control 114
Parvin award scheme 108
patronage 13, 39, 53, 94, 106, 107, 110–13, 135, 159
  see also state sponsorship
PEKA Co (publishing cooperative) 107
PEN International 112
pen names/aliases 128, 129
'pen' use of word 112

periodicals, *see* literary journals; newspapers and periodicals
Persian language 88–9, 141–2
Persian literature
  censorship figures 45
  classical 62
personal taste of censors 86
pictures in books 47, 83, 88, 90
pictures of writers on book covers 110
pig/ham references 48, 81, 90
Plato 147
playing cards/card games 82, 90
plays and playwrights 60, 92, 137
poetry 2
  after the Constitutional Revolution 21
  Ayatollah Khamenei's relationship 11, 36–8, 41
  case studies of censorship 96–104
  censorship figures 45
  collections censored 172 n.21
  cultural and lifestyle issues 83–4
  degree of censorship 60
  importance in Iran 40–1
  lyricism 66–7
  political implications 71–2
  political use 40–1
  promotion of classical style 134
  readings 36, 37, 40, 112, 135, 165–7 n.44
  refused on technical grounds 86, 97
  rejected with no reason 88, 172 n.21
poetry gatherings, meetings with Ayatollah Khamenei 36, 134–5, 165–7 n.44
political gain overcoming censorship ideals 66
political involvement in censorship 157
political references, reasons for censorship 46, 47, 67–72
postmodern (new) censorship theories 4, 5, 8, 145–6, 150–1
power and censorship 3, 4–5, 6, 7
Press Law 11, 20, 27, 43, 116–17
productive/generative force of censorship 6–7, 150–1
  see also creativity
protest against censorship
  letters 39–40, 49, 92, 115, 123–4
  other open protest 124–5
publicity
  censorship increasing 127–8, 142
  state sponsored 13, 107, 159

public libraries 43, 55, 111, 114, 133
publishers
    burnt down 116
    business licences 43, 55, 56
    closed down 92, 107
    outside Iran 128
    paper supply 114
    role in censorship 55-6, 58
punishment 99, 106, 107, 113-21

Qajar dynasty 22, 33
quality of literature
    criticised by censors 85-6
    effects of censorship 149-51, 154

radio, *see* television and radio
Rajabzadeh, Ahmad 12, 44-5, 51-2, 60, 61, 67, 86
reactions to censorship 123-32, 135
reasons for censorship, taxonomy 61-89
recognition for authors, state control 36, 38, 107, 110
relationship references, reasons for censorship 47, 48
relaxation of censorship
    historical 19-22, 24, 26
    just after 1979 revolution 53, 136
    just before 1979 revolution 26, 126, 136
    Khatami's regime 55-6
    political changes 53, 57-8
religious ideology, *see* Islamic ideology
religious references, reasons for censorship 46-7, 73-80, 90
repression as incitement to discourse 7
repressive censorship 115-21
    increasing self-censorship 117, 136
    security forces/authorities' role 10, 25, 57, 116-21, 157
    see also imprisonment; interrogation; intimidation; murders; torture
revolutionary art and culture, perceived Western view 34
rewards for approved writers 105-13
    see also literary awards; patronage; state sponsorship
Reza Shah (formerly Reza Khan) 10, 22-4, 32, 79
Rouhani, Hassan 12, 57-8, 91, 121
rule of law, opposition to censorship seen as opposing 156

Rushdie, Salman 15, 30, 92, 95, 142, 158-9
Russia
    folk tales 89
    modern literature 135, 154
    nineteenth century literature 151, 154, 155, 157
    perceived influences 34
    see also Soviet Union

Sacred Defence, *see* Iraq-Iran war
Sadegh Hedayat Foundation/Sadegh Hedayat Award 107
Saeedi Sirjani, Ali Akbar 117-18, 123
Salahi, Emran 69, 125
Salehi, Seyed Ali 72, 117, 126, 159
samizdat, *see* underground publication
Sarkoohi, Faraj 37, 93, 109, 116-17, 118, 119, 141
satirical writing 69, 111, 125
SAVAK Secret Police 10, 25, 123
Sazeman-e Tabliqat-e Eslami (Islamic Propagation Organization) 31, 39, 111, 139
SCCR *see* Supreme Council of Cultural Revolution
scientific books 44, 90
Scientific Secretary of the Book Office (Dr Motahharinia) 50-1, 59-60, 148-9
secular (*degarandish*) writers 35, 39
secular nationalism 19, 21, 23, 71
security forces/authorities, role in censorship 10, 25, 57, 116-21, 157, 172 n.27
security threats, freedom of expression 10, 25, 26, 57, 118
self-censorship
    changing regime effects 25, 56, 58
    children's literature 90
    cultural conditioning 144, 145
    fighting against 15
    impacts on quality of writing 157-8
    repression effects 117, 136
    success of censorship system 13, 142-4
    using Aesopian language 131, 154-5
Sepanlou, Mohammad Ali 93, 121, 128, 132
sexual references, reasons for censorship 7, 47, 61-7, 80-1, 102
Shāhnāmeh 62
Shakeri, Ahmad 154, 156

Shamisa, Cyrus (Dr) 127–8
Shamlou, Ahmad 93, 95, 120, 121, 126
Shams, Fatemeh 53, 134
Sharia law 56, 156
Shariati, Ali (Dr) 1, 32, 46, 70
She'r-e Enqelab (Revolution's Poetry) international festival 108
Shojaei Saein, Ali 49–50
singing 47, 80
slang language censored 83
smoking references 47, 82, 84
smuggled publications from abroad 18, 19, 127
social cohesion, role of censorship 147–8
social/cultural/lifestyle issues, reasons for censorship 47, 48, 60–1, 80–8, 149
social problems, references banned 59, 60–1, 82, 90
social structures, role in censorship 4, 5, 145
soft war, *see* cultural invasion theory
Soviet Union (USSR) 32, 34, 119, 131, 143, 149, 154
state control of paper supply 114
state sponsorship
    awards and festivals 39–40, 105, 108–9, 111, 134
    classical poetry 134
    online activism 129
    promoted books 138–9, 140
    writers and poets 13, 39–40, 53, 68, 139–40, 159
statistics from book censorship research 44–5
subjective experience of feeling censored 7, 8–9, 106, 133, 146
success of censorship, self-censorship 13, 142–4
Sufism 47, 79
suicide references 82–3
Sunnism 47
Supreme Council of Cultural Revolution (SCCR) 11, 28, 35, 52
Supreme Leader
    power over press and culture 11, 27, 28, 52, 149
    see also Khamenei; Khomeini
surrendering to censorship
    ethics 15, 155, 158
    see also self-censorship
symbolism, *see* Aesopian language; figurative language

Taghvayi, Nasser 143
Takāpu literary journal 115
Ta Siyahi ... Dar Dam-e Shah ("Into Darkness ... Trapped by the Shah") by Parvin Ghaffari 66
team leaders (senior censors) 44, 51
technical and literary issues, censorship 61, 84–9
technology
    rendering censorship futile 153
    see also Internet
Tehran International Book Fair 114, 175 n.44
Tehran Municipality Cultural and Art Organization 111
Telegram online messaging system 130
television and radio
    IRIB 105, 110–11, 119
    language 141–2
    patronage 110
    state ownership 27, 31
"The Colonel" (*Zaval-e Colonel*) by Mahmoud Dowlatabadi 67–8
theory of harm 152, 153
    see also harms
"To Be is not Easy" (*Budan Asan Nist*) by Vladimir Holan 101–4
tokenism 106, 109, 146
torture 116, 117–18, 119, 126, 157, 176 n.61
translation
    accuracy and trust 141
    idioms 76
    Persian versus Arabic words 88–9
translators, disapproved of 91, 92, 93
turbans 73, 74

underground publication and illegal sales 20, 23, 125–8
Union of Soviet Socialist Republics (USSR/Soviet Union) 32, 34, 119, 131, 143, 149, 154
universities 28, 31
unpredictability of censors 52, 60
    see also arbitrary nature of censorship

'unpublishable' (unauthorized) books, statistics 44–5
'unworthy of publication', criteria 28–9
USSR, *see* Union of Soviet Socialist Republics

valuation (*barrasi*), euphemism for censorship 12, 44
value judgements of censorship 147–59
vandalism of gravestones 121
video players banned 153
violent acts
    government supporters 116
    see also murders; repressive censorship; torture

war
    favoured literature 109, 140
    references/books censored 40, 70, 139–40
    see also First World War; Iraq–Iran war
Weblogistan (Blogistan) 128–30
Western cultural influence
    cultural invasion theory 31–5
    pre-1979 32, 33
    references to Western lifestyle banned 48, 80, 149
Westoxification (*gharbzadegi*) 32, 164 n.29

White, Harry 151–2
will to write, destroyed by censorship 136–7
women
    literary awards 108
    musicians 47, 94
    rights and status 20–1, 23, 38, 48, 121, 124
    writers and poets 38, 94, 108
    see also Behbahani; Farrokhzad
women in books, reasons for censorship 48, 63–4, 65, 66, 76
worrying about manuscripts 158
writers, works banned for personal reasons 91–5

Yazdan (God) 74
young adult literature 69, 83, 88, 89–90
Young Poetry Office (*Daftar-e She'r-e Javān*) 112
young writers
    effects of censorship 159
    relationship between generations of writers 13, 129, 159
    state sponsorship 53
Yushij, Nima 23, 37, 115

Zaval-e Colonel ("The Colonel") by Mahmoud Dowlatabadi 67

www.ingramcontent.com/pod-product-compliance
Lightning Source LLC
Chambersburg PA
CBHW072108010526
44111CB00037B/2092